The Chancellor
of the
Exchequer

DAVID LLOYD GEORGE
Max Beerbohm
(*National Portrait Gallery*)

A HISTORY OF THE ENGLISH PEOPLE
IN THE NINETEENTH CENTURY — VI

THE RULE OF DEMOCRACY

1905—1914

(BOOK I)

by

ELIE HALEVY

Translated from the French by
E. I. WATKIN

NEW YORK
PETER SMITH
1952

First published in French 1932
First published in English 1934
Second (revised) Edition 1952

Publishers' Note

This is the second edition of the book originally published as *A History of the English People in the Nineteenth Century, Epilogue Vol. II*. The first edition was published as a single book but is now split into two; Book I containing Part I and the first two chapters of Part II and Book II the third chapter of Part II and Part III.

MADE AND PRINTED IN GREAT BRITAIN

Introduction

THIS new volume of my history, or, to speak more accurately, the second and concluding volume of the Epilogue to my history, requires no preface. Though six years have passed since the publication of the previous volume I regard it as the continuation of the former. Certain topics, for instance the development of religious beliefs, I shall treat very briefly, justified in so doing by the fact that I have already said in the previous volume all that I have to say about them. On the other hand, as I pointed out then, I reserved for the present volume the detailed treatment of military and naval questions. I have kept my promise.

There is surely no need to explain why military and above all naval problems assumed a special prominence at the opening of the present century. During the years whose history I relate England was hastening alike 'towards social democracy' and 'towards war'. It was hastening towards both with equal rapidity. We must not be deceived by the noise of party strife. Apparently the Unionists were the party of opposition to Socialism, the Liberals the party prepared to make concessions to Socialism. In reality both parties, stripped of their historic significance, were yielding with a unanimity which was resigned rather than enthusiastic to the pressure of the working masses. Apparently the Unionists were the party of war, the Liberals the party of peace. But when it was a question of voting the credits for which the Admiralty asked, there was no distinction between the two parties. Neither wanted war; both yielded inevitably to the pressure which the increase in the German navy exerted upon the nation. We shall be witnessing a drama whose *dénouement* was predestined from the outset.

For me the drama comes to an abrupt conclusion on the Fourth of August 1914, when England declared war on Germany. I have not attempted in a concluding section to interpret the crisis which began that day not for England alone but for the entire world.

The contribution which I have made to its understanding will be my study of that intermediate period which though it is not the nineteenth century constitutes its epilogue, and while not yet the anxious and troubled century in which we are living to-day is its immediate preparation. The task to which I am impatient to return and to which I propose to devote the remainder of my strength and my life will be the story of that great epoch during which the British people cherished the splendid illusion that they had discovered in a moderate liberty, and not for themselves alone but for every nation that would have the wisdom to follow their example, the secret of moral and of political stability.*

ELIE HALEVY
June 1932

My thanks are due to Mr. Graham Wallas, Brigadier-General Sir George Aston, K.C.B., Sir Maurice Amos and M. H. Le Masson, who kindly consented to read particular portions of my proofs and thus gave me the invaluable assistance of their expert knowledge in the respective provinces of public education, the organization of the army, the law of marriage, and naval history.

* *Unfortunately Elie Halévy never lived to complete his great task; he died in 1937. The last volume he wrote covered the years 1841-52, thus leaving a gap in his history from the latter year to 1895. This last volume, which first appeared posthumously in 1948, is now published under the title of* Victorian Years *and contains an essay by R. B. McCallum bridging the missing years.* PUBLISHER.

Contents

PART I

PROBLEMS OF LIBERAL POLICY

Imperial and Domestic Problems

I TARIFF AND IMPERIAL QUESTIONS

I

WHEN, on December 4, 1905, Balfour tendered to King Edward his own and his colleagues' resignations, there was enacted in the political history of the British nation a rapid drama in two acts. In the first the performers were the handful of statesmen whose task it was to agree upon the composition of the new Liberal Government, in the second the anonymous mass of eight million voters invited in January to give that Government their approval. We shall briefly sketch its episodes.

Balfour's resignation had been undoubtedly determined by the sudden campaign launched against him in November by Chamberlain and his group of uncompromising protectionists. But why had it been launched just at this particular moment? And why did Balfour reply with such an air of eager haste by the resignation of his Cabinet rather than by dissolving Parliament? We may well suspect that recent events at Liberal headquarters were not without their influence upon the actions of the Unionist leaders. Until September, it had been the universal belief that the Liberal Premier would be Lord Spencer, a veteran of the Gladstonian epoch, whose titular sovereignty would give offence to nobody either among the Gladstonians or the Liberal Imperialists. On October 13, however, congestion of the brain had incapacitated him for active work. Who would take his place at the head of the party? Sir Henry Campbell-Bannerman, the pro-Boer, or Lord Rosebery, author of the watchword 'Liberal Imperialism' and founder of the Liberal League? Ever since October the question must have been frequently discussed by Unionist politicians, but when Chamberlain, on November 23, at a meeting of the Liberal Unionist Council called upon Balfour to give a clear pronouncement on the question of Tariff Reform, the quarrel between the two Liberal leaders had already been reopened on another question.

On October 21, Haldane, addressing a public meeting at Edinburgh, declared that the Irish policy of the future Liberal Cabinet would be that of Sir Antony MacDonnell and Wyndham, repu-

3

diated four months previously by the Unionist Cabinet. Four days later Lord Rosebery employed almost identical language and into the bargain explicitly rejected complete Home Rule. But Sir Henry Campbell-Bannerman, however, in a speech at Stirling a month later spoke in very different terms. He expressed his wish to see 'the effective management of Irish affairs in the hands of a representative Irish authority', that is to say, he advocated Home Rule, not mere devolution. It is true he advised the Irish to content themselves as a beginning with a measure of more restricted scope but only if this restricted concession 'was consistent and led up to their larger policy', and he stated his conviction that before long the question would receive its final solution. To this utterance Lord Rosebery decided to reply two days later by a formal protest: 'Emphatically and explicitly,' he asseverated, 'once and for all, I cannot serve under that banner,' and declared that on the Irish question he agreed with Haldane. The other leaders of Liberal imperialism—Grey and Asquith—could only reply, in language which betrayed their embarrassment, that they saw no opposition between Campbell-Bannerman's policy and Lord Rosebery's, and that heated controversy about a question which presented no practical urgency was gratuitous.[1] Maintenance of the parliamentary union between Great Britain and Ireland had been the avowed platform on which the Liberal League had been formed in the spring of 1902 in opposition to the old National Liberal Federation. Since then the two groups had become reconciled in the defence of Free Trade. But Rosebery, who for two years had lavished his energies and eloquence upon a series of important orations on behalf of Free Trade, complained bitterly that Campbell-Bannerman was depriving the Liberal party of the benefit of their reconciliation by his persistence in inscribing Irish Home Rule on his programme. Surely at a moment when the issue of a return to protection had placed all others in the shade this resurrection of the Irish question was a welcome omen for the Unionist election agents. And must we not conclude that the spectacle of this dispute confirmed Balfour in his decision to resign as soon as possible that it might be seen whether his opponents

[1] R. B. Haldane, speech at Edinburgh, October 21, 1905; Lord Rosebery, speech at Stourbridge, October 25, 1905; Sir Henry Campbell-Bannerman, speech at Stirling, November 23, 1905; Lord Rosebery, speech at Bodmin, November 25, 1905; Sir Edward Grey, speech at Newcastle-under-Lyme, November 27, 1905. Cf. Asquith, speech at Wisbech, November 28, 1905.

would be able to compose their internal differences before the General Election?

If this was Balfour's motive he was mistaken on a preliminary point. Campbell-Bannerman's declaration on November 23 on the question of Irish Home Rule had been carefully discussed beforehand not only with a representative of the Irish party, the most moderate and most Anglicized of the group,[1] but also with the most important and at the same time the most moderate of the Liberal imperialist section, namely Asquith.[2] Indeed, you had only to read its terms carefully to see that Campbell-Bannerman's acceptance of the principle of Home Rule did not involve any kind of undertaking to introduce a Home Rule Bill in the new Parliament. It was Lord Rosebery, who, in his violent eagerness to protest, had repudiated what would be the accepted programme of the entire Liberal party save himself. But even now when he had excluded himself by his deliberate choice from the Cabinet about to be formed—it is indeed possible that he had already informed the Liberal leader in October that he did not wish to be included—the Tories did not lack grounds for reckoning upon serious dissensions at Liberal headquarters.[3] It was on the morning of Monday, December 4, that Balfour handed the King his resignation. The same evening Sir Edward Grey called on Sir Henry and informed him that he would be unable to enter his Cabinet unless Sir Henry were willing to quit the House of Commons for the House of Lords. But Grey's haughty ultimatum did not take the prospective Prime Minister by surprise. As early as November 3 we find him calling Asquith's attention to the report that 'that ingenious person, Richard Burdon Haldane,' proposed to dump him on the Upper House. No one was better acquainted with the rumour than Asquith, for it concerned a project he had himself concocted in collaboration with Grey and Haldane and for which they had secured King Edward's explicit approval. Banished to the Lords, Campbell-Bannerman would be a figurehead Prime

[1] T. P. O'Connor, *Sir Henry Campbell-Bannerman*, 1908, pp. 72–5.

[2] Sir Sidney Lee, *King Edward the Seventh: A Biography*, 1925–7, vol. ii, p. 441.

[3] For the formation of the Cabinet see J. A. Spender, *The Life of the Right Hon. Sir Henry Campbell-Bannerman* (1923), vol. ii, pp. 188–204; Margot Asquith, *Autobiography* (1920), vol. ii, pp. 71 sqq; Richard Burdon Haldane, *An Autobiography* (1929), pp. 168 sqq.; J. A. Spender and Cyril Asquith, *Life of Herbert Henry Asquith, Lord Oxford and Asquith* (1932), vol. i, pp. 169 sqq; Lord Morley (*Recollections*, 1917, vol. ii, pp. 140–3); Lord Grey of Fallodon (*Twenty-Five Years*, 1892–1926, vol. i, pp. 62–3) and Sir Sidney Lee (*King Edward VII*, vol. ii, pp. 441–5) are extremely sketchy. See further the interesting details published in the *Nation*, June 4, 1921, by Gardiner.

Minister. The functions of party leadership would in fact be exercised by Asquith in the House of Commons. Sir Edward Grey would be in charge of the Foreign Office. Haldane would be Lord Chancellor, and not only would he preside in that capacity over the House of Lords but his functions would be so extended that in conjunction with the Premier he would exercise a control over the general policy of the country. Behind this staff of imperialists no one would notice a Prime Minister, by no means a marked personality, who was opposed to the policy of force and national prestige.

There were plausible arguments which could be presented to Sir Henry to dissuade him from undertaking the double task of Prime Minister and leader of the Lower House. Now seventy years old, he had never been a hard worker and for several months past his health had been seriously affected. He had just returned from a long rest cure at Marienbad. King Edward, who had met him there, advised him on Monday the 4th to spare his health, remarking that neither of them was a young man. But Sir Henry stood firm. If his health made it necessary, he would accept a peerage later, but he wished at any rate to open the session of 1906 not only as Prime Minister but as leader of the Commons. Weary of argument he postponed his decision, since his health was the objection put forward, until he could consult Lady Campbell-Bannerman on her arrival from Scotland. If the imperialist members of the party counted on her womanly fears to urge her husband to leave the Commons, they were disappointed. She loathed the clique and decided in favour of a firm front. Was the Tory opposition to have at least the satisfaction of seeing Asquith, Grey, and Haldane refuse to enter the Cabinet, since their terms had been rejected? So *The Times* believed, and raised a pæan of triumph. But the very morning the article appeared, Friday, December 8, the situation took another turn. Asquith had yielded and accepted the office of Chancellor of the Exchequer without the leadership of the Commons. Deserted by him, could Sir Edward Grey and Haldane carry on their strike? Grey seemed inclined to that course, but the 'ingenious' Haldane persuaded him to accept Campbell-Bannerman as leader, if Sir Henry would consent to give the Foreign Office to Grey, the War Office to Haldane himself. Sir Henry willingly granted Haldane an office whose importance he failed to realize. In the Foreign Office, on the other hand, he would have preferred anyone rather than Grey. But when Lord Cromer, to whom he first offered it, refused on grounds of health, he felt obliged to give way. Thus at the end of the week the Liberal imperialists had partially made good the reverse they had suffered at its beginning. They had not indeed banished Campbell-Bannerman to the Lords, but in the Treasury, the War Office, and the Foreign Office they held three offices of the first importance. I remarked one day to a prominent member of the group how easy it is to date the birth of a political association, how difficult to determinate the date of its demise; what publicity, for example, had attended the formation of the Liberal League in 1902 and how mysteriously it had vanished later. 'But the Liberal League', he replied, 'did not vanish. What happened is simply that in 1905 it absorbed the Liberal Government. That is why we went to war in 1914.'

This serious difficulty once overcome nothing prevented the formation of the Government. And formed it was on December 11. It contained in all fifty-six members, of whom twenty were in the Cabinet. The old Gladstonians were gratified by the appointment of Sir Robert Reid as Lord Chancellor, with the title of Lord Loreburn, of Herbert Gladstone, the statesman's son, to the Home Office, and of John Morley to the India Office. Bryce, the eminent historian, who had entertained hopes of the latter, found himself obliged to yield to Morley's claim and content himself with the unenviable post of Chief Secretary for Ireland. Lloyd George went to the Board of Trade. He had expected a more important ministry, was indeed believed to have entertained hopes of immediate promotion to the Home Office.[1] Winston Churchill received the first reward of his desertion from the Tories and became Under-Secretary for the Colonies (the Secretaryship itself was given to a peer, Lord Elgin). Augustine Birrell, a talented man of letters, went to the Board of Education. To attract the sympathies of the working class the Local Government Board was given to John Burns, who, although he had not accepted the programme of the Labour Representation Com-

---

[1] J. Hugh Edwards, *The Life of David Lloyd George*, vol. iv, p. 60—Campbell-Bannerman gave him the option between the Post Office and the Board of Trade. He chose the latter, which, though the salary was less, gave more scope to its occupant. His Welsh friends would seem to have dreamed of the creation in his favour of a special 'Secretaryship for Wales' analogous to the Secretaryship for Scotland. (J. Hugh Edwards, *From Village Green to Downing Street: The Life of the Right Honourable D. Lloyd George*, p. 139.)

mittee, could claim to be a Socialist of long standing and was of proletarian origin.

2

Thus the Liberals, though banished from office for over ten years, had successfully solved as expert politicians all the problems raised by the constitution of a Government. They had avoided a split between the Gladstonians and the imperialists. That Lord Rosebery's name was absent from their list hardly mattered: public opinion had become accustomed to regard this haughty aristocrat as permanently retired. And though the opposition refused to admit it, they had formed an administration far superior in the individual worth of its members to that which had just resigned. But although Sir Henry Campbell-Bannerman was now Prime Minister and leader of the Commons, the Unionist politicians cherished a forlorn hope. For the second act of the drama had still to be played. Within a few weeks, the Liberals must confront the electorate. They would emerge victorious. Of that there was no doubt. But what would be the extent of their victory? It must surely damage their cause to take the field under the command of a prominent pro-Boer, whose sole recommendation to the notice of the public was the fact that during the late war he had made common cause with men notorious as enemies of their country? Even in the Liberal camp it was regarded as dangerous to speculate on the basis of the numerous by-elections won during the past year. At a by-election voters freely allow themselves the pleasure of giving the Government a slap in the face, because they know their gesture can have no serious consequences. The utmost that could be hoped for was a majority of a hundred over the Unionists, just sufficient to prevent the eighty Irish Nationalists from dictating their terms. And many Unionists expected a less decisive result. Chamberlain prophesied that the Liberal majority would not exceed eighty, would be at the mercy of the Irish members, and that the swing of the pendulum would not be long delayed.[1]

[1] *The Autobiography of Mrs. Asquith*, vol. ii, pp. 58–9, 80. For other forecasts see the *National Review*, December 1905, vol. xlvi, p. 789, 'The Liberal Letter'; An Intercepted Letter (an imaginary letter from Campbell-Bannerman intercepted and sent to the *Review* by the Fabian Society): 'The Central Office tells me that the Conservatives of all shades cannot have more than 245 members to our 340, which gives us anyhow a clear

At this period the elections were not completed in a single day. They lasted a fortnight, and the order in which they were held ensured the Liberals from the outset an easy victory. After an isolated election at Ipswich, where they gained a seat, ten Lancashire constituencies were summoned on the following day, January 13, to elect their representatives. In 1900 all had returned Unionist members, Balfour at their head. Now all returned Liberals or Labour men, 6 Liberals and 4 Labour. And these victories were the more sensational because in several instances the successful Liberal had been faced not only with a Unionist opponent but with a Socialist as well. It was in vain that Balfour had prevaricated, and the other Unionist candidates declared against a tariff on foodstuffs—all had been irremediably compromised by Chamberlain's propaganda. It was undoubtedly a misfortune for the Unionists that the first boroughs to vote were situated in the holy land of Free Trade. But the same day in a number of other manufacturing constituencies where the Tariff Reformers flattered themselves that their propaganda had been more successful, the result was the same. The initial impulse once given, Liberal victories followed in unbroken succession so long as the borough elections continued. In London, which in 1900 had returned 8 Liberals as against 51 Unionists, 40 Liberals and Labour men were returned, and only 19 Unionists. In the remaining boroughs of England the respective positions of the two parties were almost exactly reversed. In 1900 40 Liberal members had been returned as against 127 Unionists, now 124 Liberals as against 43 Unionists. In Wales, the Unionists lost even the tiny minority returned at the last election; all the 11 representatives of the Welsh boroughs

majority, even on the rare occasions when Redmond can get over all his 85 to vote against us. And this majority of the whole House may be even as high as 70.' Lord Hugh Cecil to Mrs. Asquith, December 21, 1905: ' . . . My guess is that your party will come back 230 —giving you a majority of about 40 over us and the Irish together' (*The Autobiography of Mrs. Asquith*, vol. ii, p. 78). *The Times*, January 13, 1906: '137 seats lately held by Unionists will have to be captured by Sir Henry Campbell-Bannerman's supporters to give him a majority of 40 in the House of Commons over Unionists and Nationalists combined, whereas the great revulsion of 1895, which transformed Lord Rosebery's preponderance of 31 into a majority for Lord Salisbury of 153, was accompanied by a reversal of the previous verdict in 92 cases only.' The *Daily Mail* of December 27 ventures the following forecast: 'Conservatives and Unionists 247; Liberals 297; Labour (including Liberal-Labour) 35; Nationalists 81.' Cf. John Morley, speech at Forfar, January 10, 1906: 'This General Election is the most exciting within my experience, and probably for nearly sixty years, with the possible exception of that on Home Rule in 1886. There are three current predictions: (1) The Liberals, as in 1885, will be equal to the Tories and Nationalists combined; (2) The Unionists will number only 200; (3) The Government will have a majority of thirty or forty over the joint forces of the Tories and Nationalists.'

were Liberals. In Scotland, the Liberals reconquered the supremacy they had appeared to be losing for some years past. Instead of fifteen to sixteen, they were twenty-five to six.

On the 19th, when the borough elections were almost at an end, the county elections began. If, owing to the growth of the suburbs of large towns or the development of mining, some of these constituencies had become urban and industrial, the majority were rural, and the Unionists might well hope by maintaining their position here to mitigate the disaster which had befallen them in the boroughs. But it soon became clear that even in these areas the tide would sweep away the last dykes behind which the old Conservative party was entrenched. The agricultural labourers from dislike of the landlords and farmers, the farmers from dislike of the Education Act which had made the rates heavier, and the electors generally disgusted with a Government of aristocrats and dilettanti which had shown itself incompetent either to preserve peace or make war and after the conclusion of peace had given no proof that it had learnt the lessons of the war, voted for the Liberals. The old County families who constituted the picturesque element of the Unionist party saw themselves deserted by those whom until the dawn of the new century they had been pleased to regard as attached to themselves by a tie amounting to moral serfdom. In Dorset a Bathurst was defeated, a Kenyon in Derbyshire, a Lowther in Cumberland. Chaplin, for the last ten years Minister for Agriculture and a Lincolnshire member for thirty-two years, lost his seat. The sole comfort left to the Unionists was the fact that their defeat was not so overwhelming as in the towns. In England the counties returned 74 Liberals and 60 Unionists, in Scotland 35 Liberals and 4 Unionists; in Wales all the 19 members were Liberals.

To sum up, the new House of Commons contained 430 Liberal and Labour members, 157 Unionists, 83 Irish Nationalists. If from the 50 working-class representatives returned we subtract those who, having accepted the nomination of the Labour Representation Committee, might claim to be regarded as a group apart, there were 401 Liberals, 157 Unionists, 29 Labour members, 83 Nationalists. Any lingering hopes Unionist headquarters may have entertained on the eve of the polls had been dissipated. The Government majority was so vast that, even if the Liberals were deserted by their Labour and Irish allies, they could still dispose of

130 more votes than the hostile combination. The only strong-holds remaining in Unionist hands were the wealthy districts of London, a certain number of seats in the agricultural counties of the South (Kent, Sussex, etc.), Birmingham and its environs, where Chamberlain reigned supreme, and Liverpool, where, no doubt, the violent anti-Irish sentiment checked the Liberal advance. To find a similar electoral landslide we must go back to the General Election of 1833, which followed the passage of the first Reform Bill, and it was indeed a revolution of the same kind which was taking place at present. The paradoxical feature of the situation was that the reforms of the franchise effected as long ago as 1867 and 1884 had not borne fruit until now. Anti-Irish panics, waves of imperialist enthusiasm, the failure of the old Gladstonian party to understand the aspirations of the working masses, had kept the Conservatives in office. Their power was now a thing of the past and many, who, after 1895, had been inclined to write the Liberal party off as annihilated for the next half century, now re garded 1906 as the year one of a new era, an era of Liberalism regenerate and democratic. In the new House there were only sixteen bankers in place of fifty in the previous Parliament, and twenty-one members of railway directorates as against fifty-three.[1] There were 310 new members, almost half the total membership. And of these 310, 220 were Liberals, well-nigh three-quarters of the party representation. Among these 220 were a large number of young men, intellectuals, journalists, university professors, champions of all those eccentric causes which arouse the enthusiasm of British philanthropy. They had stood for election or allowed themselves to be put up simply in order that as far as possible the Liberal vote might be taken in every constituency. Now they found themselves returned, often to their utter amazement. On what platform? This is the question we must now examine. For the new members felt, no doubt, some difficulty in analysing the movement of vague enthusiasm which had landed them at Westminster.

3

The programme on which the new majority had been returned was undoubtedly first and foremost purely negative opposition

[1] *The Times*, February 1, 1906.

to tariff reform which the Liberals regarded as reactionary. Chamberlain had intended to give the Election the character of a referendum on the question, and the overwhelming majority obtained by the opposite party seemed a hostile verdict upon his policy from which for many a year to come there could be no appeal. But although a number of long-established Conservative organs in the provinces charged him with precipitating the Conservative defeat by his insubordination and intemperance, he obviously retained the sympathy, secret or avowed, of the London party press and the vast majority of provincial Conservative papers. The Conservative defeat, his supporters maintained, was due to the fact that Chamberlain had been compelled to play a lone hand, while the old families with Balfour at their head monopolized the official leadership of the party. The consequence was that the party had lost touch with the mass of the electorate. A new organization and a new programme were indispensable. Though he inspired this campaign, Chamberlain dared not claim the leadership of the party. The established Conservative hierarchy was too powerful. Relying, however, on the fact that of the hundred and fifty Unionists returned to the new Parliament, over a hundred had been elected on the full programme of imperial protection, he called upon Balfour to adopt it. On February 15 the papers published two letters exchanged between the official and the unofficial Unionist leaders. In the first of these Balfour informed Chamberlain that he considered fiscal reform 'should be the first constructive work of the Unionist Party', demanded 'more equal terms of competition for British trade, and closer commercial union with the Colonies', and admitted that 'the imposition of a general tariff of a moderate character upon manufactured articles and a light duty on imported cereals were not in principle objectionable' and 'should be adopted if shown to be necessary for the attainment of the ends in view or for purposes of revenue'. He was indeed careful to add that the new duties must not be imposed 'for the purpose of raising prices or giving artificial protection against legitimate competition'. And he added that to protect the British export trade and tighten the economic bonds between the mother country and the Colonies 'may be possible by other means', and that 'it is inexpedient to permit differences of opinion as to these methods to divide the party'. But these reservations did not alter the fact that by placing tariff reform upon the official programme of the party on the morrow of the *débâcle* at the polls, he had surrendered to Chamberlain. In any case, it was in this sense that Chamberlain interpreted Balfour's letter, which, he said, 'he cordially welcomed'. The following day, February 16, the reconciliation between the two leaders was sealed by a plenary assembly of the party at Lansdowne House.

Could it however be regarded as complete? Were its terms unambiguous? Balfour had no doubt accepted Chamberlain's programme in principle and that was a great deal. But he had attached to his acceptance so many reservations that their common enemies were tempted to put to the test an alliance at the best of times weak. On March 12 a member of the ministerialist majority in the Commons invited the House to pass a resolution declaring its determination 'to resist any proposal whether by way of taxation upon foreign goods, to create in this country a system of protection'. Balfour, thus driven to bay and compelled either to defend Chamberlain's entire programme or reject it categorically, evaded the issue by a speech as ambiguous, complicated, and 'balfourian' as possible. When he had finished, the Premier did not rise to reply. When, however, Chamberlain interposed to charge him with a breach of parliamentary etiquette, Campbell-Bannerman decided to speak. His speech was brief and incisive. He denounced Balfour's speech as 'futile, nonsensical, and misleading', 'only justifiable if his object had been to waste the time of the House'. 'I say, enough of this foolery. It might have answered very well in the last Parliament, but it is altogether out of place in this Parliament. The tone and temper of this Parliament will not permit it. Move your Amendments, and let us get to business.' So these two statesmen—Balfour and Campbell-Bannerman—faced each other on the floor of the House, the former unanimously regarded as a great artist, and a master of fence, the prince of the House of Commons, the latter an honourable man no doubt, but a bourgeois far from keen-witted and without prestige as a debater. And it was the obtuse bourgeois, who, at the first passage of arms, established his authority over the newly elected Parliament by informing his adversary amid the applause of his majority that he considered him a sophist and refused to waste his time by listening to him. There was indeed a third statesman to oppose Campbell-Bannerman—namely, Chamberlain himself—whose imprudent intervention had provoked the Prime Minister's withering reply.

13

Would he not very shortly give his party its revenge by employing more direct methods better suited to a democratic audience? On this point we are reduced to conjecture, for in July he suddenly disappeared from public life, a victim to the disease which made him a permanent invalid and a paralytic. But it is not likely that his ardour would have succeeded, where Balfour's subtlety had failed. The situation was too unfavourable to protectionist propaganda.

When the advocates of tariff reform opened their campaign in 1903, they had reckoned on a period of economic depression and industrial stagnation. For after three or four years of prosperity, the bad years before 1898 seemed to be returning. Their calculation had been falsified by the event. The years 1904 and 1905 had been prosperous. 1906 was better still. Imports rose from £565,020,000 to £607,889,000, an increase of 7.6 per cent; exports from £329,817,000 to £375,575,000, an increase of 13 per cent. This double increase was not wholly an increase in the amount of goods imported and exported. For there had been a general rise of prices. But there was one class of products in which this rise had not taken place. Owing to an excellent harvest throughout the entire world the price of cereals had fallen. The rise in wages therefore had not been balanced by a rise in the cost of foodstuffs. Employers and workers alike—with the solitary exception of the landowners and their farmers—were satisfied. The complaints of the tariff reformers found no echo in the world of industry.

4

The sole resource left to the defeated Unionists was to scrutinize every detail of the Government's policy, to surprise and exploit some lapse, some concession voluntary or involuntary to their ideas. Lloyd George, the new President of the Board of Trade, twice presented them with an opportunity.

The first occasion was in 1906 when an important statute was passed dealing with the mercantile marine.[1] The shipowners had taken advantage of the protectionist movement which marked the last years of the Unionist Government to bring forward two

[1] 6 Edw. 7, Cap. 48: An Act to amend the Merchant Shipping Acts 1894 to 1900 (*Merchant Shipping Act*, 1906).

distinct grievances. To examine them the Government had appointed two Committees of inquiry.[1] Both complained of the increasing number of foreign seamen employed in the mercantile marine. But a remedy was not easy to find. It was impossible to dispense with these men, especially in tropical waters, and the difficulty was all the greater because the non-British seamen, the Lascars, were Indians and therefore British subjects. The first and the more important of the Committees had recommended stricter regulations to ensure the crews better conditions on board—for example, better sleeping accommodation and food, and so attract a larger number of Englishmen to the service. This recommendation was very largely carried out by the Act of 1906. It had further recommended the introduction of a rule by which sailors in the merchant service must know sufficient English to understand orders in that language. On this point also the Act of 1906 carried out its recommendation. Actually, in the course of the debates, an amendment more directly hostile to the foreigner was inserted in the Statute. Pilots' certificates would in future be granted only to Englishmen. The shipowners had also complained that since for the past twenty years they had been subject to very strict regulations as to the amount of cargo and life-saving apparatus, it was not just to allow foreign vessels not subject to these regulations by their national laws to compete with theirs in British ports. A second Committee was appointed to investigate the question and, so far as existing international agreements permitted, its recommendations were incorporated into the Statute of 1906. The Act subjected as far as possible foreign vessels entering British ports to the regulations imposed on British vessels by English law. Of these new provisions, some, as we have seen, were obviously nationalist in character, the others, however justifiable they might appear, abandoned the orthodoxy of free trade. Foreign vessels were indeed permitted to compete with British, but only if their competition was on an equal footing. This was all the fair traders had asked for. They were quite ready to accept free trade on equal terms.

In 1907, Lloyd George took a more decided step in the direction

---

[1] Report of the Committees appointed by the Board of Trade to inquire into certain questions affecting the Mercantile Marine, with minutes of evidence, appendices and index, 1902 (Lord St. Helier's Committee)—Report from the Select Committee on Foreign Ships (Application of Statutory Powers) together with the Proceedings of the Committee, minutes of evidence and appendix, 1904 (Bonar Law's Committee).

of fair trade. For some years the question of patents had been causing anxiety to English manufacturers and the officials of the Board of Trade. Too many foreign firms, especially American and German, had taken out patents in England, often deliberately drawn up in complicated and obscure language, to prevent British industry using particular methods or machinery, or permitting their use only on payment of a royalty. The extent of the evil can be gauged from the fact that of 14,700 patents granted in 1906, 6,500 were granted to foreigners. A Committee had been appointed in 1901 to examine the problem.[1] Its report led to the passing of a Statute in 1902[2] with the object of enabling an inventor, injured by a patent wilfully misdrafted, to obtain redress from the courts. It proved inoperative. A Lancashire manufacturer brought a test case. It cost him £4,000. To a poor inventor such costs were prohibitive. The Patents and Designs Act[3] of 1907 was a more thoroughgoing measure. Not only was the procedure for modifying patents made simpler and therefore cheaper, but other provisions were laid down. In future the government would be entitled to cancel a patent, if within three years of the grant it had not been used in the United Kingdom. All applications for a patent must be accompanied by the production of specimens. And measures were taken to put an end to the system of leases which tended to subject British industry to foreign control. 'I am not afraid of foreign competition', Lloyd George declared, 'as long as British trade is free to fight it. . . . British industry shall be made perfectly free to engage on equal terms in the severe struggle with its competitors.' The German Press raised the cry of protection. From the opposition benches ironical congratulations were showered on Lloyd George. Attention was drawn to the fact that the Bill of 1907 had been prepared and its clauses worked out by the Board of Trade, before the advent of the Liberal Government, at the

---

[1] *Patent Acts*. Reports of the Committee appointed by the Board of Trade to inquire into the working of the Patents Acts on certain specified questions, 1901.

[2] Edw. 7, Cap. 34: An Act to amend the Law with reference to Application for Patents and Compulsory Licences and other matters connected therewith (*Patents Act*, 1902).

[3] 7 Edw. 7, Cap. 28: An Act to amend the Law relating to Patents and Designs (Amendment) Act, 1907. It was repealed immediately and incorporated into a comprehensive Statute which consolidated all former patent Acts. 7 Edw. 7, Cap. 29: An Act to consolidate the enactments relating to Patents for Invention and the Registration of Designs and certain enactments relating to Trade Marks (*Patents and Designs Act*, 1907). For the spirit of the new Act see Lloyd George's speech H. of C. March 19, 1907 (*Parliamentary Debates*, 9th Series, vol. clxxi, pp. 683 sqq.); also his speech on the second reading of the Bill, H. of C., April 17, 1907 (ibid., vol. clxxii, pp. 1042 sqq.).

demand of a group of industries whose leaders at least shared Chamberlain's views. Were not the Unionists entitled to surmise, as some actually did, that this young minister whom they detested so bitterly might perhaps follow one day in the footsteps of that other great demagogue, the protagonist of tariff reform? Lloyd George was certainly no doctrinaire and, more attached to democracy than free trade, was perhaps glad to prove in these early days of the new Parliament that he was not enslaved to the old formulas of Gladstonian orthodoxy.[1] But this was a very slender foundation for believing that he would shortly join the protectionists. One thing was certain; he had no political inducement to take the step. He shared his colleagues' perception that it was politics to leave the Unionist party to bear the responsibility for Chamberlain's new programme and to confront it with the alternative of disavowing it, which would leave them without a positive programme to oppose to the Liberals—or frankly adopting it as their platform, and thereby courting defeat at the polls.

We must not, therefore, ascribe to the Merchant Shipping or the Patent Acts the importance assigned to them by contemporary Unionist speakers and journalists. We must, on the contrary, draw attention to the measures ostentatiously adopted by the Government to retrace the few steps taken by its predecessor on the path of protection, tentatives so misconceived and blundering that its task was easy.

5

The Budget of 1906 abandoned the £2,000,000 yielded by the export duty on coal imposed in 1901 which had the air of an indirect concession to protectionist principles. But on what grounds could the duty be rationally defended? Its authors had argued from the necessity of preserving the reserves of coal in British soil indispensable to British industry but by no means inexhaustible. A Royal Commission, however, appointed after the

---

[1] Trustworthy witnesses tell us that Campbell-Bannerman was personally antipathetic to him (New Statesman, April 3, 1920). But the statement of his biographer, E. T. Raymond (Mr. Lloyd George: A Biography, 1922, p. 90), that in 1896 he had proposed a reduction of the duty upon tea grown in the Empire is based on a misunderstanding of this Parliamentary incident. Chamberlain, who was in office, had just declared in favour of an imperial Zollverein and Lloyd George's sole object in introducing the amendment was to embarrass Lord Salisbury's Government by compelling it to accept or reject his proposal (H. of C., July 7, 1896, Parliamentary Debates, 4th Series, vol. xlii, pp. 935, 943).

imposition of the duty to undertake a comprehensive study of the problems connected with the coal-mining industry in Great Britain, had reached the conclusion that the supply of coal was in no proximate danger of exhaustion.[1] There were a hundred thousand million tons of coal to be raised, and the annual output of the mines in England, Wales and Scotland was only two hundred and thirty million.[2] It had been argued that British industry would obtain its coal on better terms if export were rendered more difficult. The expectation, however, was not fulfilled at a time when the price of coal was rising like all other prices, and the opposition thus introduced between the interests of the manufacturing consumers and the miners sharpened the hostility of the huge mining electorate to the duty of 1901. The supporters of tariff reform could only retort that if, as the opposition implicitly admitted, the British producer suffered from the imposition of this export duty, it would be the foreign producer, not the British consumer, who would suffer from the imposition of duties on imports.[3] This logic-chopping represented the entire opposition of Unionist speakers during the debates on the Budget. The theorists of free trade, the miners, and the powerful group constituted by the merchant service were united in opposition to the export duty on coal. In fact, the opposition was a mere formality: Austen Chamberlain, Chancellor of the Exchequer in the late Cabinet, had already promised to abolish it.[4]

In 1907 a more important step was taken in the same direction. On June 6, Sir Edward Grey, in his capacity as Foreign Secretary, informed the permanent international Sugar Commission that the British Government could no longer continue to participate in the

[1] A Royal Commission appointed to inquire into the extent and available resources of the coalfields of the United Kingdom; the rate of exhaustion which may be anticipated, having regard to possible economies in use by the substitution of other fuel, or the adoption of other kinds of power; the effect of our exports of coal on the home supply, and the time for which that supply, especially of the more valuable kinds of coal, will probably be available to British consumers, including the Royal Navy, at a cost which would not be detrimental to the general welfare; the possibility of a reduction in that cost, by cheaper transport, or by the avoidance of unnecessary waste in working through the adoption of better methods and improved appliances, or through a change in the customary terms and provisions of mineral leases, and whether the mining industry of this country, under existing conditions, is maintaining its competitive power with the coalfields of other countries, 1900. *First Report*, 1903; *Second Report*, 1904; *Final Report*, 1905.

[2] *Final Report*, p. 6.

[3] H. of C. April 30, 1906, Joseph Chamberlain's speech (*Parliamentary Debates*, 4th Series, vol. xlv, pp. 560–1).

[4] H. of C., April 30, 1906, Fenwick's speech (*Parliamentary Debates*, 4th Series, vol. xlv, p. 327). Joseph Chamberlain's speech (ibid., iv, pp. 459–60).

Union under the conditions imposed by the Brussels agreement, since the agreement was 'inconsistent with their declared policy, and incompatible with the interests of British consumers and sugar-using manufacturers', and claimed for Great Britain freedom from the obligation to subject sugar which had received a bounty to the retaliatory duties it prescribed. On July 25, the Commission met at Brussels and in two days drew up the draft of an agreement supplementing the convention of 1902, which was ratified on August 28 by the adhesion of all the contracting powers. It suspended the international union for five years from September 1, 1908, and freed Great Britain during that period from the obligation to penalize sugar in receipt of a bounty, the other contracting powers merely reserving the right to require that any sugar refined in the United Kingdom and exported to their territory should be accompanied by a guarantee that no portion of it came from a country which accorded a bounty for the growth or treatment of sugar.

The Tariff Reformers protested, and their protests were similar to those they had made against the abolition of the export duty on coal. They amounted to no more than the argument that the Brussels convention had not produced all the ill-effects foretold by the Free Traders. The quantity of raw sugar imported, far from decreasing, had increased by 15 per cent. The export of confectionery had increased and had never before reached so high a figure. The plantations of cane sugar in the West Indies had been saved, which however did not prevent some manufacturers from making preparations to introduce the sugar beet industry into England. Unionist speakers further taunted the measure with being a compromise. If the Government wished to keep its election promises, why was there not a complete rupture with the international Commission?[1]

Nothing came of their protests. The Liberals had promised the electorate cheap sugar, and the pledge was fulfilled by the Brussels compromise. The Convention of 1902 was not calculated to win the British voter to the cause of tariff reform. For the only British producer it protected was not English or Scottish but the West Indian planter. The object of the Unionist Cabinet in signing it had been, by saving the West Indian colonies from ruin,

[1] H. of C., July 30, 1907 (*Parliamentary Debates*, 4th Series, vol. clxxix, pp. 799 sqq.), H. of C., August 1, 1907 (ibid., vol. clxxix, pp. 1240 sqq.).

to inculcate in the British public the belief in a solidarity of interests between the mother country and her Colonies. The problem of free trade was thus bound up with that of imperial unity. Chamberlain's revived protectionism was not and was not intended to be a parochial protection of the interests of the mother country alone; it aimed at an imperial protection, the protection of Greater Britain as a whole against the outside world. From this point of view Chamberlain had bequeathed to the new Government a legacy of singular difficulty. It was all very well for the majority of the new ministers to proclaim their opposition to imperialism; they could not escape responsibility for the settlement of imperial problems. Their anti-imperialism signified at most their unwillingness to increase a burden of responsibility, already overwhelming, by further conquests, and their belief in the desirability of applying more liberal methods in ruling the hosts of nations and races subject to the British Crown and thus perhaps consolidating the Empire by liberalizing it.

6

In April, 1907, after an interval of five years, the Colonial Conference met in London.[1] The Liberal Government did nothing to diminish the solemnity of the proceedings. Campbell-Bannerman was at pains to lay to rest any suspicions of an intransigent Little Englandism, to which his attitude during the Boer War might have given rise. He invited the Prime Ministers of the Self-Governing Colonies to his official residence in Downing Street and made the reception as imposing as he could. A special table was put up which had the shape of an E to symbolize the Empire by its very form. Above the Premier's head a likeness of Pitt lit by a projector presided over the meeting. By an innovation which did not pass unremarked, he did not leave it to the Colonial Secretary to open the proceedings, but made the opening speech himself, a profession of faith at once imperialist and Liberal. No

---

[1] For the preparations for the Conference and its work, see Colonial Conference, 1907; Despatch from the Secretary of State for the Colonies, with enclosures respecting the Agenda of the Colonial Conference, 1907 (1907); Correspondence relating to the Colonial Conference 1907 in continuance of (1907); Published Proceedings and Précis of the Colonial Conference 15th to 26th April, 1907 (1907); Minutes and Proceedings of the Colonial Conference, 1907. See further Richard Jebb, The Imperial Conference: A History and a Study, 1911, vol. ii, pp. 68 sqq.

question, he said, must be excluded from discussion, and the fact that the British Government might on one point or another find itself in disagreement with a particular Colony would not weaken the bonds of friendship which united them. Paying an ironical tribute to the statesman who had sought to cement the bond of imperial unity by commercializing it, he quoted the words in which Chamberlain had spoken of the 'sentimental' character of the tie which bound the mother country to her Colonies. In fact, the question of granting or refusing a 'preference' to the Colonies was the most important of those discussed at the Conference.

The Australian Commonwealth, New Zealand, and Cape Colony, whose Government was at the moment in the hands of imperialists of British origin, put forward resolutions advocating a system of mutual preferential tariffs between the various Self-Governing Colonies and the United Kingdom. The Prime Minister of the Commonwealth was a vehement supporter of Chamberlain's project. Alone the Canadian premier, Sir Wilfred Laurier, held aloof. Like his party, the Liberal party of Canada, he was committed to a fiscal policy entirely independent of the rest of the Empire, and reciprocity not with Britain but the United States.[1] What arguments did the other premiers bring forward? It was no longer possible, as it had been possible three or four years earlier, to argue that since the growth of commerce was more rapid between the mother country and her Colonies than between the mother country and the rest of the world, a system of preferential tariffs followed the natural line of historical development. Unfortunately for that argument the statistics for the past year yielded diametrically opposite results. But this did not prevent Chamberlain's supporters from making use of them. England, they argued, sent too much capital and too many immigrants to the United States, not enough to Canada and the other parts of the Empire. If, however, by an artificial system of protection

[1] For the Canadian tariff of 1907 sanctioned by the Ottawa Parliament on the very eve of the Conference see Edward Porritt, *Sixty Years of Protection in Canada, 1846–1907: Where Industry Leans on the Politician*, 1908, pp. 421 sqq. (written from the free-trade standpoint). For the negotiations for a treaty of reciprocity which the Canadian Government proceeded to open with the Government of the United States and which the intransigence of Congress rendered abortive, see H. A. L. Fisher, *James Bryce (Viscount Bryce of Dechmont, O.M.)*, vol. ii, pp. 62 sqq. See also Edward Porritt, *The Revolt in Canada against the New Feudalism; Tariff History from the Revision of 1907 to the Uprising of the West in 1910*, 1911 (well documented but resembling too closely a pamphlet in favour of free trade).

commerce could be diverted into colonial channels, capital and human labour would follow in the same direction; from every standpoint therefore they would be assisting the progress of the Empire.[1]

The hopes of these Self-Governing Colonies were damped by the opposition of three ministers. Asquith, speaking as Chancellor of the Exchequer, made the pronouncement in favour of the official free-trade orthodoxy which might have been expected from him. He refused to inquire whether Cobden had regarded British free trade as the prelude to universal. If he remained loyal to free trade it was because he believed it was demanded by the special and immediate interests of the British people. Lloyd George disappointed any hopes which his Merchant Shipping and Patent Bills might have aroused by defending the principle of free trade in terms as uncompromising as Asquith's. Since Winston Churchill was only Under-Secretary for the Colonies he might have kept silence. As a convert from Toryism, however, and, like all converts, suspect in both camps, he thought it necessary to state his position and put forward political arguments in favour of the complete fiscal independence of the mother country in regard to her Colonies. We have already had occasion to appreciate their gravity. Sentiments of deep affection united the different parts of the Empire and, if the mother country attempted to dictate to a Colony, or conversely, if a Colony attempted to dictate to her, the fiscal system to be adopted, everlasting conflicts of interest would result. The effect would be to weaken, not, as was hoped, consolidate imperial sentiment.

At that very moment a number of disputes brought home the danger of attempting to give a systematic form to a union which continued somehow to function in total disorganization. Asquith and Lloyd George declared their intention to do everything in their power to foster commerce between the different parts of the Empire. This, however, was not always an easy task, and the obstacles did not arise exclusively from the attitude of the mother

[1] 'Four-fifths of the capital which had built up the industries and the railways of the United States had gone from the City of London. When he thought of that, and that Canada had hardly been able to get the money to build a single line of railway across her continent, he regretted that they had not forty or fifty years ago awakened from the lethargy from which he was glad to say that they had now awakened' (Sir F. Borden: speech delivered at a banquet given by the Eighty Club to the Colonial Prime Ministers April 16, 1907).

country. It was because of the Australian Government that Imperial Penny Postage, already in operation throughout almost the whole of the Empire, did not yet extend to Australia.[1] It was all very well for Canada to advertise loudly the project of an All-Red Route between England and Australia via Montreal and Vancouver. Australia showed no enthusiasm for this piece of imperialism but put forward in London a totally different scheme, the organization of a line of rapid communications between Australia and England which would not touch Canada.[2] Moreover, for more than ten years an open conflict had existed between the mother country and the Self-Governing Colonies about the laws controlling merchant shipping and the coasting trade. In 1894, when the Liberals were in office, they had dared to violate the principle of colonial home rule, and the Parliament of Great Britain had passed a Merchant Shipping Bill[3] which, while it conferred on the colonial legislatures full powers to prescribe the conditions of coasting trade, imposed the twofold reservation that any such legislation must place British vessels on an equal footing with colonial, and must not conflict with any right granted by British treaties to foreign states. But the constitution granted six years later to Australia gave the Australian Parliament unlimited jurisdiction in this sphere.[4] This at least was the interpretation placed upon the Act in Australia. Accordingly, the Commonwealth Parliament passed in 1904 a Statute whose provisions were in conflict with those of the British Act of 1894. And in 1903, New Zealand overrode the restrictions laid down in the Act of 1894 without even troubling like Australia to justify her action by an appeal to the text of her constitution.[5] In London, a Commission[6] appointed to inquire into the Australian Statute and in particular to determine how far it was authorized by the Commonwealth Act of 1900 referred the examination of the question to a 'mari-

[1] *Colonial Conference, 1907: Minutes of Proceedings*, p. 599.

[2] Ibid., pp. 565 sqq. *The Economist* June 22, 1907, p. 1058; April 11, 1908, pp. 768, 770: 'The All-Red Route will get neither freight nor immigrants; it must pay its way on saloon passengers.'

[3] 57 & 58 Vict., Cap. 60: An Act to consolidate Enactments relating to Merchant Shipping (*Merchant Shipping Act*, 1894).

[4] 63 & 64 Vict., Cap. 12: An Act to constitute the Commonwealth of Australia (*Commonwealth of Australia Constitution Act*), 1900, Sec. 98.

[5] For the Australian Acts see *Australia, New Zealand, Correspondence relating to Merchant Shipping Legislation in Australia and New Zealand 1905*, pp. 83 sqq.

[6] Australia. *Report of the Royal Commission on the Navigation Bill of the Australian Commonwealth*, 1904. See, in particular, pp. 60 sqq., R. E. Cunliffe's memorandum 'On the powers of colonial legislatures generally in relation to merchant shipping'.

time conference'[1] which began its sessions a few days before the Colonial Conference met. It failed to reach a settlement and left England at grips with serious difficulties at two opposite extremities of her Empire. In Newfoundland the United States refused to recognize certain provisions of the local mercantile code, and the Foreign Office, siding as always with the United States against British colonists, ordered the cruisers stationed in those waters to protect American vessels against agents of the Newfoundland Government if the latter attempted to enforce its legislation on the Americans.[2] And Australia actually introduced a Bill during the following summer which not only excluded from the coasting trade all non-Australian vessels, including British, but interpreted coasting trade so widely that it seemed as though the deliberate object of the measure were to aim a deadly blow at British merchant shipping.[3] Should the British Government, to maintain the imperial order, quarrel with the United States and Australia? British diplomacy, both within and without the Empire, once

[1] Colonial Merchant Shipping Conference, 1907. *Report of a Conference between Representatives of the United Kingdom, the Commonwealth of Australia and New Zealand on the subject of Merchant Shipping Legislation, 1907*—It is worth remark that the issue raised by this dispute between the mother country and her dominions was quite different from the issue between England and foreign powers on this same question of merchant shipping. As Sir Joseph Ward pointed out (*Colonial Merchant Shipping Conference, 1907, Report* p. 2) the mercantile legislation of New Zealand was in advance of the British and could not therefore be abandoned under pressure from the mother country. On the same page Lloyd George himself pays tribute to this legislation and remarks on the borrowings from it in the British Statute of 1906: 'This country is old and moves much more slowly than her younger and sprightlier children across the seas and reforms proceed with much slower pace here than they do in all colonies. I dare say many of us regret that, and look with longing eyes to the legislation which you have been able to achieve in the Colonies without much difficulty.'

[2] For this episode see the extremely indignant speech of the Newfoundland Premier, Sir Robert Bond, West India Club, June 5, 1907. At the conference the matter was discussed with such acerbity that the speeches were omitted from the official report. The dispute between the British and American Governments respecting the Newfoundland fisheries was finally submitted to the court of arbitration at The Hague, whose decision was on the whole favourable to the British thesis (*Annual Register*, 1910, pp. 458–9).

[3] The Australian Merchant Shipping Bill formed part of an entire programme, semi-protectionist and semi-socialist, adopted by Deakin's Liberal Cabinet which depended on a Liberal-Labour coalition. Of this programme our Bill was an item. To the Australian ship-owners it offered the monopoly of the coasting trade in Australian waters, to the exclusion in particular of British vessels coming from India and manned by Lascars; to the crews of merchantmen it offered extremely advantageous conditions of employment which would cost the owners dear. The programme also comprised what was termed the New-Protection: protective duties were imposed but the manufacturer who profited by them was obliged to raise his employees' wages in proportion. On this last point the High Court decided that the measure was unconstitutional as exceeding the powers of the Federal Parliament. The decision led to the fall of the Liberal Government and in the political confusion of the following months the Merchant Shipping Bill was lost sight of (*Economist*, October 13, 1907, May 23, June 13, 1908; *The Times*, October 30, 1908; *Economist*, December 5, 1908).

more employed its favourite methods, discussion, compromise, delay.

7

On the fundamental issue of preferential tariffs the offers came from the Colonies, the opposition from the mother country. But the former were not unanimous, and even those which offered Britain a preference became suddenly hostile to any kind of preferential treatment where the regulation of merchant shipping was concerned. As regards the military organization of the Empire the proposals for unification came from London, and Campbell-Bannerman left the matter to his imperialist Secretary for War, Haldane. The opposition came from the Colonies, who were opposed both to a supreme imperial command and the permanent representation of the Colonies on the Committee of Imperial Defence. They were content to request that the Colonies might avail themselves of the Committee's expert advice on questions affecting their local interests and in such cases send a representative to participate in its discussions. As regards the political organization of the Empire the late Unionist Colonial Secretary, Lyttelton, had submitted to the Colonial Governments a proposal that the 'Colonial Conference' should be transformed into 'an Imperial Council', on which their representatives would have permanent seats.[1] The suggestion attracted the Australian Premier, Deakin, but he was faced by the opposition not only of the new Liberal Government but of the Canadian Prime Minister, Sir Wilfred Laurier. It was finally decided to retain the 'Conference'. In future, however, it should be termed 'Imperial' instead of 'Colonial'; the Prime Minister, not the Colonial Secretary, should be its President; and it should meet regularly every four years, though, if necessary, special Conferences might be summoned in the interval. In default of a council Deakin proposed a 'permanent secretariat' of which the Prime Minister should be President. His proposal was defeated, but a secretariat for the Self-Governing Colonies was formed, at the head of which the Colonial Secretary was placed. All these measures could be interpreted in two senses. They might be regarded as steps towards a federation of the

[1] Colonial Conference. *Correspondence relating to the future organization of Colonial Conferences*, pp. 3–4.

Empire. But they might equally well be regarded as tending by the constitution of the new secretariat to detach from the rest of the Empire the Self-Governing Colonies, the Dominions, or Self-Governing Dominions as they were officially entitled for the first time in 1907.[1] And the fact that the president of future Conferences would be the Premier might be taken to imply that they were nothing more than conversations between the Prime Ministers of nations completely independent of each other. If the Dominions chose to draw the federal bond tighter, so much the better. If they decided to loosen it, the parting could be effected on friendly terms. In 1907, breaking for the first time with the

[1] The Colonies were first mentioned in the official title of the sovereign in the royal proclamation issued in 1858 annulling the Charter of the East India Company in the name of the 'Queen of Great Britain and Ireland, Canada, South Africa, Australia and all the Colonies.' When, however, in 1876 Disraeli obtained from Parliament for the Queen the new title of 'Empress of India', opposition speakers (Gladstone amongst them) urged in vain that mention should be made of the Colonies. Disraeli rejected the proposal as implying that the Colonies did not form an integral part of the United Kingdom.—The word 'Dominion' was used for the first time in 1867 when the British Government decided to give it to the new federation of the British Colonies of North America. Lord Carnarvon explained that the title was adopted because of the sentiments of patriotic loyalty to the Crown which it implied, 'a designation which is a graceful tribute on the part of the colonists to the monarchical principle under which they have lived and prospered and which they trust to transmit unimpaired to their children' (H. of L., February 19, 1867; *Parliamentary Debates*, 3rd Series, vol. clxxxv, pp. 567–8). When it was decided in 1901 to introduce into the style of the new sovereign Edward VII a mention of the British Colonies Chamberlain originally proposed to add to the words 'King of Great Britain and Ireland' the words 'and of Greater Britain beyond the Seas'. The Canadian Government rejected the suggested formula and proposed 'King (or Sovereign) of Canada, Australasia, South Africa, and of all the British Dominions beyond the seas', or alternatively not to give offence to the Colonies not specifically mentioned the shorter form 'of all the British Dominions about the seas'. The latter formula secured the appro- bation of Natal, the Cape, Newfoundland, and New Zealand, and Chamberlain accepted it (*Colonies—Correspondence related to the proposed Alteration of the Royal Style and Titles of the Crown*, 1901). It was finally adopted by Parliament without opposition in the House of Commons, after a variation proposed by Lord Rosebery 'of all the Britains beyond the seas' had been rejected (H. of L., July 26, 1901; *Parl. Deb.*, 4th Ser., vol. xcviii, p. 188); see also H. of C., August 12, 1901; *Parl. Deb.*, 4th Ser., vol. xcix, pp. 457 sqq. The plural term 'Dominions' now designated all the Colonies, the Crown Colonies as well as the Self-Governing. When the text of the resolution defining the future composition of the Conference was laid before the Conference of 1907 the Prime Minister of New Zealand protested against the term 'Self-Governing Colonies' which it contained and proposed the title 'States of the Empire'. The phrase, however, was unintelligible in Australia, where the 'States' were the provinces of the Commonwealth. The term 'Dominions' was adopted, and in the text finally approved by the Conference they were termed 'Self-Governing Dominions' to distinguish them from the 'Crown Colonies' included among the Dominions in the royal title (Colonial Conference, 1907. *Published Proceedings and Principles of the Colonial Conference, 15th to the 26th April, 1907*, p. 16—*Minutes of the Proceedings of the*—pp. 79 sqq.). Strictly speaking, only Canada was a *Dominion*. Australia was a *Commonwealth*. The South African Colonies were not united. New Zealand was only a Colony but immediately after the Conference successfully claimed the title 'Dominion' (speech from the Throne, Wellington, June 21, 1907), and in September the entire country triumphantly celebrated Dominion Day.

established tradition, the Foreign Office permitted negotiations between Canada and France for a commercial treaty to be conducted at Paris, not by the British Ambassador, but the Canadian Premier, whose decisions were simply registered by a representative of the Foreign Office.[1] The solution of the question in whatever direction it might lie was left to the future. For the moment they discussed, compromised, postponed.

8

In this way, by adopting an attitude which combined generosity with caution, the Liberal Cabinet managed to emerge from the Conference with prestige unimpaired. But the problem of the relations to be established between the mother country and the Dominions was perhaps the least of those with which British imperialism was faced. Far more serious were those raised by the direct government of the different parts of the Empire. And nowhere were they more complicated than in South Africa, which had just played such a prominent part in English history. It was a compendium in which all the difficulties of imperial politics were summed up.

British South Africa contained between five and six million inhabitants, four or five million of whom were black—five or six black men for every white.[2] Among the blacks the Hottentots,

[1] For the change of attitude in this respect between the Liberal Cabinet of 1895 and the Liberal Cabinet of 1907 see Colonies (Negotiations of Treaties with Foreign Powers) Return to an address of the Honourable House of Commons, dated 13 April, 1910; for 'Return of the Correspondence between His Majesty's Governments of the self-governing Dominions and Colonies respecting the constitutional position of the latter in the negotiation of commercial and other Treaties with Foreign Powers, including the letter from His Majesty's Secretary of State for Foreign Affairs dated Foreign Office London, 4th July, 1907, addressed to the British Ambassador at Paris and laid upon the Table of the Canadian House of Commons, 1910.'

[2] According to Colonel Seely's calculation there were in South Africa 'between four and five million natives' (H. of C., August 16, 1909. Parliamentary Debates, Commons 1909, 5th Series, vol. ix, p. 953). Keir Hardie, in the course of the same debate, estimated the proportion of natives to whites as six to one (ibid., p. 988). These estimates can be no more than approximate. According to the census of 1904 there were 1,825,172 coloured persons to 580,380 whites in Cape Colony: 945,498 natives and 23,891 other persons of colour to 299,327 whites in the Transvaal; 84,541 natives and 55 other persons of colour to 898 whites in Swaziland; 241,626 coloured persons to 43,419 whites in the Orange River Colony; 79,978 natives in the employment of whites, and 6,686 'half-castes or others' to 97,189 whites in Natal in addition to 100,918 Indians counted separately. In Southern Rhodesia only the whites were included in the census. The reader can judge how difficult, in view of the diversity of methods employed, it is to determine more accurately than I have done the numerical proportion of the black population to the white. And these figures take no account of the great protectorates composed practically speaking wholly

whose culture was of a lower order, were declining in numbers and being swamped by the invasion of the Kaffirs from the north, a race morally and physically superior. The problem was further complicated by a host of mulattos, the coloured people, who regarded themselves as closer to the whites than their native ancestors. Originally, all the blacks had lived, and the majority still lived, under the tribal system. The individual was without rights, the chief of the tribe absolute master of persons and property, custom an even more despotic ruler, imposing its supreme command on the chief and his subjects alike. The men fought and spent the rest of their time in idleness, the women provided for their wants by cultivating the soil. But this indigenous system was now subject to the solvent action of new social forces. The liberal legislation of western Europe had given the blacks in the old Cape Colony equal civil rights with the white men. If they could prove that they possessed the requisite property qualification they were entitled to vote on the same footing as British or Dutch whites. And the Government furnished their children with a generous supply of schools. Where the old tribes survived steps had been taken to facilitate the transition from collective to private property. Elsewhere, the whites had pursued a different policy, protecting the tribal system against the corrosive forces to which it was exposed, segregating the blacks and refusing them access to European civilization. This method itself could be applied in different ways. In Natal, for instance, racial equality was proclaimed by the constitution, but the officials entrusted with its execution took care to render the principle nugatory. In the former Boer republics of the Orange River and the Transvaal the law sanctioned the subjection of the blacks. In the protectorates of Bechuanaland, Swaziland, and Basutoland, on the contrary, the sole object of an administration at once despotic and paternal was to maintain the tribal system intact and safeguard it against every encroachment of civilization. Almost everywhere, however, the new forces were tending to 'individualize' the blacks. Mass production, and such were the methods now used in

of blacks. In the Christian Commonwealth of February 22, 1906, we find the following statistics for Natal whose source is not given: Whites 82,542; blacks 877,388. Arnold-Forster (H. of C., March 29, 1906; *Parliamentary Debates*, 4th Series, vol. cliv, p. 1650) also estimates the whites at 82,000, the blacks however at 956,000. For the native question in South Africa there is an important official document of this date: *South Africa: Report of the South African Native Affairs Commission 1903-5*, 1905; *Natal: Report of the Native Affairs Commission 1906-7*, 1908.

gold mining, brought it well within this category—withdrew the black man for a time from his kraal to return him to it with money of his own, eager to acquire land and assert his independence. These conditions gave birth to a revolutionary agitation and the 'Ethiopian' movement, which for the first time in Africa organized blacks—the native Christians—against the whites with a programme of national claims.

On the very morrow of the General Election of 1906 a serious native revolt broke out in Natal. The blacks refused to pay a poll tax imposed by the local Parliament. But it was stated that the 'Ethiopian' propaganda played a part in the insurrection. It was repressed by the provincial Government without assistance from the imperial army. A small local force of 5,000 put it down in a campaign which continued from February until July and cost the natives 3,000 lives. The summary condemnation to death of twelve rebels as a preliminary to the suppression of the revolt outraged humanitarian sentiment in England and faced the Cabinet with a problem which on many occasions already during the past century had embarrassed British Liberals. Was the independence of the Colony, in other words of the colonists, to be scrupulously respected? Or were they to protect the freedom of the natives even against the colonists? At first the Government decided in favour of the second course and ordered the execution of the condemned men to be postponed until the Colonial Office had established the justice and legality of their sentence. But it was now the turn of colonial public opinion to rise in revolt. Protests poured in from the Cape, from Australia, and from New Zealand. The Government of Natal resigned. Then the British Government yielded and sanctioned the executions.

In point of time this was the first outstanding episode in the colonial policy of the new ministry. It was humiliating, and the Unionist opposition at Westminster raised paeans of triumph. But it was in fact important only inasmuch as it called attention, perhaps for the first time, to the gravity of the problem of the black races in South Africa. For the moment it was another racial question which clamoured urgently for solution. For the blacks were not the only 'lower race' whose presence in South Africa made difficulties for the British Government. During the last few centuries the white peoples have systematically manipulated and transported, as it served their interests, a large variety of races.

They have called into being a negro America whose slave labour was a fertile source of wealth but whose emancipation has raised grave problems for which the United States has found no other solution than the paradoxical return to a system which in some of its moral aspects resembles the Indian caste system. In South Africa, as though to continue this circulation of races around the globe, the Anglo-Saxons invited an invasion of Asiatics in constantly increasing numbers. We have already spoken of the problem created by the importation of Chinese labour into the Rand gold mines and the important place it occupied in the mind of the British public on the eve of the General Election. The invasion of coolies aroused the hostility of the workers in the Transvaal, who objected to the competition of this cheap Asiatic labour. And the British workers sympathized with their grievance. On the Rand round Johannesburg a group had been formed which entitled itself the Labour party, the first item on whose programme was the expulsion of the Chinese. The Chinese labour also gave offence to many Boer peasants instinctively hostile to strangers and who, moreover, had good reason to be alarmed for the security of their property and persons. For these workers from the East were too often the refuse of Chinese crime whom the Government had cleared from its gaols. Too frequently they escaped from the compounds where they were segregated, plundered farms, and murdered isolated Boers. The British humanitarians made common cause with these two classes of objector. 'It is a state of affairs tainted with slavery,' Campbell-Bannerman declared in one of his election speeches, and he had barely become Prime Minister, indeed his Government had not yet received the ratification of the popular vote, when he announced that he had given instructions 'to stop forthwith the recruitment and embarcation of coolies in China and their importation into South Africa'.[1]

But at the very moment when he gave this pledge he found himself faced with the fact that in November 'licences' had been granted for the importation into the Transvaal of more than fifteen thousand Chinese. How could they be cancelled retrospectively? The lawyers pronounced unanimously that it was impossible. The Liberal ministers were therefore compelled on first taking office to assist passively at a new invasion of yellow

[1] Speech at the Albert Hall, December 21, 1905.

30

labour, and make a public declaration that the settlement of the question would be postponed until the Transvaal had been provided with a responsible government. It was a humiliating admission of impotence at a moment when the Election campaign was in full swing, and when the employment of Chinese labourers in the mines was the topic with which radical speakers found it easiest to excite the indignation of the masses against the Tory candidate. Nevertheless, for a whole year the British Government could do nothing more than co-operate in repatriating individuals with a number of capitalists who had adopted an independent line of action and make preparations to replace Chinese labour eventually by a combination of white and black labour locally recruited. Then, in the spring of 1907, in the lobbies of the Imperial Conference the enemies of yellow labour at last won the day. General Botha, the Prime Minister of the Transvaal, was struggling with pecuniary difficulties which placed his Government at the mercy of the Rand magnates. He secured from the British Cabinet the guarantee of a Transvaal loan of £5,000,000. He was therefore free to gratify the wishes both of the Boer peasants and the mining proletariat by ordering the repatriation when their contracts expired of the Chinese workers actually employed. The question was thus settled without involving the mines in the catastrophe predicted by Lord Milner's friends and the Rand capitalists.

It must be added that the Chinese were not the only Asiatics whose presence in South Africa gave anxiety to the local and the imperial governments. The Hindus had traded along the entire east coast of Africa long before the first Europeans made their appearance. At present they were established in large numbers not only in Natal, where the annual number of Hindu immigrants was estimated to exceed that of the British, but even in the interior of the continent at Johannesburg, where they made a living as petty traders and artisans. The whites, however, took alarm and began to pass legislation subjecting the Asiatics to a special code, as though they were an inferior 'caste'. The Hindus replied by revolt. Mohandas Karamchad Gandhi, a devout Hindu ascetic, who, however, had studied law in London and practised at the South African bar, where he defended his compatriots' interests in the courts, had begun his formidable career as an agitator.[1] He

[1] V. D. V. Athalye, *The Life of Mahatma Gandhi*, 1923.

revolted first when he saw his fellow countrymen deprived of the suffrage and subjected to special legislation condemning them to a life of semi-slavery. For a time he enjoyed the support of the High Commissioner, Lord Milner. For the Transvaal was at this time the scene of his activities, and Milner welcomed a further pretext to oppose the aged Kruger. Gandhi had therefore throughout the Boer War displayed the most ardent loyalty to the British cause, hoping presumably to win for the Hindus the favour of Great Britain after the victory. But, if such had been his hope, he was speedily undeceived. The Hindus in South Africa were exposed to an ostracism increasingly severe and new legal restrictions were imposed upon them. In 1906 Gandhi inaugurated a novel method of resistance, not active insurrection but passive resistance, silent and inactive refusal to obey any of the regulations laid down by the law.[1]

9

The Hindu agitation in South Africa was destined five or six years later to assume formidable proportions. And it would prove the prelude to an even more serious agitation in British India, for which reason it deserved mention. For the moment, however, one question in South Africa dominated all the rest—another racial problem. How were the English and the Boers to be reconciled a few years after the war which had raged between them? In conformity with the promises embodied in the treaty of Vereeniging the Government had already begun in 1905 to bestow on the Transvaal a measure of political liberty. A preliminary constitution had been granted by letters patent of March 31, two days before the departure of Lord Milner, who had resigned on March 2, Lord Selborne leaving the Admiralty to take his place. How are we to explain the change at this particular moment? Can we avoid the conclusion that Milner, while proclaiming the grant of a constitution to which, moreover, we are told, he gave a 'general assent', did not altogether approve it in detail and preferred to leave to a successor the difficulties its introduction would involve?[2]

[1] Conflicts between Anglo-Saxons and Indians were not confined to the African coast of the Indian Ocean. In Canada in 1907 anti-Japanese riots were complicated by anti-Indian disturbances. For the Vancouver disturbances see *The Times*, September 12, 13, 14, 1907.
[2] Notice the ill-humour with which Milner announced the reform of April 5, 1901, while admitting it to be inevitable, in his speeches at Germiston, March 15, 1905, and

One thing at least is certain: his resignation was a godsend to the Liberal Government, which thus escaped the necessity of dismissing a few months later an orthodox disciple of Chamberlain. Lord Selborne was no doubt a very conservative statesman, but a man of moderate temper with whom Campbell-Bannerman could get on well. In the December of 1905 the need to take a further step in the Transvaal was urgent. For the constitution of 1905 had completely failed to satisfy the Boer population. A legislative council of forty members, of whom the majority were elected: this at first sight seemed a considerable concession. But the franchise was based on a property qualification determined in such a way as to give the vote to a far larger number in the towns than in the country districts, to the benefit of the British element and the detriment of the Boer. Moreover, the powers of this council were limited. The British Government had the right to 'disavow' within two years any law it might pass, and the initiation of financial measures was strictly reserved to the governor.[1] A formidable agitation against the measure was organized by General Botha. He announced that he and his friends would enter the legislative council only to make any regular work impossible by their obstruction. He demanded—not only for the Transvaal but also for the Orange River Colony—the immediate establishment of a system of unrestricted democratic self-government with a responsible cabinet. The Liberals had barely entered office when they decided that the constitution of 1905 should not be put into operation and despatched a Commission to South Africa to conduct a rapid inquiry and report before the summer. By July 31 the Government was able to lay before both Houses the main lines of the constitution, definitely granted to the Transvaal by letters patent of December 6.[2]

The suffrage was for all practical purposes universal. The constituencies were arranged in such a way that no one could claim that old traditions were outraged, for the former boundaries were

Johannesburg, March 31, 1905 (Transvaal, Further Correspondence relating to affairs in Transvaal and Orange River Colony . . . 1905, pp. 188 sqq.). See, however, W. Basil Worsfold, The Reconstruction of the New Colonies under Lord Milner, 1913, vol. ii, pp. 259 sqq., who maintains that the entire text of the constitution had Lord Milner's approval. If this is the case it was the mere fact of granting representative government to the Transvaal which aroused his antipathy.

[1] Transvaal. Despatch transmitting letters patent and order in council providing for constitutional changes in the Transvaal. April 1905.

[2] Transvaal. Transvaal Constitution, 1906. Letters patent and instructions relating to the Transvaal and Swaziland Orders in Council. December 1906.

respected. And though the English would possess a slight majority in the new assembly it was only because they possessed it in the population. In the debates the two languages were to be on an absolutely equal footing, whereas under the provisions of the constitution of 1905 Dutch would merely have been tolerated. A second chamber nominated by the Executive was reluctantly set up and the Government was at pains to defend it. It was indeed an arrangement 'of which nobody is particularly enamoured'. But all the Colonies possessed such a chamber, and this second chamber, avowedly moreover of a temporary nature, might serve as a useful check in the interest of the Kaffirs on the native policy of the popular assembly. The two speeches in which on the same day Lord Elgin in the Lords, Churchill in the Commons,[1] explained the intentions of the Cabinet, met with violent protests from the opposition. But the Unionist Press was more reserved and when in December the matter came once more before Parliament the protest of the opposition in both Houses seems to have been merely formal.[2]

During this same December the Government promised to extend self-government to the Orange River Colony. The following June it carried out its pledge. It was an even bolder experiment, for in this case the population was homogeneous and completely Dutch. But in the Transvaal itself, to the great disappointment of the British Government, the Boers secured the majority of seats. This did not necessarily mean that the Boers were the majority of the population. But it proved to the hilt that the Pro-Boers had been right in condemning a war undertaken in the interest not of the British inhabitants but the mineowners. For an entire section of the British population, particularly among the working class, rejecting the 'progressive' party which entitled itself the English party and was manipulated by the mineowners, voted for the candidates of Het Volk, the Boer nationalist party. In this way it came about that 'General' Botha, a general of the Boer army, represented his country at the meetings of the Imperial Conference. He received from the Secretary for War the honours British courtesy owed to the valour with which he had fought England on the battlefield.

[1] July 31, 1906 (*Parliamentary Debates*, 4th Series, vol. clxii, pp. 611 sqq., 729 sqq.).
[2] H. of L., December 17, 1906 (*Parliamentary Debates*, 4th Series, vol. clxvii, pp. 939 sqq.); H. of C., December 17, 1906 (ibid., pp. 1063 sqq.).

10

The great problem remained to be solved—the union of all these free states into a single state. From the economic standpoint it was intolerable that customs and railroad charges should form a perpetual source of conflicts between them, suspended from time to time by laborious and precarious agreements. From the political standpoint it was absurd that a white man should acquire or lose the right to vote by changing his domicile from one state to another, or black men be subject to a different system. Circumstances were particularly favourable for settling the problem. The imperialists of Milner's school favoured a federation of South Africa, as the first stage to the federation of the entire Empire. It was to make it possible that they had engineered the forcible destruction of the two independent republics. It was in fact the group of Lord Milner's former subordinates in South Africa, headed by the youthful Lionel Curtis, who undertook a serious examination of the question and drew up the important memorandum communicated by Lord Selborne to the home Government in January 1907.[1] The British Liberals on their part wished to prove that their methods, not those employed by Chamberlain and his disciples, provided the true solution of imperial problems and that, by granting a system of complete political independence to the Transvaal and Orange River, they were taking the quickest road to reconcile the two races throughout the whole of South Africa. If Milner had not left Africa, if there had been no General Election in 1906, would Lionel Curtis and his friends have carried out their task with the same freedom? And the Boers expected the unification of South Africa to compensate them for the treaty of Vereeniging by establishing their predominance by peaceful and legal means throughout the entire country. For the Orange River Colony was wholly theirs, in the Transvaal they disposed of the majority of seats, and if Dr. Jameson, the hero of the raid, was Prime Minister at Cape Town, it was an accident due to the disenfranchisement of so many rebels. The amnesty had supervened, once more they would be masters, an expectation actually verified in 1908.

[1] *The Selborne Memorandum: A review of the Mutual Relations of the British South African Colonies in 1907.* With an Introduction by Basil Williams, 1925.

The task of framing the constitution of the future British South Africa was entrusted to a national convention of representatives of the various South African Governments which sat from October 1908 to February 1909, and whose labours resulted in the Statute by which the Imperial Parliament granted the constitution of September 1909.[1] No general solution of the native problem could be found and for that reason the different systems of franchise obtaining in the various states, henceforth 'provinces' of the Union, were left intact. Where the blacks already possessed the franchise (as in Cape Colony) they continued to possess it for the elections to the new federal Parliament, and the constitution even laid it down that they could be deprived of it only by a majority of two-thirds. But they were ineligible for membership of the Union Parliament, and the utmost the home Government could wring from the Boer representatives was the nomination by the Governor-General of a limited number of senators on the ground of their special knowledge of the 'needs' and 'wishes' of the coloured people, an extraordinarily indirect form of representation. All the economic difficulties on the other hand were overcome by a political unity so complete that it exceeded Milner's federal ideal and eventually enabled the Boers to override all opposition by English Natal.[2] The capital was the Cape; the Supreme Court sat at Bloemfontein and the executive departments were established at Pretoria in the Transvaal. The Statute was passed without amendment in an almost empty house,[3] at a moment indeed when the attention alike of the nation and of Parliament was absorbed by questions nearer home and exciting

[1] 9 Edw. 7, Cap. 9: An Act to consolidate the Union of South Africa (*South Africa Act*, 1909)—For the Union of South Africa and the work of preparation see R. H. Brand. *The Union of South Africa 1909*—also an excellent chapter in Sir John A. R. Marriott, *The Mechanism of the Modern State: A Treatise of the Science and Art of Government*, 1927, vol. i, pp. 257 sqq.

[2] Lord de Villiers, president of the National Convention, visited Canada in 1908 and found that too much autonomy had been left to the provinces. 'In Quebec', he wrote, 'the result has been to establish a distinctly French province without any prospect of its being ever merged into a Canadian as distinguished from a purely French nation' (Eric A. Walker, *Lord Villiers and his Time: South Africa, 1842–1914*, 1925, p. 434). At first sight it may seem strange to find a Boer so unsympathetic to the successful efforts of the French Canadians to preserve their independence. The reason is that he was thinking of the similar efforts the English in Natal might make to retain their independence against the Dutch majority. It was a curious fact that in both instances the British Government adopted the constitutional arrangement (federation in Canada, unification in South Africa) most unfavourable to the British element.

[3] H. of C., August 16, 1909, Arthur Balfour's speech: 'The House is a thin one and a weary one' (*Parliamentary Debates*, Commons 1909, 5th Series, vol. ix, p. 1000).

political passions more directly. Nevertheless, this easy acceptance of the South African constitution eighteen months after Campbell-Bannerman's death was a triumph for that Gladstonian liberalism of which he had been the convinced exponent.

II

In Northern Africa, Egypt[1] from the juridical standpoint formed no part of the Empire, and Egyptian affairs, therefore, came within the competence not of the Colonial but the Foreign Secretary. For Egypt was simply 'occupied' by a British army and the British Consul-General at Cairo possessed only the influence the presence of the army of occupation conferred upon him. This, however, was very great and the Consul-General was, in fact, the Imperial Governor of the country. A legislative council which met every month and of whose thirty members only fourteen were nominated by the Government, the remainder elected at second-hand on the basis of a franchise practically universal, had the right to criticize but not to reject or amend the bills submitted to it by a cabinet entirely subject to British influence. A General Assembly, composed, in addition to the thirty councillors and six ministers, of forty-six elected 'notables' of whom eleven represented the towns, thirty-five the country districts, had the right to refuse its assent to any new tax. But the Khedive's government, subject for twenty years to Lord Cromer's beneficent supremacy, had never found itself obliged to ask the assembly for new sources of revenue. The Budget always showed a surplus, and the country enjoyed a prosperity unknown until the arrival of the English. The Soudan was completely pacified, and by the agreement of April 1904 France had finally recognized England's privileged position in Egypt. When, therefore, the Liberals took office at the end of 1905 they had no reason to expect trouble from this quarter. A keen supporter of the Anglo-French agreement, Lord Cromer was certainly convinced at this period that, free at last from the con-

[1] For the condition of Egypt under British control see Lord Cromer's excellent annual reports. *Egypt: Reports by His Majesty's Agent and Consul General on the finances, administration and condition of Egypt and the Soudan in* . . . See also, for the period immediately preceding that with which we are dealing, Alfred Milner (Lord Milner), *England in Egypt 1892* . . . 11th Ed. *with additions summarizing the course of events to the year 1904*, 1904. See also The Earl of Cromer, *Modern Egypt*, 2 vols., 1908.

stant difficulties caused by the opposition of the French Colony with the more or less open support of the Quai d'Orsay, he could pursue without further obstacle the complete anglicization of Egypt. But suddenly a native agitation sprang into existence more embarrassing and possibly more dangerous than the French obstruction had been. In one aspect it was a nationalist movement. A powerful group belonging to the elite of the native population —doctors, men of business, barristers, journalists—argued that since the British Government claimed that the object of its occupation of Egypt was to bring that country the benefits of western civilization, it should not stop half-way but grant Egypt those parliamentary institutions of which the legislative assembly was a mere shadow but which, it would seem, constituted the pith and marrow of European civilization. In another aspect it was a panislamic movement, not confined to Egypt, but active along the entire northern coast of Africa. As such it appealed to the lower strata of the population, untouched by western influences. The panislamic agitators, their eyes fixed on the Sultan, preached a revolt of all Moslems against the oppression of the colonizing powers and their culture.

In the opening months of 1906 the relations between the Anglo-Egyptian Government and Turkey were disturbed by a serious diplomatic incident. It concerned the frontier between the Turkish and Egyptian territory in the region of Sinai. The Turkish Government sought to extend its jurisdiction to the east coast of the peninsula. The British Government not only contested this claim but maintained that the territory under its control extended to the Mediterranean coast, to a point east of El-Arish. France and Russia supported Britain at Constantinople. The admiral in command of the Mediterranean fleet informed the Porte that he had made all arrangements to land a force in the most important islands of the Archipelago. In Egypt, the army of occupation was reinforced. Finally, on May 14, the Sultan, faced with an ultimatum, submitted. It was a diplomatic and military incident belonging to the foreign relations of the United Kingdom rather than to the administration of the Empire. If it concerns us here, it is on account of its strange repercussion on the domestic situation in Egypt. Reading the contemporary British press we receive the impression that the British Government was defending the interests and rights of Egypt to the east of the Suez Canal. But in Cairo and Alexandria the episode by no means appeared in that light. It was regarded as a reinforcement of British control over Egyptian foreign policy, a machination to embroil the Egyptian with the Turkish Moslems. In the Soudan an Arab rising had to be suppressed by bloodshed, and Lord Cromer recognized that the troops hastily summoned from Malta to Cairo would be better employed in keeping order on the spot than in making war on Turkey. They were exposed to the hostility of native mobs. On June 13 at Denshawai, near Tanta, in the Delta, five officers attempted to shoot pigeons without first obtaining permission from the inhabitants. Their imprudence provoked a riot in which one of them was mortally wounded.

Fifty-two arrests were made and after a summary trial twenty-one of the accused were condemned, four of them to death. The death sentences were immediately carried out. But would Lord Cromer be content with repressing the disorders by force? Aware of the increasing gravity of the insurrection against British rule, he must surely perceive that concessions were inevitable. He categorically refused to admit this: the utmost he was prepared to concede was that it was desirable, though difficult, to give the natives a larger share in the administration, and he appointed Zaglul Pasha Minister of Education. He also admitted in principle the possibility of convoking the provincial councils more frequently, and increasing the number of their members, possibly even to some very slight extent their jurisdiction. But he would take no step in the direction of transforming the legislative council into an Egyptian Parliament.[1] Such a Parliament would be unworkable. It would soon be superseded by a despotism of the oriental type which would destroy all the fruits of the twenty years of British administration and whose first victims would be the 'blue shirted fellahs'. Lord Cromer would not allow that he was himself a despot for he was subject to the control of the Foreign Office and the British Parliament, where Radical opinion was always on the alert to denounce abuses in the administration of the Colonies, and was liable to the censure of the Egyptian press, against which he refrained from invoking the protection of

---

[1] *Egypt No. 3* (1907). *Despatch from the Earl of Cromer respecting proposals of the Egyptian General Assembly*, May 8, 1907. See, a year later, the scheme for reforming the provincial councils worked out by the new Consul-General, Sir Eldon Gorst, in conformity with his predecessor's suggestions (pp. 3, 4). Cf. Lord Cromer's reflections in 1908 in his *Modern Egypt*, vol. ii, pp. 275–6.

new laws.[1] In any case the grant of a constitution worthy of the name could not be contemplated until an indispensable preliminary reform had been effected—the abolition of the system of capitulations and mixed tribunals which enabled criminals to escape the clutches of the law if they could claim foreign nationality, and made a host of administrative acts dependent on the consent of seventeen governments. He suggested the establishment of a council composed exclusively of Europeans to draw up the laws governing the relations between natives and foreigners. He suggested at the same time a reform of the mixed tribunals. Their composition, while remaining international, would no longer be exempt from the control of the imperial government, and they would apply a code which the government with the assent of the legislative council could alter from time to time as local needs might require.[2] But this reform would itself be extremely difficult, requiring as it did the assent of seventeen states. In any case, it was not Lord Cromer's task to carry it through. At the opening of 1907 he resigned on grounds of health. Ten years earlier his departure would have been a triumph, in 1907 it appeared almost a flight. To be sure, his successor, Sir Eldon Gorst, the son of Sir John, declared his intention not to depart from the line of action followed by his predecessor. But did he believe what he said? Confronted with the problems of the new Egypt could he succeed where a greater than he had abandoned the field?

12

Keir Hardie, the leader of the Labour party, declared in July 1906 that 'the terrible event which happened in the Soudan the other day, with its attendant brutalities, reduced the administration of that country under British rule to the level of that of the Congo Free State', and he could not think of the massacre of the natives in South Africa 'without shame and horror'.[3] Were we to witness a revolt of British humanitarianism against the excesses of

---

[1] *Report . . . on the finances, administration and condition of Egypt . . . in 1905*, p. 12.

[2] The question had been already raised in the report for 1904. For the detailed plan of reform Lord Cromer had in view, see his report for 1906, pp. 10 sqq.

[3] Letter to a black domiciled in England: *Daily News*, July 5, 1906—Keir Hardie's reference to the Soudan betrays an obvious confusion in his mind between the repression of the Soudanese rebellion and the executions which followed the Denshawai incident.

British imperialism? What actually happened was the diversion of humanitarian indignation into another channel. It turned against the atrocities of a foreign imperialism, atrocities whose theatre was that state of the Congo to which Keir Hardie alluded. In 1884 at the Berlin Conference the great Powers having agreed to renounce for themselves the annexation of the Congo basin had decided to set up in those regions an independent State whose administration was entrusted to the King of the Belgians. He had governed the Congo as his private property with the greed of a very astute man of business. And he had delegated the administration of entire districts to companies who, to compel the natives to cultivate the rubber forests, had employed the most brutal methods, not even shrinking from massacre. British humanitarian sentiment was outraged and found vent in an outburst of indignation when in 1902 at the close of the Boer War liberalism once more prevailed over the imperialism popular during the preceding years.

The agent of an important Liverpool shipping company, Edmund Morel, resigned his post to devote himself entirely, with the financial support of the Liverpool mercantile magnates, to a campaign of propaganda against the abuses in the government of the Congo. He denounced as violations of freedom and humanity, violations also of the conditions laid down by the Berlin Conference, the exactions to which the natives were subjected and the closure of markets to European commerce by the monopolies granted to the companies.[1] He won the support of the political groups and the churches; in fact, British public opinion was solidly at his back. The King of the Belgians, against whom the campaign was primarily directed, decided to shelter himself by transferring the responsibility for the government of the Congo to the Belgian Parliament. Morel and his friends were willing that the British Government should approve the transfer, but only provided no reservations were made with the aim and effect of perpetuating all the abuses he denounced.[2] The struggle would

[1] E. D. Morel, *The Congo Slave State: A Protest against the new African Slavery; and an Appeal to the Public of Great Britain, of the United States, and of the continent of Europe,* 1903; *Red Rubber, The Story of the Rubber Slave Trade flourishing on the Congo in the year of grace 1906,* 1906; *Great Britain and the Congo: The Pillage of the Congo Basin,* 1909. For the author's biography see E. Seymour Cocks, *E. D. Morel: The Man and His Work,* 1920.
[2] E. D. Morel, *The Future of the Congo: An Analysis and Criticism of the Belgian Government's proposals for a reform of the condition of affairs in the Congo, submitted to His Majesty's Government on behalf of the Congo Reform Association; with Appendices.*

continue for several years. Success was at last in sight when at the end of 1909 Leopold's death raised to the throne of Belgium King Albert, more humane than his uncle and less of a man of business. But it was not until 1913 that the militant philanthropists of Liverpool obtained complete satisfaction on the two points in dispute: protection of the natives against the exploitation of which they were the victims; freedom of trade by the abolition of the monopolies.

This campaign of aggressive humanitarianism aroused little sympathy on the Continent. When the British Government called upon the other signatories of the Berlin convention to support its demands France and Germany refused. England found support only in Washington, the other capital of the English-speaking world.[1] In Paris and Berlin, as at Brussels, it was pointed out that Morel, far from being a martyr to the cause he espoused so zealously, lived by it and lived very well, and moreover that his financial backers were merchants, not apostles. Lord Cromer was loud in his denunciations of the disgraceful administration of the Congo. Was it to cover Denshawai? Or was it perhaps because he wished England to regain possession of the Lado enclave on the Upper Nile which she had too generously abandoned to the King of the Belgians? Lord Lansdowne on behalf of the Unionist party had called upon the British Government to intervene on the Congo between the negroes and the whites. Why had his attitude been so different when in Natal the white men were of British race? But when all this is granted, it remains true that the abuses denounced by the Congo Reform Association were hideous facts, that when Morel called upon the Belgian (and also the French) Government to abolish in their Colonies the privileges granted to private companies, he was only asking them to follow the example England had lately given in her own, and that England was not pursuing any secret design of conquest but simply claiming equal freedom of trade in the Belgian Congo for her own subjects and the entire world. Moreover, if his campaign directly served the interests of some exceedingly influential groups of business men, in other respects it ran counter to the policy pursued by Great Britain. At a moment when the Foreign Office in its fear of Germany was working hard to conciliate all

[1] Where E. D. Morel succeeded in securing Mark Twain's collaboration. *King Leopold's Soliloquy*; A Satire, 1907.

the European powers, his denunciations had aroused the indignation of the Belgian public against British hypocrisy and arrogance, and though Sir Edward Grey did his best to sweeten the pill by the courteous language in which he couched his Government's demands, he could not prevent Belgian foreign policy from remaining consistently pro-German until the eve of the Great War.

13

But why at this particular moment did this problem of the government of the native races suddenly assume such importance at the two extremities of Africa? What was the underlying cause of the 'Ethiopianism' and the 'Panislamism' which in South and North Africa alike caused such embarrassment to British imperialism? We might be tempted at first sight to see in the phenomenon a reaction to the British General Election of January 1906. If British imperialism had begun to mistrust itself, what wonder if the subject peoples began to doubt the solidity of the edifice? But we cannot believe that the Election played such an important part in the history of our planet. We should rather, we think, regard this African agitation as the offshoot of a general insurrection of the non-European races against western domination. The movement had its centre in Asia, its origin in the victories won by Japan at an interval of ten years. Over China first; an Asiatic nation had proved itself capable of sharing in the partition of China on an equal footing with the Christian nations. Now over Russia: an Asiatic nation had successfully resisted a Christian empire whose power was then regarded as more formidable than that of any other and on Chinese soil had replaced by its own imperial sway the dominion of the European power it had defeated.

The lesson given by Japan to Asia had been further enforced by the Russian revolution. On the frontier between Europe and Asia the spectacle was witnessed of a mighty nation rising on the morrow of its defeat against a military and administrative despotism of venerable antiquity. For several months the overthrow of the Czardom was believed to be imminent. Why should not the Oriental nations follow the example set by the Russian revolutionaries and overthrow either, as in China, a corrupt monarchy which had proved incapable of defending its people against the aggression of four or five foreign Powers, or, as in India, a foreign Government established by conquest? From 1899 to 1905 British India had been governed by a statesman who was one of the most typical representatives of the Imperialist spirit and creed. Already distinguished when appointed Viceroy of India for his expert knowledge of the problems of the Far East, Lord Curzon had displayed during his seven years' rule the qualities and the defects whose combination composed the perfect Chamberlainite: industry, obstinacy, ostentation, despotism, and an overbearing harshness. But in Lord Curzon the overbearingness passed all bounds and involved him in actions which, whether justifiable or not, arrayed everyone against him. He had hardly entered upon office when he claimed for himself, as Viceroy over three hundred million subjects, an independence comparable with that possessed by the freely elected Parliaments of the Dominions, and pursued in the north around and beyond the passes of the Himalayas a policy of aggression which caused no little anxiety to the home Government. He had antagonized the natives by taking steps to check the influx of candidates for the university examinations with the aim of retarding the growth of that intellectual proletariat whose temper alarmed the supporters of order in India. In 1905 he decided to divide Bengal into two separate parts, consolidating one of them with Assam. It was a measure for which excellent administrative arguments could be advanced. But its effect was to create a province of 'Eastern Bengal and Assam' in which two-thirds of the population were Mohammedans, thereby arousing what was nothing short of an insurrection among the Hindus. At least he might have won for his policy the support of the solid mass of 'Anglo-Indians'. But in the hope of conciliating the native population he had ordered that the ill usage to which they were subject at the hands of the conquering race should be punished as severely as the sporadic acts of violence committed by the natives against their masters. He had thus alienated the Anglo-Indians also. By a final caprice he quarrelled in 1905 with Lord Kitchener, who after signing the peace treaty in South Africa had secured the command of the Indian army. The original ground of quarrel was a dispute as to the respective authority of the Commander-in-Chief and the military member of the executive council, whom we may regard as the Viceroy's minister for war. Kitchener claimed complete independence in all purely military questions.

Lord Curzon refused to admit the claim and demanded a measure of control for his military member, in other words for himself. A commission of inquiry was appointed in London which pronounced in favour of Kitchener's contention, attributed only minor functions to the military member and called upon Lord Curzon to appoint a new official to fill a post in future subordinate. He proposed a candidate whose name appeared to spell defiance to the report of the Commission and who was not accepted. Lord Curzon thereupon resigned.[1]

14

He was succeeded by Lord Minto, an old soldier who had been Governor-General of Canada. If he belonged to a family which like so many other great families had gone over to Unionism some twenty years ago, the family tradition of the Elliots was Whig, and, moreover, he had performed with tact in Canada duties identical with those of a constitutional sovereign. He might, therefore, be expected to bring to British India a period of calm after the seven troublous years inflicted upon the country by Lord Curzon.[2] Thus, when it took office, the Liberal Cabinet had been freed from Lord Curzon in Asia, as in Africa from Lord Milner. Even before the landslide of January 1906 the militant imperialism of 1898 was crumbling.

Half a century earlier British India had already experienced its revolution. Having suppressed it at the cost of much bloodshed, England had pledged herself to govern the country with a scrupulous impartiality, to respect native beliefs and customs and appoint 'so far as was possible' native subjects to administrative

[1] For Lord Curzon's viceroyalty see *The Life of Lord Curzon, being the authorized biography of George Nathaniel, Marquess Curzon of Kedleston*, by the Right Hon. the Earl of Ronaldshay, 1928, vol. ii, *Viceroy of India*; Lovat Fraser, *India under Curzon and after 1911*; see also the anonymous work extremely hostile to Lord Curzon's government entitled *Twenty-eight Years in India*. For the quarrel between Lord Curzon and Lord Kitchener see the *Life of Lord Kitchener* by Sir George Arthur, 1920, vol. ii, pp. 199 sqq.

[2] 'For the last few years—this is a very important point—the doctrine of administrative efficiency has been driven too hard. Our administration—so shrewd observers and very experienced observers assure me—would be a great deal more popular if it was a trifle less efficient, a trifle more elastic generally. We ought not to put mechanical efficiency at the head of our ideas. . . . Perfectly efficient administration, I need not tell the House, has a tendency to lead to over-centralization; it is inevitable. The tendency in India is to override local authority and to force administration to run in official grooves' (H. of C., June 6, 1907, John Morley's speech; *Parliamentary Debates*, 4th Series, vol. clxxv, p. 881).

posts. She had kept her promise, though very slowly and very incompletely. Official regulations, whose terms, however, had often been altered, had reserved for the natives the monopoly of certain posts in the local government and had even admitted a proportion of them to more important positions. An Act of 1892, couched however in very ambiguous and indirect language, had empowered the Viceroy to introduce into the provincial councils a proportion of elected members.[1] These concessions had not been uninfluenced by an agitation whose mouthpiece was a body which met annually and entitled itself the Hindu 'National Congress'. Its adherents demanded for British India swaraj, Home Rule, a Hindu Parliament, freely elected and governing the three hundred million Indians by means of a responsible Cabinet. They did not declare war on British sovereignty or civilization. They simply claimed for the natives the right to collaborate on an equal footing with the civil servants of British birth in the westernization of India. They confined their agitation to strictly legal methods—public speeches and the press. They made little impression on the imperialists of the Chamberlain school, who were convinced at the close of the nineteenth century that the concessions already made were more than enough to satisfy the native races. 'My own belief', wrote Lord Curzon in 1900, 'is that the Congress is tottering to its fall, and one of my great ambitions while in India is to assist it to a peaceful demise.'[2] During the last year of his viceroyalty he would not have used the same language.

For the repercussion of the Japanese victories made itself felt and a new party of extremists soon came into being. Who were the leaders of this new movement? There was a certain Tilak, the author of learned works in which he sought to prove that the Vedic culture was the oldest and the most nordic of all cultures.[3] He began his career as an agitator by organizing a movement of protest against the law which had been passed prohibiting the marriage of Hindu girls before the age of twelve.[4] And his col-

---

[1] 55 & 56 Vict., Cap. 14: An Act to amend the Indian Councils Act, 1861 (*Indian Councils Act*, 1892).

[2] Lord Ronaldshay, *The Life of Lord Curzon*, vol. ii, p. 152.

[3] *The Orion or researches into the antiquity of the Vedas*, 1893. *The Arctic Home of the Vedas being also a new Key to the interpretation of many Vedic texts and legends*, 1903.

[4] For Tilak and his political career see D. V. Athalve, *The Life of Lokomanya Tilak; with a foreword by C. R. Das, president-elect of the 36th National Congress*, 1921; and the collection of his political speeches: *Bal Gangadhar Tilak, His Writings and Speeches. Appreciation by Babu Aurobindo Ghose* (no date). For the revolutionary agitation in general see Valentine

league was the Gandhi whose acquaintance we have already made. He came from South Africa, famous throughout India for his defence of his fellow Indians there against English persecution. He had brought with him the programme the agitation must follow. It was 'non-co-operation', swadeshi, the boycotting of everything English or European, institutions as well as goods. In itself this method did not involve the use of violence. But it was not long before the malcontents, not content with refusing to buy British goods, publicly burned them. And very soon they grew tired of these attacks on property, and assassinations by shooting or bomb took their place. The movement was a return to the national traditions, a revolt against western materialism and utilitarianism, a movement to preserve Brahmanism in its integrity.[1] It attached itself to the avowed anti-Mohammedan agitation to which the separation of the two Bengals had given birth. The leaders, however, perceived the danger to their cause which would be involved by a civil war between the Hindus and Moslems of which the British would reap the benefit, and sought for a banner that would unite both against the common oppressor. Moreover, both the Tolstoyan programme of passive non-co-operation and the dynamite outrages betrayed Russian influence. The difference between the movement by which Japan had successfully asserted her hegemony in the Far East against the supremacy of the European powers and this movement by which India was attempting to throw off the British yoke may be summed up as follows. In Japan a monarchy and an hereditary aristocracy of ancient and proud traditions borrowed from Europe her industrial and military methods the better to resist the invasion of her culture. In India an entire people, also the heir of an immemorial tradition, borrowed from the European nations, though we must admit from the least European of these, namely Russia, their methods of revolutionary agitation to achieve the same end.

Under these circumstances it was an act of courage for John Morley to accept, even perhaps to ask for, the post of Secretary of State for India. He regarded himself as the official representative

Chirol, *Indian Unrest: A Reprint, revised and enlarged from 'The Times'*, with an introduction by Sir Alfred Lyall, 1910. For a general view of the social and political problems connected with the government of British India at this period see the excellent work by Joseph Chailley, *L'Inde Britannique; Société indigène; Politique indigène; Les idées directrices*, 1910.

[1] For the attempts made at this period in India to reinvigorate Brahmanism, see Dr. J. N. Farquhar, *Modern Religious Movements in India*, 1915.

in the Cabinet of the Gladstonian tradition. Perhaps in playing this part he was a little too obviously conscious of his own importance. He was a great Liberal, a Liberal veteran, a survivor of the golden age of Liberalism, and as such his attitude towards the new tendencies of the younger generation was an indulgent pity not the less irritating for a tinge of disdain. Moreover, he was not very popular with his colleagues, beginning with Campbell-Bannerman, who had given him the amusing nickname Priscilla, suggestive of a spinster and a bluestocking. But it cannot be denied that he acquitted himself of the formidable task with firmness and prudence and as successfully as the circumstances permitted. He had the good fortune to deal with a Viceroy of modest personality and tractable temper, content in his relations with him to adopt the attitude of a subordinate rather than an autocrat.[1] He had also the good fortune to be faced in the House of Commons by a leader of the opposition who had nothing of Chamberlain's spirit. Balfour passed the word to his followers not to molest Morley, and his orders were obeyed without difficulty at a time when the right of the sword was no longer the fashionable creed in England.[2]

[1] For Morley's Indian policy see *Recollections by John Viscount Morley, Book V: A Short Page in Imperial History* (vol. ii, pp. 147 sqq.). The reader will find there copious extracts from his daily memoranda and his letters to Lord Minto. See also John Morley, *Speeches on Indian Affairs*, Second Edition revised and enlarged; and on the other hand John Buchan, *Lord Minto: A Memoir*, 1924. It is the life story of Lord Minto published by his family after his death. The author does his best to prove that Lord Morley's recollections place the facts in a false light. According to Buchan the real author of the policy which Morley would have us regard as his personal choice and imposed by him on Lord Minto was on the contrary Lord Minto who, by flattering Morley's senile vanity, contrived to make him believe that he was the originator when he was really obeying the Viceroy's dictation. In fact Lord Morley does not conceal so often as Buchan would have us believe the points on which he took Lord Minto's advice—for example, the appointment of a native member of the Viceroy's executive council. He even admits that in certain instances he was less bold than the Viceroy. The latter wanted a majority of non-official members in the Viceroy's legislative council. Morley opposed it. (H. of C., December 17, 1908; *Parliamentary Debates*, 4th Series, vol. cxcviii, pp. 1984-5.) On the other hand as regards the composition of the new executive councils and on the question of an amnesty, whatever Buchan may say, Minto was the conservative, Morley the reformer. And it remains doubtful whether Lord Minto's liberalism was the result of deep convictions or mere indolence. See for instance the account of him preserved by W. S. Blunt in his Diary for October 25, 1909: ' . . . He also told us about Minto, as Viceroy of India, a mere nonentity in the Government, not even reading the most important documents laid before him. On one occasion they tested this by gumming the leaves slightly together, which he returned unopened' (*My Diaries*, vol. ii, p. 292). For a good summary of the reforms accomplished by Morley see E. Major, *Viscount Morley and Indian Reform*, 1910. Some interesting details may be found in Syed Sirdar Ali Khan, *The Life of Lord Morley* . . . 1923, pp. 194 sqq. For a general survey of British legislation affecting India consult Sir Courtenay Ilbert's compendium, *The Government of India: A brief historical survey of Parliamentary Legislation relating to India*, 1922.

[2] Morley's Diary, August 2, 1906: 'I will take care that Balfour and Percy are kept well informed of the truth of things. I don't think there is any predisposition in any quarter to

15

Whatever hopes the formation of a Liberal ministry, when the Unionist Cabinet resigned in favour of Campbell-Bannerman and his colleagues, aroused in some quarters, whatever fears it aroused in others, were enhanced a few months after the General Election by the incidents of the Fuller affair. Certain schools in Eastern Bengal had taken part in the agitation of the extremists. The Lieutenant-Governor of the province, Sir J. Bampfylde Fuller, called upon the University of Calcutta to take disciplinary measures against them. Lord Minto disapproved of this demand and asked him to withdraw it. Rather than obey he offered his resignation. It was accepted and he was immediately replaced. The incident caused a great stir among the Anglo-Indians, which found an echo in London. But Morley made it plainly understood that his Indian policy would not be a mere exhibition of weakness. He systematically carried out a perfectly definite policy, on the whole the reverse of that which Lord Cromer had followed in Egypt. Lord Cromer had scrupulously respected the freedom of the press: Morley repressed its excesses. Lord Cromer had refused pointblank the nationalist demand for a representative Parliament at Cairo: Morley, on the contrary, answered the claims of the National Congress by a policy of concessions.

Yielding to Lord Minto's arguments and braving the wrath of the hundred and fifty Radicals who under the title of the Indian Committee constituted themselves the advocates at Westminster of the Hindu rebellion, Morley authorized the Governor-General to put into force regulations dating from the days of the East India Company, by which his agents were empowered to prosecute the authors of seditious articles; public meetings could be prohibited at his discretion in particular districts, and dangerous agitators even deported without trial. On May 10, 1907, a vice-regal ordinance subjected public meetings in certain 'proclaimed' areas to a severe control. On June 3 the Viceroy gave full powers to the local authorities to prosecute seditious articles. But at the same time Morley informed Parliament and the nation that his

think ill of us.' May 3, 1907: 'Balfour is behaving well, as might have been expected. He told me that he had passed the word to his men that they are not to molest me. (*Recollections*, vol. ii, pp. 83, 213.)

determination to liberalize the political institutions of British India remained unshaken.[1] The Government intended to carry the elective and representative principle throughout the entire constitutional edifice of India. It also intended in fulfilment of the promises made in 1861 to give the natives access even to the highest ranks of the civil service. We may remark the conception, inspired by Burke rather than by Mill[2] and perhaps suggested to Morley by Lord Minto, of a species of consultative senate or council of notables (Imperial Advisory Council) in which the great landowners would sit side by side with the native princes. This arrangement would give its due weight 'to one of the great conservative forces which the bureaucratic structure of an alien government has to some extent inevitably tended to overshadow'.[3] To prepare the public mind for these impending reforms Morley took the further step of nominating two Indian members of the 'Council of India' which assisted him at Whitehall. He thus initiated the important measures which the British Parliament adopted during the following years in execution of a prearranged programme. On the one hand, there was a press law which authorized the police to suppress revolutionary organs and confiscate copies of the newspaper and its printing apparatus, an Act, based in fact on a statute passed in 1883 to repress the activities of Irish anarchists in England, inflicting severe penalties for the fabrication and even, if it gave grounds for 'reasonable suspicion' the mere possession of explosives, and a Statute withdrawing acts of anarchist violence from the ordinary procedure of the courts and trial by jury.[4] On the other hand, a solemn message was sent from the King-Emperor to the princes and people of India on the fiftieth anniversary of the date when the British Government took over the territories hitherto governed by the East India Company. It announced a very wide amnesty and at the same time a 'prudent' extension of the liberties granted to

[1] H. of C., June 6, 1907 (*Parliamentary Debates*, 4th Series, vol. clxxv, pp. 883–4).
[2] See in the speech delivered by Morley at Arbroath, October 21, 1907, the extremely involved passage in which the aged Radical advises young Hindus to seek the inspiration of their liberalism in Burke rather than in Mill. In his speech of June 6, 1907 (ibid., p. 880) he appeals to Mill—whom he calls the teacher of his generation—only to support the legitimacy of Britain's paternal government in India.
[3] Parliamentary Papers, August 26, 1907 (*The Times*, August 27, 1907).
[4] The Act regulating the Press and the Act dealing with explosives June 8, 1908; for the detailed provisions of these two Statutes see *The Times*, July 9, 1908. Act subjecting anarchist plots to a special jurisdiction, December 11, 1908; for its provisions see *The Times*, December 11, 1908.

India by the Indian Councils Act of 1892. The new Indian Councils Act[1] passed in 1909 by the British Parliament without any very serious opposition[2] did not alter the strictly advisory character of the provincial legislative councils. Nor did it alter their distinctive system of representation—a representation not of individuals, but of interests effected in accordance with complicated rules laid down by the Viceroy. And in yet other respects the Bill was a less ambitious measure than the important measure of decentralization previously contemplated, less ambitious even than the measure announced in December 1908. Lord Morley declared with the utmost emphasis that the new Act must not be regarded as a step towards parliamentary government, that neither now nor at any later date would he take the responsibility of setting up a parliament in India.[3] But the membership of the legislative councils was considerably increased so that they bore a closer resemblance to parliaments. In future the election would be a genuine election, not the mere recommendation to the Viceroy of a candidate whom he was free to reject, and the competence of the councils, particularly in matters of finance, was guaranteed and extended.[4] And measures were taken to secure that on all the legislative councils except the Viceroy's the non-official members should always be in a majority.[5] Further, Morley, with Lord Minto's full support, appointed a native to the Viceroy's executive council,[6] and the new statute empowered the Viceroy to set up in conjunction with every organ of provincial government an executive council to which Indians would be eligible on the same terms as Europeans. It was not enough to satisfy the extremists:

[1] 9 Edw. 7, Cap. 4: An Act to amend the Indian Councils Acts 1861 and 1892 and the Government of India Act, 1833 (*Indian Councils Act*, 1909).

[2] For the Indian Councils Act of 1909 see H. of L., December 17, 1908. Lord Morley's speech (*Parliamentary Debates*, 4th Series, vol. cxcviii, pp. 1,974 sqq.) and the parliamentary papers published at the same time; the report of the Royal Commission appointed in December 1908 which appeared in March 1909; also H. of C., April 19, 1909, T. F. Buchanan's speech (ibid., 5th Series, vol. iii, pp. 496 sqq., 1266 sqq.).

[3] H. of L., December 17, 1908 (ibid., 4th Series, vol. cxcviii, p. 1995).

[4] The second clause of the Act of 1892 granted the Viceroy's legislative council and the provincial legislative councils the right to discuss the Budget. But on this point it imposed restrictions abolished by Clause 5 (b) of the Statute of 1909.

[5] Critics remarked that the non-official members need not be natives and, therefore, that the Councils though not containing a majority of officials might contain nevertheless a majority of Europeans (Wilfred Blunt, *My Diaries*, November 22, 1909).

[6] The decision had been approved by the Cabinet on May 3, 1907. But it had taken two years to overcome the opposition of the King and a powerful section of the House of Lords who considered that the step would give offence to the native princes (Sir Sidney Lee, *King Edward VII*, vol. ii, p. 38).

they were still a long way from swaraj. Nevertheless, the British Government had good reason for satisfaction. It had conciliated the moderate element of the population and without taking any imprudent risk had given a more liberal character to the government of India.

Outbreaks of rebellion in Egypt; swadeshi in Bengal. Despite differences of creed and language these were two different forms, African and Asiatic, of an identical phenomenon, the revolt of nationalities against empires, two repercussions of the same important historical event, the victory won by Japan on land and sea, the breakdown of Russian imperialism in the Far East. We have found it necessary to emphasize the grave significance of these events, whose unexpected issue we shall witness in 1914, the world war. And it is the more necessary because they show what difficulties faced the new Liberal Cabinet from the outset. Tied by its Gladstonian traditions to an anti-imperialist policy, it was nevertheless responsible for the administration of the vast Colonial Empire it had inherited, the largest the world had ever known. Opposition speakers were in a position to exploit these difficulties against Campbell-Bannerman's ministry, offer embarrassing congratulations on the vigour with which it repressed revolutionary plots in Bengal, and force the Government to yield when it attempted to protect the Kaffirs in Natal from the violent methods of repression adopted by the local authorities. But these difficulties did not threaten the existence of the Government. At the end of two sessions its formidable majority had not been seriously impaired, and no one could claim that its method of governing the Empire had disappointed the expectations of the electorate. It had granted a system of complete self-government to the Boers of South Africa and had actively promoted political and administrative reform in India. Moreover, its predecessors had pursued too systematically the policy of diverting popular feeling to imperial questions. The British public was heartily weary of their policy of national honour and expensive victory, and this weariness which contributed so powerfully to the Liberal victory of January 1906 was no less evident two years later. There remained the problems of strictly domestic concern, whose importance was the greater since the country displayed less interest in colonial affairs. There was the Irish question, always a deep line of cleavage between the two parties. There was the religious and educational question, once more acute since the Education Act of 1902. And finally, there was the labour question, also acute since the Courts and finally the House of Lords, sitting as the supreme court of appeal, had undermined the privileged position of the trade unions.

II DOMESTIC QUESTIONS:

IRELAND, EDUCATION, LABOUR

I

We should hesitate to call the Irish question, in the strict sense, a domestic question concerning the mother country. No doubt, when the twentieth century opened England, Scotland, and Ireland were parts of a single 'United Kingdom'. But the Irish, or at least the vast majority of Irishmen, belonged to it in spite of themselves. At the very door of Great Britain, Ireland was still a 'Colony', and a Colony which demanded the independence a Conservative and 'Unionist' England refused. Twice we have seen the Unionist Cabinet attempt a policy of concession, and twice retreat when faced with the opposition of the Ulster 'colonists', who resented the grant of too much liberty to the 'natives' of the rest of the island. A change of Government supervened. Lord Aberdeen returned from Canada to replace Lord Dudley as Lord Lieutenant. Bryce, the eminent historian, and a recognized authority on the American Constitution, succeeded Walter Long as Chief Secretary. Sir Antony MacDonnell, the Under-Secretary, never vacated his post; he remained under Bryce as under Walter Long, under Walter Long as under Wyndham. What Irish policy would the new Cabinet adopt? They had pledged themselves 'to govern Ireland according to Irish ideas' and the Irish idea of government was first and foremost that Ireland should be governed by the Irish, the genuine Irish, the Irish Nationalists. Bryce yielded to their demands and appointed government officials and magistrates only on the recommendation of Redmond and his friends. Even so, he did not transform the administration rapidly enough to satisfy their impatience. He made them wait over a year before he could be brought to sacrifice Sir Horace Plunkett, whom John Dillon pursued with implacable hate, regarding his policy of conciliation as more prejudicial to the claims of Irish nationalism than the brutal opposition of the old Tories. There remains the question of legislation in the strict sense. In the first place, what would be the effect of the important Statute of 1903 which, if carried into execution without a hitch, would transfer all the arable land from the landlords to the tenants?[1] From the very beginning it had encountered more or less avowed opponents among the Irish politicians, afraid lest they might be compelled to witness the success of a reform of which they had not been the authors, designed by those who had planned it to divert the Irish from the pursuit of their political claims by satisfying their economic. The confusion which followed its enactment, the arrest of the policy of devolution, the fall of the Unionist Cabinet, and the General Election favoured their opposition. They had no difficulty in finding in the country districts of Ireland a host of people whose discontent was easily inflamed.

The Act of 1903 contained clauses intended to prepare the way for the resettlement on the land of the tenants previously evicted by the landlords. But the funds provided were insufficient to enable them to be put into execution. An agitation was organized to secure the amendment of the Act of 1903 on this point, and the enactment of another statute. And the tenants of urban properties in their turn embarked on an agitation demanding the same safeguards against the threat of eviction as the rural tenants possessed.

The Act did not compel the sale of land and although it promised landlords who sold and tenants who purchased advantages which fully compensated for any loss they might sustain, there were landlords who nevertheless preferred the security of the *status quo* to the risks and vexations of a sale. The word of command went round to the tenants in many parts of Ireland to refuse in future to pay their landlords a rent in excess of the annuity paid to the State by the tenants who purchased their land. This would compel the landlords to sell, and the land purchase legally optional would become, if the order were universally obeyed, for all practical purposes compulsory.

---

[1] For the history of the Irish land laws, particularly during the period with which we are concerned, see W. F. Bailey, *The Irish Land Acts: A Short Sketch of their History and Development*, 1917. John E. Pomfret, *The Struggle for Land in Ireland, 1800–1923*, 1930.

The Act dealt only with arable land and did not extend to pasture. But in those western districts which the statute termed 'congested' there was no lack of space on which to settle the poverty-stricken crowd huddled in the villages. The cultivators had been evicted from their smallholdings, which had been absorbed in large estates, vast solitudes abandoned to herds of cattle. Did these unfortunates owe their dispossession solely to human wickedness? Was it not chiefly due to the operation of economic laws under the system of free trade common to England and Ireland? If these areas were no longer under cultivation, was it not because their cultivation was no longer profitable? If new cultivators were reinstalled, would they not be condemned to inevitable bankruptcy and the land soon return to pasture once more? Notwithstanding, public opinion clamoured for a resettlement and a plan of campaign was arranged to intimidate the graziers. Cattle were not mutilated: this cruel method adopted thirty years earlier had unnecessarily revolted humanitarian feeling in England. But at night the fences surrounding the pastures were removed and the animals driven off. The following morning the grazier could not find his beasts or, if he found them at all, it was only after a tiring search, several miles from their pasture, scattered along the roads. The cattle-driving first organized during the winter of 1906–7 steadily increased till the following autumn. The magistrates, unfortunate choices from the village politicians, either went on strike by refusing to sit on days when cases of cattle-driving would come before the bench or refused to condemn. The London press gave these disturbances all the publicity the agitators could desire and called upon the Government to take severe measures.

This was a policy which it was not easy for a Liberal Cabinet to adopt. The General Election was scarcely at an end when the operation of the Crimes Act of 1887 had been suspended in the districts, certainly very few, where it was still in force, and after a few months' opposition Bryce yielding to his colleagues' wishes[1] agreed to abandon the Arms Act of 1881, hitherto annually renewed, which enabled the Government to prevent anarchy by disarming seditious agitators. After he had exchanged at the end of 1906 the thankless task of governing Ireland for the more bril-

[1] Bryce to Lord Fitzmaurice, November 30, 1908 (H. A. L. Fisher, *James Bryce, Viscount Bryce of Dechmont*, vol.i, pp. 35 sqq.).

liant and easier post of Ambassador at Washington, the Cabinet found itself compelled to adopt repressive measures. But loyalty to Liberal principles forbade enforcement of the provisions of the last Crimes Act. The Cabinet could not forget that this statute, like all its predecessors of the same kind, had been passed by a Unionist Parliament in the teeth of Liberal protests. Steps were, moreover, taken to give the disaffected a measure of satisfaction. A Royal Commission was appointed, with Lord Dudley as chairman, to inquire into the laws dealing with the congested districts and discover what could be done to extend and improve them.[1] A Labourers Bill[2] and a Town Tenants Bill[3] were passed in 1906; an Evicted Tenants Bill[4] in 1907. Moreover, to better the conditions of the Irish lower classes within the limits of the existing legislation and secure valuations of the land more favourable to the tenants, the regulations governing the appointment of the Estates Commissioners were modified, so that to be appointed to the Board it would no longer be necessary to pass the prescribed examinations. And four of the commissioners were deprived of their posts to make room for men more agreeable to the Irish politician. But the agrarian legislation had given birth to a problem graver than those of which we have just spoken. The machinery of the statute of 1903 broke down.

[1] A Royal Commission appointed to inquire into and report upon, the operation of the Acts dealing with Congestion in Ireland, the working of the Congested Districts Board, and the Land Commission under these Acts, and the relations of the Board with the Land Commission and the Department of Agriculture and Technical Instruction; what areas (if any) outside the districts now scheduled as congested, require to be dealt with as congested; what lands are not conveniently situated for the relief of Congestion; what changes in law and administration are needed for dealing with the problem of Congestion as a whole, for facilitating the migration of the surplus population from congested areas to other lands and generally for the bettering the condition of the people inhabiting congested areas. Appointed July 2, 1906, it presented its report May 5, 1908.

[2] 6 Edw. 7, Cap. 37: An Act to amend the law relating to Labourers in Ireland and to make provision with respect to the application of a portion of the Ireland Development Grant (*Labourers [Ireland] Act*, 1906). The object of the Statute was to authorize the building of cottages at the public cost and make it easier for farm labourers to acquire pieces of land.

[3] 6 Edw. 7, Cap. 54: An Act to improve the position of Tenants of certain Houses, Shops or other Buildings in Ireland (*Town Tenants [Ireland] Act*, 1906). The object of the Statute was to give the tenant the right to be indemnified for any improvements of the property he had made during his lease, and also when the refusal to renew the lease was judicially declared 'unreasonable'.

[4] 7 Edw. 7, Cap. 56: An Act to facilitate the possession of land for certain Evicted Tenants in Ireland and for other purposes connected therewith, and to make provision with respect to the tenure of office by the Estates Commissioners (*Evicted Tenants [Ireland] Act*, 1907). The Act empowered the Estates Commissioners to acquire land by expropriation and settle on it farmers evicted by their landlords. But an amendment introduced in the House of Lords restricted the number of possible beneficiaries to 2,000.

The Act could not be said to have failed in view of the fact that by 1907 one-third of the cultivated area had changed hands as a result of the combined operation of the Land Act of 1903 and the earlier land purchase Acts. But from one point of view it had been too successful and the host of land-hungry peasants who took advantage of the law to demand land was so numerous that the funds available to satisfy them were giving out. In 1903 the Government had undertaken to issue land bonds to the annual value of £5,000,000 bearing interest at 2¾ per cent. But as a result of the general depreciation of government securities it now found itself obliged to borrow below par; in July 1907 the value of the bonds fell to 83. To make up the difference between the real price of issue and the nominal value of the bonds a clause in the Act of 1903 which no one seems to have noticed when it was passed[1] empowered the Government when certain allocations from the imperial budget had been exhausted to obtain the necessary funds from the Irish ratepayer. This actually happened in 1907. We can well imagine the indignation of these ratepayers, committed as they were to the principle that the entire United Kingdom, not Ireland alone, must pay the cost of a measure which they regarded as a reparation due to Ireland from Great Britain. What was to be done? Pay the landlord in bonds instead of cash? Make the sum required a first charge on the premium of 12 per cent which according to the provisions of the original statute was to be added to the money obtained by the loan? Issue bonds in future bearing 3 instead of 2¾ per cent interest? Or simply make the Treasury bear the entire cost of the fall in Government securities? The Chancellor of the Exchequer, Asquith, informed the House that he was studying the question. He explained in language sufficiently mystifying that they were in search of an arrangement which would burden neither the British nor the Irish taxpayer. In any case, he added, the financial arrangement made in 1903 must be revised; he intended to reform it on 'a sounder and more equitable basis'.[2] In other words, the Land Act of 1903 was declared bankrupt. No one in the Nationalist party was displeased by the bankruptcy.

[1] If we can believe Wyndham (H. of C., July 5, 1907; *Parliamentary Debates*, 4th Series, vol. clxxvii, pp. 1,019–20) he never intended to impose this burden on the Irish ratepayer. But his explanations are very involved and, when all is said, prove only that when the Bill was passed in 1903 everyone expected a rise not a fall in the value of Government securities. See Asquith's trenchant reply. (Same sitting ibid., p. 1,026.)

[2] H. of C., July 5, 1907 (*Parliamentary Debates*, vol. clxxvii, p. 1029).

2

While the economic problems, for which the late Government had hoped to find a solution acceptable to all parties, were becoming once more a source of discontent, the great political and national question of Home Rule remained unsolved. On this point the Liberal party seemed bound by Gladstone's former pledge to the Nationalists which it had been prevented from performing already only by the opposition, twice repeated, of the House of Lords and the opinion of the majority of Englishmen. On the eve of forming his Cabinet Campbell-Bannerman, as we have already seen, had refused to yield to Lord Rosebery's demand and had solemnly declared that on this point, as on all others, he remained faithful to the tradition of Gladstone. Would he then reintroduce in its integrity, immediately after his accession to office, a Home Rule Bill on the lines of those rejected in 1886 and 1893 ? If the Liberal majority had not been so overwhelming and the eighty Irish members had held the fate of the Government in their hands they might perhaps have dared to demand it and the Cabinet have been compelled to obey their orders to its own ruin. But, as we know, this was very far from the case. Campbell-Bannerman was, therefore, in a position to restrict himself to the more prudent programme he had traced in November 1905, and secure for it the preliminary approval of the Nationalist leaders. He would persuade the Irish to accept a partial measure, an 'instalment' of representative control and administrative reform, by convincing them that not only was it no obstacle to a more radical programme but a step towards its accomplishment. What would be the nature of this 'payment on account' with which the Irish electorate was asked to be provisionally content? Bryce, the analyst of the American constitution, seemed at first sight better fitted than any other man to devise the necessary formulas and it would appear that during the summer of 1906 he opened negotiations through the channel of Sir Antony MacDonnell with the two heads of the National Irish League, Redmond and Dillon. In November it was rumoured that the Government had no intention at present of granting Ireland a Parliament and simply proposed to pursue the policy of 'devolution' the late Cabinet had adopted and dropped, by setting up in Dublin a body partly elected, partly nominated by the executive, not to legislate but to supervise the execution of statutes passed at Westminster.[1] The negotiators no doubt found themselves faced by two problems. Should the new body be entrusted with the control of the police? What control should be given or refused to the clergy of the various denominations, particularly to the Catholic hierarchy, over the administration of the educational system set up by the British Parliament? When in December Bryce resigned his Secretaryship to go to the United States, the Unionists spread the report that it was because on the former question he had met with the successful opposition of Sir Antony MacDonnell. They went so far as to prophesy that Sir Antony would replace him as Chief Secretary.[2] It was an idiotic rumour. Sir Antony had never been a *persona grata* with the Nationalists, who regarded him as a traitor, who had espoused in Asia the cause of British imperialism and was only too ready to treat his Irish compatriots as Hindus. If they had accepted such a man their policy could have been indistinguishable from O'Brien's. In fact, according to reliable Nationalist testimony, Bryce had not been in the least disposed to grant the Irish more than MacDonnell advised, and his relations with Redmond and Dillon had been the reverse of cordial.[3] When he was succeeded by Augustine Birrell, a witty man of letters and a professional sceptic, who exchanged the Board of Education where he had not been a success for the Irish Secretaryship, the appointment was certainly regarded as a victory by the Nationalist leaders. Had he renewed negotiations with them? If he had, had at least a conditional agreement been reached? In any case, on May 7 Birrell, in whose honour the Nationalist members of Parliament had given a banquet the previous night, expounded the ministerial scheme.

The Bill introduced that day set up a central representative Council of 106 members, of whom eighty-two would be elected, twenty-four nominated by the executive. Of the forty-five Irish administrative departments, eight would be subject to its control. This seems very little, but we must remember that by reason of

---

[1] *The Times*, November 9, 1906.

[2] *The Times*, December 22, 1906.

[3] T. P. O'Connor, *Sir Henry Campbell-Bannerman*, p. 131. Cf. T. M. Healy's letter to his brother, March 16, 1906: 'Redmond is cogitating over some plan but what it is I don't know! Bryce is a Belfast man—without Morley's Irish sympathies. Antony MacDonnell is the driving power and his models are Hindu' (T. M. Healy, *Letters and Leaders of my Time*, vol. ii, p. 476).

their importance these eight departments, which included the Local Government Board, the Department of Agriculture and Technical Instruction, the Congested Districts Board, and public education in all its branches, amounted to over half the Irish Administration.[1] It was estimated that these departments cost the nation £2,000,000 a year. To this estimate the Government proposed to add £650,000, and with this annual revenue of £2,650,000 to form an Irish Fund to be placed at the disposal of the Council, which if it had no legislative powers would at least possess within the limits of the eight departments specified by the Bill, entire control over the administration of the existing Irish Statutes, the sole reservation being the Lord Lieutenant's veto absolute or suspensory at his discretion upon any decision the Council might take. Of the police there was not a word. Birrell was content to point out that the number of departments subject to the Council's control might be subsequently extended and to remark that 'if the new Council after some years is a success, why, then, I dare say it may pave the way to Home Rule'. Nor was anything said about any right of the clergy to be elected to the Council, or any control they might be granted over the educational establishments of the country. On the contrary, it would seem that this control was abandoned unreservedly to an assembly of laymen elected by a suffrage practically universal.[2]

Redmond had no desire to oppose openly a Bill he personally liked. But he saw immediately how unlikely it was to win the approval of Irish public opinion. His language was therefore hesitating and he referred the decision to a national Convention of the party to be held within a few days in Dublin. A movement of opposition to the Bill was at once organized in Dublin, headed by the clergy. On May 14 the *Freeman's Journal* published the names of 107 priests who declared their intention to participate in the Convention. It met on the 21st. No Convention hitherto held in Ireland had been so well attended. It was Redmond who opened the proceedings by proposing a resolution which declared that Ireland could not be satisfied with half-measures and that 'they

---

[1] Augustine Birrell, speech at Queen's College, Belfast, November 23, 1907: 'He had done his best to enable the Irish people to administer their own affairs over seven-twelfths at least of the great departments of the Irish State.'

[2] The real short title of the Bill was 'Irish Council Bill'. But it became usual to refer to it as the 'Irish Councils Bill', which did much to prejudice Irish public opinion against it. The completely false impression was given that the Government was seeking to divide authority among several different councils.

should press upon the British Government with all their strength and power to introduce a measure for the establishment of a native Parliament, with a responsible Executive, having power over all purely Irish affairs'. The resolution was passed unanimously. In these circumstances, the Government had no choice but to withdraw the Irish Council Bill. Balfour was ready with ironical congratulations, calling the attention of Parliament to the queer experiment made by Campbell-Bannerman and his colleagues in 'governing Ireland in accordance with Irish ideas'.

Once again the policy of moderate concessions, of 'devolution', had failed. In 1905 it had been defeated by the intransigence of the Ulster loyalists. In 1907 it was faced by the intransigence of the Nationalists which was now assuming the novel form of a propaganda, mentioned this year for the first time in the London press, though actually Sinn Fein was already eight years old. But it had made its first appearance during the great outburst of nationalism which marked the centenary of the rebellion of 1798 and during the following years, when revolutionary feeling had temporarily died down in Ireland and the followers of O'Brien were working with Lord Dunraven's group to carry out immediate measures of economic reform, the stream of Sinn Fein, though its source did not dry up, flowed more or less underground. What was the creed of the new group? The leading figure of the movement, Arthur Griffith, in his paper, *The United Irishman*, made no direct attack on any form of Irish agitation. He was full of sympathy for the Gaelic League and its efforts to revive the Irish language. In principle he condemned neither parliamentary action nor armed revolt if circumstances should recommend either. But as things were they were both inopportune, and he advocated the employment of another method, borrowed, he said, from the Hungarians of 1861. The latter, who at that time were agitating for the re-establishment of the constitution of 1848, had acted as though it were still in force, taking the oath according to the forms then prescribed, paying no attention to official documents, and refusing to pay taxes. In a few years they had gained the victory. If the Irish wished to restore the constitution of 1782, illegally abolished by the Act of Union of 1800, they should follow this Hungarian example. No more members should be sent to Westminster, a council of Three Hundred should be set up in Dublin which would constitute a *de facto* Irish Parliament, and courts of arbitration to whose jurisdiction loyal Irishmen would submit their disputes instead of employing the regular courts. The British Army, whose ranks and prestige had been swelled too long by Irish recruits, must be boycotted, also British goods whose importation had so long prevented the growth of a national industry. Foreign rule must be destroyed by a species of political strike or passive rebellion, refusal to co-operate with the established authority in any shape or form, the determination to do everything 'ourselves', 'ourselves alone', Sinn Fein. This was the programme publicly adopted by a National Council which met at Dublin on November 28, 1905, barely a week before the fall of Balfour's ministry, to embody Griffith's policy in a distinct organization. It was a programme, to speak Hindustani, of complete swadeshi.[1]

The moderation displayed during the following months by the Nationalist leaders, and their close alliance with the Liberal Government, assisted the propaganda of Sinn Fein. In the autumn of 1906 the movement counted only twenty 'branches',[2] two years later there were over a hundred.[3] The Nationalists noticed a falling off in the financial contributions received from America. It was because Sinn Fein was recruiting American subscribers to its funds. In January 1907, when the Corporation of Dublin was re-elected, Sinn Fein for the first time put forward candidates in opposition to the Nationalists. After the failure of the Irish Council Bill three Nationalist members of Parliament resigned on the ground that they had joined Sinn Fein and, when in September the Nationalist party wished to call a large public meeting in Dublin, they were obliged to transform it into a private meeting to prevent its capture by the Sinn Feiners.

There was no reason indeed to take too seriously a movement led by men who were cranks, even more than fanatics. But the success of their propaganda was nevertheless ominous. On the outskirts of the official Nationalist party Tim Healy made advances to Sinn Fein. The United Irish League broke away from the control of its founder, William O'Brien. Michael Devlin, who

[1] For the origins of Sinn Fein see Robert Mitchell Henry, *Modern Ireland in the Making: The Evolution of Sinn Fein*, 1920; George Lyons, *Some Recollections of George Griffith and his Times*, 1923; also Griffith's pamphlets, *The Sinn Fein Policy*, 1904; *The Resurrection of Hungary, A Parallel for Ireland*, 1905.
[2] Robert Mitchell Henry, *Modern Ireland in the Making* . . . p. 77.
[3] *Annual Register*, 1908, p. 257.

had just refurbished an old revolutionary association, the Ancient Order of Hibernians, with a programme less strictly Catholic but not less nationalist, introduced Hibernians into the local branches of the League. They prevented O'Brien from speaking at public meetings and finally compelled him to sign at Dublin on December 25, 1907, a formal treaty of peace with Redmond which amounted to a surrender, since it began by professing the creed of nationalism whole and undiluted. Under the potent influence of these heated nationalist passions Redmond's imagination caught fire; he celebrated the memory of the rebels of 1798 and held them up as an example to the rising generation. *The Freeman's Journal* paid homage to Sinn Fein and hinted that after all its programme was perhaps not irreconcilable with that of the party which looked to the *Journal* for guidance. At Westminster the Nationalist members officially declared that they reserved entire freedom of action unhampered by any engagement or obligation towards the Liberal majority. At Jarrow-on-Tyne, where a seat had fallen vacant, a Labour candidate had come forward in opposition to the Unionist and Liberal candidates. He was an Irishman by birth and expected on that ground to win from the Liberal candidate the votes of the large body of Irish workmen in the constituency. But the Irish would give their confidence only to a candidate completely their own. The presence of four rival candidates in this English constituency gave the momentary impression that the arrangement of parties had been totally dislocated. Was there then a complete rupture between the English Liberals and the Irish Nationalists? No. Personal relations between Redmond and Dillon on the one hand, and Campbell-Bannerman on the other, remained friendly. The former were therefore suspected of having adopted a more favourable attitude than they would admit towards the compromise proposed in May, and the latter, on the other hand, of willingness to advance further on the path of concession to Ireland, the moment circumstances became more propitious. When the session of 1908 opened, the latter suspicion proved well founded.

The Prime Minister and the Nationalist leader agreed that the latter should introduce in the House of Commons a motion affirming the principle of Home Rule, and that Campbell-Bannerman should accept it. The arrangement could not be fully carried out. Redmond was obliged to dispense with the presence of Campbell-

Bannerman, overtaken by the disease which would carry him off.[1] Nevertheless it was evident, two years after the General Election, that the mere fact that a Liberal Government was in office had made a compromise impossible, and that sooner or later, as at the close of the last century, England must decide for or against the programme of complete Home Rule.

3

Sooner or later, but certainly not immediately ! For the Liberal statesmen on the morrow of the General Election, the Irish question was not urgent. It was not on that question that the election had been fought. The claims of other clients must be met before those of the Irish Home Rulers, who did not even possess the means of putting pressure on the Liberal leaders. For the overwhelming Liberal majority swamped their eighty-four representatives. These clients were first and foremost the Nonconformists, aroused, as we have seen, from their political inertia by the Education Act of 1902. They had not been content with the agitation they conducted throughout the country by their 'passive resistance' to the rate collector when he called upon them to contribute by paying their rates to the support of the denominational schools. In every constituency they had organized the Liberal victory of 1906. They had never before sent so many members to a British Parliament. In this respect the Election of 1906 had effected nothing short of a revolution. Some 180 Dissenters sat in the new House.[2] The Congregationalists were best represented— as might have been expected of the most political and republican

---

[1] T. P. O'Connor, *Sir Henry Campbell-Bannerman*, 1908, pp. 156 sqq.; L. G. Redmond Howard, *John Redmond*, 1910, p. 217; J. A. Spender, *The Right Honourable Sir Henry Campbell-Bannerman*, 1923, vol. ii, p. 38.

[2] *Free Church Year Book*, 1906, p. 306: At a luncheon given by the Liberation Society on February 27, 1906, the chairman gave the following detailed figures, amounting to a slightly smaller total: Congregationalists 65; Wesleyans 30; Baptists 14; Presbyterians 22; Unitarians 14; Calvinistic Methodists 8; Primitive Methodists 7; Friends 7; United Methodists 3. To these figures we must add the seven or eight Nonconformists (probably Wesleyans or Unitarians) who were Unionist members. Nor was this simply a temporary phenomenon. At the General Election of January 1910 the number of dissenters elected was still no less than 125 (53 Congregationalists, 25 Wesleyans, 8 Calvinistic Methodists, 7 Primitive Methodists, 3 United Methodists, 15 Baptists, 7 Unitarians, 6 Quakers, 1 Presbyterian) (*Free Church Year Book*, 1910, p. 214)—that is to say, dissenters were returned for 125 of the 315 seats won by the Liberal and Labour parties, instead of 180 out of 430. The proportion is practically the same.

of the sects—but all had their representatives. When to these Dissenters we add thirteen Scotch Presbyterians,[1] sixteen Jews,[2] eighty Irish Catholics and a handful of English Catholics (less than ten), the number of members not belonging to the Church of England reaches 300. With a loss of only forty more seats, the Established Church would not have possessed a majority in the Commons. Nothing similar had been witnessed since the days of Cromwell. The Chancellor of the Exchequer, Asquith, and the President of the Board of Education, Augustine Birrell, were at least of Nonconformist origin. Lloyd George was the hero of Welsh Nonconformity. The entire Protestant world outside the Church of England expected as its strict right the immediate repeal of the Act of 1902.

On April 6, 1906, Augustine Birrell expounded in the House of Commons the main features of the Government's Bill. The first clause would lay down the principle that no school should be recognized as a public elementary school unless it was a school provided by the local educational authority. In other words, no denominational teaching would be given in any public elementary school. This did not mean that public education would be strictly secular. An amendment introduced in this sense when the clauses of the Bill were being discussed received only sixty-three votes, and an amendment moved by Chamberlain—he had never liked the Act of 1902 and this intervention was his last escapade before he disappeared from political life—relieving teachers from the obligation of giving religious instruction, while giving parents the right to secure for their children whatever denominational instruction they preferred, to be given in school but at their own cost, received only 172. The only form of religious instruction which would be legal in future and would, in fact, be given almost universally would be undenominational teaching, simple Bible teaching it was usually termed, to be given by the teacher himself. Special arrangements could still be made with those non-provided schools which were compelled by lack of funds to seek financial aid from the State. Clause 2 of the Bill laid down the principles by which they would be governed. The local authority would become responsible for the upkeep of the buildings and would

[1] *Free Church Year Book*, 1906, p. 306.
[2] There were 32 Jewish candidates (15 Unionists, 17 Liberals). Of these 16 were returned (12 Liberals, 4 Conservatives). There had been 12 Jews in the House of Commons returned in 1900, 8 Unionists and 4 Liberals (*Jewish World*, quoted by *The Times*, February 1, 1906).

have the right to alter or enlarge them. Outside school hours they would remain at the owners' free disposal, but during school hours the local authority would have entire control—that is to say, in country districts the Nonconformist child would no longer be obliged to receive Anglican instruction. The Bill, in the language of a Liberal speaker, was the Magna Carta of the village Nonconformist.

The measure was not in reality quite so simple as this. Those former free schools, which in 1902 had become the non-provided schools of the new system, if they wished to remain public elementary schools, could nevertheless obtain special facilities for the denominational teaching they had given hitherto. It must not exceed two hours a week. The cost could not be defrayed by the local authority and it could not be given during the hours when the children were obliged to attend school nor by a teacher employed by the public authority. These 'ordinary facilities', to use the jargon of the Bill, of which the Anglican Church might take advantage, were obviously extremely restricted. It was not the same with the 'extended facilities' granted in urban areas, that is in every borough or urban district whose population exceeded 5,000, if four-fifths of the parents asked for them, and provided there were in the same locality other schools which could be attended by children whose parents objected to this religious instruction. What in fact were these schools to which this clause accorded special privileges? With the exception of the Jewish schools in the East End of London they were Catholic schools founded for the use of the Irish proletariat of all the large towns in the kingdom. The Liberals could not dispense with the Irish vote, the Labour party still less. This curiously illogical concession was the result. The Government hoped by this Bill to satisfy the Nonconformists in the country districts without depriving the Irish Catholics of the advantages conferred upon them by the Act of 1902. In the event the Bill roused the opposition, as violent as it was legitimate, of the Anglican Church without satisfying either the militant Nonconformists, indignant at the favour shown to Roman Catholicism, or the Catholics themselves, who were not content even with the 'extended facilities' they were offered. Clause 4, which defined these facilities, left the local authority free to grant or refuse them. The Catholics demanded that it should be compelled to grant them. The Bill passed its third reading on

Monday, July 30, by a majority of only 169. It was a considerable majority, no doubt, but far less than the normal majority for a Government measure. The Irish Nationalists had voted solidly against the Bill. And if the Nonconformists had voted for it, it was with reluctance.

4

The Bill had now to face the House of Lords, where the Anglican Church was supreme and Catholicism well represented, but the Nonconformists the merest handful. The House of Lords did not throw out the Bill straightaway. It passed the first and second readings at the beginning of August. But when the House reassembled in October and it was debated clause by clause, the Lords transformed it into a measure of a totally different character. They 'extended' the 'extended facilities' to rural as well as urban areas, requiring moreover the consent of only two-thirds of the parents instead of four-fifths. They authorized the teachers to give denominational instruction, and this not only in the non-provided schools under the Act of 1902, but also in the provided schools. The Bill, as shaped by the joint labours of the Government and the House of Commons, empowered the local authorities to take over the free schools on certain conditions; as remodelled by the House of Lords it obliged them to do so. Indeed, the Lords went still further and repealing a provision of the Act of 1870 which the legislature had not dared to touch in 1902, deprived the local authorities of the right, of which a very small minority had taken advantage,[1] to give no religious instruction

---

[1] Not, however, from the point of view we should call in France '*laique*'. See the interesting remarks by Ramsay MacDonald, 'The Education Bill; the Secular Solution' (*Fortnightly Review*, vol. lxxxix, p. 715: April 15, 1908): 'It is of some interest to observe that the areas in England and Wales where no religious instruction in public schools is given are found mostly in districts where "conversion" is regarded as the essential characteristic of religion. Out of the 70 schools in Cardigan for instance, 66 have no such instruction; out of the 100 in Carmarthen, 62 are purely secular. The fact that in Wales there are over 160 schools with a time-table which is purely secular, so far from condemning the religious indifference of the Principality, ought really to be put in the forefront of the reasons showing how religiously minded the Welshman is.' Clause 7 of the *Code of Instructions for Public Elementary Schools* 1906 authorized teachers to add to their lessons of English history lessons, in citizenship. But the Cabinet categorically rejected Chiozza Money's proposal to make this instruction in citizenship compulsory (H. of C., July 5, 1906; *Parliamentary Debates*, 4th Series, vol. clx, p. 237). The *Report of the Board of Education* quotes the language used in this clause of the code when it lays down that this secular moral instruction may be 'either incidental, occasional and given as opportunity arises, or given systematically as a course of graduated instruction. The teaching should be brought home to the children by

whatever in the schools. In future, no school would be supported by public money, which did not find a place in its time-table for religious instruction.

What would the Government do? Work through the Bill again clause by clause, making concessions to the Upper Chamber on a particular clause, refusing them on another? It would be an endless task. The Cabinet decided to ask the Commons to reject the Lords amendments *en bloc* and on December 12 the House voted accordingly by a majority of 416 to 107. Nevertheless, there was still hope of saving the Bill. Why not attempt to reach a compromise between the two Houses by private negotiations? It would seem that the Archbishop of Canterbury was in favour of the suggestion. He remained throughout on friendly and even intimate terms with the Prime Minister. But Balfour thought otherwise, and rejected the proposals made by the Government, though they were in fact so conciliatory that they would no doubt have rendered the Bill unacceptable to the Radicals if by chance the Unionist leaders had accepted them. He regarded the Act of 1902 as his own work, possibly his masterpiece, and wanted it preserved in its entirety. Moreover, as an expert parliamentary tactician he perceived that it was a favourable opportunity to avenge his crushing defeat at the polls the previous January. Apparently, the country was up in arms for or against the Bill. The debates in the House of Commons had been heated. Only a ruthless application of the closure had enabled them to be concluded in three months. And the galleries had been crowded throughout. The Established Church, the Catholics, the Protestant sects had multiplied public meetings, petitions, demonstrations of every description. But, despite appearances, the agitation was superficial. The great mass of the electorate took no interest in the struggle, and the Anglican Church and the supporters of the *status quo* could take advantage of their indifference. By refusing any amicable arrangement he defied the Government to appeal to the country by dissolving

reference to their actual surroundings in town or country and should be illustrated as vividly as possible by stories, poems, quotations, proverbs, and examples drawn from history or biography'. The report adds: 'The whole subject of Moral Instruction needs careful handling. . . . Though few would care to deny that morals can be taught to children apart from the truth of revealed religion, yet as they are closely bound up with religion and derive their surest sanctions from religion, great care must be taken to avoid any conflict of laws or clashing of canons. To do this may seem difficult until the experiment is made' (pp. 24-5).

Parliament. 'They will not dissolve,' he declared; 'they know better.'[1]

And in fact, when the House of Lords on December 17, on the motion of Lord Lansdowne, maintained its amendments by a majority of 142 to fifty-three, the Prime Minister simply dropped the Bill on which both Houses had wasted so many months. After this, it was all very well for Campbell-Bannerman to dub Balfour in irony 'director-in-chief' of both Houses.[2] He only enhanced his opponent's prestige. Chamberlain banished by ill-health from the party arena, and the Act of 1902 saved from the grave peril which threatened it at the beginning of the year, he was in truth the hero of the hour. Lloyd George might deliver attacks on the Upper House which King Edward regarded as a breach of constitutional usage.[3] And the Premier might arouse the applause of the Commons by his declaration, 'that a way must be found, a way will be found, by which the will of the people expressed through their elected representatives in this House will be made to prevail'.[4] These were but distant threats. The Constitution did indeed provide a means to enforce immediately the will of the nation, an appeal to the country by dissolving Parliament. But it was a step which Campbell-Bannerman and his colleagues dared not take.

5

The King's speech which opened the session of 1907 did not even allude to education. It merely contained a passing threat addressed to the House of Lords and the announcement that the Cabinet had under consideration the best method of settling disputes between the two Houses. But something must be done to repair the disastrous effect produced by the defeat of the Education Bill. The West Riding County Council had refused in 1906 to pay the teachers of four non-provided schools that portion of their salary which in the Council's opinion was the remuneration for their denominational instruction. The refusal had been pro-

[1] Speech at the Junior Constitutional Club, November 28, 1906.
[2] H. of C., December 11, 1906 (*Parliamentary Debates*, 4th Series, vol. clxvii, p. 157).
[3] Speech at the Palmerston Club at Oxford, December 1, 1906. For the King's protests see J. A. Spender, *The Life of the Right Hon. Sir Henry Campbell-Bannerman*, vol. ii, pp. 313 sqq.
[4] H. of C., December 20, 1906 (*Parliamentary Debates*, 4th Series, vol. clxvii, p. 1740).

nounced illegal by the Court of first instance, legal by the Court
of Appeal, and finally illegal by the House of Lords in its capacity
as supreme court of appeal at the very moment when as a legislature it had defeated the Education Bill in December. Why not
legalize by an express Statute a procedure as to whose present
legality the judges were divided? A Bill to this effect, consisting
of a single clause, was introduced on February 26 by MacKenna,
who had just succeeded Birrell at the Board of Education. The
Bill relieved the local authorities of the cost—estimated at a
fifteenth of the education rate—of the religious instruction given
in non-provided schools. It was sufficient to alarm the Anglicans,
too little to placate the Dissenters. Nothing more was heard of
the Bill, which was silently dropped by the Government at the
close of the session.

If, however, legislation was evidently extremely difficult, indeed practically impossible, could not some indirect method be
found by which the Ministry might achieve its object without
having to face the opposition of the House of Lords? By a series
of administrative regulations the Board of Education laid down
the principle that no financial assistance should be given to the
training colleges, often private foundations of an Anglican complexion,[1] unless they undertook not to impose any denominational
test upon their pupils.[2] It extended the application of this rule to
institutions for secondary education and without going back on
the past decided that no financial aid should be given to them
unless the majority of the board of managers were nominees of
the public authority and if any denominational test was imposed

[1] The *Report of the Board of Education* for the year 1909–10 gives interesting statistics as
to the training colleges of both descriptions, denominational and undenominational—for
the three preceding school years. In 1907–8 the denominational training colleges provided
4,945 places, the undenominational 6,001; in 1908–9 the denominational 4,903, the undenominational 6,974; in 1909–10 the denominational 4,862, the undenominational 7,431
—that is to say, the undenominational training colleges had made indisputable progress,
the denominational had remained stationary. The insignificant decline in the number of
places is explained by the transfer of two colleges from primary to secondary education.
During the following years, as a result of the financial aid given by the Board of Education
to the foundation of new training colleges, the balance in favour of the undenominational
colleges steadily increased. In 1914 there were twice as many places available in the undenominational training colleges as in the denominational (S. J. G. Moore, *The Schools and
Social Reform: The Report of the Unionist Social Reform Committee on Education, with an introduction by the Right Hon. F. E. Smith*, 1914, p. 37).

[2] This, we must once more assert, was not secularism. In 1907 the Government officials
even attempted, though the attempt failed, to reinforce in training colleges for primary
school teachers the obligation of religious though undenominational instruction. See two
articles by Graham Wallas, *The Nation*, July 10, 24, 1909.

on managers or teachers. Moreover, the Government could have recourse to the expedient of introducing into the Budget a special credit which constitutional usage would not allow the House of Lords to reject, since by universal consent it could not amend the Budget. Admittedly in violation of a clause in the Education Act of 1870 a credit of £100,000 was provided to enable the local authority to construct a school in any district where it seemed desirable to destroy the monopoly of the Anglican Church.[1]

This was all, and despite the indignant protests of the opposition speakers it did not amount to much. The Bill to settle disputes between the two Houses, which the speech from the throne had seemed to foreshadow, never made its appearance. The only step taken was to introduce on June 24 a motion which affirmed that the right assumed by the Upper House to amend or reject Bills sent up by the Lower must be so restricted as to secure that the will of the Commons should prevail before the life of the Parliament had expired. After animated debates which occupied three sittings the motion was carried amid loud applause by 432 to 147 votes—that is to say, by a majority of 285. English Nonconformists and Irish Catholics at enmity for the past eighteen months made a united front against the common enemy. But it was nothing more than a declaration of principle. When would the Government attempt to apply it? When would it dare to give battle?

A final attempt was made in 1908 to solve this question of religious teaching in primary schools—a permanent sore of English politics. During the closing months of 1907 the President of the Board of Education had promised a simple and short Bill. But the Bill whose principles he explained to the House of Commons on February 24, 1908, was in fact as complicated as its predecessor of 1906. The first clause laid down that there should be only one category of public elementary school, in which the teachers should not be subject to any religious test and the only type of religious instruction permitted would be the simple Bible teaching given in all or almost all board schools since 1870. As was pointed out in the debate which followed, this provision marked a greater departure from secularism than the Act of 1870, for the

---

[1] H. of C., July 11, 1907, Arthur Balfour's speech and MacKenna's explanations (*Parliamentary Debates*, 4th Series, vol. clxxviii, pp. 67 sqq.). H. of L., July 25, 1907. Lord Londonderry's speech and Lord Crewe's reply (ibid., vol. clxxix, pp. 17 sqq.).

elementary schools lost the right, which they had hitherto possessed, to give no religious instruction.[1] The continued existence of the free schools was recognized and they could even be assisted by grants from the central government on a scale more liberal than before 1907, but only if they did not possess the monopoly of teaching in a particular locality, that is to say if the parish, to use the current phraseology, was not a single school parish, if the number of pupils was not less than twenty, and the standard of such a school both hygienic and educational should be certified by an inspector as not inferior to that of the provided schools supported by the rates. When free schools were transferred to the public authority, denominational teaching would still be permissible provided it was not given by the teacher and was given out of school hours or on a Sunday or holiday.

Faced with this new Bill the Anglican episcopate was not content with a mere *non possumus*. On March 30 the Bishop of Saint-Asaph introduced an alternative Bill in the House of Lords, inspired on certain points by the advice given at the end of 1906 by the Archbishop of Canterbury. It was a compromise based on mutual concessions. While recognizing that the Nonconformists had a legitimate grievance in the country districts, it asked them to recognize in their turn the legitimacy of the Anglican counterclaim in the urban areas where the former board schools, the provided schools of 1902, were in a majority. There would, therefore, be only one category of school in which the teachers would be free to give or not to give the religious instruction, and the normal religious instruction would be undenominational, but on three days a week those children whose parents desired it might receive denominational instruction provided it was not at the public expense. Whereas the Bill of 1906 might be regarded as an attempt to unite Nonconformists and Catholics against Anglicanism, a compromise was now proposed between Nonconformists and Anglicans from whose benefit the Catholics would be excluded. Lengthy negotiations were carried on throughout the spring and summer. Campbell-Bannerman had been dead for several months and MacKenna had been replaced at the Board of Education by Runciman when the latter began an official correspondence with the Archbishop of Canterbury with the object of drafting a Bill acceptable both to the Liberal majority in the

[1] Graham Wallas: Letter to the *Manchester Guardian*, November 1, 1908.

House of Commons and to the House of Lords. In its amended form the Bill was made public on November 20. To ensure its success a settlement committee was formed at the request of the Archbishop of Canterbury which was immediately joined by seven bishops and several leading Nonconformists. But when the Representative Church Council met on December 3 the bishops were faced with the opposition of their own laity.

The motive which had brought together the Archbishop of Canterbury, the Bishop of London, the Wesleyan, Scott Lidgett, and the Congregationalist, Sylvester Horne, was fear lest Parliament, weary of their disputes, might cut the knot by secularizing the provided schools. The stalwarts of the Anglican Church, the followers of Lord Halifax and the Cecils, were not so timid, and with good reason. They perceived that in exchange for the right of admission given to Anglican clergymen in the provided schools, they would sacrifice the monopoly hitherto possessed by the parsons in the rural areas. When a motion opposing the Bill was submitted to the Council, only three bishops out of twenty-one supported it, but it was carried nevertheless by 189 to 99 votes. The Bill was therefore dropped by the Government amid universal indifference.[1] No one wanted to hear anything more of this dispute between the Church and the sects about religious education in the schools.

6

This abandonment by the Radical party of its educational programme will not surprise our readers if they recall what we said in our last volume of the decline of Nonconformity in England at the close of the nineteenth century. The shock given by the Edu-

[1] Though the public cared nothing, the small group for whom the question had a special interest continued to discuss it. See Athelstan Riley, Michael Sadler, Cyril Jackson, *The Religious Question in Public Education: A Critical Examination Scheme Representing Various Points of View*, 1911. In most districts an agreement would seem to have been reached to recommend to the teachers a syllabus of religious teaching which, though undogmatic, and from one point of view for that reason, was less biblical and therefore more remote from the traditional Nonconformist creed and more acceptable to Anglicans. For this movement, which we cannot study in detail here, see Sir G. Croydon Mark's speech in the House of Commons, March 8, 1912 (*Parliamentary Debates*, Commons, 5th Series, vol. xxxv, pp. 692 sqq.); also A. J. Mundella, *The Place of Religious Teaching in a National System of Public Schools: 'Hard Facts for Legislators'*; *Address to the Education Settlement Committee*, July 11, 1912; *The Cambridgeshire Syllabus of Religious Teaching for Schools*, Ed. 1, 1924, the prototype of the new type of syllabus. For the spread of the new methods see *Religious Instruction in Provided Schools in England and Wales*, 4th Edition (revised), November 1931.

cation Act of 1902, the violent reaction of the sects, the passive resistance movement and the victory at the polls in January 1906, may well have fostered among the Nonconformists the illusion that the progressive decline of their sects had been checked and the Anglican Church would pay the penalty for presuming on their weakness. In support of this belief they could still appeal to many healthy signs. The Welsh 'revival' was one. Another was the 'new movement' organized among the Wesleyans by Hugh Price Hughes, which sought to regain contact with the masses by founding 'missions' in the suburbs of the large towns. Moreover, the Wesleyans had opened a subscription on a large scale to purchase a property in the heart of London next door to the Anglican Westminster Abbey and the Catholic Westminster Cathedral, on which to install their administrative and religious headquarters. Finally, at Selly Oak, near Birmingham, the Quakers had founded their admirable institution for free theological teaching, training for foreign missions and peace propaganda. But the final, and to all seeming irremediable, defeat of the agitation against the Education Act, in spite of the powerful Nonconformist representation in Parliament, was a bad symptom, so bad that it seemed to outweigh all the favourable symptoms. And it was not the only one.

In the first place, there was the decline which we have remarked already, but which continued to make progress, of those fissiparous tendencies which constitute the very essence of what the English call Congregationalism and distinguish the English sects from the Protestants of the Continent. This Congregationalism had enabled the sects to develop by multiplying independent groups, by division and schism rather than by organization. Now, however, the Roman principle of unity began to attract these religious anarchists. The Baptists furnished themselves with superintendents, a term borrowed from the Wesleyan body, the Congregationalists with moderators, who were nothing less than a species of bishops exempt from the control of the independent groups. And the same tendency manifested itself in the appointment of special ministers to administer the large funds collected from Baptist and Congregational subscribers to maintain the central organization, support the pastors and provide retiring pensions for them. Besides this movement towards a more unified organization within the individual sects, there was a movement towards reunion between the sects themselves. Among the Methodists the scheme sponsored by Hugh Price Hughes for a general reunion of their branches had indeed failed, for the moment at least. But the union of three sects, the United Methodist Free Churches, the Methodist New Connexion and the Bible Christians, sanctioned in 1907 by a Statute, constituted a preliminary success for the advocates of 'Methodist Union'.[1] In Scotland the same tendency was displayed by the reunion of the two great branches of free Presbyterianism —the Free Church of Scotland and the United Free Church. It was effected in 1900. Though faced in 1904 with an adverse decision of the courts to which a dissident minority of the United Free Church had appealed, the union finally triumphed over these difficulties, and a movement was already taking shape for a reunion with the Established Church itself.

The sects, as we should expect, interpreted this movement towards unity as a sign of life. That it was in reality the reverse is proved by the annual statistics of the Free Churches. In the closing years of the last century their numbers had grown very slowly, all out of proportion to the rapid growth of the population. Even this slow increase had now ceased. After the temporary stimulus caused by the Welsh revival, every year witnessed a constant decline in the number of those who communicated, in other words, regularly attended the services of the Free Churches. From 1906 to 1907 there was a decrease of 27,000 communicants, from 1907 to 1908 a decrease of 6,000, from 1908 to 1909 a decrease of 7,000 and from 1909 to 1910 a decrease of 24,000. While honestly publishing these disconcerting figures, whose effect was doubly disastrous at a moment when they were being defeated by the Anglicans on the education question, the Nonconformists attempted to dispute their significance. The fact, they argued, that their

---

[1] An Act to authorize the union of the Methodist New Connexion, the Bible Christians and the United Methodist Free Churches under the name of 'The United Methodist Church', to deal with real and personal property belonging to the said Churches or denominations, to provide for the vesting of the said property in trust for the United Church so formed and for the assimilation of the trust thereof and for other purposes (*United Methodist Church Act*). There had been seven Methodist Churches, there were now only five. The new group which took the name of United Methodist Church with 88,801 communicants (increased in 1908 to 164,071) ranked fourth after the Wesleyans with 628,693 communicants, the Primitive Methodists with 203,128, and the Calvinistic Methodists with 189,164. Apart from these four powerful Methodist Churches with a total communicant membership exceeding 1,000,000, there remained only two tiny groups, the Independent Methodists with 9,754 communicants and the Wesleyan Reform Union with 8,689. It is obvious how much easier complete reunion had now become. Yet it was not effected until 1929.

figures were computed on a stringent basis, far more stringent than the Anglican statistics, placed them at a disadvantage. Among the Wesleyans or Baptists, to be classed as a 'communicant' it was not sufficient to communicate once a year, at Easter, as in the Anglican body.[1] But this had always been the case, and on whatever basis, lax or stringent, the figures were calculated, the decrease in Nonconformist membership remained an incontestable fact. The Nonconformists also pointed out that their Churches were becoming steadily more wealthy, that a subscription organized by the Baptists in the opening year of the century had produced £250,000, a Wesleyan subscription a little later £100,000, and that the Nonconformist Churches were spending on their Sunday Schools and social activities of every description more than they had ever spent.[2] But this fact, when taken in combination with the decline in the number of members, proves that the Free Churches had become richer only because they had become more middle-class, suggests that the public spirit which impelled all these wealthy men to subscribe so liberally should not be confused with profound religious conviction, and in any case makes it plain that the Free Churches were not only out of touch with the labouring masses among whom a century and a half before the new-born Wesleyan movement had won such amazing victories, but were losing the allegiance of the classes which till lately had given it. 'More chapels are being built,' we read in the *Free Church Year Book for* 1911, 'and more churches too.... The Churches are vying with each other to attract worshippers; music, lecture programmes, comfortable seats, and, generally speaking, well-prepared sermons, beckon the people in, but do they come? We are again face to face with the old tragedy, the tragedy of our work—the masses of the people, all immortal souls, are not touched. It used to be the fashion to make this lament, as relating to the working classes; the truth is—and we must face its startling reality—the educated middle-class, especially the young people, are losing touch altogether with the House of God.'[3]

---

[1] *Free Church Year Book*, 1913, p. 289.
[2] Letter from Dr. Clifford to *The Times*. *The Times*, May 6, 1913.
[3] *Free Church Year Book*, 1911, p. 290. Cf. *Free Church Year Book*, 1910, p. 270: 'It will be seen that the Evangelical Free Churches now provide 8,662,691 sittings, an increase of more than 100,000 over last year's figures, without reckoning the unclassified; while there is a decrease of nearly 7,000 in the number of communicants.'

Was the ground lost by the sects won by the Church of England? For a moment it would seem Anglicans were disposed to cherish this pleasing belief. Their victory on the education question encouraged optimism, and statistics confirmed it. For some years the number of Anglicans continued to increase, while the Nonconformist 'communicants' decreased. But in the first place, the increase was extremely slow, very far from keeping pace with the growth of population. And it was soon followed by a fairly rapid decrease, whereas the decrease in Nonconformist membership tended rather to slacken. Moreover, the Established Church was still faced with a shortage of clergy. And it was threatened by a danger far more serious than the competition of the sects, namely that revival of Catholicism, Anglican and Roman, whose progress we have already had occasion to relate.

A Royal Commission, appointed in 1904 to inquire into the growth of ritualism,[1] reported that the serious nature of the conflict was the impotence of the bishops to prevent all these ritual innovations which were in effect repudiations of Protestantism, and that the only way in which their authority might perhaps be strengthened was to legalize, if necessary by an express statute, a host of practices which the rigid Protestantism of half a century before would have regarded as intolerable. But at what point was it possible to fix the limits of this legal toleration? Alone among the Churches throughout the world the Church of England presented the paradox of an episcopal Church whose bishops traditionally lacked power to coerce. Moreover, not satisfied with the toleration they enjoyed, certain Anglo-Catholic clergymen had themselves ordained priests and the public witnessed with increasing equanimity conversions to Roman Catholicism.[2] A cousin of

[1] A Royal Commission appointed to inquire into the alleged prevalence of breaches or neglect of the Law relating to the conduct of Divine Service for the Churches of England, and to the ornament and fitting of Churches; and to consider the existing powers and procedure applicable to such irregularities and to make such recommendations as may be deemed requisite for dealing with the aforesaid matters, April 23, 1904.

[2] For the movement towards Catholicism see two interesting compilations. *Roads to Rome: Being personal records of some of the more recent converts to the Catholic Faith, With an Introduction by His Emminence Cardinal Vaughan, Archbishop of Westminster, 1892–1903*, compiled and edited by J. Godfrey Raupert, Edition 3, 1908. It contains sixty-five short accounts of converts who give the reasons for their conversion. Also *Converts to Rome: A biographical list of the more notable converts to the Catholic Church in the United Kingdom during*

the King was converted to marry the King of Spain. A Eucharistic Congress was held in London, and although yielding to protests the Government refused to allow a public procession of the Blessed Sacrament, a large Catholic procession nevertheless took place in the London streets in the neighbourhood of Westminster Cathedral. It was known that King Edward had asked to be released from the obligation of declaring the worship of the Virgin and the sacrifice of the Mass 'superstitious and idolatrous',[1] and though the Parliament of 1906 could not find time to deal with the question, it would shortly be settled to the satisfaction of the Catholics.[2] How unreal the battle between the Church and the Sects must have been when the only question which seriously fluttered the ecclesiastical dovecots was the battle in the Church of England between the Evangelicals and the Liberals on the one hand, and the Anglo-Catholics on the other, or rather, since within the Church the Anglo-Catholic victory was well in sight, if indeed it had not already been won, the battle between the entire church, including the Anglo-Catholics and Roman Catholicism.

Protestantism was on the decline. Hilaire Belloc and Chesterton were doing their utmost to bring it into ridicule while rehabilitating Catholicism and it was a sign of the times that in popular drama the Catholic priest was no longer the traitor, the Jesuit unmasked at the close by the combined efforts of honest folk. Now the playwright very often made him the providential instrument of dramatic justice. In the world of affairs, the Jewish financier bent on luxury and display was replacing the Puritan man of business who toiled conscientiously to acquire wealth as though fulfilling a stern duty. Throughout the great mass of the population, more indulgent than formerly to Catholicism, but more remote than ever from conversion, there prevailed an increasing hostility to asceticism or religious pessimism of any kind. That Catholicism left man the hope of purgatory was put to its credit, but it was blamed for leaving him exposed to the fear of

the last sixty years, compiled and edited by W. Gordon Gorman, new and enlarged edition, 1910. This is the tenth edition, containing 6,700 names. The first, which bore the title *Rome's Recruits*, was published in 1876. 'This list', the author explains, 'is in no way a numbering of the people, but a record of a spiritual change among the intellectual classes of these islands' (p. 10). And again: 'It will be found by a cursory inspection of the list that there is hardly an English noble family that has not given one or more of its members to the Roman Catholic Church' (p. 1).

[1] Sir Sidney Lee, *King Edward VII*. . . . Vol. ii, pp. 22 sqq.

[2] 10 Edw. 7 and 1 Geo. V, Cap. 29: An Act to alter the form of the Declaration required to be made by the Sovereign on Accession (*Accession Declaration Act*, 1910).

hell. Religion was expected to foster a humanitarian optimism, to offer the human race and even the individual a guarantee of health and happiness on earth.[1] H. G. Wells and Bernard Shaw, whose readers were ten or rather a hundred times more numerous than those of Belloc and Chesterton, professed a sort of religion of progress which borrowing ideas from Bergson's *Evolution Créatrice* and confining itself strictly to the sensible universe, attempted a spiritual interpretation of evolution. Powerful currents from the warm countries of the south, Jewish, Catholic, but above all pagan, were battering and crumbling the wavebeaten cliff of Nordic Protestantism.

From all this it is clear that the Nonconformist campaign against the Education Act was defeated far more by the general apathy than by the obstinate resistance of the Anglicans. And this apathy was nowhere more profound than in the Government departments. We must not imagine that the Education Bills successively introduced by the Ministry only to be defeated by the Lords or dropped in the Commons were the work of the Board of Education, resentful that its freedom of action had been hampered since 1902 by Anglican interference. In fact, the Education Act of 1902 had been drafted under the aegis of Sir Robert Morant, who was still the autocrat of the Board and whose despotism would continue until 1911 when he would be driven from his throne by a revolt of the Union of Teachers.[2] Others less kindly disposed towards the Church of England were quick to perceive the advantages the Board derived from the concordat of 1902. So far as secondary education was concerned, these were in-

[1] See, for example, Margaret Ethel MacDonald's quaint criticism of a friend who lived a life of remarkable self-sacrifice and had no religious faith: '. . . I should imagine, if Christ's teaching is true, or if there is anything divine in our moral sense and in human love and self-sacrifice, that ——'s life is more acceptable to God than that of the majority of orthodox religious people of whatever sect. *Only I think if she believed in God she would take more care of herself, she is rather weary of life and does not trouble to take proper food and rest.*' (Quoted by J. R. MacDonald, *Margaret Ethel MacDonald*, p. 70).

[2] For the episode of the Holmes circular which condemned the practice of choosing elementary school inspectors too exclusively from the pupils of elementary schools and thus arousing the formidable antagonism of all the teachers, see F. H. Hayward, *Educational Administration and Criticism: A Sequel to the Holmes Circular, with a preface by John Adams*, 1912. Also H. of C., April 4, July 13, 1911 (*Parliamentary Debates*, Commons 1911, 5th Series, vol. xxiii, pp. 2155 sqq.; vol. xxviii, pp. 434 sqq.). 'We have a new Minister of Education, supported, we have no doubt, by a new permanent secretary. Sir Robert Morant, who has been so long the dominant figure of the Board, watching Minister after Minister flit before him like shadows in the cave, has passed on to another task, taking with him, we believe, the thanks of many friends of educational progress and perhaps hearing, as he goes, a sigh of relief from those who found his hand too heavy' (*Times Educational Supplement*, January 2, 1912).

disputable. The old independent grammar schools in which the influence of the Anglican Church was predominant had been swept away, to be replaced by new schools where the authority of the Church was reduced to a minimum, if not completely destroyed. Midway between elementary and secondary education the rapidly multiplying technical schools, and classes for adults, had literally no place for religion in their curricula. And even in the domain of elementary education the Act of 1902, which had been so widely regarded as the salvation of the denominational schools, turned out as time went, to be less favourable to the Church than had been originally believed. The right possessed by the Board of Education to inspect the denominational schools, who now received their share of the rates on the same footing as the undenominational, provided a thousand pretexts, if the Board wished, for making their existence hard. Moreover, these schools were usually village schools. As the depopulation of the country districts proceeded the number of children attending them diminished. Some had even to be closed. On the contrary, in the crowded urban centres, which were steadily growing, the new schools opened belonged to the category of the old board schools. An increase was therefore soon witnessed in the number of children attending the provided schools, a decrease in the number attending the non-provided, and the Church of England suffered under the new system as under the old.[1] The change to be dreaded was a compromise of the kind arranged in 1908 between certain Anglican bishops and Nonconformist leaders, by which the parsons would lose their monopoly of the village school in return for the right of entry into all schools without exception. This, however, was just what the teachers in the public elementary schools would not brook. They were willing to submit to the obligation of giving their pupils every day a perfunctory religious lesson, if at that price they could prevent intruders invading premises they regarded as their exclusive domain. Thus the *status quo* found an increasing number of defenders, not only among those who took no interest in education but among those who, precisely because

[1] When the Bill of 1902 was passed 2,000,000 children were being educated in the board schools, 2,000,000 in the voluntary schools. (For the figures in 1895 see my *History of the English People*, vol. v, p. 165.) In 1913–14, 3,313,488 children were attending the provided schools as against 2,069,136 attending the non-provided (*Board of Education. Statistics of Public Education in England and Wales. Educational Statistics.* 1913–14, p. 271). In 1930 the figures were respectively 4,049,263 and 1,943,893 (*Education in 1930. Being the report of the Board of Education and the Statistics of Public Education for England and Wales*, 1931, p. 113).

they were enthusiastic educationalists, were disgusted with these ecclesiastical bickerings. Loud as was the din of the combat, after all completely barren, which during the years that followed the election of January 1906 raged between Anglicans, Catholics, and Nonconformists, it was matched by the silence which enveloped the extensive work of reform accomplished by the joint labours of Parliament and the Board of Education.

8

When the Liberal Cabinet on the morrow of its advent to power was confronted with the many questions connected with public education, it was not content with attempting to satisfy the Nonconformists. When Birrell introduced his Bill he expressed his regret that the problem of religious instruction occupied public attention so exclusively to the neglect of other and more important educational problems. In addition to a number of provisions dealing with endowments, his Bill contained a clause which empowered the County Councils to devolve a portion of their educational functions to subordinate bodies functioning over a more limited area, thus effecting a species of decentralization which would amount to a partial return to the system of school boards. The Bill was also accompanied by a further Bill 'consolidating' all previous Education Bills including the new Bill of 1906 if it were passed. Officials of the Board of Education would no longer be in danger of losing their way in a maze of enactments, some of them three-quarters of a century old. They would have to apply only a single comprehensive Statute. Of all these ambitious projects not one survived the defeat of Birrell's Bill. But we have already seen how after 1907 partly by administrative regulations, in part also by legislation, the Government contrived to effect a series of partial reprisals. And these reprisals were not solely concerned with the everlasting battle over denominational teaching in the schools. In the purely secular sphere they did much to render the elementary schools more efficient, the secondary schools more democratic.

To take first the improvements effected in elementary education. Already in this year 1906, otherwise so barren, the Government carried an act authorizing the Scottish school boards to provide for the education and conveyance to school of epileptic and crippled children.[1] Another Act which attracted more attention empowered the English education authorities to provide meals for children attending the schools. If it were proved that their under-nourishment was due to their parents' poverty, the meals might be given at the cost of the school.[2] In 1907 an important measure of administrative reorganization was passed,[3] an Act, observed the annual report of the Board, which, 'though it attracted but little public attention, may without exaggeration be described as an event of the first educational importance'.[4] It gave the local educational authorities extended facilities for raising loans and purchasing land. It proceeded to impose upon them the obligation of arranging for the medical inspection of the children, authorized them to set up holiday schools and play centres, and for the first time gave them unrestricted powers to make whatever provision was necessary for the education of deaf, deaf and dumb, and blind children.[5] In 1908 a novel experiment was undertaken, a first step towards a compulsory post-elementary education such as had lately been introduced in Germany. A Statute authorized the local Scottish authorities—the measure was temporarily confined to Scotland—to enact for their respective districts by-laws making attendance at school obligatory up to an age not exceeding seventeen.[6] What results would these statutes

[1] 6 Edw. 7, Cap. 10: An Act to provide for the Education and Conveyance to School of Epileptic and Crippled and Defective Children. (*Education of Defective Children* [*Scotland*] *Act*, 1906.)

[2] 6 Edw. 7, Cap. 57: An Act to make provision for Meals for Children attending Public Elementary Schools in England and Wales. (*Education* [*Provision of Meals*] *Act*, 1906.)

[3] 7 Edw. 7, Cap. 43: An Act to make provision for the better administration by the Central and Local Authorities in England and Wales of the enactments relating to Education. (*Education* [*Administrative Provisions*] *Act*, 1907.)

[4] *Report of the Board of Education for the Year 1906–7*, 1907, p. 8.

[5] Before a special school for blind or deaf and dumb children could be sanctioned the Statute of 1893—56 and 57 Vict., Cap. 42: (*Elementary Education* [*Blind and Deaf Children*] *Act*, 1893) required that at least a third of the cost should be provided by private subscription. The stipulation was abolished in 1907.

[6] 8 Edw. 7, Cap. 63: An Act to amend the laws relating to England and Scotland and for other purposes connected therewith (*Education* [*Scotland*] *Act*, 1908). For the problem of post-elementary education which the Education Bill of 1919 finally attempted without success to render compulsory in England see my article on '*La Nouvelle loi Scolaire anglaise*' (*Revue de Paris*, October 1, 1919; *26th année*, vol. v, pp. 596 sqq.). To complete this account of the educational legislation during the years following 1907 we must also mention 8 Edw. 7, Cap. 67: An Act to consolidate and amend the Law relating to the Protection of Children, and Young Persons, Reformatory and Industrial Schools, and Juvenile Offenders and otherwise to amend the Law with respect to Children and Young Persons (*Children Act*, 1908): Part IV, Reformatory and Industrial Schools. 9 Edw. 7, Cap. 13: An Act to provide for the recovery by Local Education Authorities of Costs for Medical Treatment of Children attending Elementary Schools in England and Wales (*Local Education Authori-*

produce? And in so far as they were permissive what employment would the local authorities make of them? In any case, the Liberal Government had opened up the way.

9

The provision of education for those above the age for leaving school has taken us beyond the boundary of elementary education. This is equally true of the so-called higher elementary education which the Code of 1905 empowered the local authorities to provide and of which the central schools founded in London and Manchester would present excellent models.[1] It is true also of the permission given to the local authorities by the administrative Statute of 1907 to provide scholarships for pupils of public elementary schools 'from the age of twelve up to the limit of age fixed for the provision of instruction in a public elementary school by sub-section 2 of section 22 of the 1902 Act'. But although in these three instances the standard of elementary education, as hitherto understood by the public, was outstepped, the education these various provisions envisaged was nevertheless treated by the Government as something which came within the competence of the officials in charge of elementary education, not of those concerned with secondary. In other words, their authors consistently regarded the distinction between elementary and secondary education as one not of age but of class. There was an elementary education which you might carry as far as possible, but which remained throughout a preparation for manual labour. And there was a secondary education begun as soon as possible by the children of the middle-class which prepared them for all those professions which were the reserve of the ruling class. Would the Liberal Government continue to maintain this point of view? Suddenly they made it known that they would not, but intended to develop the principle contained in germ, though only in germ, in the Educa-

ties [*Medical Treatment*] *Act*, 1909). 10 Edw. 7 and 1 Geo. 5, Cap. 37: An Act to enable certain Local Education Authorities to give boys and girls information, advice and assistance with respect to the choice of employment (*Education* [*Choice of Employment*] *Act*, 1910).

[1] For the foundation and first beginnings of these schools see the excellent article entitled 'Central Schools. A London and Manchester Experiment' in the first number of *The Times Educational Supplement*, September 6, 1910, p. 5.

tion Act of 1902—by making secondary education democratic.

The report of the Board of Education published at the end of 1906, after announcing that the sum provided in the budget for the development of secondary education had been increased and that the Government was engaged in framing the necessary regulations for its allocation, explained the principle on which it would proceed. 'Education is one. . . . It ought to be continuously progressive from the time when a child first passes beyond the home and goes to school up to the time when school life ceases, when the boy or girl ceases to be under educational tutelage, has been taught how to learn for himself or herself. In an ideal commonwealth, this process would be complete for the whole youth of the nation. This is a high ideal, and how far removed it is from existing facts, or from any state of facts which can be contemplated, as soon to be possible, is at once obvious. But short of it there is no finality: and the higher the aim is fixed, the higher the attainment is likely to be.'[1]

There was no intention of complying with the demand of the youthful Labour party and making secondary education free straightaway. For that the time was clearly not ripe. Only four years had passed since the Act of 1902 had made it possible to organize in Great Britain a system of public secondary education, and only two since the Board of Education had created a body of inspectors to control the standard of education given in those secondary schools which sought Government grants. But in 1907 the budgetary provision for secondary education was further increased and the regulations distinguished between two categories of secondary school which would receive respectively a higher or a lower grant. To receive the higher, five pounds a year for every pupil, two conditions which we have already mentioned must be fulfilled: the board of managers must contain a majority of representatives of the local authority, and no religious test must be imposed on teachers or pupils. But a further condition was imposed—subject to certain exceptions laid down by the regulation —that at least a quarter of the places should be free, reserved for pupils from elementary schools who passed the examination for a scholarship.[2] And those schools in which the proportion of scholar-

---

[1] *Report of the Board of Education for the Year 1905–6*, 1906, p. 61.
[2] H. of C., May 15, 1907, R. MacKenna's speech (*Parliamentary Debates*, 4th Series, vol. clxxiv, p. 1054).

ships might be less than a quarter of the places were exceedingly few. In a much larger number of schools it was higher, sometimes 30 or 40 per cent or even more.[1] On this point however the figures are not easy to interpret. Even before 1902 the county and borough councils had begun to grant scholarships more liberally. After as before 1902 we must take into account, besides the children in receipt of these scholarships, those who received scholarships from private foundations; and in addition to those who came up from the elementary schools with a scholarship, there were children who came up without one. But the extent of the effort made by the public authorities to provide a bridge between the elementary and the secondary school will be evident when we reflect that in 1900 scholarships at a total cost of £80,000 were granted to some 5,500 children, in 1911 to 38,000 at a cost of more than £400,000.[2]

The new system involved its special problems. Should the standard of the entrance examination qualifying a boy or girl for a scholarship be so high that only exceptionally gifted children went on to the secondary school, children whose abilities merited a place among their wealthier companions? In that case, the proportion of a quarter would be out of the question and the object in view, to open secondary education to the lower classes, would not be achieved. Or should it merely ensure that the standard of the children in receipt of free places should not be lower than that of the paying pupils? The proportion of a quarter would be speedily and enormously exceeded. And would this host of newcomers prove industrious and keen workers? Or would they drop out at various stages, whatever undertakings might have been given, before the five years' course of study was completed? And even before they proved laggards would not their presence pro-

---

[1] 'To insist all at once upon so large a proportion as 25 per cent "free places", *ex-hypothesi* boys and girls from working-class parents . . . is under present conditions "a large order," especially when, owing to a peculiar administrative interpretation by the Board of its own regulation, the number at a given moment in a new and rapidly growing school might be nearer 40 per cent and actually does in many schools reach 30 per cent (*Times Educational Supplement*, September 6, 1910; 'The New Secondary Education. Some Dangers Ahead'). In the year 1908–9, in the seven schools for which the Durham County Council was the responsible authority, the percentage required by the Board was 25 in each case but the percentage actually given in the case of one school was 67 in 1907–8 and 39 in 1909–10; in another 46 in 1909–10 and 45 in 1910–11; and in a third 51 in 1910–11 (*Report of the Board of Education for the Year 1909-10*, 1911, p. 70).

[2] Of which it is true, as a critic points out, more than half were provided by the London County Council and more than half the remainder by a small number of large towns (S. J. G. Hoare, *The Schools and Social Reform*, 1914, p. 33). It was indeed the London County Council which inaugurated this lavish distribution of scholarships, a policy due surely to the influence of Sidney Webb.

voke an exodus of the paying pupils? Would not the intellectual as well as the social standard of these secondary schools be lowered in consequence? These were difficult problems. But their difficulty did not daunt either the Liberal Ministers or the experts at the Board of Education.[1] To connect elementary with secondary education was the outstanding achievement of the Government during these years. But we must not forget that they made use of the instrument which, when they drew up the Act of 1902, the Conservatives intentionally or unintentionally had placed in their hands.

10

But if secondary education were brought within the reach of the working class would education have been rendered completely democratic? When a child of middle-class parentage had finished his secondary education about the age of seventeen his parents did not usually regard his education as complete, but sent him to the University for three or four years. Must this higher education remain permanently the privilege of the middle- and upper-class minority? Could nothing be done to bring its benefits within reach of the proletariat? Two experiments had been made in this direction without any assistance from the State during the years immediately preceding the advent of the Liberals to power.

The first of these was the foundation at Oxford of Ruskin College.[2] An American philanthropist provided the original funds in 1899. His intention was to found at Oxford, but this time for the benefit of the working class, an institution similar to the halls which had grown up round the new universities of London and Manchester to make it possible for poor students to live more cheaply because they lived together and assisted each other in their studies. Ruskin College was therefore called at first Ruskin Hall. But it was also a 'college', because the 'Ruskin' students, prevented by mixed feelings of pride and shyness from attending the University and College lectures, were determined to have their own

---

[1] For these educational and social problems and others not discussed here connected with the provision of secondary education, see the excellent *Report of the Board of Education or the Year 1906–1907*, pp. 8 sqq.

[2] For Ruskin College see Henry Sanderson Furniss (Lord Sanderson), *Memories of Sixty Years*, 1931, pp. 82 sqq.; also an interesting article entitled 'A College for Workmen' in he *Speaker* for February 24, 1906.

teachers to teach them political science, political economy, and economic history. There were between thirty and fifty students, closely packed in an unpretentious building, doing their own housekeeping and, at first, their own cooking. Endless discussions conducted in an atmosphere thick with the smoke of pipes followed each lecture. There was one long term lasting forty-eight weeks, the only vacation being four weeks at Christmas, though the students were allowed to devote the week-ends to Labour propaganda in any locality they might choose. Correspondence courses which reached some 6,000 workmen throughout the country enabled the governing body of the college not only to bring its influence to bear upon a host of very young men for whom there was no room within its walls—many of them indeed too young for admission—but also to discover among this large body the *élite* who later on would be chosen as actual students.

This governing body was composed in part of members of the University of Socialist sympathies, such as Professor York Powell, Sidney Ball, and the Rev. A. J. Carlyle, in part of trade-union secretaries such as Barnes and Bowerman, whose task it was to see that the new institution was not, like the University Extension Movement, annexed by the middle class. If, however, the Principal, Dennis Hird, an eccentric ex-clergyman who had been deprived of his living for writing a book in praise of polygamy, claimed to teach the complete Socialist creed, many of the tutors thought it their duty to inculcate in their simple audience a salutary scepticism and weaken their faith in revolutionary dogma. This produced considerable friction. But the predominant influence was that of the trade-union officials, who were neither Marxian nor anti-Marxian, but, dispensing with theories of any kind, were content to defend the corporate interests of their class. It was they who provided the greater part of the funds, not only the annual payment of £52 to every student for his support but whatever further sum was required to meet the expenses of the college. And they sent up to Oxford young men of twenty-eight to thirty who for five or six years had proved themselves good workers in the cause of the unions, to learn English purer than their local dialect and the phraseology of politics and political economy so that when they went back to their unions they would be able to furnish the working class in the urban and county councils, and eventually in the House of

Commons itself, with all the leaders it required, so that it could dispense entirely with middle-class interference.

The second experiment was the foundation of the Workers' Educational Association.[1] Like Ruskin College, the movement was intended by its founder, Albert Mansbridge, a Lancashire co-operator, to renew the attempt made thirty years earlier by the University Extension Movement, which had in a sense been too successful, since its very success had made it turn its back on its proletarian origins and become a purely middle-class institution. He sought to inaugurate on novel lines a movement for the higher education of the working class by effecting an alliance between the University Extension Movement, on the one hand, and the co-operators and the trade unions on the other. The project, brought for the first time in 1899 without much success before the University Extension Summer School, was revived in 1902 immediately after the Boer War. At the end of 1905 the Association possessed 'branches' in eight towns and 'district committees' throughout the north-west and south-west of England. And in November, a few days before the resignation of the Cabinet, Sir William Anson, President of the Board of Education, with Sir Robert Morant at his side, received a working-class deputation introduced by Will Crooks which asked for financial help from the Board. For the moment nothing was done; the matter was simply referred for examination to the Advisory Committee. But when the Workers' Education Conference held its annual meeting at Oxford on August 10, 1907, Morant attended.

The subject of discussion was 'What Oxford can do for the people'. A young Scotch workman from the Clyde dockyards, S. R. Mactavish, voiced, in language almost threatening, the attitude of the working class: 'I have not come here as a suppliant. . . . I refuse to sit down at the rich man's door and beg for crusts. . . . I demand for my class all the advantages that Oxford has it in her power to offer, and I claim it as a right of which we have been unjustly deprived—unjustly for us and for Oxford too. . . . For, remember, democracy will be achieved with or without the assis-

---

[1] For the Workers' Educational Association and the Tutorial Classes, see Albert Mansbridge, *An Adventure in Working Class Education: Being the Story of the W.E.A. 1903–1915*, 1915; also *University Tutorial Classes: A Study in the Development of Higher Education among Working Men and Women*, 1913. The Workers' Educational Association is mentioned in the *Report of the Board of Education for the year 1906-7*, p. 91; and the Tutorial Classes in the report for the year 1910–11, p. 79.

tance of Oxford; but if the University of Oxford continues to hold herself aloof from the working classes, then we shall end by thinking of her, not for what she is, but for what she has been.' And he found fault with the too conservative spirit in which the University Extension taught political economy and history.

'In point of fact,' he declared in conclusion, 'workmen's sons come to Oxford to escape their class, not to relieve it. . . . We want her in future to inspire them, not with the desire of succeeding, but with that of serving society—we have need of you. But you have need of us.'

Such language alarmed a portion of his audience, but only a minority. The real enemies of the new organization were the extremists, ill-pleased to see among its officers not only such extremely moderate trade-unionists as Henderson and Bowerman but politicians of every party and Anglican clergyman and bishops. Ruskin College also took umbrage at these new schemes, whose very existence seemed to imply that it had failed to fulfil its founders' hopes. Dennis Hird, supported by all his students, raised the entire college in arms against the moderate policy of the governing body. Indirectly, the revolt was aimed at the youthful Workers' Educational Association.

But after a two years' struggle Hird was driven from Ruskin College and obliged to found in London a rival college supported by the subscriptions of a few trade unions more revolutionary than the rest. Meanwhile, the Workers' Educational Association carried out its programme, whose details had been settled by a committee of fourteen, of whom seven represented the universities, seven the working class. Tutorial classes were organized and regular weekly lectures given in all centres where they were asked for. The complete course lasted two years. Every year twenty-four lectures were given. An hour's lecture was followed by an hour's open discussion. In the interval between the lectures the tutor was at the students' disposition to give them advice and correct their essays. Subsidized by grants from trade unions and co-operative societies, the universities, the local authorities, and the Board of Education, and staffed by young and enthusiastic tutors, sufficiently well paid to be able to devote themselves entirely to the work, the new educational movement prospered.[1]

---

[1] 'The Oxford Committee held that a tutor could undertake five classes, and decided to pay £80 per class or £400 per annum for full work. Cambridge pays £72 a class and

The students learnt much from their tutors, but the tutors learned little less from their pupils. For both alike—the Tutorial Classes, like Ruskin College but on a far larger scale—were schools in which they were preparing themselves to become the future leaders of the Labour party.

II

Thus, the most important measures adopted by the Liberal Government in the sphere of public education—the provision of free meals to poor children in elementary schools, the steps taken to render secondary education democratic and higher education accessible to the working class—were all directly borrowed from the programme of the Labour party. It would be incorrect to say that this new party won an important success at the election of January 1906, for that election gave it birth. Hitherto, there had been no Labour party, but merely a Labour Representation Committee, whose stalwarts asked themselves, not without anxiety, what the result of the appeal to the nation would be. They were still a tiny group, very unimportant in comparison with the two powerful party organizations, the Liberal and the Unionist. A small room in the flat occupied by Ramsay MacDonald and his family on the second floor of a house in Lincoln's Inn Fields; a table; two or three chairs; if a fourth or fifth visitor turned up, he was given a seat on the piles of newspapers and magazines which littered the floor—this was the headquarters of the future Labour party. The three victories at Clitheroe, Woolwich, and Barnard Castle[1] had for the moment inspired the members of the Committee with unbounded hope, and the Liberals on their side, impressed by these unexpected successes, had in many constituencies made haste to conclude alliances with the Labour group. When the election campaign opened, in twenty-one one-member constituencies the Liberal had retired in favour of the Labour

London £60. Other Universities have hitherto paid less' (A. Mansbridge, *University Tutorial Classes*, p. 116). 'In 1905 the Workers' Educational Association counted eight branches, a hundred affiliated organizations and 1,000 individual members, in 1914 179 branches, 2,555 affiliated organizations, 11,430 individual members. The Tutorial Classes began in the school year 1908–9 with 234 students attending eight classes. . . . In 1913–14 there were 3,234 students attending 145 classes' (A. Mansbridge, *An Adventure* . . . pp. 67–8). For the grants from the Board of Education see A. Mansbridge, *University Tutorial Classes*, Appendix II, p. 136, also the *Board of Education Regulations for Further Education*, an annual publication which began in 1907–8.

[1] See vol. v, pp. 278–9, 363.

candidate, and in ten two-member constituencies the Labour candidate shared the same platform with the Liberal. Later, however, the question of tariff reform had seemed to relegate Labour questions to the background. A considerable number of by-elections were held between the Barnard Castle election and the General Election and only one working-class candidate was returned, a miner named Richards in Monmouthshire, and he stood as a Liberal. Two Labour candidates, on the other hand, who stood in opposition to the Liberal and Protectionist candidates at Norwich and in Lancashire, found themselves at the bottom of the poll and did not even prevent the election of the Liberal. In consequence, the Liberals became less tractable, negotiations between the old party and the new group more difficult.[1] In January 1906 there was a considerable number of three-cornered contests. The total number of candidates supported by the Labour Representation Committee was fifty-one[2]—that is to say, the Committee made itself responsible for a quarter of their election expenses and undertook, if they were elected, to provide an annual salary of £200 a year while they remained in Parliament. What would be the result at the Election of this friction between the Liberals and Labour men? Would it prove damaging to either or to both?

In the event the Government majority was so overwhelming that neither suffered. In two Lanarkshire constituencies, at Wigan in Lancashire, at Stockton-on-Tees, and at Grimsby a split vote between the Liberals and Labour resulted in the election of the Unionist candidate. But almost everywhere the Liberal or the Labour candidate was returned.[3] Of the 51 candidates put up by the Labour Representation Committee 29 were elected and immediately formed themselves at Westminster into a special group which called itself 'the Labour party' and to show its entire independence of the Government sat on the opposition benches. Parliamentary statisticians, however, did not regard these 29 as

[1] For the negotiations conducted in the autumn of 1905 through the channel of George Cadbury, the great Quaker chocolate-manufacturer, see A. G. Gardiner, *Life of George Cadbury*, p. 81.

[2] Besides eighteen candidates representing the miners and seven candidates put forward by the Social Democratic Federation. For a complete account of the working-class candidates, see J. Keir Hardie, 'Labour and the forthcoming Election' (*Nineteenth Century*, January 1906; vol. lix, p. 12 sqq.).

[3] For a good analysis of the election results see Keir Hardie, 'The Labour Party' (*National Review*, February 1906; vol. xlvi, pp. 1002 sqq.).

the only Labour members in the new House. Some even reckoned 54, among them 14 miners who had their separate electoral organization and persisted in forming a group apart. Of these 54, 45 were of working-class origin.[1] If among the members of the Independent Labour party Ramsay MacDonald had been a pupil teacher, Snowden a clerk in the civil service, and Jowett was an employer, this does not alter the fact that the victory of Labour at the polls was the victory of a class rather than a party. At first sight these 50 working men seemed an unimportant group in comparison with the 200 Nonconformist members. But if at Westminster these Nonconformists were a formidable body of representatives, they represented only the 'sects', swamped in the twentieth century by a vaster and more powerful electorate. The 50 working-class members, on the other hand, could regard themselves with good reason as the genuine representatives of the enormous majority of the voters. If the Cabinet proved too obedient to the orders of the representatives of Nonconformity, it ran the risk of alienating the sympathies of the electorate. On the other hand, not only the Liberal members of Parliament but all the members without exception, even the Conservatives, were aware after January 1906 that, if they refused to take the grievances voiced by the Labour members seriously, they might lose their voters *en masse* to Labour. 'We have here', wrote Balfour on January 17, 1906, to the King's private secretary, 'to do with something much more important than the swing of the pendulum or all the squabbles about Free Trade and Fiscal Reform. We are face to face (no doubt in a milder form) with the Socialistic difficulties which loom so large on the Continent. Unless I am greatly mistaken, the Election of 1906 inaugurates a new era.'[2] Balfour no doubt was not sorry to make this observation, for it was the Liberals who would be the first to suffer from the birth of the Labour party. It was none the less true, as also was the parenthesis about the 'mild' character of English Socialism. For if in the whole

---

[1] Thirty members who refused to join the Labour party (in fact, they complained bitterly that the Labour party had stolen their title, for a Labour Group had existed in the previous Parliament) constituted a Trade Union Labour Group within the ranks of the Liberal party (G. M. Alcock, *Fifty Years of Trade Unionism*, p. 365). But the group lost much of its importance when the fourteen miners left it for the Labour party and it soon disappeared.

[2] Arthur Balfour to Lord Knollys, January 17, 1906 (Sir Sidney Lee, *King Edward VII* ... vol. ii, p. 449). Cf. Arthur Balfour to Lord Saint-Aldwyn, January 26, 1906 (Lady Victoria Hicks-Beach, *Life of Sir Michael Hicks-Beach (Earl Saint-Aldwyn)* 1932; vol. ii, p. 224).

of Europe there was no Socialist party which was so completely representative of a class, in spite of this (or was it because of this?), there was not one so undoctrinal. It was a significant fact that the few 'Socialist' candidates who had come forward in one or two constituencies, whether Social Democrats of Hyndman's group or independent Socialists, had been defeated without exception. At Burnley, Hyndman had not even the satisfaction of preventing the election of the Labour candidate. The new Labour members, men who owed their political education to long years of trade-union negotiation, flattered by their membership of the first Parliament in the world and the courteous reception they received, felt almost overawed as they listened to the discussion of questions of general policy which transcended their professional competence.[1] They were guiltless of any desire to identify the interests of their class with those of the human race, or achieve their aims at the cost of overthrowing the entire fabric of society; they were devout Christians and moderate patriots. What then were their demands? In the first place they demanded that the wrong inflicted upon the trade unions by the hostile judgment in 1901 of the House of Lords should be righted, and that since the supreme court of appeal had decided to interpret the statutes of 1871 and 1875 dealing with the unions in a sense opposed to the plain intention of their authors they insisted that these statutes should be recast in such terms that the judges' ill-will should never again be able to nullify the intention of the legislature.

12

As we have already seen, the Unionist Government, anxious lest the discontent aroused among the working classes by the

[1] Winston Churchill (speech at Hartlepool, May 12, 1906) mentions as one of the distinctive features of the new Parliament 'the strength and influence of the Labour party'. He continues: 'The interests of the country were greatly advantaged by the increase in the number of Labour representatives. They were a stable and not an unstable element and added greatly to the wisdom and the earnestness and consequently to the dignity of the House.' Cf. Sir Almeric Fitzroy, August 14, 1907: 'Haldane's and Grey's comments upon the relations of Ministers to their large and heterogeneous following were full of interest. They were both agreed that the Labour Members gave them much less trouble than gentlemen in close political connection—a fact which they were inclined to ascribe to the circumstance that most of the Labour party had through their Trade Unions become men of affairs, capable of apprehending any practical issue submitted to them. Haldane declared that, in relation to military administration, he had found individual Labour members most ready to listen to reason and accept explanations offered in a reasonable spirit, and Sir E. Grey instanced Mackarness, Colton, and Bellairs as types of an opposite tendency' (*Memoirs*, vol. i, pp. 329–30).

judgment of the House of Lords might have disastrous consequences at the polls, appointed a Royal Commission of five members to inquire into the question of trade disputes and combinations.[1] It would have reported in the autumn of 1905, on the eve of the General Election, if the Cabinet had not objected to the report being used as a source of political capital by the candidates of all parties.[2] It was not therefore published until January 15 under another Cabinet when the rout of the Unionists had already begun. In substance the report proposed that three points which the late judgments had rendered doubtful should be determined by fresh legislation. These decisions had restricted the right of picketing—that is to say, the right of strikers to make the strike effective by making it complete. The Commission proposed that it should be expressly declared lawful 'to persuade to strike—i.e. to desist from working, apart from procuring breach of contract'. It further proposed to delete from the statute of 1875 the too indefinite offence of watching and besetting a house and to substitute for it a prohibition 'of acts in such a manner as to cause a reasonable apprehension in the mind of any person that violence will be used to him or his family, or damage be done to his property'. In the second place, to restrict the right to strike, the judges had taken advantages of an omission in the statute of 1875. The statute had laid down that an act committed in the course of a strike by several persons should not be deemed an act of criminal conspiracy, if it would not constitute a crime, when committed by a single individual. But it had not laid down that they were not liable to a civil action, and civil proceedings had actually been taken. The Commission proposed that they should be expressly barred. Finally, these limitations upon the right to strike had been rendered a very serious menace to the trade unions by the celebrated Taff Vale Decision which held the unions liable to damages for offences committed by their members in the course of a strike. Until 1901 the judges had interpreted the intentional silence on this point of the Act of 1871 as implying non-liability. Now that the courts had adopted the contrary view what steps should be

[1] *A Royal Commission appointed to inquire into the subject of Trade Disputes and Trade Combinations and as to the law affecting them, and to report on the law applicable to the same and the effect of any modification thereof*, June 6, 1903. *Report of the Royal Commission on Trade Disputes and Trade Combinations*, January 15, 1906.

[2] Sidney and Beatrice Webb, *The History of Trade Unionism* (revised edition extended to 1920), 1920, p. 605.

taken? It was one thing not to declare the trade unions liable, quite another to lay down positively that they were not, even when the acts adjudged illegal by the courts had been committed by their express orders. The Commission recoiled from such an enormity and suggested a device which betrayed the systematic and elaborate workmanship of the Webbs. It proposed to legalize unions and strikes, and give the legal union a constitution which would protect it from responsibility for its members' acts if unauthorized and immediately disavowed. It further proposed that the unions should be permitted to separate their benefit fund from the rest of their funds so that it could no longer be confiscated during a strike, and become, if they wished, 'corporations' capable of concluding legal agreements with the employers and their own members. It was proposed, in short, not to abolish the liability of the unions, but to restrict it by defining it, and thus take the first steps towards remodelling their entire status.[1]

When on March 28 the Attorney-General, Sir John Walton, expounded in the House of Commons the principles of the Government's Bill, they were obviously identical with those on which the commission had based its report. In the first place the Bill, reviving the phraseology of a statute of 1859,[2] inadvertently repealed by the Act of 1871, declared 'peaceful persuasion' during a strike lawful. It extended to civil proceedings the protection against criminal given by the statute of 1875. Finally, it dealt with the vital question of the unions' financial liability by imposing upon them the obligation to form 'executive committees'. Acts committed by these committees themselves or by their regular agents acting within their instructions would alone render the union liable for damages. To this solution only one alternative was possible, the total abolition of liability. In an impassioned peroration the Attorney-General pointed out the dangers of the

[1] According to S. and B. Webb the Commission 'reported in favour of the Trade Union accepting full responsibility for its own action, subject to considerable, *but far from adequate*, amendment of the Law' (*The History of Trade Unionism*, revised edition, 1920, p. 600). But in spite of the fact that apparently he did not regard these amendments as 'adequate' Sidney Webb was one of the three members to sign the majority report. In a short note appended to the report he pointed out that he desired to go further and contemplated a system of trade unionism which would render strikes impossible (*Report of the Royal Commission on Trade Disputes and Trade Combinations*, p. 18). For the views of Professor William Ashley, closely akin to Webb's, see his article entitled 'Trade Unions and the Law' (*National Review*, January 1906; vol. xlvii, pp. 56 sqq.).

[2] 22 Vict., Cap. 34: An Act to amend and explain an Act of the sixth year of the reign of George the Fourth to repeal the Laws relating to the Combination of Workmen and to make other provisions in lieu thereof. (*Combination of Workmen Act*, 1859.)

latter course. It was anti-democratic because it placed the trade union in a privileged position at law. And it would expose the unions to the risk of being committed by their most irresponsible agents to actions they disapproved.[1]

But the champions of the proletariat were up in arms at once. They could not forget that in 1905 a Unionist House of Commons had voted by a very large majority in favour of the complete abolition of liability; that during the Election campaign it had been made clear at every public meeting at which the question was raised that the workers demanded nothing less, and that many candidates, beginning with Sir John Walton himself, had pledged themselves, if returned, to secure the unions against liability under any circumstances. Sir John had in fact contrived to introduce into his peroration language which seemed intended to cover a retreat. It was for Parliament, he had pointed out, to decide whether it approved the solution proposed by the Government or preferred another. And he had refused to determine beforehand the form the Bill would finally assume. The Labour speakers therefore did not oppose the first reading of the Bill on the understanding that the Government would not oppose its future amendment in accordance with their wishes. They were aware of the voting power at their back and knew that all the members of the House were equally aware of it. 'It was a more serious question than simply a question of party politics, inasmuch as it was a question which affected the great mass of the workers in the country.'[2]

Two days later the House of Commons was invited to discuss the second reading of a Labour Bill dealing with the same question and which, while agreeing with the Government's Bill on the first two points, proceeded to lay down that a trade union could never be made liable for damages on account of illegal acts committed by its members.[3] An extremely heated debate was in progress when the Prime Minister intervened. He asked permission to speak the language not of law (he was no lawyer) but of common sense. The solution put forward by the Labour Bill possessed, he admitted, the advantage as compared with that proposed by the Government two days before that, if adopted, it gave less scope for litigation. After all, it simply restored the condition of affairs

---

[1] H. of C., March 28, 1906 (*Parliamentary Debates*, 4th Series, vol. cliv, pp. 1295 sqq.).

[2] H. of C., March 28, 1906, Shackleton's speech (ibid., vol. cliv, p. 1316).

[3] H. of C., March 30, 1906: Hudson's Motion (*Parliamentary Debates*, 4th Series, vol. clv, pp. 21 sqq.).

which had existed for the last thirty years of the nineteenth century and which had favoured the growth, on the whole beneficial, of the trade unions. Twice already, in 1904 and in 1905, he had voted for it himself. Why then should he reject it now that he was Prime Minister? He asked the House of Commons to pass the second reading of the Bill. Its principle would then be embodied in the Government's Bill.[1] This course was adopted. When the Government measure came up once more for discussion, it was no longer in charge of the Attorney-General but of the Solicitor-General, Sir William Robson. He left the question of the absolute non-liability of the unions to the free vote of the House, admitting that the Government could not maintain the original form of the Bill 'without considering or consulting the opinions of the trade unions'.[2] The debate which followed in July, August, and November was rapid. The opponents of the Bill, thus altered to satisfy the demands of labour, never amounted to a hundred, only once exceeded fifty, and on one occasion, and moreover when the decisive issue of liability or non-liability was put to the vote, were no more than twenty. The champions of the privileges of labour even won a further victory. Sir Charles Dilke, with the assent of the Government, carried an amendment that no judicial proceedings could be taken even if a strike involved a breach of contract.[3] Balfour delighted to humiliate the Cabinet by pointing to its disgraceful retreat on March 30.[4] But if the legal members of the Cabinet had indeed been compelled to retreat—among them it was said Asquith and Haldane—Campbell-Bannerman had asserted his authority and his personal prestige emerged enhanced from the debates. And had not Balfour himself retreated along with the rest? When the Bill came up for the third reading he refused on behalf of his party to challenge a division. He had always, he said, believed that the existing law required amending, so as to safeguard the benefit funds of the

---

[1] H. of C., March 30, 1906 (*Parliamentary Debates*, 4th Series, vol. clv, pp. 51 sqq.).
[2] H. of C., April 24, 1906 (ibid., vol. clv, pp. 1482 sqq.).
[3] Clause 3 of the measure lays down that 'an act done by a person in contemplation or furtherance of a trade dispute shall not be actionable on the ground only [that it induces some other person to break a contract of employment or] that it is an interference with the trade, business or employment of some other person, or with the right of some other person to dispose of his capital or his labour as he will'. The words placed in brackets were added on the motion of Sir Charles Dilke, H. of C., August 3, 1906 (ibid., vol. clxii, p. 1678). For the serious legal consequences of this amendment see M. W. Geldart 'The Present Law of Trade Disputes and Trade Unions' (*Political Quarterly*, May 1914, p. 33).
[4] H. of C., April 24, 1906 (*Parliamentary Debates*, 4th Series, vol. clv, pp. 1527–8, 1535–6).

trade unions. He would not make himself responsible for imperilling those funds by voting against the Bill.[1] The House of Lords could not oppose the unanimous decision of the Lower House. At the opening of December, at the very moment when under his leadership the Lords were engaged in garrotting the Education Bill, Lord Lansdowne pointed out that the country had spoken, that if they sent back the Trade Disputes Bill, it would be returned to them in a more embittered spirit, and therefore that the only possible course was to pass it.[2] Thereupon this important measure,[3] a scandal to the lawyers, was passed without division or debate less than a year after the Liberals had come into power. Its enactment was a victory not of the Liberals over the Conservatives, but of the proletariat over the bourgeoisie.

13

The working class put forward at the beginning of 1906 a further claim. This time they did not demand that the policy followed by the Unionist Government should be reversed, but that a policy which in their opinion had been pursued too timidly

[1] H. of C., November 9, 1906 (ibid., vol. clxiv, pp. 906, sqq., esp. p. 909).

[2] H. of L., December 4, 1906 (ibid., vol. clxvi, p. 702).

[3] 6 Edw. 7, Cap. 47: An Act to provide for the regulation of Trade Unions and Trade Disputes (*Trade Disputes Act*, 1906). It would be interesting to know how it was administered. It appears to have applied most strictly. The judges, and not only Tories like Darling, but such an advanced Liberal as the Chancellor, Lord Loreburn, were content with lamentations and protests when called upon to apply it. See a list of their protests in a letter over the signature of C. Arthur Buckley in the *Spectator* for February 17, 1912. As the years went on, the Courts became increasingly favourable to the contentions of the unions. At first they refused to grant immunity to illegal Acts not expressly specified in the Statute of 1906 (Conway v. Wade, 1908; Lark v. Belfast Harbour Commissioners, 1908). But in 1913 in Vacher & Sons v. The London Society of Compositors, the House of Lords refused to condemn the Compositors' Union for defamation, though the defamation was not in connection with a labour dispute. It regarded the defamation as itself constituting such a dispute (S. and B. Webb, *History of Trade Unionism*, revised edition, 1920, p. 606). If, however, the employers were thus disarmed by the Courts, they took their revenge in other ways by making use of the police during a strike, especially when the military replaced the ordinary police force. General Macready relates how, when called upon to keep order during a strike in South Wales at the end of 1910, he decided on his responsibility that the strike pickets must not exceed six persons, that they should not be permitted to light fires to keep themselves warm within a given radius of an inhabited building, that their members must be distinguishable by white bands on the arm, and might only exercise their right of peaceful persuasion under police supervision, as otherwise the police would be unable to determine whether the persuasion was genuinely peaceful (General the Right Hon. Sir Nevil Macready, *Annals of an Active Life*, vol. i, pp. 147-8). For the restrictions to which the right of picketing remained subject, see also C. Watney and J. A. Little, *Industrial Warfare, The Aims and Claims of Capital and Labour*, 1912, pp. 307-8.

should be carried further. We have seen how in 1897 the Unionist Government passed a Workmen's Compensation Bill which the unions regarded as a victory. And the extension of its benefits in 1900 to the agricultural labourers had been a second success.[1] But they were not satisfied. They demanded more,[2] and the Government, to prove that it had no objection in principle to their claims, appointed in 1904 a committee of inquiry. The latter, however, was perhaps obeying the unavowed wishes of the Cabinet when it reported adversely on almost every point.[3] Render the application of the statute universal? It was out of the question. It would involve the absurdity that if a private person paid a passer-by to sweep the snow from his doorstep, he would be deemed, in case of accident, a responsible employer. Moreover, what ground was there for bringing within the scope of the law occupations devoid of professional risk of any kind? It would be better to follow the German precedent, followed hitherto, and gradually extend a statute originally applicable to particular categories of workers to other categories, one at a time. Pay benefit not only from the fifteenth day as prescribed by the Act of 1897 but from the first? It would be a premium on idleness, a direct encouragement to a worker to go on the sick list and, if in addition he was in receipt of benefit from a union or friendly society, he might, thanks to the indemnity paid by his employer, receive a total sum in excess of his wages. Extend the benefit of the law to the victims of those 'industrial diseases' due in the opinion of experts to the unhealthy nature of certain occupations? A dangerous experiment, the report declared. Experts were not infallible. It was better to keep to the common-sense distinction between accident and 'disease'; and if it were desired to protect the worker against the risk of 'industrial diseases' to incorporate that risk in a general measure of insurance against sickness.

These negative conclusions were not calculated to appease the unions at a moment when they were becoming increasingly hostile to a Cabinet and party that were losing their hold over the country.

[1] See vol. v, p. 237.
[2] H. of C., May 19, 1904. Shackleton's speech. (*Parliamentary Debates*, 4th Series, vol. cxxxv, p. 408.)
[3] *Home Office Departmental Committee on Workmen's Compensation: Report of the Departmental Committee appointed to inquire into the Law relating to Compensation for Injuries to Workmen*, vol. i, *Report and Appendices 1904 (Sir Kenelm Digby's Committee)*, vol. ii, *Minutes of Evidence with Index*, 1905, vol. iii, *Supplementary Index*, 1906.

The pressure of the working class compelled the Government to introduce a Bill at the opening of the session of 1905.[1] It simply extended the benefits of the Act of 1897 to several categories of employment. And on one point it restricted its application. Complaints were made that the Act had made it harder for elderly men to find work: less robust and more liable to accidents, their employment involved too much risk to the employer. The Bill proposed that workers over the age of sixty should be entitled to conclude special contracts with their employers, less costly for the latter. Moreover, the introduction of the Bill in the House of Lords seems to have been an empty gesture. Once introduced, it was dropped immediately. In September the Trade Union Congress once more protested against the Government's inertia and demanded the establishment of a system of compulsory insurance.[2] The resignation of the Unionist Cabinet followed and the Liberal victory of 1906. Labour was to receive satisfaction.

In the first place—and this was a novelty in the history of British labour legislation—the Workmen's Compensation Act of 1906,[3] a statute of consolidation and amendment, was a measure of universal application. It embraced 'any person who has entered into or works under a contract of service or apprenticeship with an employer, whether by way of manual labour, clerical work or otherwise, and whether the contract is expressed or implied, is oral or in writing'. The only categories excluded from its scope were non-manual workers whose annual remuneration exceeded

---

[1] H. of L., April 4, 1905, Lord Belper's motion (*Parliamentary Debates*, 4th Series, vol. cxliv, pp. 263 sqq.).

[2] The measure which would be passed in 1906 did not depart from the system set up in 1897, the French as opposed to the German system which required the employer to ensure himself against the risk of compensating his employee. The system had its drawbacks and the report of Sir Kenelm Digby's committee had pointed them out. Many small employers failed to insure themselves—whether from economy or mere neglect and many workmen who were victims of accidents neglected to make use of their rights. The law often remained a dead letter, at Sheffield for example, a town of small workshops (*Report* pp. 12–13). Throughout the debates the representatives of labour continued to demand a system of compulsory insurance (see H. of C., March 26, 1906, Barnes' speech; *Parl. Deb.*, 4th Ser., vol. cliv, p. 902). But the Cabinet, while not refusing an inquiry, insisted on the difficulties involved and on this point the only satisfaction the champions of compulsory insurance received was the insertion in the clause dealing with occupational diseases of a provision enabling the Government by a provisional order which must be subsequently ratified by Parliament to introduce compulsory insurance in any industry where there existed a society insuring against the risk in question and containing the majority of the employers.

[3] 6 Edw. 7, Cap. 58: An Act to consolidate and amend the Law with respect to Compensation to Workmen for Injuries suffered in the course of their Employment (*Workmen's Compensation Act*, 1906).

£250, casual labourers, workers who did not work for the trade or business of their employer, those who worked in their own homes, in the language of the Act 'outworkers', and members of the employer's family. Step by step in the course of the debates several restrictions imposed by the Bill in its original form were dropped. Shop assistants were given the right to compensation. Domestic servants also, a concession proposed by Campbell-Bannerman. The statutes of 1897 and 1900 were jointly applicable to 7,250,000 workers. It was the intention of the Liberal Government to extend their benefits to a further 2,000,000. Finally, no fewer than 6,000,000 became entitled to compensation for the first time.

In the second place the Bill reduced from a fortnight to a week the period at the end of which the employee who had met with an accident began to receive compensation, a sum equal to half his wages. The Labour members asked for a further reduction to three days and, though they failed to secure it, were at least successful in obtaining that when the victim of an accident was kept from his work over a fortnight the compensation should be reckoned from the day of the accident. The Government, on the other hand, attempted in vain to re-insert into the Bill, subject to certain restrictions, the clause the Unionists had inserted in the Bill of 1905, permitting employers to conclude special contracts with workers over sixty years old. It was dropped during the debate on the Bill. Moreover the original Bill reproduced a provision of the Act of 1897 which refused compensation to a workman guilty of 'serious or wilful misconduct'. The Labour members disliked this restriction and even a worker guilty of misconduct had the right to compensation in the event of 'death or serious and permanent disablement'.[1]

Thirdly, 'industrial diseases' would give the workers the same right to compensation as accidents in the strict sense. A schedule enumerated six of these: anthrax, poisoning by lead, mercury, phosphorus, or arsenic, and ankylostomiasis.[2] The ministry was empowered to add other diseases to the list by departmental orders. And a committee was immediately appointed to inquire into the desirability of doing so. It reported in favour of adding

---

[1] H. of C., November 29, 1906 (*Parliamentary Debates*, 4th Series, vol. clxvi, pp. 367 sqq.).
[2] A disease, caused by hookworm, affecting miners (*Trs. note*).

eighteen other diseases to the six mentioned in the original schedule.[1] This was done by a departmental order on May 22, 1907.[2]

14

After 1906, so important in the history of British Labour legislation, 1907 was a barren year. Among the measures of social reform brought forward by the Cabinet the most interesting were those which attacked the monopoly of the great landlords, always odious to the masses. In his election programme of December 21, 1905, Campbell-Bannerman had pledged himself to deal with the problem. The speech from the throne which opened the new Parliament had announced an inquiry into 'the means by which a larger number of the population may be attracted to and retained on the soil', and had promised that it should be carried out without unnecessary delay. In 1907 three Bills were introduced in the Commons. The Opposition had the pleasure of pointing out that each was based on a different principle.[3] The first concerned Ireland. As we have already seen[4] its object was to settle on the land as owners farmers evicted by their landlords. Therefore, if it were passed and successfully put into operation, it would buttress private property in land. The second concerned Scotland. Its object was to extend to the Lowlands measures already adopted in the Highlands on behalf of the small tenants, the crofters. Like Gladstone's Irish Land Act of 1882 it did not confiscate property but simply limited the amount of rent payable and protected the farmer against unjustifiable eviction. The third concerned England. Its spirit was distinctly Socialist. It obliged the County Councils, if the Board of Agriculture on inquiry deemed it necessary, to purchase land for small agricultural holdings on which to settle not independent owners but tenants of the Council.[5] The

---

[1] *Report of the Departmental Committee on Compensation for Industrial Diseases*, 1907. (Herbert Samuel was chairman.)

[2] A further report published in 1908 advised the inclusion of three additional industrial diseases. This was done, December 2, 1908.

[3] H. of C., August 13, 1907, Arthur Balfour's speech (*Parliamentary Debates*, 4th Series, vol. clxxx, pp. 1105 sqq.).

[4] See above, pp. 53-7.

[5] 7 Edw. 7, Cap. 54: An Act to amend the Law with respect to Small Holdings and Allotments (*Small Holdings and Allotments Act*, 1907). The Bill was based on the work of a committee appointed by the previous Government in April 1905 (Lord Onslow's Committee) which reported in 1906: (*Departmental Committee on Small Holdings*). *Report of the*

House of Lords threw out the Scottish Bill, but let the two others pass. The English Bill appears to have produced interesting results at least during the years which immediately followed its enactment.[1] An Act of 1908 reinforced its provisions and completed them by further provisions authorizing the local authorities to divide the land they purchased into allotments which the poor inhabitants of large towns could rent to grow vegetables.[2] These, however, were petty reforms ill adapted to arouse popular enthusiasm.

Nor was it more likely to be kindled by the Factory and Workshop Act,[3] which extended the provisions of the Factory Act of 1901 to laundries, or the Employment of Women Act,[4] which modified on two points of detail the provisions of the Factory Act of 1901 and the Coal Mines Regulation Act of 1887 regulating female labour. A comprehensive statute dealing with industrial and financial companies whose object was to make illegal certain current practices which defrauded the public was more important and obviously of Socialist tendency, as indeed had been the Companies' Act of 1900, since it gave the State a larger measure of

---

Departmental Committee appointed by the Board of Agriculture and Fisheries to inquire into and report upon the subject of Small Holdings in Great Britain; With copy of the Minutes appointing the Committee, 1906. The Committee's terms of reference were 'to inquire into the administration and working of the Small Holdings Act, 1892; to examine the various arrangements made by landowners in recent years for the provision of smaller agricultural holdings; and to report as to the condition under which such holdings are more likely to be attended with success and as to measures which may most advantageously be taken, either by legislation, co-operative association, or otherwise, to secure the increase of their number'. The preceding Statute of 1892 which was permissive and left County Councils the option of buying or leasing, selling or letting to tenants had yielded very poor results. In ten years only 652 acres had been acquired.

[1] For the execution of the Statute see from 1908 onwards the annual reports of the Board: *Board of Agriculture and Fisheries: Annual Report of Proceedings under the Small Holdings and Allotments Act, 1908: The Universities and College Estates Act; The Glebe Lands Act, 1888; The Improvement of Land Acts; The Settled Land Acts; The Agricultural Holdings Acts and certain other Acts; In the year* . . . The number of acres acquired annually by the operation of the Act rose from 21,417 acres in 1908 to 39,472 in 1909, fell to 33,335 in 1910, rose again to 36,358 in 1911. After this we note a constant fall until the war: 33,493 acres in 1912; 24,493 in 1913, 16,537 in 1914.

[2] 8 Edw. 7, Cap. 36: An Act to consolidate the enactments with respect to Small Holdings and Allotments in England and Wales (*Small Holdings and Allotments Act*, 1908).

[3] 7 Edw. 7, Cap. 39: An Act to amend the Factory and Workshop Act, 1901 with respect to Laundries and to extend that Act to certain Institutions and to provide for the inspection of certain premises (*Factory and Workshop Act, 1907*). The influence exercised by the Catholic Church in the House of Commons generally and over the Labour party in particular made itself felt during the debate, when the Catholic members obtained the exemption of convents from inspection by the Home Office.

[4] 7 Edw. 7, Cap. 10: An Act to repeal Section 57 of the Factory and Workshop Act 1901, and part of Section 7 of the Coal Mines Regulation Act, 1887, relating to the Employment of Women and Children (*Employment of Women Act*, 1907).

control over private companies.[1] But it was a Socialism which did not directly affect the proletariat, a class from which company promoters and stockbrokers drew no shareholders or victims.

This slackening of the Government's legislative activity coincided with the appearance of a marked coolness between Liberal and Labour politicians. Important Liberals denounced the Socialist peril.[2] Labour circles took offence. The Liberal leaders with anxiety, the Unionist with hope, saw the Labour party assume a more distinctively Socialist character and constitute itself definitely a third party strictly independent of both the older parties. If the Liberals lost votes, and the tide of enthusiasm which had swept them into power must inevitably recede, the Conservatives might profit in the constituencies by this division of votes between Liberalism and Labour. Their hopes were indeed actually fulfilled in April 1906 at Cockermouth in Cumberland. The Independent candidature of the miner Smillie enabled the Unionist candidate to defeat the Liberal.

Would the same thing happen the following summer at Jarrow-on-Tyne when a Labour candidate and an Irish Nationalist came forward against the Liberal candidate, already faced by a Unionist? The result of the election took everyone by surprise. The Liberal candidate was indeed defeated, but it was by the Labour candidate, Peter Curran, who received 5,000 votes as against 4,000 given to the Conservative, only 3,500 to the Liberal and 2,000 to the Nationalist. Six weeks later at Colne Valley in the West Riding of Yorkshire when a Socialist presented himself against a Liberal and a Conservative he was returned at the head of the poll, though it was a very close contest. Both were seats which the Liberals had been accustomed to regard as safe. In the Colne Valley a Liberal had been returned unopposed in 1906. Moreover, if at Jarrow the Labour candidate had been the official candidate of the Labour party, neither at Cockermouth nor at Colne Valley was this the case. In both instances the Labour candidates—Smillie at Cockermouth, Victor Grayson at Colne Valley—were independent candidates and revolutionaries. Victor Grayson, origin-

[1] 7 Edw. 7, Cap. 50: An Act to amend the Companies' Act, 1862 to 1900 (*Companies' Act,* 1907). It reinforced a number of details and completed the provisions of the Act of 1900, thus carrying out the recommendations of a Commission appointed by the Unionist Cabinet in 1905. We must call attention to a section imposing certain conditions on foreign companies operating in Great Britain. It betrays the same inspiration as particular clauses of the Patent Act and Merchant Shipping Act.

[2] The Master of Elibank, speech at West Linton, Peeblesshire, August 25, 1906.

ally a mechanic, had studied theology with the intention of becoming a minister, but had abandoned theology (it was a sign of the times) for political economy and become a Socialist journalist. In the House of Commons the violent scenes he provoked attracted the attention of England, indeed of the whole of Europe.

It is not surprising that the popular discontent which found expression at the polls also manifested itself in the Socialist Groups. On the very morrow of its defeat in January 1906, the Social Democratic Federation resumed its revolutionary campaign, changed its name to the Social Democratic *Party* and advocated 'the fusion of all the organizations ready to work on a definite democratic basis, for the realization of Socialism'. Its membership increased rapidly and when at the opening of 1908 the founder of the Federation, Hyndman, proposed to effect this fusion by union with the Labour party—that is to say, by adopting the very policy he had himself repudiated in 1900, he was defeated by a large majority. The Labour party was led by a Henderson and a MacDonald, and the extremists of Social Democracy refused to lower the red flag. At the opposite extremity of the Socialist camp the Fabian Society was roused from its conservative tranquillity by the sudden incursion of H. G. Wells, who for two years, until he wearied of the enterprise and returned to novel-writing, attempted to transform the Society into a political group employing its election agents and putting forward candidates in as many constituencies as possible, its programme being the abolition of private capital and the destruction of family selfishness. Finally, the Independent Labour party, which was led by the same moderate men who led the Labour party, made life difficult for its leaders. It was in vain that in 1907 Ramsay MacDonald, to retain some authority over the group, used language verging on revolutionary. Grayson's election brought the disorder which prevailed in the party to a climax. It was only by resigning from the executive in April 1909 that MacDonald, Keir Hardie, and Snowden could escape responsibility for his excesses.

But the Social Democratic party proved as weak as the Federation had been. Wells' attempt was but a flash in the pan, a passing episode quickly forgotten in the history of the Fabian Society. The opposition of the Independent Labour party to the moderate policy of the Labour party was never very violent during the next few years. The Labour party strictly so called remained the faithful mirror of the British proletariat. MacDonald soon became its official leader in the House of Commons, without therefore ceasing to be a member of the Independent Labour party. How are we to describe this Labour party? Was it Socialist or Anti-Socialist? The party itself did not know. At the annual conference held at Hull in January 1908 it rejected by an overwhelming majority a motion accepting Socialism, only to pass the very next day a motion which stated that 'the Labour party should have as a definite object the socialization of the means of production, distribution, and exchange'. At bottom it was completely indifferent to theory, concerned simply to defend the immediate interests of the working class. It was before everything else moderate and chose Henderson as its chairman instead of Keir Hardie because Hardie's sentimental utopianism did not express the party's views. It contemplated making itself a political party with a regular organization in every constituency but hesitated to take the step for fear of diminishing the authority of the Trade Union Congress. The unions, on their part, would seem to have intended at one moment to strengthen their authority by excluding, from the body of officials whose function it was to maintain permanent contact between the party and the Congress, anyone who was not himself a member of a union. They shrank however from the prospect of losing the services of such indispensable workers as MacDonald and Snowden. Nevertheless, the Labour party was fundamentally the party of the trade unions, a corporative and professional party. If we would understand the character of the working-class movement at this period we must not make too much of two or three by-elections, or two or three doctrinal disputes in the groups representing labour. We must rather fix our attention on the strikes which the unions—whose members now exceeded 2,000,000—began to call the moment the Trade Disputes Act of 1906 had restored their liberty.

On December 21 the Bill became law. A month had not gone by before a strike broke out in London which attracted the attention of the general public, not only because it occurred in the capital, but even more by its unexpected nature. It was a strike of music-hall artists which soon spread to the entire staff. The artists objected to certain conditions, in their opinion too severe, which the managers inserted in their contracts. The musicians and mechanics—in fact music-hall employees of every description—

followed suit. The great music halls of London were obliged to close. In a hall which happened to be vacant the strikers organized a monster entertainment in aid of their strike and 2,500 pickets triumphantly asserted the right of peaceful persuasion the law had just conferred upon them. The strike, during which strict discipline was maintained, and which did not interfere with the material welfare of the nation, had the sympathy of the public. The managers gave way and a 'board of conciliation' decided to ask for the services of the Board of Trade's professional arbitrator, George Askwith. When the twenty-two variety theatres concerned had re-opened, the arbitrator held twenty-two meetings, heard a hundred witnesses and finally drew up and got accepted by both parties the Music Hall Award of 1907 which, though altered several times later, constituted the first labour code for all music-hall employees. It comprised a standard form of contract and regulations for settling future disputes. It would seem that the President of the Board of Trade, Lloyd George, was tempted at first to give the intervention of his Board a more picturesque garb and had therefore offered the post of arbitrator to a personage much in the limelight in London, T. P. O'Connor, a man half Irish, half English, half politician, half journalist and man of letters. O'Connor refused.[1] But Lloyd George would soon be occupied with other arbitrations, involved in conflicts of a far more serious nature and would descend into the arena in person.

15

There was in the first place the threat in the autumn of 1907 of a general strike on the railways. It was the first occurrence of its kind and caused a sensation. Throughout the nineteenth century practically nothing had been heard of the railwaymen. The battle of the proletariat had been fought by the workers of the engineering, building, and textile trades. In 1872 the railwaymen had formed for the first time a union intended to comprise all their branches, the Amalgamated Society of Railway Servants. It stagnated, was soon nothing more than a friendly society, and

[1] Lord Askwith, *Industrial Problems and Disputes*, pp. 103 sqq. Lord Askwith has kindly explained at my request a passing allusion in the text.

would seem never to have had more than 10,000 members until the Socialist agitation of 1889 gave it a new lease of life, while creating on its left wing a union of unskilled workers, the General Railway Workers' Union. In 1891 it contained 30,000 members, in 1900 60,000. But it was still badly organized and the strikes which broke out among the railwaymen in the closing years of the century were partial and spasmodic, uncontrolled by the executive committee of the Union. They merely endangered its funds without benefiting the working class. One of these local strikes was responsible for the counterstroke of the Taff Vale Decision, which for several years effectively reduced to impotence the Amalgamated Society of Railway Servants like the other unions. Nevertheless, even under these circumstances it accomplished useful work and under the extremely moderate leadership of Richard Bell saw that the statutes protecting labour were enforced. The General Election of 1906, by revealing to the proletariat the extent of its power, gave its activities more aggressive turn. The Union leaders devoted the year 1906 to drawing up a national programme of claims, which was published at the close of 1907 immediately after the Trade Disputes Bill had restored to the Union complete freedom to strike.

What were these claims? The railwaymen complained that their wages were too low. Thirty-eight per cent of them were paid one pound a week or less; 50 per cent between one pound and thirty shillings.[1] On the Scotch railways two-thirds of the men were paid twenty-three shillings a week or less, a third nineteen shillings a week or less.[2] The railwaymen also complained that their hours were too long—though they had already been considerably reduced by statute.[3] In one single month in 1906 the total number of hours worked on the railways amounted to 48,000 days of thirteen hours, 16,000 of fourteen, and some of the employees worked fifteen, sixteen, seventeen, even eighteen hours.[4] These long hours endangered the safety both of travellers and of the men themselves, who succumbed to fatigue. A delegation which the railwaymen had chosen to approach the owners in

---

[1] *The Green Book*, 1907, quoted by S. and B. Webb, *History of Trade Unionism*, revised edition 1920, p. 527.

[2] Richard Bell, speech at Glasgow, November 4, 1907.

[3] 63 & 64 Vict., Cap. 27: An Act for the better Prevention of Accidents on Railways (*Railway Employment* [*Prevention of Accidents*] *Act*, 1900.)

[4] G. W. Alcock, *Fifty Years of Railway Trade Unionism*, p. 348.

their name was still remembered, for it had been composed almost wholly of maimed men.[1] The companies disputed the Union's figures. They pointed out that in estimating the wages received, no account had been taken of the special advantages enjoyed by railway employees as compared with those of other companies. They received clothing, often also lodging, were secured against the risk of unemployment and provided with a retiring pension. They also pointed out that the hours of a railwayman could not be fairly compared with those of a miner or textile worker, for the former was frequently on duty without any work to perform. As regards accidents, the men had obtained protective legislation which had cost the companies dear. The latter could not compensate themselves by raising their rates, for these were fixed by law in the public interest. Indeed, without a previous inquiry the companies could not even charge the maximum rates permitted by statute.[2] The shares of every company were falling as the direct result of the decrease in dividends. In 1907 the average dividend did not exceed $3\frac{1}{2}$ per cent, in ten years it had fallen by $2\frac{1}{2}$ per cent. If the workers' claims were granted it would fall to 2 per cent.[3]

The companies searched for a way out of a position disastrous in itself, even if no concessions were made to the men. At first the British railway system had been one of genuine competition. The companies had multiplied competing routes between the same cities and for as long as possible sought to attract travellers by lowering their rates to the advantage of the public, if not of their employees. Now, however, when the common desire of all the companies was to increase their rates, competition was no longer a reality. Working agreements were concluded between several companies, sometimes relating to rates, sometimes extending to the speed of the trains, and sometimes enabling the companies to divide the traffic according to a fixed proportion. Why not take the final step? This very year 1907 the Great Northern, the Great Central, and the Great Eastern railways were engaged in working out a scheme of amalgamation for which in 1909 they sought in

[1] T. A. Brocklebank, *Mammon's Victims: A Revelation to the Nation; A Text-Book for Workers and Coroners*, 1912, p. 75, which on this point refers to a pamphlet published by John Burns in 1899.

[2] Edwin A. Pratt, *Railways and their Rates* . . . 1906, pp. 12 sqq.

[3] Ibid., p. 42; *The Times*, September 16, 1907, 'The Railway Dispute'; *The Economist*, May 11, 1907, 'The Railway Position'.

vain legal sanction.[1] It was defeated by the hostility of the Labour members. They did not object in principle to the amalgamation of some 200 British railway companies in one large organization. But they did not want that organization with its monopoly of the national railway system to be a private company working to make profit at the expense of the public and its employees alike. In the interest of both they demanded that the railways should be nationalized. Until 1906 the nationalization of the railways had been the Utopia of a few cranks. It now became a plank of the Labour platform, passionately defended and attacked in an entire series of articles and pamphlets.[2]

Nationalization however did not figure among the claims which the Railwaymen's Unions put forward in 1907 and which they termed 'the national programme'. They were content to demand reductions of hours and increases of wages. They asked for a regular eight-hours' day for certain classes of workers, a ten-hours' day for the rest, and a minimum rest of nine hours between the work of two consecutive days, the laying down of definite conditions for overtime work, an immediate increase of two shillings in the wages of all men working more than eight hours a day, and an additional three shillings a day for all employed in the London stations.[3] These were the demands which they invited the companies to discuss with their representatives and this last request was itself a claim, more important perhaps than those contained in the programme. The railwaymen called upon the railway companies to follow the example of the coalowners and textile manufacturers and recognize the Union leaders freely chosen by the men as their authorized representatives. Where that prac-

[1] See the debates H. of C., April 5, 1909 (*Parliamentary Debates*, Commons, 1909, 5th Series, vol. iii, pp. 798 sqq.). The amalgamation was sanctioned in principle but the clauses were never discussed and the entire question referred to a select committee which reported in 1911 (*Report of the Departmental Committee on Railway Agreements and Amalgamations*, April 11, 1911).

[2] For nationalization: William Cunningham, *Railway Nationalisation*, 1906; Clement Edwards, *Railway Nationalisation*, 1898, 2nd edition revised with preface by Sir Charles Dilke, 1907; G. L. Wardle, *Railway Nationalisation*, 1908; W. Bolland, *The Railways and the Nation, Problems and Possibilities*, 1909; Emil Davies, *State Purchase of Railways*, Fabian Tract No. 150, 1910; *Nationalisation of Railways*, 2nd edition, 1911; *The Case for Railway Nationalisation*, I.L.P. Pamphlet, 1912. Against: Edwin A. Pratt, *State Railways*, 1907; *Railways and their Rates with an appendix on the British Coal Problem*, 1903; *Railway Nationalisation*, 1908. For arguments on both sides see the debates H. of C., February 11, 1908; G. A. Hardy's motion (*Parl. Deb.*, 4th Ser., vol. clxxxiii, pp. 1612 sqq.); Lloyd George's speech (ibid., pp. 1637 sqq.).

[3] The programme is reproduced in full in Charles Watney and James A. Little, *Industrial Warfare, The Aims and Claims of Capital and Labour*, 1912, pp. 55-7.

tice had been adopted what bad results had followed? Did not the chairman of the Amalgamated Society, Richard Bell, show as much wisdom and moderation as the officials of the miners' and textile workers' unions? Indeed, his moderation went so far that he refused to join the Labour party, a refusal which provoked an organized opposition in his Union, led by a young Welshman, J. H. Thomas. The companies, however, refused to negotiate with the Union officials. They regarded themselves as a public service in which the interest of the community required a military discipline. The weapon employed by the Union was the strike or its threat; to recognize the Union would be to recognize implicitly the lawfulness of a general strike in so important a national service. It was a strange argument in the mouths of men who obstinately opposed nationalization of the railways. And it was brought forward at a particularly inopportune moment, since the Postmaster-General under the new Liberal Cabinet, Sydney Buxton, had just recognized the Postal Clerks' Association. The directors of the great companies stood firm. The Railwaymen's Union, they said, represented only a minority of their employees, less than 100,000 out of some 600,000. Why should this minority be given the right to speak on behalf of all the railwaymen?[1] The railwaymen replied by contesting the directors' figures. The total number of men employed by the companies, eligible for membership of the Amalgamated Society, did not exceed 200,000. Half of these were therefore already members and the number was continually increasing. It had almost doubled during the last five years. Why should it not double itself again during the next five? Nor had the companies any right to regard the railwaymen who were not members of the Union as its convinced enemies. The vast majority consisted of shirkers, only too glad to let others fight their battles. But this did not alter the fact that when Richard Bell presented the national programme he was not yet supported by compact battalions. Not only had his Union much leeway to make up before its organization equalled that of the great Mining and Textile Unions. The railwaymen's forces were also divided among several Unions. There were separate Unions for Scotland and Ireland. There was a separate Union for the unskilled workers. There was a Railway Clerks' Association founded in 1897 to contain all the clerical workers. And above all there had been in

[1] *The Economist*, September 21, 1907; *The Times*, September and October 1907.

existence since 1880 an Associated Society of Locomotive
Engineers and Firemen, a wealthy and compact Union of the
engine drivers and mechanics, concerned only with the interests
of its own group and extremely conservative. It stood resolutely
apart. On the other hand, the companies did not present a solid
front. An association of companies had indeed been formed to
consult on the best methods of defending their common interests.
But among the great companies one, at least, the North-Eastern,
separated itself from the others on the vital question of recognizing
the Union. In short, when for the first time on all the railways of
the United Kingdom employers and men were arrayed in battle
against each other, the concentration of their respective forces was
still in progress. It had not yet been completed.

Bell, assisted by two expert economists, published a large
volume of statistics dealing with the conditions of labour on the
railways. The companies replied to his 'green book' by a 'red
book' in which they tried to disprove his figures. They also published a pamphlet denouncing 'the national programme and all
it stands for', which Bell answered in a counter-pamphlet entitled
The Railwaymen's Charter. But the conflict did not stop at a war
of pamphlets. In March, the House of Commons adopted a motion
which declared the hours of work on the railways excessive, demanded a stricter execution of the existing laws and the passage
of new legislation, if the existing statutes were proved to be inadequate.[1] In May, Lloyd George, making use of the powers conferred upon him by an Act of 1889, called upon the companies to
submit to him an account of all the days of more than twelve
hours worked by their staffs during the preceding month and
announced his intention to repeat the demand every three months.
On May 11 the railwaymen, encouraged by these expressions of
sympathy by the majority in Parliament and the Board of Trade,
organized a mass meeting to present 'the national programme'.
There was anxiety on the Stock Exchange. Railway shares fell
two and a half to five points. And the anxiety increased when on
September 15 the Committee of the Union announced its intention to take a vote of its members on the question of a strike.
Since the companies persisted in their refusal to recognize the
Union, the vote was taken. Lord Claud Hamilton, Chairman of

[1] H. of C., March 6, 1907, Harvey's motion (*Parliamentary Debates*, 4th Series, vol. clxx,
pp. 885 sqq.).

the Great Eastern Railway, caused widespread indignation by a manifesto in which he denounced not only the Amalgamated Society of Railway Servants but trade-unionism as a whole and maintained that war had been openly declared upon individualism by the Socialist forces. When at the close of October the result of the voting became known it appeared that 76,925 votes had been given in favour of striking, only 8,773 against it.

It was at this point that Lloyd George intervened, determined to prevent a strike. No doubt from the outset he had good reason to feel confident that the negotiations he was undertaking would have a favourable issue. Among the companies and their supporters Lord Claud's intemperate language was not generally approved. In these circles, as in the House of Lords, it was clearly understood how dangerous it was from the political standpoint to arouse the hostility of the working class. On the other hand, the Union, or at least the Committee, was not sufficiently certain of victory really to desire a strike. Though the General Railway Workers' Union had joined the movement and had voted almost unanimously for the strike, the Society of Locomotive Engineers and Firemen had adopted a totally different attitude, refusing even to take part in the referendum. Finally, a way out of the impasse was found. The authorized representatives of the companies did not meet the authorized representatives of the Union, but both in turn met Lloyd George and his assistants at the Board of Trade, and the agreement worked out at these separate meetings was separately signed by the 'authorized representatives' of both parties. The Union was recognized without being recognized. The actual agreement was conceived in the same spirit. It did not settle the question of hours and wages but referred them for settlement to an entirely new organization set up for 'conciliation' and 'arbitration'. Hitherto, the men had to present their grievances to the head of their department. He in turn referred the matter, though not until he thought fit, to a board on which the employees were in a minority; and there was no appeal from the decision at which he arrived after consultation with the board. In future there would be an entire hierarchy of 'conciliation boards' at which both sides would be equally represented. The men's representatives must be employees of the company's. The board would sit twice a month. From the boards which dealt with disputes in the first instance an appeal lay to 'sectional' boards and from these in turn to a 'central board'. And if the men were still unsatisfied by its decision, they could demand that the dispute should be referred to an umpire. The Union was not actually recognized, for the provision that the members of the board must be employees excluded its committees. But the latter could use their constantly increasing authority to secure that all the men's representatives on the boards were union men and the settlement undoubtedly constituted for the railwaymen a considerable advance on their previous position. Moreover it could be denounced only by a previous notice of twelve months and in any case not for six years. Peace was thus ensured until the end of 1914[1].

16

By his Merchant Shipping and Patent Acts Lloyd George had made himself popular with the shipowners and manufacturers. By his striking and skilful intervention in the railway dispute he established a reputation for statesmanship both with politicians of every party and in the world of business. A month later he again intervened in a trade dispute and won another victory. Among the Lancashire cotton spinners, on the whole better paid than they had ever been, the fine spinners of Oldham complained that their wages were too low in proportion to those received by their fellow spinners and claimed their share of the considerable increase of wages in their branch of the industry. In vain they attempted to negotiate. The millowners refused even to consider their claims, which they denounced as a breach of the Brooklands Agreement. The spinners on their side announced their intention to take a referendum of the Union on the question of a strike. Lloyd George made a personal visit to Manchester and, though he did not succeed in his apparent desire to be appointed umpire, he was at least successful in overcoming the millowners' obstinacy and persuading them to agree to a joint meeting of owners and operatives. At the opening of December an agreement was concluded which, though it did not grant the operatives everything they had asked, raised their wages by 9 per cent, an increase of from

[1]For the struggle see *Strikes and Lock-outs: Board of Trade (Labour Department), Report on Strikes and Lock-outs in the United Kingdom 1907,* 1908, pp. 49 sqq.; Lord Askwith, *Industrial Problems and Disputes,* 1920, pp. 113 sqq.; M. Alfassa, *Une Solution nouvelle des Conflits,* 1908

five shillings to six shillings a week. Some 8,000 operatives benefited by this quasi-arbitral award.[1]

A third success followed, two months later. Its field was the
engineering and shipbuilding industry. The agitation began in the
Clyde dockyards and among the carpenters—known as the
White Squad in contrast to the Black Squad, the iron and steel
workers. A year earlier they had considered a strike for higher
wages. Now they were on the defensive, refusing to accept a
reduction accepted by the Black Squad. Four thousand men went
on strike and as they were receiving strike pay from the General
Federation of Trade Unions, the employers threatened to reply to
the strike by a lock-out in all the industries of the district whose
employees were affiliated to the Federation. The Union Executive advised submission. The strikers refused, and the strike spread
to the important Amalgamated Society of Engineers. The Society,
which had been reconstituted and had gathered new strength after
its defeat in 1897, had just concluded a comprehensive and detailed
agreement for the amicable settlement on an equal footing of all
disputes between employers and men in the engineering industry.
The workers refused to agree to wage reductions, accepted, in
accordance with the terms of the agreement, by the local committees of the Union. If partial concessions made by the employers
satisfied the engineers on the Clyde, they did not satisfy the
engineers on the Tyne where 12,000 went on strike. Once again
Lloyd George offered the services of the Board of Trade, and on
February 20, 1908, had the satisfaction of seeing the terms of a
provisional settlement accepted by Sir Andrew Noble, the employers' representative, and the representatives of the Unions.[2]

'By the force of his personality,' *The Economist* wrote, 'Mr.
Lloyd George has made his office transcend the statutory duties
imposed upon it. Three times within a few months Mr. George
has successfully settled disputes in the largest industries of the
country, and in each case averted a disturbance to trade which
would have spread beyond the immediate area affected.'[3] The
agitation did not in fact cease immediately either on the railways
or in the cotton industry. The struggle was still continued by the

[1] *The Economist*, December 7, 1907; *Strikes and Lock-outs: Board of Trade (Labour Department) Report on Strikes and Lock-outs . . . in 1907*, pp. 55 sqq.
[2] *The Economist*, February 8, 22, 1908; *Strikes and Lock-outs: Board of Trade (Labour
Department) Report on Strikes and Lock-outs . . . in 1908*, pp. 41 sqq.
[3] *The Economist*, February 29, 1908.

carpenters on the Clyde, and among the engineers of the Clyde and Tyne the strike broke out afresh in spite of the efforts of the men's leaders. If, nevertheless, after a longer or shorter interval the policy of compromise finally prevailed, it was due not so much to the skilful handling of Lloyd George, as to the unfavourable condition of trade, the crisis into which British industry was suddenly plunged.

The crisis did not originate in Great Britain nor was it most acute there. It was the repercussion of a crisis which had occurred in the two countries—the United States and Germany—which were now the most progressive industrial nations of the world. In those countries the progress of industry had been so rapid once the difficulties of 1902 had been overcome that they had not only ceased to export their iron and steel to Great Britain but actually imported British iron and steel. Now, however, a new glut had been produced, first in the United States, then in Germany. Money became scarce, manufacturers went bankrupt, banks failed. Not only were the American and German markets closed to British goods, but the British market was once more threatened with dumping. Prices fell steadily from a maximum in May 1907, until the end of the year, when for the first time for many years the general price level was lower than the year before. In April 1908 prices reached their lowest level, but as winter succeeded autumn and the year 1909 opened no perceptible rise had taken place. As before in 1902 but with greater anxiety, men were asking whether the rise of prices witnessed for several years had not been after all a temporary phenomenon and a new period of low prices and industrial stagnation were not beginning for Britain, for Europe, indeed for the entire world. The hopes of the tariff reformers revived, and a few by-elections won by Unionists seemed to sanction their optimism. The workers, on the other hand, lost heart. They had failed to take advantage of the boom in trade when it set in at the turn of the century; they had been defeated by so many unsuccessful strikes and adverse decisions of the courts. The Election of January 1906 and the passing of the Trade Disputes Bill had restored their confidence. Must they now witness the sudden check of a movement so full of promise? We may say at once that the tariff reformers' hopes were speedily disappointed. For they depended on the trade depression. And from March 1909 prices began once more to rise, and trade revived.

After a year in which exports and imports had achieved a record, only 1908 had witnessed a diminution of foreign trade. The figures for 1909 were already improving, those for 1910 would exceed the record established in 1907 and the expansion of trade would continue until the eve of the Great War. The improvement was due in part to an increase in the amount of exports and imports, in part to an increase in their value. In the decade from 1904 to 1914 prices rose by 22 per cent. This was undoubtedly because of a fall in the value of gold. A similar phenomenon had occurred about the middle of the nineteenth century following on the discovery and development of the Californian goldfields. Subsequently, these goldfields had become exhausted and the fall of prices had been so rapid that to remedy the scarcity of gold economists had advocated bimetallism. Now, however, new methods of gold mining had been invented by which the ore could be extracted from beds at a deeper level, and the more these were perfected the greater became the number of beds—not only in South Africa but in North America and Australia—where gold existed in sufficient quantities to be worth mining. In a work published in 1912 the economist Layton pointed out that since 1896 gold had been mined to the value of £1,000,000,000 sterling, four times the amount mined during the first fifty years of the nineteenth century and almost half the total stocks of gold available.[1] The formidable dislocations of currency we have experienced of recent years have made us forget those of the period before the war. The latter would have been more severe than they were if Asia on the one hand, the United States on the other, had not absorbed far larger quantities of gold than had been expected. Even so, they were sufficiently serious to cause anxiety to a considerable number of expert economists and induce them to inquire whether some other standard of exchange should not be substituted for gold, lacking as it did the indispensable stability. And the workers enrolled under the banner of the trade unions after the discouragement and hesitation of the winter of 1907–8 renewed their campaign with even greater vigour, demanding by strikes or threats of striking their share in the increasing prosperity of trade, and calling upon Parliament to pass new legislation to protect the interests of their class.

[1] Walter T. Layton, *An Introduction to the Study of Prices with special reference to the History of the Nineteenth Century*, 1912, pp. 83–4.

17

What then, everything considered, was the political situation when Parliament met at the opening of February 1908? The Government's majority, slightly reduced by a few by-elections won by Labour or Unionist candidates, was still practically speaking as overwhelming as it had been two years earlier. But the Conservative Opposition, impotent in the Commons, possessed in the Lords a permanent majority as large as that which since 1906 the Radicals had possessed in the Lower House. The entire strategy of the two official leaders of the Unionist party, Balfour and Lord Lansdowne, consisted in using the House of Lords as an instrument to exert a permanent pressure on the Liberal majority, by rejecting among the Bills sent up to it all those and no more which it could safely reject without endangering the popularity of the party in the present House of Commons and ruining its chances at the next Election The Irish question did not come before the House of Lords, since Irish intransigence had brought the Irish Council Bill to a premature demise. Asquith's budgets, to which we shall return later, prudently democratic, very economical, and always disposing of a surplus, were universally popular after years of extravagance. Moreover, was it not accepted that in finance the House of Commons was absolute master and that for the House of Lords financial questions did not even exist? There remained the question of religious education in the schools. Also the question of Labour legislation. Undeniably the House of Lords during the last two sessions in handling these two problems had taken skilful advantage of the power conferred upon it by constitutional custom to 'sift' the Bills sent up by the Liberal Government.

On the Education Bill the victory had undeniably lain with the Lords. The Cabinet never retrieved the defeat it had suffered at the close of 1906. Admittedly, it did not dare to dissolve Parliament and appeal to the electorate to implement its desire to satisfy the Nonconformist claims. It was obvious that the nation had no interest in their claims. No doubt the Government continued to announce by the mouth of the Premier or one of his subordinates that it had prepared all its plans to alter the constitution on the first opportunity and in particular to curtail the powers of the

House of Lords. Would it dissolve on this issue itself? It had no intention of doing so. A conflict must first be provoked between the two Houses on some other question better adapted than the question of religious education in the schools, to arouse popular feeling. Should it be the question of reforming the franchise? In 1906 the Government had attempted to carry a Bill to abolish the plural vote which by enabling wealthy voters to vote during the same election under different qualifications in several constituencies benefited the Unionist party. The House of Lords had thrown out the Bill without a debate, refusing to pronounce on the question until a measure dealing comprehensively with the franchise as a whole was sent up. Should the Government accept the challenge and bring forward such a measure? Should it attempt to make Great Britain a country of universal suffrage in the full sense of the term by giving every citizen an equal vote and equalizing the constituencies? It was however far from certain in 1908 that a reform of this kind would arouse popular enthusiasm. Compactly organized in their unions the workers had secured under the existing franchise, in spite of the fact that it was not yet universal, the passage of the Trade Disputes Bill with a most significant speed. Surely they would be well advised, instead of waiting for a reform of the franchise, to obtain from Parliament, as at present elected, further legislation from which they would reap immediate and practical benefit? A measure, for example establishing a system of workers' old age pensions. Chamberlain had promised it but had broken his promise. Was it not a duty strictly incumbent upon the Liberal party to repair this breach of faith by setting up that system of universal old age pensions without contribution from the workers which the Trade Union Congress demanded every summer? Or again a statute or body of statutes ensuring the workers against unemployment? The suggestion had been put forward in 1902 and 1903, when industry was suffering from a depression that was almost a crisis, and the Unionist Cabinet had even taken some steps in this direction, though they did not amount to very much. Now, when a severe industrial depression once more prevailed, more serious than that of 1902, the workers' demands became more insistent. In 1902 John Burns had criticized the Government's attitude. What would he do at present when he was President of the Local Government Board?

The speech from the throne which opened the new session at the close of January 1908 gave the most prominent place to the question of old age pensions for workmen. But would it provide the opportunity for a victorious battle with the Lords? Would not the reform be carried too easily, because the Unionist Party and the Lords would vie in its support with the Liberal majority in the Commons? This indeed had been the tactics pursued by the Lords for the last two years. They had accepted the Workmen's Insurance Act and the Trade Disputes Bill, yielding, like the ministerialists themselves, to the pressure of the working masses from outside, officially represented in the House of Commons by a tiny group of fifty members. The Church of England, whose stronghold was the House of Lords, had adopted the same tactics, and the bench of bishops had been careful to dissociate itself from the attacks upon Socialism delivered by politicians, whether Liberal or Conservative, provided the Socialism in question were not hostile to the family or the Christian religion. The Liberal leaders therefore found themselves in a quandary. They were faced with the problem of devising a measure of social legislation whose effects would be so far-reaching that the House of Lords could neither accept it without humiliation, nor reject it without imperilling its prerogatives and even its existence. After two years of Liberal legislation one fact at least was established beyond doubt. The Election of 1906, on the surface a victory of free trade, and apparently a Nonconformist victory, had been in reality and at bottom a victory of the proletariat.

CHAPTER II

Foreign Policy:
The Army and Navy

I FROM THE CONFERENCE OF ALGECIRAS TO THE ANGLO-RUSSIAN AGREEMENT

I

To understand how the international situation was regarded by the British Government and people at the opening of 1906 we must begin by speaking not of England, but of Germany, the leading Continental nation, whose power focused the attention of all the other nations, and had begun to create universal anxiety. What had been for more than thirty years the guiding principle of German foreign policy? At first, when Bismarck was at the helm, Germany's sole desire was to consolidate in peace the unity conquered within a few years by two wars, startling alike in their speed and decisive results. She had pursued a policy ungenerous to be sure, but not in the least aggressive, selfish but prudent. Friendly towards all the powers, even France, if France would accept her friendship, she was content to foster their mutual rivalries in order to prevent the formation of such a coalition as had previously been fatal to the French hegemony. Then William II had succeeded to the throne, had dismissed Bismarck and soon inaugurated a more ambitious programme. He wished to give Germany a strong navy. His policy had therefore been anti-British. He had entertained the dream of uniting under his overlordship all the nations of Europe to challenge Britain's naval supremacy. His grandiose project had been defeated by the opposition of France and, while still hoping to resume it at some later date when France had forgotten the loss of Alsace and he had completed the construction of his fleet, he had returned temporarily to Bismarck's policy of prudence. It had been completely successful so long as the Boer War continued. Now, however, when the war was at an end and England no longer preoccupied with South Africa, the British Government had inaugurated the new policy of an *entente cordiale* with France. How

E   121

could Germany apply to this *entente*, which upset all the traditions of European diplomacy, the old principles which had given Europe thirty years of peace, herself thirty years of steadily increasing power? Alternatively, what new principles should she adopt? To the men who decided German foreign policy the change of Government in England in December 1905 was a welcome augury.

The 'Tangier' episode a few months before had been her first attempt to break the Anglo-French *entente*, scarcely a year old, and detach France from England by demonstrating the dangers and humiliations to which her friendship with England exposed her. Delcassé had fallen, at a nod from the Emperor William, and in January the powers were to meet, at Germany's request, to restrict the freedom Britain had undertaken to bestow on France in Morocco, thus inflicting indirectly on the British Government an abasement almost equal to that suffered by the French. But at this very moment Balfour and Lord Lansdowne disappeared from the scene and their successors—so it was hoped in the Wilhelmstrasse —would be well placed to abandon without the humiliation of a retreat the principles on which their predecessors' policy had been based. Moreover, the new cabinet was a Liberal cabinet, in which the pro-Boers of yesterday seemed the preponderating element.

Morley, whose creed was peace at any price, and who in 1898 had broken with the official Liberal party because in his opinion its opposition to Chamberlain's imperialism was too feeble, came back in triumph. Bryce, like Morley, an old Gladstonian, was the historian of the Teutonic Holy Roman Empire and the American Republic, an intellectual 'Protestant' whose sympathies were with the Teutonic rather than the Latin peoples. Sir Robert Reid, now Chancellor under the title of Lord Loreburn, shared this point of view. So did John Burns, an inveterate enemy of France, whose authority in the cabinet was indeed far less than Morley's or Bryce's but who was highly respected by the middle class. Everyone regarded Haldane as the typical pro-German. Finally, the Prime Minister, Campbell-Bannerman, had shown himself throughout the Boer War the determined foe of a bellicose policy. He was, it is true, anything but an enemy of France. He was a lover of French culture, and an enthusiastic reader of French novels, more capable than any British premier for many a long year of addressing in excellent French delegations from across the Channel who were given an official reception in London. But he wanted the reconciliation with France to be the prelude to a general reconciliation with all the European powers, Germany first of all. The overwhelming victory the Liberal party had won in the January Election had visibly augmented his influence from this point of view, both in the Cabinet and the House. That victory indeed was due to the numerous domestic issues we have already studied. But it signified also, many observers would have said first and foremost, that the entire nation—workers, business men, and intelligentsia—was weary of the aggressive imperialism which ten years earlier had brought the revived Conservative party into power. To please the crowds one must no longer talk of conquests, colonial expansion, national honour.

How then are we to explain the fact that after the revolution at the polls of January 1906 British foreign policy remained exactly what it had been before? In the first place we must remember the influence exercised within the Cabinet by the imperialist group. Its members had secured offices of exceptional importance. They were younger, more brilliant, and everyone expected them to be more active than such veterans as Morley, Bryce or Campbell-Bannerman. It was their conviction, a conviction proclaimed emphatically more than once by Lord Rosebery, that the foreign policy of the United Kingdom must be 'continuous', unaffected by the vicissitudes of the party struggle; and the prudent Asquith and the restless Haldane, who dressed his window with German goods but sold merchandise of a very different character, gave wholehearted support to the new Foreign Secretary, Sir Edward Grey, who was himself the more ready to continue the policy of an understanding with France, because he had been one of its first advocates, even before the Unionist Cabinet and the officials at the Foreign Office had perceived its advantages. Finally we must not forget the presence of King Edward at the head of the executive. Despite the constitutional fiction that the monarch must always conform his personal views to those of his responsible ministers, public opinion saw in him the true author of the *entente cordiale*. It was believed that the strong dislike he entertained for his nephew, the Emperor William, entered into his desire to see England follow an anti-German policy, that he was using his influence to complete the Anglo-French *entente* by an understanding with Russia, and that it was on his recommendation and with this end in view that Sir Charles Hardinge had been appointed Ambassador at Petersburg and returned to London in January 1906 to become permanent Under-Secretary for Foreign Affairs.[1]

2

We must not, however, exaggerate the part played by any individual, whether Grey at the Foreign Office or King Edward on the throne. We have already had occasion to call attention to the fact that King Edward had been reigning for two years before he perceived the necessity to substitute for the policy of friendship with Germany a policy of friendship with France. In reality, he guided neither public opinion nor the policy of the Foreign Office. He simply made up his mind towards the end of 1902 to follow the lead given by both. Thenceforward he had the good fortune to make himself useful by actions which at the same time made him popular. A lover of travel and public ceremonies, he was the itinerant ambassador of the Foreign Office, its 'super-ambassador'. But he was nothing more than an agent and never initiated a policy which could be called with truth, as it was so often without justification, King Edward's policy. The case of Sir Edward Grey is different, if his conversion to the new foreign policy really

[1] From this it was a short step to regard Edward VII as a man of genius, who operated behind the scenes the machinery of British foreign policy, and many people both in France and Germany took it. See Rudolf Marten, *Kaiser Wilhelm II und König Edward VII*, 1907, p. 31: 'King Edward is the soul of British policy. . . . He is England's unavowed Emperor. The powerful position attributed to the German Emperor by the Prussian and Imperial Constitution, and by constitutional custom and tradition, is occupied by the present King of England without constitutional authority or the sanction of tradition or custom. Whether the Conservatives or Liberals are in office is a matter of indifference. King Edward who stands behind both, rules'; p. 91: 'Edward VII, King of England and Emperor of India, is England's secret Emperor. In him the British nation possesses for the first time a Cæsar.' Emile Flourens, *La France conquise: Edouard VII et Clemenceau* [1906] (a clerical and anti-English work), p. 105: 'Edward VII has nothing of the commonplace tyrant. A despot who makes his will obeyed he has made the concealment of the iron hand in a velvet glove a fine art. He detests the manner of a despot and the pose of a conqueror. With a subtle perception which long experience has rendered more acute he knows the exact moment when the opposition must be crushed by brute force and he never shrinks from employing it. But his favourite weapon is persuasion which he wields in every conceivable shape with the dexterity of a past master. His expert knowledge of the human heart and of the French character in particular has taught him how to use with unerring skill the method of persuasion most appropriate to the tastes and desires of the individual in question.'

preceded that of the Foreign Office, if he was among its originators, and if it was for that reason that in December 1905 the Foreign Office wanted to have him as its chief. But when this has been granted, we must not misconceive Grey's political calibre. He was not of the lineage of Canning and Palmerston, one of those men with an innate genius for diplomatic intrigue and the manipulation of public opinion, who are happy only in their office, as the ideal sea captain is happy only on the poop of his ship. The ten years of Unionist government had been for him ten years of repose, during which he had performed, not too strenuously, the ritual of an opposition speaker. When he achieved the summit of his ambition he found himself, as it were, caught in the wheels of the formidable machine he had hoped to control and carried along by them. Even the loss in 1906 of a wife with whom he had lived in a close communion of tastes and ideas did not plunge him in despair into a maelstrom of activity. On the contrary, we receive the impression of a weary and disillusioned man. He continued a lover of the country, a student of bird life who looked forward the entire week to the week-end which would allow him to forget the affairs of Europe and escape to his beloved nature. And this phlegmatic temper which had nothing in common with the temperament of a Canning, a Palmerston and still less of a Chamberlain explains the fact that he was able to pursue the new policy which had been followed by the Foreign Office for the past two or three years with the utmost possible moderation. He appears indeed to have given it an interpretation predominantly negative, and his object was not so much an alliance with a particular European power against Germany as to prevent Germany from forming such an alliance against England. If, therefore, the Foreign Office sought on occasion to draw too close the bonds uniting Britain with her new friends, and his colleagues were alarmed from time to time by the prospect of the conflicts with Germany which the British foreign policy might involve, Sir Edward was just the right person to mediate between the Cabinet and the Foreign Office, and blur the features of the new policy without ever giving it up. Moreover, the balance of power which was his political creed of its very nature excluded a permanent alliance with one power against another, since the shifting equilibrium of national forces in Europe required that England should as far as possible remain free to transfer her weight from one scale to the other.[1] And since Chamberlain's imperialism had until 1902 been deliberately hostile to France and Russia, the subsequent change of friendships could be interpreted in two different ways. It might be regarded as a new orientation of British imperialism, and it was in this sense that it was understood by Asquith, Haldane, and Grey himself. Or it could be interpreted as an entire repudiation of the preceding imperialism, and it was because it was presented in this light that it escaped the censure of the Gladstonian veterans in the Cabinet. Assisted by so many favourable circumstances, Grey managed to acquire in a few months an amazing prestige not only in England but on the Continent,[2] and the candour, honesty, and entire disinterestedness to which everyone paid tribute invested a policy often ambiguous with the halo of his personal honour.[3]

In any case there can be no question of King Edward's policy, or Sir Edward Grey's, if by that is meant a policy imposed upon the Foreign Office or even suggested to it by either. There was a policy of the Foreign Office with which the private views of the King and the Foreign Secretary happened to coincide. It was in truth the policy which circumstances dictated and against which they would have attempted in vain to rebel. 'The Germans', Sir Edward wrote with truth, 'do not realize that England has always drifted or deliberately gone into opposition to any Power which establishes her hegemony in Europe.'[4] We have already witnessed

---

[1] 'So long as England remains faithful to the general principle of the preservation of the balance of power, her interests would not be served by Germany being reduced to the rank of a weak Power, as this might easily lead to a Franco-Russian predominance equally, if not more, formidable to the British Empire. There are no existing German rights, territorial or other, which this country could wish to see diminished. Therefore, so long as Germany's action does not overstep the line of legitimate protection of existing rights, she can always count upon the sympathy and good will, and even the moral support of England . . .' ('Memorandum by Mr. Eyre Crowe,' Foreign Office. January 1, 1907; *British Documents* . . . vol. iii, p. 417).

[2] Metternich to Prince von Bülow, March 23, 1909: 'In questions of foreign policy no one exercises such great influence over his fellow countrymen as Sir Edward Grey. His word is its own guarantee' (*Die Grosse Politik* . . . vol. xxviii, p. 126). *Daily News*, September 2, 1907: 'It is with reluctance that a Liberal newspaper criticizes the act of a minister whose personality exercises a magnetism amounting almost to fascination over the House of Commons.'

[3] For Sir Edward Grey's policy see Gilbert Murray, *The Foreign Policy of Sir Edward Grey, 1906–15*, 1915 (a defence with which we may contrast Hamilton Fyfe's satirical reflections, *The Making of an Optimist*, 1921, p. 40); also Herman Letz, *Lord Grey und der Weltkrieg: Ein Schlüssel zum Verständnis der britischen aemtlichen Aktenpublikation uber den Kriegsausbruch 1914*, 1927 (English translation 1928), a work which if perhaps not sufficiently impartial is nevertheless well documented and contains many acute psychological observations.

[4] Minute written on June 9, 1906; *British Documents* . . . vol. iii, p. 359.

and shall continue to witness Germany's efforts to break the *ententes* which were forming around her, efforts whose sole result will be to strengthen them until at last the circle which surrounds her is drawn tight and firm. Indeed, Russia, France, and England will themselves on occasion attempt to loosen the framework of the new system. In vain: it will resist all attempts to destroy or weaken it. We cannot conceive the statesman of genius or the master stroke of policy that during these critical years could have diverted the fatal course of events. The system was Europe's automatic reply to the growth of German power.

3

Picture the situation in January 1906. The Conference of Algeciras was about to meet to determine the future status of Morocco by a common agreement between all the signatories of the convention of Madrid. England, however, was in the throes of a General Election. The newspapers wrote of nothing else, and the Ministers had not even the leisure to hold a Cabinet Council. Every Minister had his hands full, courting the voters in his constituency half the week, and getting into touch with the business of his department the rest of the time. Sir Edward Grey, however, while assuring the German ambassador that the policy of friendship with France pursued by the Foreign Office for the last three years implied no distrust of Germany, expressed his personal conviction that, if Germany made the question of Morocco a pretext for declaring war on France, British public opinion would not allow the Government to remain neutral, and even, if we may believe Metternich, expressed himself in plainer terms than Lord Lansdowne had used six months before.[1] On the other hand, it would seem that the Liberal victory at the polls exceeded his expectation and made him doubt whether under any circumstances the British public would entertain the prospect of war. And on January 31 he advised the French Ambassador, Paul Cambon, to that effect.[2] And King Edward himself seems to have been im-

---

[1] Sir Edward Grey to Sir F. Lascelles, January 9, 1906 (*British Documents* . . . vol. iii, pp. 209–10); Metternich to Prince von Bülow, January 3, 1906 (*Die Grosse Politik* . . . vol. xxi,[1] pp. 47–50).

[2] Sir Edward Grey to Sir F. Bertie, January 31, 1906 (*British Documents* . . . vol. iii, pp. 180 sqq.) especially p. 181: 'M. Cambon must remember that England at the present

pressed by the vigorous disavowal by the electorate of imperialism in any shape or form. On January 23 he wrote to the Emperor William in extremely cordial terms suggesting a meeting in the near future and offering his services as mediator to settle by an amicable compromise the dispute between France and Germany in Morocco.

But the Kaiser's reply, though couched in polite language, was a flat refusal of the proffered mediation.[1] The purpose of his action at Tangier had been to prevent England from acting as arbitrator in Morocco. It was not for him to give way eight months later. The King of England and his ministers had therefore no option but to give the French claims unreserved diplomatic support, to which indeed they were pledged by the agreement of April 1904. A journalist, Sir Donald Mackenzie Wallace, was the King's private agent at Algeciras; Sir Arthur Nicolson, the British Ambassador at Madrid, the official representative of the Government. The Cabinet allowed the King to give British support the same theatrical setting as a year earlier. On his way to Biarritz he stopped at Paris. He visited the President, Loubet's successor, Fallières, ignored the Prime Minister, and had a long interview in a private house with Delcassé. The conversation was a significant step eight months after Delcassé's fall and four months after the indiscreet revelations of the Parisian press which, even if not accepted as reliable in every detail, had implanted in every country in Europe the firm belief that military measures against Germany had been concerted between England and France the previous spring.

What were these French claims which England pledged herself to support? By the very fact of going to Algeciras, France admitted that she had been wrong in not asking all the signatories of the Madrid Convention to sanction her establishment of a quasi-protectorate in Morocco. But she intended to seek that sanction and the sole difference between her intentions in 1904 and the demand she put forward now was that the more-or-less avowed protectorate for which she asked would be exercised under the control of the powers, would be a 'mandate' conferred upon her by them

moment would be most reluctant to find herself engaged in a great war, and I hesitated to express a decided opinion as to whether the strong feeling of the Press and of public opinion on the side of France would be strong enough to overcome the great reluctance which existed amongst us now to find ourselves involved in war.'

[1] King Edward to the Emperor William, January 23; the Emperor William to King Edward, February 5 (*Die Grosse Politik* . . . vol. xxi[1], pp. 108 sqq.). Cf. William II's observations on a telegram from Count Bernstorff of January 16 (ibid., p. 95).

and subject to certain conditions ensuring more effectively than the agreement of 1904 freedom of trade for all nations. To this programme Germany opposed a system of complete internationalization under which no power, least of all France, could enjoy a privileged position. It was the system the European powers had attempted to set up in Macedonia a few months before, and whose failure was already reported. Alone among the powers of Europe, Germany had refused to agree to it. In Morocco the position was reversed. But in both instances the German Government was pursuing the same policy. Champion in its own interest of the independence of the Mediterranean powers, it regarded the installation of an international police force in Macedonia as a violation of the Sultan's sovereignty which it sought to maintain unimpaired. In Morocco it was the inevitable minimum of interference which it would advise the Government of Fez to accept to avoid a worse fate.[1] Between the two proposals compromise was impossible. If before the Conference France and Germany could have reached an understanding for the settlement of the Moroccan question, how quickly its work would have been completed! And how much time would have been gained for the pacification of Europe! But Berlin had rejected all the proposals for an agreement whether official or unofficial which had been received from Paris after Delcassé's fall. Was it because the German Emperor and his Chancellor were deliberately hostile to the French policy in Morocco? A year after Algeciras, when a leading French statesman renewed the proposal already made in the autumn of 1905—that French control in Morocco should be recognized in return for compensation in some other part of Africa—the Congo for example—the Emperor William replied that he was not opposed to French suzerainty in Morocco, that he did not even want any compensation: what he wanted was 'an alliance'.[2] He thus revealed the secret of his policy, as he had already revealed it to the Czar Nicholas in August 1905 at their Bjorköe conversations. The Emperor's policy, which among other

[1] For German attempts to effect an understanding between the Sultans see the strange rumours reported from Constantinople by Sir N. O'Connor on February 12 (*British Documents* . . . vol. iii, p. 248).

[2] The Emperor William to Prince von Bülow, June 16, 1907 (*Die Grosse Politik* . . . vol. xxii, pp. 571 sqq.). For this conversation and the rumours current on the subject see the interesting details in two despatches from Sir F. Bertie to his Government, September 12 1907, and the minute, dated the 16th, attached to the first of these (*British Documents* . . . vol. vi. p. 55 sqq.).

faults suffered from his inability to state it openly on the eve of the Algeciras Conference, was to effect through the mediation of the Russian Government an understanding between France and Germany which would be understood by everyone as a breach with England.

No French statesman dared risk such a policy and the only effect the German Government produced at Paris by suggestions of this kind, implied in every step it took, was to make the position of the advocates of peace difficult, and equally difficult the position of the party, stronger than is recognized to-day, which desired to return to the policy of settling all colonial questions by amicable arrangement with Germany. On the contrary, it strengthened the party which refused to be reconciled to the loss of Alsace and for whom hatred of Germany was the substance of French patriotism. Moreover, while it refused to conclude a preliminary agreement with France, it did not even promise to abide by the free decision of the Conference. It demanded that the Conference should ratify its policy of internationalization. If the demand were refused, the German representative would leave the Conference, and war might be the result. At the unveiling of a monument to Moltke on October 26, 1907, the Emperor William delivered as a toast at the banquet one of those bellicose speeches with which from time to time he liked to flutter Europe. A phrase about 'dry powder and a whetted sword' was never forgotten. Once more panic reigned in French political circles. In feverish haste urgent measures were taken to renew the defences of the eastern frontier which had been neglected for some years.

4

In fact, the German Government did not expect the Conference to break down. When it instructed its representatives never to allow Germany to appear 'isolated' during the proceedings, it evidently regarded its system of internationalization as the most likely to win the approval of all the Governments concerned, with the exception of the French. Did it not serve the interests of all the other nations, even of Great Britain? The attitude adopted by the Foreign Office wore an air of paradox. To honour the pledge given in 1904, avoid a false move in the diplomatic game, and escape the snare laid by Germany by abandoning its support of the French claim, the British Government sacrificed in Morocco the immediate interests of British trade and industry.[1] The Germans noted with satisfaction that British opinion was not so unanimously favourable to France as it had been at the time of the Tangier episode. One important organ, the *Manchester Guardian*, departing on this question from the bulk of the Liberal Press, openly opposed the French point of view and the more vigorously as the Conference protracted its sessions. At Algeciras on February 3 Count von Tattenbach attempted to win over the British representative and detach him from the cause of France.[2]

His advances met with an extremely cold reception. Sir Arthur Nicolson, who deliberately kept in the background, was content to give his silent support to France, and it soon became evident that Germany's diplomatic position was far worse than Berlin had expected. All the powers who two years before had readily acquiesced in the establishment by France of a sphere of influence in Morocco now found themselves gathered at Algeciras not of their free will to defend their respective rights but to obey the summons of Germany and serve her political interests. It was therefore Germany, not, as she had hoped, France, who found herself the object of universal hostility. Though Italy was bound to Germany by the Triple Alliance, which she had twice renewed, she was also bound to France by an agreement on the question of Morocco. And if Italian opinion could only guess the exact contents of the agreement, it entirely approved of its spirit. Combe's anti-clericalism had demolished once for all the legend that France was in league with the Vatican against the unity of Italy, and France was extremely popular with the lower classes. To England, Italy was bound by even closer ties. It had concluded the Triple Alliance only with the approval, indeed almost on the advice, of England, and if that Alliance should prove to be directed against England, Italy, placed by her geographical condition at the mercy

---

[1] See the remarkable communication the Foreign Office found itself obliged to transmit on July 3, 1905, to the Manchester Chamber of Commerce: 'I am directed by the Marquess of Lansdowne to acknowledge the receipt of your letter of the 26th ultimo on the subject of the Anglo-French convention of the 18th of April 1904 and to state that the Board of Directors of the Manchester Chamber of Commerce appears to be under a misapprehension in supposing that an opportunity is likely to be afforded for revising that Agreement. The Declaration in question has been signed by the two Governments and has already been put into execution and cannot now be altered.' (*British Documents* ... vol. iii, p. 112).

[2] Sir A. Nicolson to Sir Edward Grey, February 4, 1906 (*British Documents* ... vol. iii, p. 241).

of the British fleet, would be obliged to denounce it. In Spain, the Government's policy of agreement with France and England had many more enemies. But France assured herself of Spanish support by substituting a Franco-Spanish gendarmerie for the purely French force of her original plan, and by its actions the Spanish court showed its approval of the new arrangement. At the opening of February the rumour was current that King Alphonso XIII had gone to Biarritz to meet Princess Victoria-Eugénie of Battenberg, King Edward's cousin. On March 7 the Princess was received into the Catholic Church and the English monarch came out to Biarritz to arrange a marriage which would place an English princess on the Spanish throne. The situation had changed since the days, still recent, when England, loathed by all the nations of the Continent, had offered Germany an alliance she had refused with disdain. The Emperor William was furious. 'All these Latin nations,' he wrote, 'miserable degenerates that they are, are mere weapons in the hands of England to combat German commerce in the Mediterranean. Not only have we no friends left, but this emasculate race, this scrap-heap of Latin peoples, heartily detests us. As it was in the days of the Hohenstaufens and the House of Anjou so it is now. The Latin riff-raff betray us on every hand and throw themselves into the arms of England, which intends to use them against us.' And as though he had entertained the dream of a pan-Teutonic alliance, he added: 'War between Teutons and Latins on the entire front. And the former, alas, are divided.'[1]

In Russia, England had many foes; the Anglo-French *entente*, concluded in the midst of the war with Japan, was unpopular. William II and Bülow therefore hoped to find in Russia support for their anti-British policy. But even the statesmen most hostile to England—Count Witte at their head—pressed a conciliatory policy upon the Emperor. For in the first place they knew that Russia, ruined by the defeat and revolution, had more need than ever of French money. And in fact the Russian Government would soon be rewarded for not refusing France its diplomatic support by a loan the French banks and, for the first time, the London banks would take up. And the loan would enable her to defeat the revolution.[2] And secondly, Witte and his friends per-

[1] Note to a despatch from the German chargé d'affaires at Madrid, Wilhelm von Stumm, to Prince von Bülow, March 9, 1906 (*Die Grosse Politik* . . . vol. xxii, p. 268).

[2] *The Memoirs of Count Witte* (1849–1916), translated from the original Russian manuscript and edited by Abraham Yarmolinsky, pp. 292 sqq.

ceived that the brusque methods employed by William II were producing the opposite effect to that which he expected, tightening instead of loosening the Anglo-French *entente*. Austria, Germany's ally, had no direct interests in Morocco. She complained at Washington that Germany's attitude was too unyielding and sought to discover a compromise which would be generally acceptable. But of President Roosevelt's attitude we must speak at greater length. For it was very different from what it had been in 1905, and the difference has perplexed historians.

A determined foe of Delcassé's policy, he alone, among the rulers of the great Powers, had supported the German Emperor's demand that the question of Morocco should be submitted to an international conference. Now, in 1906, through his representative at Algeciras he became the opponent of German intransigence whose intervention finally compelled the German Government to capitulate on the fundamental question of the gendarmerie. How are we to explain this change of front? By the change in the diplomatic situation during the interval. In 1904, the Japanese victories, following so close upon the conclusion of her treaty with England and the signature of the Anglo-French agreement, had seemed to make Britain the arbiter of world politics. In 1905 the treaty of peace between Russia and Japan had been signed in the United States under the ægis of the President, who had been supported by German diplomacy, and on the other hand it was with his support that the Emperor William had annulled that portion of the Anglo-French agreement which concerned Morocco. Therefore, when 1906 opened it was no longer King Edward who was overlord of the world, but the Emperor William and President Roosevelt. But Roosevelt had not humbled King Edward in 1905 to minister to the Emperor William's conceit; to humble the latter monarch in his turn, he wished to make himself if possible the umpire between Germany and France on the question of Morocco. If we would understand the troubled history of these years we must be careful not to classify France among the powers of the first rank. France was simply the greatest among the powers of the second class, by turns beneficiary and victim of the struggle for world hegemony carried on above her head by a small group of giants—England, Germany, and the United States of America. In 1906 we cannot add Russia, for her power was at the moment under eclipse.

The question was therefore finally settled by a compromise. The discussions at the Conference bore chiefly on two points: the institution of a state bank and a gendarmerie. In the matter of the bank France was defeated. She claimed a preponderant share in its control, pleading the amount of French investments in Morocco. She secured only three out of the fourteen seats on the board of directors. In the matter of the gendarmerie, on the other hand, her claims were far more successful. Germany proposed an international gendarmerie, to be organized by the Sultan under the control of the diplomatic corps. France had the wisdom to put forward from the very beginning an extremely moderate proposal. The gendarmerie should be confined to the eight open ports of Morocco and not entrusted to France alone but divided between Spain and herself. Germany refused, as she refused when Italy proposed that the Franco-Spanish gendarmerie should be placed under the control of some neutral power. But when Roosevelt adopted the Italian proposal she suddenly changed her tone and accepted a compromise put forward by Austria at her suggestion, that the policing of certain ports should be entrusted to France, of others to Spain, and at Casablanca to a neutral power, whose chief representative should have the right to inspect the French and Spanish gendarmerie in other ports. It was now the turn of France to refuse and be blamed for her intransigence by London and Petersburg. But Roosevelt intervened a second time, and more francophil than Grey and his subordinates, rejected the policing of one port by a third power. For the second time Germany submitted. Nevertheless the argument Roosevelt brought forward against the Austrian compromise was a double-edged sword. To give the policing of certain ports to France, of others to Spain, and of one port to a neutral power was, he argued, the first step towards a partition of Morocco, and therefore a threat to the sovereignty of the Sultan. But for the same reason he must condemn at the same time the Franco-Spanish proposal that the gendarmerie should be French in some ports, Spanish in others. In every port there must be a force of mixed nationality, French and Spanish. France however persisted in her claim and since she had now the unreserved support of England and Russia and since Roosevelt did not wish to appear in any respect less francophil than England, he yielded, though with bad grace. For the third time Germany gave way.

By the terms of the final agreement the inspector, who was to be Swiss, would not command in any port. At Tangier and Casablanca the gendarmerie would be a mixed force, French and Spanish. At Larache it would be Spanish, French at Rabat, Safi, Mazagan, and Mogador. When compared with the gains France had expected from the agreement of 1904, this was little. When compared with the losses Germany had expected to inflict upon her it was a great deal. It was the first instalment of that Franco-Spanish occupation of the coast of Morocco England had sanctioned in 1904.[1]

5

May we then regard the question of Morocco as finally settled after these twelve troublous months? In Morocco friction continued between the French and Germans until the French army occupied Casablanca in 1907, and as a result of the occupation the Sultan Abdul Aziz was overthrown by a national rising and replaced by Abdul Hamid. And on the other hand did the agreement do anything to diminish the rivalry between England and Germany on all the seas of the globe? British naval and military circles were so sensitive that the least incident was sufficient to arouse indignation and alarm. Were the Germans carrying on in their colony of South-West Africa a difficult campaign against a native revolt? It was a mere pretext. They had designs on the British possessions in that part of the world.[2] Did a German company negotiate with the Portuguese Government the purchase of land in Madeira for the construction of a sanatorium, another obtain a concession from the Spanish Government for a cable

[1] For the Conference of Algeciras see, in the first place, André Tardieu, *La Conférence d'Algésiras: Histoire diplomatique de la Crise marocaine* (15 Janvier–7 Avril 1906), a work very indiscreet at the time of publication, and very informative, but the polemics of a contemporary too closely mixed up with the events he relates for the historian to make uncontrolled use of his statements. The book has also lost its importance since its revelations have been verified and completed by the important German and English diplomatic publications (*Die Grosse Politik . . .* vol. xxii—*British Documents . . .* vol. iii, pp. 204 sqq.). For the part played by Roosevelt and his representative at Algeciras, Henry White, the American Ambassador in Rome, see J. B. Bishop, *Theodore Roosevelt and His Time*, 1920, vol. i, pp. 488 sqq.; also Allen Nevins, *Henry White, Thirty Years of American Diplomacy*, 1930, pp. 261 sqq.

[2] H. of C., July 31, 1906, Lyttleton's speech (*Parliamentary Debates*, 4th Series, vol. clxii, p. 757). Sir Percy FitzPatrick's address to the members of the Empire Parliamentary Association, July 9, 1919 (Sir John A. R. Marriott, *The Mechanism of the Modern State . . .* vol. i, p. 259 n.). Sir C. Hardinge to Sir Edward Grey, August 16, 1906 (*British Documents . . .* vol. iii, p. 367).

passing through the Canaries? The German navy, of course, was seeking a base for its cruisers. It was evident that the Anglo-French *entente* had not been weakened. Contrary to German hopes, Algeciras had proved that the *entente*, far from being the caprice of a cabinet or party was based on the facts of the international situation and therefore remained as firm under a Liberal Government as it had been when the Conservatives were in office.

Nevertheless, neither the two months during which the Conference was in session nor the months which followed it were a period of war fever. The British had just emerged from a struggle which at the outset they had regarded as nothing more than a punitive expedition of the colonial type, but which had ended by attaining or almost attaining the scale of a great war. Some had even been afraid it would expand into a European war. At no price would they incur a similar risk. This was the fundamental significance of the January election. They wished to put war out of their minds and they succeeded. During the Conference at Algeciras an occasional article expressed the opinion of the leading English newspapers in favour of France, but in the interval a host of other questions concerning domestic politics occupied their readers' attention, at a time when the first session opened of a Parliament whose aspect was almost revolutionary. When the Conference had closed with results not very satisfactory to the German foreign office, England made it clear that while she wished to maintain 'the *entente cordiale*,' she would do nothing that would give it a too openly anti-German aspect. London, which during the Conference had sent her county councilllors on an official visit to Paris, gave a cordial reception during the following summer to a delegation of German journalists and a delegation of German burgomasters. King Edward, after an official visit to President Fallières at the beginning of May, stopped in August at Homburg on his way to Wiesbaden to pay William II. the visit of a relative and friend. These manifestations of friendly feeling between England and Germany alarmed certain political circles in France.[1] Not so many years before England had been

[1] Their mistrust had already found expression during the Conference at Algeciras, especially when the British Government differed from the French in its attitude towards the compromise proposed by Austria. See two despatches from Sir Francis Bertie to Sir Edward Grey of March 15, 1906 (*British Documents* . . . vol. iii, p. 306). For its persistence see Sir Edward Grey to Sir Francis Bertie, July 9, 1906; Sir F. Bertie to Sir Edward Grey, July 12, 1906; C. Spring-Rice to Sir Edward Grey, August 31, 1906 (*British Documents* . . . vol. iii, pp. 361, 362, 374).

virtually the ally of Germany against France. Might not that time return? But these fears were as superficial as they were ill-founded. The predominant sentiment in France, as in England, was the desire for peace almost at any price. Of this Delcassé's fall in June 1905 had been a striking proof. The French had feared lest England's friendship for France might force her into an armed struggle with Germany. After that, how could France be genuinely alarmed to see England remove what she regarded as her greatest danger by entertaining, side by side with the *entente cordiale*, as friendly relations with Germany as the situation permitted? Moreover, many signs proved that French feeling had changed very little since the previous June. The Chamber expressed the profound indifference of the nation to the question which was being discussed at Algeciras by overthrowing the Rouvier Cabinet at one of the most critical moments of the Conference, on a question of domestic policy. The general election which followed a few weeks later was almost as sensational as the British election of January. It resulted in the rout, almost the total annihilation, of the party which represented a bellicose patriotism. Paris therefore did nothing to encourage the French in Morocco to adopt an aggressive attitude. Clémenceau, who became Prime Minister in October, an old opponent of colonial expansion, was perfectly sincere when he informed the German Ambassador that Morocco left him 'completely indifferent'.[1] If, however, it was obvious to everybody that the French Government and Parliament had not the least wish for incidents to occur in Morocco, and in no case could conceivably provoke them, incidents which might nevertheless take place would lose much of their gravity.

6

The new foreign policy inaugurated by the Foreign Office at the end of 1902 and to which even after the change of government it had remained faithful, and the nation with it, has appeared in our account of Algeciras as simply a policy of friendship with France and the Latin nations. But the reconciliation with France had still to be completed by a reconciliation with Russia. In

[1] Prince Radolin to Prince von Bülow, March 15, 1907 (*Die Grosse Politik* ... vol. xxiii, p. 547).

fact, the Foreign Office had done everything in its power to reach an understanding, not only with France, but also with Russia from 1895, when Lord Salisbury took office, till 1898. But the Russian occupation of Port Arthur in March 1898 had brought the negotiations with Russia to a sudden end and it was then that England had made the advances which Germany had rejected so arrogantly. When the policy of an Anglo-German *entente* failed, those politicians who about 1901 first perceived the necessity of finding Continental allies against Germany thought first of Russia, and it was because there seemed no hope of success in that direction that they turned in despair to France. Unfortunately the *entente cordiale* had hardly been achieved when it led to the Tangier episode and Delcassé's fall, humiliations of France and almost equally of Great Britain. To what did the Wilhelmstrasse owe this success? Surely to the fact that Russia, weakened by its defeat in the Far East, had left France defenceless before the threat of a German invasion?[1] Was it not a matter of vital importance to court Russia once more? Since the day must come, five or ten years hence, when she would have recovered from the disasters that had befallen her, must not England take steps to assure that she would not be, as so often in the past, her enemy, but her friend, and form an alliance between France, Russia, and herself sufficiently strong to put a stop to this German bullying?

The task was far from easy. The renewal of the Anglo-Japanese alliance had strengthened Russian dislike of England, and if no one in London had discovered the secret of the Bjorköe interview, the French diplomatists, now friends of the Foreign Office, brought Sir Edward Grey disquieting reports of the favourable attitude of Lamsdorff and Witte towards the project of a Continental combination against Britain.[2] But the more alarming these reports, the more pressing the need to take action, and perhaps the weakness of Russia at the close of 1905 was actually favourable to the opening of negotiations. Now that British imperialism had become more pliable, the same might be expected of Russian.[3]

[1] Memorandum by Sir Edward Grey, February 20, 1906; and the accompanying notes by Sir C. Hardinge (*British Documents* ... vol. iii, p. 267), also a minute bearing Grey's signature of September 18, 1906 (*British Documents* ... vol. iii, p. 389).

[2] Sir Charles Hardinge to the Marquess of Lansdowne, October 4, 8, 14, 21, 1905; the Marquess of Lansdowne to Sir F. Bertie, October 25, 1905 (*British Documents* ... vol. iv, pp. 205, 208, 211, 214, 217).

[3] Lieutenant-Colonel Napier to Sir A. Nicolson, April 27, 1907: '... she is still smarting from the Japanese defeat that we were the indirect means of inflicting upon her, and the

Lord Lansdowne had been putting out feelers for several weeks when the Unionist Cabinet resigned, but official negotiations were not opened until December 1905. The *rapprochement* with Russia was the achievement of Sir Edward Grey and the Foreign Office during the first eighteen months of the new Government.

When Sir Charles Hardinge agreed to leave the embassy at Petersburg to become permanent under-secretary at Downing Street, it was because he believed that in that capacity he could do more to promote an understanding with Russia.[1] He was succeeded by Sir Arthur Nicolson, who having worked hard at Tangier, Madrid and Algeciras to promote the *rapprochement* with France went to Petersburg to continue there the same anti-German policy. He was accompanied by Sir Donald Mackenzie Wallace. Sir Donald had been King Edward's agent at Algeciras. Speaking Russian fluently and with a thorough knowledge of the country, he became the counsellor and guide of the new ambassador, who might otherwise have been at a loss in surroundings so completely strange. The more so that he arrived in the midst of a revolution. After long months filled with repeated risings brutally repressed the first Duma met. A new cabinet was appointed to meet it in which Lamsdorff was replaced by another minister for foreign affairs, Isvolsky. The British, well satisfied with Lamsdorff, with whom they had concluded in January by word of mouth a species of 'tacit agreement', an accord between the foreign policies of the two powers,[2] were afraid that Isvolsky might prove more open to German influences.[3] The hopes of the Germans, exceedingly displeased by the Russian attitude at the Algeciras Conference, rose in proportion to the English fears.[4]

loss of prestige of an unsuccessful war coupled with the revolutionists at home has evidently greatly shaken her hold upon her Central Asian Mohammedan subjects and it is of the greatest importance that we should take advantage of this frame of mind' (*British Documents* . . . vol. iv, p. 532).

[1] Sir Charles Hardinge to Sir Arthur Nicolson, September 4, 1907: '. . . I felt that I could do more by impressing my views on people at home, and I promised both Lamsdorff and the Emperor that I would do my level best to bring it about [an agreement with Russia]' (*British Documents* . . . vol. v, p. 580).

[2] Sir A. Nicolson to Sir Edward Grey, September 1, 1906: '. . . Mr. Isvolsky observed that he wished to act in harmony with the spirit of what he termed the "tacit agreement" of January last' (*British Documents* . . . vol. iv, p. 386). For the tacit agreement itself see Spring-Rice to Sir Edward Grey, January 26, 1906 (*British Documents* ' . . vol. iv., p. 223).

[3] Sir A. Johnstone to Sir Edward Grey, Copenhagen, May 27, 1906 (*British Documents* . . . vol. iv, p. 235). See, however, the reassuring account communicated by Léon Bourgeois of his conversation with Isvolsky at Paris in April (Reginald Lister to Sir Edward Grey, May 21, 1906; *British Documents* . . . vol. iii, p. 356).

[4] Von Schön to Prince von Bülow, May 14, 1906 (*Die Grosse Politik* . . . vol. xxii, pp.

But the former were speedily reassured, the latter disappointed. Isvolsky, who, the first perhaps among the agents of the Russian Government, had received King Edward's confidence at Copenhagen in 1904, showed himself from the outset determined upon a policy of understanding with England. The negotiations for the conclusion of an Anglo-Russian *entente* on the same lines as the *entente* concluded with France in April 1904, continued without interruption and from November were actively pressed forward. They led to the convention of August 31, 1907. They had proved a more difficult task than the Anglo-French negotiations. This is easily understood when we remember the many conflicts of interest and opinion which divided the two countries.

In Russia the pro-British party was the Liberal party, the party which supported the revolution. All its sympathies lay with the three countries of Western Europe—England, France and Italy—where parliamentary government was established, and which, moreover, were drawing so closely together. If Isolvsky, the foreign minister, was in favour of an agreement with England, it was because at home he supported a liberal policy of loyal co-operation with the Duma. To all these groups of the left Germany was an object of hatred. William II was accused of encouraging the weak Nicholas II to adopt a policy of reaction. When the Duma was dissolved in July 1906, the Government thought it prudent to guard the German embassy with troops.[1] It was afraid it might be sacked by a mob of rioters. On the other hand the party of reaction was pro-German. The reconciliation between England and France, Russia's official ally, far from producing an immediate *rapprochement* with England accentuated at first the hostility entertained towards France in military circles. These circles cherished the hope that the old project of an alliance between the three Emperors might be revived. Russia had learned by bitter experience the cost of war, defeat, disaster and revolution. The efforts of the Panslavists to break up the Austro-Hungarian monarchy should therefore be discouraged. And the

22–4). Count von Metternich to Prince von Bülow, July 31, 1906 (*Die Grosse Politik . . .* vol. xxxi[11], p. 448). See on the other hand Count Henckel's report of May 17, 1906 (*Die Grosse Politik . . .* vol. xxii, p. 23). For the uncertainty felt in London see Von Stumm's ambiguous despatch to Prince von Bülow, May 19, 1906 (*Die Grosse Politik . . .* vol. xxii, pp. 24–6).

[1] Or rather, fearing a hostile demonstration against the German Embassy and not wishing to single out this particular Embassy for protction it had them all guarded (Alexander Isvolsky, *Memoirs*, p. 208).

Russian Emperor should accede to the alliance between the German and the Austrian Emperors. Peace would be assured, directly in Eastern and Central Europe, indirectly throughout the entire Continent by this revived Holy Alliance, this league of three monarchs against the danger of popular insurrection.

In England it was just the opposite. If the imperialists—whether they belonged to the Unionist or the Liberal party—objected to particular concessions to Russia the Foreign Office found it politic to make, they were taken as a whole, obsessed by fear of the German fleet, stronger every year and stationed at the very gates of Britain, and in their anxiety to possess an ally sufficiently powerful to intimidate Germany were seriously troubled by the collapse of Russia, which a few years previously they had so eagerly desired. Among the advanced Liberals on the other hand, in spite of their indifference to the expansion of the British Empire in Asia, the prospect of a *rapprochement* with Russia was greeted with an outburst of indignation. To be sure they sympathised with the Russian people. But they witnessed their impotence to overthrow the Czar, and after, as before, 1905, Russia was incarnate in a Government they abhorred, which completely stifled all freedom of thought and massacred the workers and the Jews. Their denunciations not only filled the Radical press but found utterance in the House of Commons itself. To enter into friendly relations with the Russian Government was to give the latter British support in the struggle against the revolution, to assist the cause of reaction in Russia and indirectly throughout the entire Continent.

From this source countless difficulties arose. At the opening of 1906 the Russian ministers asked King Edward to pay a visit to the Czar. Either they wished to give some pledge to Liberal opinion or hoped to compromise the King by the support to the cause of order his visit would appear to give. From every point of view the proposed visit was dangerous, and he declined the invitation.[1] Instead Sir Edward Grey suggested that the British fleet should visit Cronstadt. This time it was the Russian Government which asked the British to postpone the proposed visit.[2] The same year the Inter-Parliamentary Union was to hold its Congress in London and for the first time a Russian delegation would be

---

[1] Sir Sidney Lee, *King Edward VII* . . . vol. ii, pp. 564–5. Spring-Rice to Sir Edward Grey, January 16, March 15, 1906 (*British Documents* . . . vol. iv, pp. 221, 227).
[2] Sir Sidney Lee, ibid, p. 565.

present, since Russia at last possessed a Parliament. But on the very day, July 23, that Campbell-Bannerman, as Prime Minister, was to give the Congress an official welcome the news arrived that the Czar had dissolved the Duma. '*Je ne fais pas de commentaires,*' declared Sir Henry, who spoke in French,[1] '*sur les nouvelles qui ont éclaté ce matin, ce n'est ni le lieu ni le moment. Nous n'avons pas une assez grande connaissance des faits pour pouvoir blamer ou louer. Mais ceci du moins nous pouvons dire—nous qui fondons notre confiance et notre espoir sur le régime parlementaire. Les nouvelles institutions ont souvent une jeunesse accidentée sinon orageuse. La Douma revivra d'une forme ou d'une autre. Nous pouvons dire avec toute sincérité: La Douma est morte. Vive La Douma.*'[2] The Russian court took offence, and the Russian ambassador protested. Sir Henry was obliged to explain, almost excuse, his words.

During the following months the Russian Government strengthened its authority. The Stolypin cabinet, formed after the *coup d'état* of July, seemed likely to last and displayed a measure of energy and consistency both in repressing disorder and in carrying out some useful measures of social reform. The visit of two Russian men-of-war to Portsmouth in the spring of 1907, followed by a visit of the crews to London, proved that war and revolution had not completely annihilated the Russian navy and was a sign of the friendly relations which now existed between the two Governments. Since Isvolsky remained at the Russian foreign office the negotiations for an agreement were pushed forward, the more actively since the Russian cabinet offered firmer guarantees of stability. On August 31 the Convention was signed. Both for its positive contents and its omissions, and for the reception it met with in both countries, it merits detailed examination.[3]

---

[1] J. A. Spender, *The Life of the Right Hon. Sir Henry Campbell-Bannerman*, vol. ii, p. 264.

[2] 'I do not propose to comment on the sudden news received this morning. This is neither the place nor the time. We do not know the facts sufficiently for blame or approval. But this at least we can say—who base our confidence and our hope on parliamentary government. New institutions have often a chequered, if not a stormy, youth. Under one form or another the Duma will revive. In all sincerity we can say "the Duma is dead, long live the Duma".'

[3] For the Anglo-Russian Convention see *British Documents* . . . vol. iv, pp. 232 sqq. (See also *Die Grosse Politik* . . . vol. xxvi, pp. 1 sqq.) There is nothing on the subject in Isvolsky's (unfinished) memoirs. Nothing either in Witte's, who, however, was no longer in office after May 1906 and whose sole interest before that date in a *rapprochement* with England was to obtain a loan from the English banks. There is only the following bitter comment of a dismissed minister: 'The Convention inaugurated the policy of philandering with England. . . . It was due to my opposition that it was not concluded until 1907' (*Memoirs*, pp. 432–3).

7

The preamble of the Convention laid down that its purpose was to settle by mutual agreement certain questions relative to the interests of the signatories on the continent of Asia, and 'the removal of every cause of dispute between Great Britain and Russia in respect of the aforesaid questions'. It comprised three sections, 'an agreement concerning Persia', 'a convention concerning Afghanistan', and 'an agreement concerning Tibet'.[1]

The agreement concerning Tibet and the Convention concerning Afghanistan dealt with the northern frontier of India. The imperialist school wanted England, in order to safeguard India against the danger of a Russian invasion, to cross the Himalayas and establish to the north a series of 'bulwarks' or 'glacis' against an enemy considered so dangerous. On this point Lord Curzon and Lord Kitchener, however they might dispute the limits of their respective jurisdictions, were agreed. The new Viceroy, Lord Minto, adopted the views common to the entire Anglo-Indian world, and King Edward was of the same opinion. But the Russo-Japanese war had changed the face of Asia. For a long time to come there would be no Russian peril in this region. The Foreign Office had not waited for the advent of the Liberal Government to disavow Lord Curzon's policy in regard to Afghanistan and Tibet. This, no doubt, even more than his quarrel with Lord Kitchener, was the reason of his recall.[2] Morley, therefore, sup-

[1] For the meaning given to these terms 'convention' and 'agreement' see the memorandum drawn up by Isvolsky on August 6, (19,) 1907 (*British Documents* ... vol. iv, pp. 300–1, 499–500).

[2] On this point see Lord Midleton's revelations in a speech delivered at Guildford on November 20, 1930. The speaker wished to correct mistakes contained in a recent biography of Lord Curzon by reference to confidential statements made to him by Balfour shortly before his death. 'His difficulty with the home Government was that he claimed to direct the foreign policy of India in relation to her neighbours without sufficient regard to its effects on British policy throughout the world. Most unfortunately he felt it necessary to advise operations in Tibet and Afghanistan, which the Russian Government and our ally the Ameer regarded with the greatest anxiety. Mr. Balfour's Cabinet neither shared his fears nor were willing to acquiesce in the strong measures he proposed. It happened that in that body of twenty men all of whom were his admirers and probably at least half were his intimate friends, one and all were unanimous that a crisis must be avoided, and in both cases they unanimously refused to authorize the serious steps which he proposed to take and our successors in office entirely concurred with us.' In spite of Edward VII' s repeated requests neither Balfour at the end of 1905 nor Campbell-Bannerman at the beginning of 1906 would give Lord Curzon the English peerage which would have enabled him to sit in the House of Lords as an inconvenient critic of the Government's policy (Sir Sidney Lee, *King Edward VII* ... vol. ii, p. 379). He did not obtain it until 1908

ported not only by his colleagues, but also by the Committee of Imperial Defence, had no difficulty in overcoming Anglo-Indian opposition and checking without danger to the Empire the innate tendency of imperialism to a policy of aggrandisement. By the terms of the Convention of 1907 Russia recognized Afghanistan 'as outside the Russian sphere of influence', and undertook not to send diplomatic agents to that country but to negotiate with it through the channel of the British Government. In return England pledged herself not to interfere in the domestic government of Afghanistan so long as the latter respected the pledges she had given to England not to annex any portion of Afghan territory and to maintain equal commercial rights for both countries, any privilege secured for British or Anglo-Indian trade to accrue automatically to Russian. As regards Tibet both Governments promised to abstain from any interference with the domestic affairs of the country, to send no representatives to Lhassa, or seek any concessions, such as railways, roads, telegraphs, or mines, either for themselves or for their subjects. Even the despatch of a scientific expedition by either of the two Governments should be subject to the consent of the other. Protests were raised in Russia against the Afghan Convention, because it recognized England's established right of exclusive control over the foreign policy of Afghanistan. Protests were made in London by a section of the Conservative opposition against the Tibetan agreement. For when Lord Curzon was Viceroy England had despatched a military expedition to Tibet and imposed upon her a quasi-protectorate in which China had just acquiesced, and the fruits of these successes were now surrendered. But this portion at least of the Convention was loudly applauded by the Radical press; the cost of the Indian army could now be reduced.

That part of the Convention which concerned Persia met with a far more mixed reception in Russia and still more in England. Persia was one of those half-civilized, half-barbarous countries which were attempting to raise themselves to the European level, getting into debt as a result of their ill-advised efforts, and as they piled up their indebtedness becoming the mark and finally the prey of their creditors' greed. Russia had already laid hands on

when the Government had no more reason to refuse him this gratification of his personal ambition since he had just entered the House of Lords as a representative Irish peer (see the letter to the Irish peers offering himself as candidate, December 27, 1907).

the northern portion of the country and intended to extend her grasp to the Persian Gulf, where one day, if she recovered her strength, she might find that open port she had lost in Port Arthur. Here, however, she was faced by the ambitions both of Germany, who was extending in this direction her railway from Bagdad, and of England, who, as mistress of the seas, regarded herself as entitled to exercise suzerainty over the coast of the Gulf. How could an agreement be achieved on this point between England and Russia? Russia wanted two vertical zones of influence, the eastern of the two Russian, the western British. The Persian coast of the Gulf would be divided between both. England wanted two horizontal zones, the southern, which would be British, would include the entire Persian coast of the Gulf. But the British Government, not daring to put forward this claim, proposed the compromise on which the agreement was based. The two powers agreed to divide Persia into three zones.[1] In the northern zone, which included Teheran, England would leave Russian influence a free field. In the southern, or rather the south-eastern, zone, which ran from a line drawn from the Afghan frontier to Bender-Abbas, on the coast, Russia would leave England a free hand. In the intermediate zone, which comprised the entire Persian coast of the Gulf, England and Russia mutually undertook not to prevent the grant of concessions to the subjects of either power without a preliminary agreement between both.[2] The British Government, with the support or rather under the pressure of the Government of India, attempted to insert in the agreement a formula by which Russia recognized England's 'special interests' in the Persian Gulf. But the attempt was defeated by the refusal of the Russian Government, which maintained that, since this was a problem which concerned other nations besides Great Britain and Russia, it had no place in a bilateral agreement. There were moments during the summer of 1907 when this difference

[1] In the document they were careful not to term these zones 'spheres of influence' or even 'of interest' so as to avoid the appearance of violating the sovereignty of Persia at a moment when in the preamble of this very agreement both powers pledged themselves 'to respect' her 'integrity and independence'. See Sir Edward Grey to Sir Arthur Nicolson, October 31, 1906; Sir Arthur Nicolson to Sir Edward Grey, November 4, 1906 (*British Documents* . . . vol. iv, pp. 407, 409).

[2] Grey had wanted a special arrangement for Teheran, the capital of the entire country. See the minute signed by Sir Charles Hardinge, February 26, 1907 (*British Documents* . . . vol. iv, p. 433). But he abandoned the claim almost immediately in return for guarantees given to British interests in the neutral zone—Sir Edward Grey to Sir Arthur Nicolson, March 8, 1907 (*British Documents* . . . vol. iv, pp. 43–5).

seemed likely to bring the negotiations to an end. Sir Arthur Nicolson found himself obliged to visit London, apparently to urge counsels of moderation on his Government. Finally England gave way. All that Sir Edward Grey was able to secure was the publication, at the same time as the agreement, of a letter from himself to Nicolson, in which, after recalling the existence of special rights in the Gulf guaranteed to England by their exercise for more than a century, he pointed out that during these negotiations the Russian Government had implicitly recognized these rights and expressed his belief that 'this question will not give rise to difficulties between the two Governments' if it should ever prove necessary to raise it. This did not satisfy the uncompromising imperialists in England. And in Russia on the other hand complaints were raised that she obtained by the agreement nothing she did not possess already. But both sides were so weary and Russia so exhausted that these complaints found little echo.[1] In England it was the Radical group, a powerful section of the ministerialists, who regarded the convention as committing the British Government to an enterprise closely resembling the French enterprise in Morocco, and to a dismemberment of Persia to be effected in concert with a Government which was the sworn foe of freedom and civilization.

8

When, in May 1906, the *Standard* revealed to its readers for the first time the secret that England was seeking an agreement with Russia, the paper informed them that the question of the Bagdad railway would be among those discussed.[2] And when the *Daily Telegraph*, in September, made further revelations, often true even in detail, the article, after representing the Tibetan question as on the point of settlement and admitting that the negotiations on the subject of Persia would be far more difficult, added: 'In time, and

[1] As early as 1903 Valentine Chirol one of the principal architects of the *entente cordiale* wrote as follows: 'Are we to run the risk of seeing Eastern Persia converted into another Manchuria, with a military railway on the Manchurian model, running down to another Port Arthur on the Gulf or on the Indian Ocean, and turning the flank of Afghanistan and British Baluchistan, or are we to draw a line at which by mutual consent or otherwise, Russia's policy of peaceful penetration from the north shall be met by a British policy of peaceful penetration?' (*The Middle Eastern Question, or some Political Problems of Indian Defence*, p. 404).
[2] May 19, 1906.

doubtless very soon, the question of the Near East will be reached, and I may say, without laying claim to the gift of prophecy, that when it is disposed of, Russian warships will no longer be excluded from the Dardanelles.'[1] Nevertheless, the Convention of August 31, 1907, contained no mention either of Asia Minor or Turkey in Europe. On these points an agreement, or at least a public agreement, was so difficult to reach that silence had been found preferable.

At Constantinople England continued to follow the complicated policy she had pursued for more than a century. On the one hand by constituting herself protector of the Christian populations oppressed by the Sultan she continued to augment her prestige in a way which served her honour and interests at the same time. On the other hand she shrank from weakening the Sultan's power to such an extent as to strengthen Russian influence on the Bosphorus, for she was afraid that Russia might one day occupy Constantinople and restore the old Byzantine empire. But the appearance of a new factor had made her policy more difficult. At the period of the Crimean War, Germany did not exist. In 1878, Germany, still new-born, had not yet entered upon a policy of expansion and Bismarck had expressed the sentiments of the entire nation when he declared that Macedonia was not worth the life of a Pomeranian grenadier. In the interval the situation had changed. Throughout the Mohammedan world Germany was pursuing a policy which though, as we know to-day, destined to fail, appeared at the time clever and cautious. German imperialism sought no annexations. It offered its protection to the native monarchs in return for compensations of a purely economic nature—banking, railway, or mining concessions. In this way Germany had made herself extremely popular at Fez, as a bulwark against French or Spanish imperialism, at Teheran as a bulwark against Russian or British, and again at Constantinople as a defence against the Russians and still more against the English.

Of this policy of peaceful penetration the Bagdad railway was the principal achievement. When the Anglo-Russian negotiations opened at Petersburg, the first section from Konieh to Eregli had just been opened. When the second section had been completed and the line taken across the Taurus the construction

---

[1] *Daily Telegraph*, September 29, 1906, 'England and Russia. An Understanding on Asiatic Policy'. Persia and Tibet. Petersburg, September 25.

of the remaining section over a vast plain to Mosul would be an easy task. If it were carried further still the railway would reach the Persian frontier, and German trade and finance were already engaged in a systematic attempt to obtain a footing in Persia. There was a German bank at Teheran, a German line of shipping in the Persian Gulf. The negotiators of the Anglo-Russian Convention were therefore obliged to deal with the problem of Bagdad. On the Russian side Isvolsky proposed that by a friendly agreement the German railways in Mesopotamia should be linked up with the system of railways which Russia was constructing in northern Persia. Sir Edward Grey was disturbed by the German project of extending the line to Koweit on the Persian Gulf. Would Germany agree that from Bagdad or at least from Bassora traffic should proceed by water in vessels owned by a British line? Or that the final section of railway from Bassora to Koweit should be built and worked by England? Or alternatively that the entire line should be placed under the management of an international board? Negotiations followed. Germany indeed could not refuse to negotiate, for she knew that the undertaking could be completed only with the help of British and French capital, and that it would not be forthcoming without the sanction of Downing Street and the Quai d'Orsay. But the negotiations failed both between Germany and Russia, and Germany and England. They failed because the German Government insisted that the undertaking should remain altogether, or at least preponderantly, German. And they failed for another reason—because Germany was afraid that their success would endanger her credit with the Sultan. He was convinced that England, mistress of Egypt and India, was preparing to embark upon a further project of aggrandisement, nothing less than to unite these two possessions by annexation of all the intervening territory. He looked to a German Bagdad to plant itself in this territory as a barrier blocking the road against this new advance of British imperialism.[1]

As regards European Turkey, Isvolsky, hostile as he was to the Asiatic policy the Russian empire had pursued for the last twenty years and anxious to see Russia once more turn her face towards Europe, might be expected to revive the question of the Dardanelles. Russia had just lost Port Arthur. Might she not obtain by friendly agreement with England, if not a port in the Persian

---

[1] For these negotiations see *Die Grosse Politik* ... vol. xxvi, pp. 175 sqq.

Gulf, at least a free passage for her navy into the Mediterranean? It was with this object in view that he regularly supported the English standpoint at Constantinople, whether in the matter of an international gendarmerie in Roumelia or of the higher tariff the Porte wished to impose? Though British commerce protested against the latter England consented. But if in concert with Germany the Porte demanded this higher tariff, it was to finance the Bagdad railway. And England gave her consent on the express stipulation that the money it yielded should be spent in Roumelia.[1] She thus contrived while satisfying the demands of British humanitarianism to put an obstacle in the way of German expansion in Mesopotamia. But on the question of the Dardanelles no agreement was reached.

It seems in fact that the original conception entertained at Petersburg of an *entente* with Great Britain was an agreement about the Straits. This once achieved, it would be easy to reach an understanding on the questions at issue between the two countries in Asia.[2] But false reports, circulated by German agents at Constantinople and deliberately intended to make the negotiations difficult by bringing up the question of the Dardanelles, warned both the English and the Russians of the dangers involved, and for months those in charge of the negotiations on both sides tacitly agreed not to raise it. Isvolsky, knowing England's traditional attitude on the question, shrank from the risk of a refusal. In fact, circumstances had changed more than he realized. At the beginning of 1903 Balfour, in a report submitted to the Committee of Imperial Defence, had stated that a passage of the Russian fleet from the Black Sea into the Mediterranean would no longer endanger the European balance of power, as would have been the case fifty years earlier.[3] But Grey did not wish to show his hand by raising the question first.[4] When Benckendorff, the Russian ambassador in London, on a visit to Petersburg, attempted to discuss it with Nicolson, the latter replied that the Darda-

---

[1] *British Documents* . . . vol. v, pp. 168 sqq. *Die Grosse Politik* . . . vol. xxii, pp. 327 *n*.

[2] Spring-Rice to Sir Edward Grey, January 26, 1906: he reports a conversation which he had held with Count Benckendorff (*British Documents* . . . vol. iv, p. 222).

[3] Extract from Defence Committee Paper I B (*Report by Mr. Balfour of the conclusion arrived at on the 11th February in reference to Russia and Constantinople, February 12, 1903.* Quoted in a memorandum by Sir Charles Hardinge, November 16, 1906 (*British Documents* . . . vol. iv, p. 59).

[4] Sir Edward Grey to Sir Arthur Nicolson, November 1906 (*British Documents* . . . vol. iv, p. 414). Minute by Sir Edward Grey following a despatch from Sir Arthur Nicolson, January 30, 1907 (*British Documents* . . . vol. iv, p. 523).

nelles did not come within his instructions.[1] This was tantamount
to referring him to Sir Edward Grey. Benckendorff, therefore, on
his return to London, informed Grey of the Russian claim that
she should have the right to send her men-of-war into the Mediterranean, but the other powers should be not allowed to send theirs
into the Black Sea. His astonishment equalled his delight when
Grey told him frankly that the British Government had determined to abandon her former policy of closing the Straits to
Russia. He added, however, that it could not safely translate this
declaration into a public and documentary engagement. It would
arouse a storm of indignation in the country. Moreover, Russia
and England would act imprudently if they claimed to settle by
themselves a question which concerned all the powers.[2] Isolvsky
recognized the weight of these arguments. And he returned them
against England when the latter wanted a formal document recognizing her 'special interests' in the Persian Gulf. He was content to
take note of Grey's declaration, reserving the right to act upon it
when circumstances permitted.[3]

9

From all that has been said it is clear in what respects the Anglo-
Russian Convention of 1907 differed from the Anglo-French
entente of 1904. In both cases the superficial purport was the same,
nothing more than the settlement of outstanding colonial questions. But in the former case all, or at least all which presented a
serious character, were settled. In the latter some were deliberately
passed over and they were precisely those which, to judge from

[1] Sir Arthur Nicolson to Sir Edward Grey, February 10, 1907 (*British Documents* . . . vol.
iv, p. 272).
[2] Memorandum by Sir Edward Grey, March 15, 1907; Sir Edward Grey to Sir Arthur
Nicolson, March 19, 1907 (*British Documents* . . . vol. iv, pp. 279, 280).
[3] Sir Arthur Nicolson to Sir Edward Grey, March 27, 1907; Note by Sir C. Hardinge,
April 2, 1907; Sir Arthur Nicolson to Sir Edward Grey, April 14, 1907; Sir Arthur Nicolson to Sir Edward Grey, communicating a memorandum of Isvolsky's—same date; Sir
Edward Grey to Sir A. Nicolson May 1, 1907, enclosing a memorandum to be submitted
to Isvolsky; Sir A. Nicolson to Sir Edward Grey, July 10, 1907, communicating a memorandum of Isvolsky's; Sir Edward Grey to H. J. O'Beirne, July 31, 1907. In September
Isvolsky raised the question of a free passage through the Dardanelles by Russian men-of-
war during a series of interviews with Aehrenthal: Baron von Aehrenthal to Prince von
Bülow, October 31, 1907 (*Die Grosse Politik* . . . vol. xxii, p. 80). Cf. Prince von Bülow to
Baron von Aehrenthal, December 8, 1907; Baron Marschall to Prince von Bülow, December 14, 1907 (ibid., pp. 81 sqq., 83 sqq.).

past experience, were likely to prove serious later on. In the former case the reconciliation was not merely political. Public feeling in both countries became friendly, in spite of the reluctance displayed in certain quarters, particularly in France. In the latter there was nothing of the kind: not a word was heard of an *entente cordiale.* Moreover the Russians were very careful to maintain contact with Germany, to keep her in touch with the negotiations and remove any anxiety she might feel as to the nature of the new relations between England and Russia. Even explicit declarations by German statesmen that they had no objection to raise were insufficient to reassure Isvolsky. He remembered that Bülow had said the same when the agreement between England and France was published in April 1904, and all Europe knew what had followed. This constant anxiety to keep Germany's friendship disturbed the Foreign Office, and its alarm reached a head when, in October 1906, Isvolsky visited Berlin and Paris while excusing himself from a visit to London.[1] The alarm will seem justified when we remember what powerful friends Germany possessed at the Russian court. Many in the Czar's *entourage* resigned themselves to the Convention only because it allowed Russia to liquidate on the most favourable terms possible the vast enterprise of imperial expansion in Asia which was on the verge of failure, made it easier for her to obtain from the West the money necessary for her recovery and left her perfectly free later on when she regained her strength to pursue whatever policy she might choose.[2] Like the war itself, the policy which led up to it had its two fronts, an eastern and a western, distinct from each other and very imperfectly linked.

Nevertheless Germany had cause for anxiety. The more so since

---

[1] *British Documents . . .* vol. iv, pp. 243 sqq. Even in the summer of 1907 when the Convention was ready for signature the British representative at Munich, Cartwright, could write to his Government on August 7: 'The dream of reconstituting the Alliance between the three Emperors undoubtedly exists in some quarters. . . . The part that Monsieur Isvolsky may play in bringing this about is still uncertain, but he is generally credited with not being adverse to Russia following such a course. . . . If one is to believe what one hears Monsieur Isvolsky's sympathies lean more towards Germany than towards France' (*British Documents . . .* vol. vi, p. 41).

[2] In 'September 1907 Russia and Great Britain concluded a treaty relating to Persia, Afghanistan and Tibet. The convention inaugurated the policy of philandering with England. Since we did not give up our traditional flirting with Germany, the situation became rather ambiguous. At present we are trying to adjust ourselves to it by assuring Germany that of course we love her best and that we are flirting with England merely for appearance's sake, while to England we say the reverse. I believe we shall soon have to pay for this duplicity' (*Memoirs of Count Witte,* p. 432).

the Convention was preceded by the conclusion of two treaties of friendship between France and Japan and between Russia and Japan. These two treaties, of which the former was signed on June 10, the second on July 30, had presumably been concluded under the auspices of the Foreign Office. Nor was this all. On June 16 the text was published of two declarations couched in identical terms and exchanged respectively on May 16 between England and Spain, and France and Spain, which undertook to maintain the territorial *status quo* in the Mediterranean and that portion of the Atlantic which washed the coasts of Europe and Africa,[1] and the rumour was current that a secret pact of the same kind had been concluded between England and Germany's official ally, Italy. Germany determined to reply to these agreements by another to be concluded with Russia, Sweden, and Denmark for the maintenance of the *status quo* in the Baltic and, to make the agreement possible, obtained from France and England a renunciation of the right of control over the Baltic won by their joint victories in the Crimean War. Though the French Government consented, because it did not wish to refuse a request of its Russian ally, it was a very grudging consent. But when Germany sought to push her advantage further and proposed an agreement between England, Denmark, Sweden, Holland and Belgium for the maintenance of the *status quo* in the North Sea, Sir Edward Grey insisted that France should be included, as mistress of Dunkirk.[2] German policy had missed

---

[1] We know today the complete history of these agreements. In 1898 England had attempted to force upon Spain an alliance, directed against France, which would have amounted to a naval and military control of Spain by England. When in June 1905 the King of Spain visited the King of England Lord Lansdowne made a similar but far more moderate suggestion for an alliance, to be directed this time against Germany. Sir Arthur Nicolson, British Ambassador at Madrid, communicated Lord Lansdowne's proposal to Jules Cambon, the French Ambassador. The brothers Cambon took it up and transformed it eighteen months later (December 1906) into a project for an agreement between France, England, and Spain to maintain the *status quo*. The proposal met with a hostile reception in London, since the British Government did not desire to make the negotiation of the Anglo-Russian agreement more difficult by negotiating another anti-German pact. Finally, as the result it would seem of the visit which Edward VII paid to Carthagena in April accompanied by Sir Charles Hardinge, England put forward the suggestion which was accepted by the French and Spanish Governments of two agreements to be drawn up in identical terms and signed simultaneously, between England and Spain on the one hand, between France and Spain on the other (*British Documents* ... vol. vii, pp. 1 sqq.; especially pp. 1–3, 6–9, 21–2). This is an instance in which the application of their new policy led Sir Edward Grey and the Foreign Office a little further than they had intended to go.

[2] The two agreements were signed at Berlin on April 23, 1908. For the circumstances under which they were concluded see Viscount Grey of Fallodon, *Twenty-Five Years 1892-1916*, vol. i, pp. 143 sqq.; *Die Grosse Politik* ... vol. xxiii[11], pp. 400 sqq.

its mark. Germany was obliged to content herself with the Baltic agreement, a very feeble reply to so many achievements of British diplomacy which she could not but regard as manifestations of hostility towards herself. All or almost all the nations of the world had concluded agreements with one another; Germany was left in isolation.

Agreements, no doubt, not 'alliances'. But with an indiscreet jubilation a section of the Parisian press represented the agreements between France, England, and Spain as amounting to nothing short of an alliance,[1] and an English Conservative organ betrayed the secret wishes of one section at least of the public by announcing the signature of the Anglo-Russian Convention as the conclusion of a 'treaty' and the formation of an 'alliance'.[2] Moreover, the Convention had hardly been signed when a series of visits to Russia by officers of the British staff began—visits without precedent in history. General French visited Russia in the autumn of 1907, General Ian Hamilton the following spring.[3] And these visits were paid at a time when it was being rumoured on the Continent that a military convention had been secretly concluded between France and England, and that the staffs of both countries had agreed upon the measures to be adopted in the event of a joint campaign against the German army. How much truth was there in this rumour? And if it were well founded,

---

[1] Von Mühlberg to Prince von Bülow, June 22, 1907: 'I took the opportunity to observe to M. Cambon that even if the contents of the agreements did not directly affect our interests, the manner in which they were staged—publication on the day when The Hague Conference opened, two inaccurate despatches of the Agence Havas, the secrecy with which they were concluded, jubilant utterances in the French Press—could not fail to arouse considerable anxiety in Germany. It was not surprising that such comments as had appeared in the *Matin*, that questions of European policy would be settled without consulting Germany, were ill-received by German opinion. We had taken pains to restrain the language of our Press. The French Press had adopted a different attitude to the transaction from the English. The *Standard* had even pointed out that any attempt to read into the declarations a significance hostile to Germany would be folly' (*Die Grosse Politik* . . . vol. xxi[11], p. 571).

[2] '. . . A treaty has been concluded. . . . In fact the new Convention perfects and completes the imposing edifice of alliances which now enshrines the peace of the world' (*Daily Telegraph*, September 2, 1907).

[3] Von Miquel to Prince von Bülow, October 9, 1907; note by William II: 'The policy of investment proceeds noiselessly and inevitably in spite of the invitation to Windsor which is a mere blind intended to throw dust in the eyes of fools in both countries.' 'French's mission to Petersburg three weeks before my visit to London is *unprecedented*, the more so since it is well known that no German general has been officially invited to Russia for the last forty or fifty years' (*Die Grosse Politik* . . . vol. xxv[1], p. 48). A report circulated in Berlin which Reuter's Agency was obliged to contradict that a formal alliance had been concluded between Russia, France, England and Japan (*Die Grosse Politik* . . . vol. xxv[1], pp. 53 sqq.).

what was the character of the arrangements concluded between the staffs of the two armies? Before answering, we must study as a whole the measures adopted to reorganize the military defences of the United Kingdom by the new minister for war, Richard Burdon Haldane.

II HALDANE AND ARMY REORGANIZATION

I

To understand the bearing of the reforms which Haldane accomplished at the War Office during his seven years as Secretary for War we must know the exact nature of the problem with which the British Government had been faced, since the experiences of the Boer War had compelled it to recognize that a thoroughgoing reform of the army must be effected to prepare for the eventuality either of another war of the same kind or of the European conflict in which it seemed inevitable that England would one day be involved. What pattern should this work of reorganization follow? Here as everywhere else the model nation exercised its attraction. Germany had created an original type of large standing army, an object of alarm to her neighbours, which by summoning to the colours all healthy young men for a period of two or even three years, seemed to combine the advantages of a professional army and a militia. There were indeed many—especially since the Boer War—who wished to see England adopt conscription. But this demand, of considerable strength so long as the war lasted and with which moreover the Government appeared to agree,[1] lost much of its force when peace had been restored and dislike of war and the military profession regained the ascendancy over fear of the enemy and martial enthusiasm.

---

[1] H. of C., March 8, 1901, Brodrick's speech: '. . . I do not doubt that man for man a voluntary army is better than a conscription army, but man for man a trained army of conscripts is better than an incompletely trained army of volunteers and especially if it happens to outnumber them. Therefore, my adhesion to the voluntary system is strictly limited by our ability to obtain under it a force with which our military authorities can satisfy the Government that they have sufficient force to resist invasion and can maintain it to their satisfaction. At the same time, the Government fully recognize that while the country is willing to pay heavily to escape invasion, it is incumbent on the Government to exhaust every means before coming forward with any such proposals, and especially under the circumstances of the present time' (*Parliamentary Debates*, 4th Series, vol. xc, p. 1060).

Moreover, conscription of the Prussian type found very few supporters in England.[1] Those who were regarded as its advocates were usually content to ask for something very different.

Some asked for national training—that is to say, compulsory military exercises during which the men would not be quartered in a barracks or instruction camp. The Webbs, faithful to their principle of combining a Nationalist and Conservative policy with a policy of social reform of a Socialist tendency, advocated that the school age should be raised to seventeen or even eighteen, and military training given in connection with the curriculum. And a system of the same kind was supported by Blatchford, the Socialist jingo.

Others asked for what they called 'national service'. This was the programme of an important league founded in 1903 by Lord Roberts, who, in spite of his protests, was regarded by the public as the champion of 'conscription'. The four years of compulsory military service which he demanded for young men between eighteen and thirty involved nothing more than two months' training in an instruction camp in the first year, a fortnight in the following three.[2] But even in this extremely attenuated form conscription aroused invincible opposition.

This repugnance to compulsory military service was a sentiment of which the vast majority of Englishmen had learned to be proud; it came from the heart of their liberalism. It was in vain that the defenders of conscription pleaded that the system was in no way opposed either to the spirit of Anglo-Saxon civilization, since the Australian Commonwealth had accepted it, or even to the British Constitution, since balloting had been the old method of recruiting the militia, and if the system had long since fallen into desuetude it was only because every year Parliament automatically suspended the Ballot Act. It was equally useless to remind the opponents of conscription that the England of Crécy and Agincourt had known compulsory military service, that Wellington's

---

[1] Spencer Wilkinson, *Britain at Bay*, 1909, asked for two years of military service for the infantry and artillery, three years for the cavalry and mounted infantry, the men in some cases to remain in the service up to the age of thirty-nine.

[2] *The National Service Journal*, No. 1, November 1903. For schemes of a similar nature see further G. C. Coulton, *A Strong Army in a Free State: A Study of the Old English and Modern Swiss Militia*, 1900. Richard Benett of Liverpool, *Two Million Civilian Soldiers of the Queen*, 1900; Samuel Smith, 'National Defence', a letter in *The Times* and an article from the *Spectator*, March 1, 1902. See further the Utopian and imaginative scheme sketched by Rudyard Kipling in four articles entitled 'The Army of the Dream' (*Morning Post*, June 15, 16, 17, 18, 1904).

troops in part, Nelson's sailors wholly or almost wholly, had been 'conscripts' and that until 1870 the Liberals had been as strongly opposed to compulsory education as to conscription. It was labour lost. These arguments fell on deaf ears, for popular prejudice was stronger than any argument. We must not be deceived by the fact that a number of English Socialists advocated in a modified form a system of conscription. They were but a handful of eccentric individuals. The existing system of voluntary enlistment had no more hearty defenders than the trade unions which detested conscription. The same divergence of outlook became evident whenever the question of the army was discussed at an international Socialist congress. All the Continental Socialists advocated a militia system, the 'nation in arms' in place of an army trained in barracks. But it was in vain that they attempted to persuade the Labour party to accept a programme identical with that which was being advocated by the British Conservatives. Popular prejudice was, moreover, reinforced by the serious financial and even military arguments invoked by the opponents of conscription in support of their instinctive dislike.

In the first place, we must remember that in the case of Great Britain the problem of national defence presented a totally different aspect from that which it possessed in the case of the great Continental Powers. Because the latter were Continental, they were obliged before all else to maintain large standing armies to protect their soil against the possible invasion of their land frontiers. Only when this had been done could they bear the expense, if sufficiently wealthy, of supporting a fleet to increase their prestige on distant seas, annex a colonial empire and protect its communications with the mother country. The United Kingdom, on the contrary, had only maritime frontiers. Its first necessity therefore was a navy, and an army was but a secondary weapon, whether for the defence of the mother country or the annexation and defence of Colonies. Throughout the whole or almost the whole of the nineteenth century the army had indeed cost more than the navy. But this was because of the fact that a professional army, however small, is expensive and that England had only one rival at sea—namely, France, and she was far less formidable than she had been in the seventeenth and eighteenth centuries. From the moment when, towards the close of the century, the number of great naval powers increased, England had found herself compelled to increase her navy so as to be in a position to meet a possible combination of hostile fleets. The cost of the navy had equalled, then exceeded, the cost of the army. The demands of the South African War had once more increased to a formidable extent the expenditure upon the army. But this was an abnormal and a temporary phenomenon. In 1904 the army estimates fell to £29,225,000 as against a navy estimate of £36,830,000.[1] Would it now be found necessary to reverse the proportion? Possibly, if England must indeed maintain an army comparable in size with those of France and Germany and at the same time a navy stronger than the French and German combined. But was such an army necessary? Yes, if England were in fact exposed to the danger of invasion, the landing on her shores of a large Continental army.

The question engaged the attention of the Committee of Imperial Defence created at the beginning of 1903 by Arthur Balfour, the Prime Minister. It would seem that originally the composition of the Committee was not fixed and that to each meeting the Premier, the sole permanent member, invited whatever members of the cabinet, Generals, Admirals or experts in a particular department he thought fit. Gradually, it seems to have become the custom that any person once invited should be invited every year, and that the inner Committee should be composed of permanent members, a number of highly placed functionaries, Ministers or otherwise, civilians and soldiers. The custom grew up of inviting the heads of the Government Departments and also, when opportunity offered, statesmen from the Dominions. Five years after its creation Lowell, in his study of the British

---

[1] Taking as typical those years during which the British Government was able to reduce the expenditure on national defence to a minimum, we find the following proportion between the army and navy estimates—Financial year 1858–9: Army estimates £13,295,000, Navy estimates £19,215,000; Financial year 1870–1: Army estimates £14,124,000, Navy estimates £8,970,000. Then both figures rise, but the second more rapidly than the first. In 1895–6 the cost of the navy for the first time exceeded the cost of the army: £19,724,000 as against £18,460,000. Period of the Boer War—Budget of 1901–2: Army estimates £92,542,000, Navy estimates £31,030,000. Budget of 1904–5: Army estimates £29,225,000, Navy estimates £36,830,000. We must remember that in the case of an 'imperial' power like Great Britain such figures can be disputed. If the Colonies contributed nothing or almost nothing, to the normal defence of the Empire, it was not the same with the land forces. Sir Charles Dilke (H. of C., February 23, 1903, *Parliamentary Debates*, 4th Series, vol. cxviii, pp. 543–4) estimated that when India, the Dominions, and the forces under the control of the Foreign and Colonial Offices were taken into account, the total sum expended by the British Empire on her land armaments exceeded £50,000,000. These and the following calculations are therefore true only of the mother country, the United Kingdom.

Constitution, still expressed doubts as to the future of the Committee.[1] But the following years would prove it a hardy and vigorous institution. When war came the Committee would assume supreme control of military operations on behalf of the United Kingdom and the entire Empire. Meanwhile, in peacetime it functioned as the supreme council for military and naval defence, to whose decision both the War Office and the Admiralty submitted their often conflicting plans. To transcend the professional limitations of the military and naval experts and co-ordinate army and navy in the wider interest of the nation and Empire was the principal function of the Committee. But it rapidly tended to become a sort of super-cabinet, half civilian, half military, whose institution constituted an important innovation in British constitutional history.[2] It had not been in existence for two years when this critical question of the danger of invasion was brought before it. The supposition was made that the regular army was engaged in a foreign campaign far from Britain and the naval squadrons were all in distant waters. Lord Roberts was asked what was the size of the army with which, in his opinion, in view of all the difficulties and risks of transport, an enemy might contemplate invading Great Britain. He replied that he thought it possible to land a foreign army of 70,000 men. The Committee came to the conclusion with, it would seem, at least the provisional agreement of Lord Roberts, that a force of 70,000, supposing it were possible to land it, would be too small to attempt an attack upon London. And it was far from certain that the landing would be possible. Steam transport, wireless telegraphy, submarines were all inventions which favoured the defence. In short, a foreign army fighting on British soil was not a serious possibility.[3] Balfour in the speech in which he explained the Committee's

---

[1] 'The Committee is intended to deal not only with estimates, but with larger questions of military policy. But whether the result will be permanently attained, or whether the Committee will meet with the usual fate and find itself absorbed by details of administration and of expenditure is yet to be seen.' (A. Lawrence Lowell, *The Government of England*, vol. i, p. 105.) For the origins and development of the Committee see the interesting information in Arnold-Forster, *The Army in 1906*, 1906, p. 388; and General Sir Ian Hamilton, *Compulsory Service: A Study of the Question in the Light of Experience*, 1911; Introduction by the Right Hon. R. B. Haldane, pp. 15–17.

[2] For the serious nature of this innovation which might be regarded as violating the principle of ministerial responsibility see the debate in the House of Commons, March 5, 1903 (*Parliamentary Debates*, 4th Series, vol. cxviii, pp. 1570 sqq.).

[3] H. of C., May 11, 1905 (ibid., vol. cxlvi, pp. 62 sqq. especially p. 70). Balfour's language is clearly calculated to give the impression that Lord Roberts agreed with the Committee. But was this anything more than a rhetorical artifice? This at any rate is

views to the House of Commons considered the possibility—he was careful to add immediately 'purely hypothetical'—of a French army, embarked at Brest or Cherbourg, landing on the south coast. The supposition was a transparent device which deceived nobody barely a month before Delcassé's fall when the Tangier incident held public attention. It was Germany which was in the mind of Balfour and his audience. But because fear of Germany continued to grow during the years which followed, the Committee found itself obliged in November 1907 to study the question afresh to reassure the public. As in 1905 it reached the conclusion 'that invasion (so long as our naval supremacy is assured against any reasonably probable combination of Powers) by a force assumed, for purposes of calculation, to be 70,000 men, is impracticable'.

We must be careful not to misunderstand the argument which Balfour developed on May 11, 1905—a speech in which he expounded the views of what was known as the Blue Water School—because it regarded the 'blue water' surrounding Britain as her rampart. Balfour did not say 'the fleet is there, sleep in peace'. This would not have met the contention of the advocates of conscription that a conscript army by mounting guard over the coast would release the fleet for distant operations. It was the view of the Admiralty, shared by the Committee of Imperial Defence, that even in the absence of the fleet, mines and submarines were sufficient to defend the coast. As for the ill-organized reserve forces, militia, volunteers, and yeomanry, neither soldiers nor sailors took them into serious consideration. Professional soldiers had no interest in the militia except as a recruiting ground for the regular army. They were content to leave the volunteers, whom they despised, to their customary disorganization. This was a source of considerable embarrassment to the advocates of con-

certain. Six years later at a time, moreover, when the creation of the territorial army had strengthened the reserve forces, his point of view was entirely different (*Fallacies and Facts* 1911, pp. 120 sqq.). Cf. the article signed Master Mariner in the *Contemporary Review* for February 1909, inspired, Lord Roberts affirms in his criticism of the article, by the War Office. Further, Balfour in his speech did not seem to contemplate an invading force of more than 5,000. The question was again submitted in November 1907 to a sub-committee of the Committee of Imperial Defence. Its conclusions were given to the House of Commons by Asquith on July 29, 1909 (*Parl. Deb.*, Commons, 1909, 5th Ser., vol. viii, pp. 1356 sqq.), who on this occasion envisaged once more the possibility of a force of 70,000 invading England. But the implications of such a figure must be realized. 'We should', he said, 'have a home army not only adequate to repel raids . . . but a much more serious thing—to compel an enemy which contemplates invasion to come with such substantial force as to make it impossible for them to evade our fleet' (ibid., p. 1388).

scription—they were unwilling to avow openly that, if they wanted a citizen army, it was for entirely different reasons. They were obliged to admit that the needs of the navy took precedence over those of the army, and accept the proportion laid down as normal by the Navy League between the respective expenditure on the army and the navy, twenty-four as against thirty-six million. They were content to urge the necessity of increasing the expenditure on the army *pari passu* with the increase in naval expenditure to provide for other needs than those we have mentioned hitherto. What were they? To answer the question we must first study the various and complicated functions which the regular army fulfilled.

2

The primary function of the British army was to garrison the vast extent of the British Empire, to maintain internal order, and protect the frontiers. In North America there were garrisons in Bermuda and at Halifax. On the route to India and the Far East garrisons were stationed at Gibraltar, in Malta, at Singapore, in Mauritius, and at Hongkong. A brigade—three battalions, in all over four thousand troops—constituted the army of occupation in Egypt. After the restoration of peace in South Africa it had been necessary to leave a force of twenty-five thousand in the country and there was no reason to suppose that it could be reduced in the near future. Finally there were fifty-two battalions —seventy-six thousand men—in British India and at Aden. Obviously these outposts could not be permanently occupied by an army of young conscripts serving two or three years with the colours. More seasoned troops, inured to a lengthy period of life in barracks, were necessary. The system of short service enlistments in existence at the period of the Boer War was only a system of *short* service by comparison with the *long* service of the period before 1872. Measured by Continental standards the seven years' enlistment substituted for the previous twelve was an extraordinarily long service. And it was to furnish the necessary troops to replenish the foreign garrisons, constantly reduced by disease or as the men's term of service expired, that Cardwell, the Secretary for War, had devised in 1871 that system of linked battalions whose principle we have already had occasion to explain. Each regiment was composed of two battalions. One of these was on service abroad. The other, the home battalion, while kept in constant readiness to take part in a campaign abroad, served as a recruiting ground and training barracks for the foreign unit.[1]

The system was not always easy to work. When after 1895 the Government embarked on a policy of imperialist annexation the number of battalions serving abroad increased so considerably that it was no longer possible to provide each with a home battalion. And home battalions had been despatched to distant Colonies. On one occasion, against all precedent, a battalion of the Guards had been sent to garrison Gibraltar. But the system had broken down completely when, in 1899, it became necessary to rush a large army to South Africa. This was a problem for which it was plain that Cardwell's system of linked battalions could provide no solution, and the British nation began to realize the danger to which it would be exposed, sooner or later, of a war far more serious than the Boer War, in which to resist a European foe it would be necessary to employ not only the entire navy but the entire army as well.

To what quarter did it seem likely that this expeditionary force, which had to be improvised at the end of 1899, would be sent? The traditional view, common to the War Office and the Admiralty, envisaged its despatch after the conclusion of the Boer War to British India to meet the Russian menace.[2] The British navy

[1] For Cardwell's system see the excellent chapter by General Sir Robert Biddulph, *Lord Cardwell at the War Office: A History of his Administration 1868–1874*, 1904, pp. 161 sqq.

[2] L. S. Amery, *The Problem of the Army*, 1903 (the preface is dated November 1) p. 146: 'The Russian Empire can fairly be described as our most formidable and also most probable military adversary.' H. of C., March 7, 1904, Arnold-Forster's speech: '. . . We propose to complete during the next year 108 field guns and eighteen Royal Horse Artillery guns . . . India is the only possible place of contact with a great European Army. . . . There will be greater value for these guns in India than there would be here, and therefore we propose to assign to India practically the whole of the output of these guns for the coming year' (*Parliamentary Debates*, 4th Series, vol. cxxxi, pp. 342–3). H. of C., March 9, 1904, Balfour's speech: '. . . Though I do not believe that this landing of a great organized force . . . is possible, no man can blind himself to the fact that the whole trend of circumstances in the East is to make us a Continental Power conterminous with another great military Continental Power, and that is the dominating circumstance which we have to take into account in framing our Army Estimates' (ibid., vol. cxxxi, pp. 623–4). H. of C., June 28, 1904, Arnold-Forster's speech: '. . . We have had the guidance of the Committee of Defence . . . upon the general problem as to the work the Army has to do outside the United Kingdom and we have realized that oversea work would be the great demand on our Army. Of all the problems of oversea the most pressing, the most definite in one sense, the most indefinite in another sense, must be the problem which may arise on the only great land frontier we have. The Indian problem is a very complicated one. . . .' (ibid., vol. cxxxvi, p. 1497). H. of C., May 11, 1905, Balfour's great speech (ibid., vol.

would therefore be responsible for conveying an enormous army from Europe to Asia, either by rounding South Africa or traversing the Mediterranean, where, as in a closed vessel, the ambitions of a host of different nations clashed. The transport of the British troops to South Africa had been a brilliant success, which had aroused universal admiration at a time when Britain's military organization was the object of severe and well-merited criticism. But it would have been impossible if the seas had been scoured by hostile cruisers and submarines, and the German naval law of 1900, while increasing the danger of this, suggested new possibilities to British sailors—the despatch of an expeditionary force to Flanders to meet a German invasion, side by side with the French army and the small Belgian army, or preferably to Hanover to create a diversion.

It was a new problem which at once involved a concerted plan between the army and the navy. The Admiralty laid down as a fundamental principle that an expeditionary force could not be transported abroad until the seas had been cleared of the enemy. It must have time to win another Trafalgar. This would require nine months at most. It would then be able to undertake the transport of an army. It was an obstacle which the impatience of the War Office could ill brook. But an obstacle perhaps which had its advantages in the eyes of the champions of conscription. The latter, as we have seen, did not advocate conscription in the full sense. They did not claim that the short periods of military service which their programme demanded would enable those who had performed them to go to the front immediately a war was declared. But if they were mobilized at once the delay imposed on the War Office by the tactics of the Admiralty would give time for an intensive training. When after some months the Admiralty declared the seas clear they could be profitably amalgamated with the old professional army. Thus, without daring to say so publicly for fear of alienating still further a public opinion already hostile, the advocates of National Service contemplated the possibility of sending British conscripts on active

cxlvi, pp. 78 sqq.). Ten months later the tone has completely changed: H. of C., March 8, 1906, Haldane's speech: '. . . A short time ago we were menaced on the N.W. frontier of India by Russia. Are we menaced by Russia today? (Cries of No.) Have circumstances changed or have they not? Are they not different from what they were? If circumstances have changed, is it necessary to maintain that vast establishment in India, which causes us at home inevitably to incur a large expenditure in keeping up the materials from which to supply drafts for the Indian Army?' (ibid., vol. cliii, p. 675).

service abroad. Not to India, indeed; that was out of the question. But possibly to the Continent. If in 1805 England had possessed a conscript army, it would not have taken herself and her allies ten years' hard struggle to complete Trafalgar by Waterloo.

3

The task of reorganizing the army was begun in 1901 in the midst of the Boer War by Lord Lansdowne's successor at the War Office, St. John Brodrick. For the moment he refrained from asking for conscription. Without adopting that extreme measure he determined to imitate the German model and put an end once and for all to the condition of sheer chaos which had come to seem the natural state of the British army—nothing but isolated regiments, no regular grouping of brigades, divisions, or army corps, and no centre of organization except the War Office. He proposed, and actually began to carry into effect, the establishment of six army corps in the United Kingdom. There were to be three in the South of England, one in the North, one in Ireland, and one in Scotland. Each army corps constituted a complete and permanent unit with its staff, its infantry, its cavalry, its artillery, its medical corps, and its commissariat. A valuable work of decentralization would thus be accomplished. The fact that so much would be done within each army corps would relieve considerably the congestion at the War Office. And on the other hand a sudden international crisis would not find the country unprepared as it had been in 1899. Three of these army corps would be kept in readiness for active service, which would mean a force of twenty thousand available for immediate despatch abroad. Several measures were taken to obtain the necessary number of recruits. The pay was raised from 7d. in 1896 to 1/6 in 1904. The conditions of life in barracks were improved; the soldiers were treated a little more as men, a little less as machines. Brodrick further devised a new system of short-service enlistments—three years with the colours, nine in the reserve—which had the advantage of attracting more recruits. And if their period of service was shorter, they remained liable to be called up at any moment. Here too—conscription apart—the German model was followed. Finally, to prevent the constant depletion of the home battalions to replenish those on foreign service, Brodrick, abandoning for the first time the system of linked battalions, created a Royal Garrison Regiment to invite the enlistment of soldiers who, having completed their period of service, were willing to lead at Gibraltar. for example, or in Malta an easy and inactive life as sentinels of the empire.[1]

But the scheme immediately aroused lively criticism,[2] both from the Gladstonians, who thought that it went too far, and the Imperialists, who thought that it was on the wrong lines. The former protested against the serious cost of maintaining permanently six army corps. It would involve, they argued, when the system was in full working, an annual expenditure upon the army of £40,000,000. The latter denounced Brodrick as an illusionist. Only the first three army corps were genuine army corps. The other three existed only on paper and were a mixture of professional soldiers and volunteers. It was to a motley force of this kind that it was proposed to entrust the defence of Great Britain when the expeditionary force had gone abroad! And finally there was one point on which everyone agreed, that Brodrick's scheme must be modified. The enlistments for three years had worked well when recruits were wanted in large numbers for a war which could not last very long. But the system became unworkable when soldiers were needed to relieve the garrisons in distant colonial possessions. Soldiers were actually being sent out to India to serve only ten months, And about the summer of 1903 the War Office began to find itself unable to obtain recruits even on these terms. These distant garrisons were rapidly becoming depleted.[3]

---

[1] For an account of Brodrick's system see his speech, H. of C., March 8, 1901 (*Parliamentary Debates*, 4th Series, vol. xc, pp. 1052 sqq.).

[2] H. of C., February 24, 1903, debate on Beckett's amendment to the address (ibid., vol. cxviii, pp. 682 sqq.). Winston Spencer Churchill, *Mr. Brodrick's Army*, 1903. L. S. Amery, *The Problem of the Army*, 1903, Chap. II, pp. 19 sqq.

[3] 'I have had means of finding out for certain, what the newspapers have so often guessed at, that the first four War Secretaries have with the greatest difficulty been able to supply sufficient drafts for India. Sums of so much as £15 of the taxpayers' money—what were they but bribes?—have been paid to soldiers in India, to get them to extend their service. Men suffering imprisonment in military prisons here in England have been released before the expiration of their sentences, on condition that they would "volunteer" for some regiment in India' (Robert Edmondson, Ex-Squadron Sergeant-Major, *John Bull's Army from Within, with an Introduction by Arnold White*, 1907).

4

When the Cabinet was reconstituted in September 1903, Brodrick was banished from the War Office, like his predecessor Lord Lansdowne at the end of 1900. He went to the India Office and was succeeded at the War Office by Arnold-Forster, who had made a reputation as an expert student of the problem of army reform.[1] It was a problem whose solution seemed more urgent than ever when the report of the Royal Commission appointed at the end of 1902 to inquire into the preparations for the Boer War and the conduct of the early operations had just been made public.[2] In its report, which appeared in August, the Commission had censured the absence of a plan of campaign, and of an expeditionary force ready for immediate embarkation, the lack of information, the insufficient supply of horses and means of transport, and the disorganization of the War Office. Arnold-Forster's position at the War Office was in one respect easier, in another more difficult, than Brodrick's had been. Easier, because unlike his predecessor he was not obliged to prepare his plans for reorganization in the middle of a war. More difficult because in 1903 the public, war-weary, had begun to demand economies rather than reforms, the reduction of the expenditure upon the army rather than its organization. Arnold-Forster was faced with the problem of achieving more than his predecessors with less money.

His work of reform was twofold. It was in the first place a reorganization of the War Office, secondly a reorganization of the army itself.

The Commission of Inquiry into the Boer War had denounced abuses rather than proposed remedies. It had however indicated the general lines on which a reform of the War Office should proceed,[3] and one of its members, Lord Esher, in a special appen-

[1] See his work, *The War Office, the Army and the Empire: A review of the Military Situation in 1900 . . . with a Preface by the Rt. Hon. The Earl of Rosebery,* 1900.

[2] *Royal Commission on the War in South Africa: A Commission appointed to inquire into the military preparations for the War of South Africa and into the supply of men, ammunition, equipment and transport by sea and in campaign and into the military operations up to the Occupation of Pretoria.* Appointed in October 1902, it consisted of Lord Elgin, the Chairman, and eight other members, among them Lord Esher. It heard a hundred and fourteen witnesses and reported on August 25, 1903. A very complete summary will be found in *The Times* for August 26.

[3] *Report,* p. 132 sqq.

dix[1] had given a more definite shape to the plan suggested by the Commission. Lord Esher and his colleagues had criticized the anomalous position of the Commander-in-Chief, in relation to the Secretary for War. It had not been defined by law or custom. The Commission also recalled that Lord Hartington's Commission had in 1890 advised the abolition of the post, that it had nevertheless been retained, although with reduced powers, by the Unionist Government of 1895 and that the Commander-in-Chief, Lord Wolseley, had taken advantage of the Boer War to extend his authority, an attempt which had led to considerable friction. The Commission recommended that the Commander-in-Chief should be replaced by an Inspector-General wholly independent of the War Office whose function it would be to present an annual report, showing how far the wishes of Parliament had been carried out in the organization of the army. Further, the Commission, repeating recommendations made both by the Hartington Commission[2] and a Committee of 1901[3] advised that to secure unity and continuity of policy, the joint authority of the departments of the War Office should be reinforced by combining the various branches of the service in an organization which would occupy a position in regard to the army similar to that of the Board of Admiralty in regard to the navy. Arnold-Forster had scarcely entered the War Office when, in concert with the Prime Minister, Balfour, he appointed a small committee of three —Lord Esher, Admiral Sir John Fisher, and Sir George Clarke, the future Lord Sydenham, to work out these recommendations in a detailed form. Three long reports published in rapid succession satisfied the reformers.[4] At the same time to strengthen the Committee of Imperial Defence and protect it against the possible whims of some future Liberal premier, the Committee recommended that it should be turned into a regular department of state by setting up a 'permanent secretariat' to consist of a repre-

---

[1] *Report*, p. 144 sqq.

[2] *Preliminary and further Reports of the Royal Commissioners appointed to inquire into the Civil and Professional Administration of the Naval and Military Departments, and the relations of these departments to each other and to the Treasury*, 1890, p. xxi.

[3] Its chairman was Sir Clinton Dawkins. Its object was among others to inquire 'whether the present method of conducting the administrative and financial business of the War Office and its distribution as between the Civil and Military Departments is satisfactory' and to suggest methods 'which would bring the work of the War Office more into harmony with that of large business undertakings'.

[4] *War Office (Reconstruction) Committee. First Report*, January 18, 1904. *Second Report*, February 26, 1904. *Third Report*, March 9, 1904.

sentative of the army and a representative of the navy with their subordinates. Its function would be to furnish the civilian members of the Committee with all the technical information they might require and also—though this was not directly stated—to enforce conformity to the official policy if the civilians were suspected of deviating from it.

On this, as on other points, the recommendations of the Committee were immediately carried into effect. The first report had scarcely been published on February 1, when Arnold-Forster instituted the Army Council, a copy of the Board of Admiralty, for which the Committee had asked. The Committee had recommended that all its members should be new men. He carried out its recommendation. So far as the three civilian members were concerned, this was effected automatically, since he had brought with him to the War Office a new under-secretary and a new financial secretary. But the four military members were also newcomers, not one of whom had previously been at the War Office. They were the Chief of General Staff, responsible for collecting information and making the strategic preparations for a war, the Adjutant-General in charge of the personnel, the Quarter-Master General in charge of supplies, and the Master General of the Ordnance responsible for the artillery and fortifications. There was no longer any Commander-in-Chief, and the first Inspector-General, whose functions were very strictly limited, was the King's brother, the Duke of Connaught. The Government attempted to obtain for the new council the express sanction of a statute. But the Bill was dropped, it would seem because the opposition of constitutionalists who disliked this supervision of responsible ministers by a bureaucratic institution had proved embarrassing.[1] The Army Council was set up notwithstanding by letters patent and an order in council. It was a permanent institution, altogether different from the War Office Council set up during the Boer War by Brodrick, which derived all its authority from the Prime Minister, or the Army Board, of which the Commander-in-Chief, not the Secretary for War, had been chairman and which, revived in 1900, had disappeared once more

---

[1] For this opposition see H. of L., July 29, 1904, Lord Spencer's speech (*Parliamentary Debates*, 4th Series, vol. cxxxix, pp. 71 sqq.), and for the entire question the explanations given by R. B. Haldane, H. of L., April 6, 1909 (ibid., 1909, 5th Ser., vol. iii, pp. 934 sqq.).

with the restoration of peace.[1] In 1905 all the detailed arrangements of the various branches of the service were reorganized and brought into conformity with the four new departments.[2] The reform marked an epoch in the development of British military bureaucracy, and British bureaucracy in general. Arnold-Forster was less successful when he tackled a vaster problem, the reform of the army itself.

5

We might have expected that his work of reform would have been made easier by the Royal Commission on the militia and volunteers appointed in 1903, which reported on May 20, 1904.[3] But if the report established the urgent necessity of reform, it contained practically no useful suggestions as to the reforms which should be made. As regards the militia the Commission suggested that the periods of training and of service should be lengthened and brigades and divisions set up; as regards the volunteers, an alteration of the system according to which the Government grants were made, the institution at the War Office of a special department for the volunteers, and again the establishment of brigades and divisions. But it made these recommendations with great hesitation, or rather with indifference. The real conclusion the Commission reached was that since the five great Continental powers had possessed a conscript army for the last quarter of a century, England by her refusal to follow their example placed herself in the event of a war with any one of them in an inferior position from the start. Conscription therefore should be adopted —not even the modified system of the Swiss militia. This proves what a strong hold the principle of conscription possessed over military opinion. But how fantastic a suggestion of this kind was!

It is sufficient to read the report to perceive that the all but

---

[1] *Report of Royal Commission on the War in South Africa*, pp. 138 sqq.
[2] *Memorandum of the Secretary of State relating to the Army Estimates for 1905–6*, pp. 7 sqq.
[3] *Militia and Volunteers (Royal Commission) Report of the Royal Commission on the Militia and Volunteers with Appendices*, May 20, 1904. The Commission which consisted of eight members, its chairman being the Duke of Norfolk, had been appointed 'to inquire into the organization, numbers, and terms of service of the Militia and Volunteer Forces; and to report whether any and if any, what changes are required in order to secure that these forces shall be maintained in a condition of military efficiency and at an adequate strength'.

unanimous recommendations of the Commission were doomed from the outset to remain a dead letter, and that throughout the inquiry its members had been faced with departmental hostility when they attempted to obtain the information which would enable them to estimate exactly the risks of invasion against which the country should take precautions. After the War Office had informed them that the question they had to consider was the provision for home defence of an army of three hundred thousand, including sixty-six thousand regulars, they had consulted the Committee of Imperial Defence, which had pointed out that since the Admiralty declared it impossible to land more than five to ten thousand troops on the English coast there was no reason to ask for these three hundred thousand. They had thereupon betaken themselves to the Admiralty itself, which had declined to give evidence, and then once more to the Committee of Imperial Defence, whose chairman had been content to ask the Commission not to enlarge unduly the field of its inquiries.[1] It was very soon evident that the recommendations of the Commission had no practical importance, and when the question was raised in the House of Lords, Lord Lansdowne stated that in recommending conscription the Commission had exceeded its powers.[2] Arnold-Forster's system was totally different.

An admirer and student of the German army, as with good reason were all military experts, Arnold-Forster had reached the conclusion that an army quartered in barracks is superior to a militia. This had been sufficiently proved by the way in which General Chanzy's army had crumpled up in 1870 before the army of Prince Frederick-Charles. It was out of the question to introduce the Prussian system into England and make all physically-fit youths into soldiers living in barracks. The system already established in England must therefore be preserved—a professional army quartered in barracks and recruited by voluntary enlistment. Its organization, however, must be improved, while the number of soldiers was reduced. This would satisfy at once the Conservative demand for efficiency and the Liberal demand for economy. He abandoned the system of linked battalions which necessitated the maintenance at home of a number of battalions equal to that of the battalions serving abroad. He announced his

[1] *Report of Royal Commission on Militia and Volunteers*, pp. 4–5.
[2] H. of L., June 27, 1904 (*Parliamentary Debates*, 4th Series, vol. cxxxvi, pp. 1210 sqq.).

intention to abandon Brodrick's expensive system of six army corps. What the army reformers demanded, and in particular the Committee on the reorganization of the War Office, was a wide measure of administrative decentralization. But to place the entire burden of administering the army on the generals in command of the army corps would merely relieve the War Office by over-burdening the generals. He divided the United Kingdom for military purposes into a number of purely administrative districts. As regards the command he announced his intention to substitute for the army corps a too ambitious system which did not answer the genuine needs of the country, a system of divisions, and at the same time he promised to organize a striking force of sixteen thousand men ready for immediate despatch abroad. He dissolved nineteen battalions and proposed to equip the country with two distinct military organizations. On the one hand there would be a hundred and four 'general service' battalions with good pay and service enlistments—nine years with the colours, three in the reserve. On the other hand there would be seventy-one 'home service' battalions stationed in the counties and bearing their names, commanded by subalterns of the general service army and by officers interchangeable with officers of the latter. It would be the old militia but amalgamated with the regular army, the sole difference being the easier conditions and far shorter terms of service—two years with the colours, six in the reserve, and lower pay. The number of volunteers was reduced. The figure, reached in 1904, of two hundred and fifty thousand was too high. A hundred and eighty thousand would be enough. Arnold-Forster proposed to divide them into two classes. Sixty thousand, well paid, compactly organized, and subjected to a more severe training would constitute a genuine fighting force. The remaining hundred and twenty thousand, who would receive only the training given hitherto to all volunteers, would form a reserve which could be profitably employed in the event of war.[1]

As will appear later Arnold-Forster's scheme was not without its good points. It was a failure nevertheless. This was primarily

[1] Arnold-Forster explained his system at Liverpool on January 28, 1904, to the House of Commons on July 14 of the same year (*Parliamentary Debates*, 4th Series, vol. cxxxviii, pp. 52 sqq.), and in 1906 in a volume entitled *The Army in 1906: A Policy and a Vindication*, 1906. Cf. Lord Haliburton, *The Army Organization: The Arnold-Forster Scheme*, 1905, and Mrs. Arnold-Forster, *The Right Honourable Hugh Oakeley Arnold-Forster—A Memoir*, 1910, pp. 224 sqq.

due to defects inherent in a system which experience would compel his successor to abandon. These long-service enlistments of nine years had been adopted to satisfy the pressing need to replenish the garrisons depleted by the three-years' system which the necessities of the Boer War had forced on Brodrick. They had proved successful; in India and elsewhere in 1905 the battalions were at their full strength. But the system must inevitably break down the moment the nine-years' enlistments had to compete with the two-years' enlistments required to furnish the home-service battalions.

Arnold-Forster therefore postponed the latter scheme and a Militia Bill introduced in 1905 was a mere gesture. It was never even debated. The reorganization of the volunteers was also postponed.[1] And he had further difficulties to face. A member of a Conservative Cabinet, he did not find it easy to overcome the opposition of a host of vested interests. The speeches he delivered in Parliament during 1905 give the impression of an animal hunted down by a pack. 'I find I am dealing with at least six armies. I am dealing with the Army in India, the Indian Army, the Army at home, the Militia, the Volunteers, and the great army of those who have left the colours and are now entrenched in the clubs of this city.'[2] In the Cabinet itself he had to suffer from the intrigues of Lord Lansdowne and Brodrick, the two former Secretaries for War, who had no wish to see Forster succeed where they had failed and who spread the report that his plan represented only his personal views not those of the Government as a whole. Moreover, he belonged to a party in rapid decline and hastening towards the defeat at the polls whose imminence no one doubted. He was therefore exposed to a cross-fire, from the opposition speakers and from the irregulars of his own party. He vanished in 1905 in the general rout of the Unionists without having had time to effect anything. In the new Cabinet Richard Burdon Haldane took his place.

---

[1] *Memorandum of the Secretary of State relating to the Army Estimates for 1905–6*, p. 6; also Arnold-Forster, *The Army in 1906*, p. 211.

[2] H. of C., March 28, 1905 (*Parliamentary Debates*, 4th Series, vol. cxliii, pp. 1419–20). For the objections brought against his plan see especially the debate in the House of Lords on July 29, 1904 (ibid., vol. cxxxix, pp. 45 sqq.), and in the House of Commons, March 28, 1905 (ibid., vol. cxliii, pp. 1398 sqq.).

6

We have witnessed Haldane's attempt to make himself Lord Chancellor. When he saw him accept the War Office, Campbell-Bannerman believed he had entrapped a colleague who hated him, and whom he hated with equal cordiality. 'Serve him right,' an old friend wrote gleefully to the Premier on receipt of the news.[1] For Sir Henry knew better than anyone how dearly the War Office might cost a British politician. It was his conduct of the department which in the summer of 1895 had been, if not the real cause of the overthrow of the Liberal Cabinet, at any rate the immediate pretext. Since then he had been the amused and often sarcastic witness of the unfortunate efforts made by his successors —Lord Lansdowne, St. John Brodrick, and finally Arnold-Forster. 'Leave the old army alone and don't make war.' The device sums up his policy of inaction.[2] Haldane was a politician of the most active type. He was far too intelligent not to perceive the difficulties of the task he had so lightly assumed, as a member of a cabinet on principle indifferent to the army, and serving under a chief who distrusted him. But he believed himself capable of overcoming them. Moreover, he was aware of the unprecedented importance which attached to this question of army reorganization in the light of the inevitable conflict with Germany. By giving him the War Office Campbell-Bannerman flung him a challenge. He took it up.[3]

His first reform was the creation in September 1906 of a General Staff.[4] It consisted of seventy-two officers who met at the War Office with the Chief of Staff presiding to study problems of

[1] J. A. Spender, *The Life of the Right Hon. Sir Henry Campbell-Bannerman*, vol. ii, p. 198.

[2] See his speech H. of C., February 5, 1904 (an amendment to the Address was being debated complaining of England's unpreparedness for the Boer War): '. . . The right honourable gentleman says that in the time of his predecessor the defences of the colonies were so neglected that there were only two battalions or 3,000 men in South Africa and the Government had to raise the force. Yes, Sir, because the force depends upon your policy. At that time there was no ground for fear whatever. The force was adjusted to the policy. There are two policies that you can pursue in a case such as this. There is the policy of force and of threats resting upon force and on the other hand there is a policy of patience and of peaceful and conciliatory negotiation' (*Parliamentary Debates*, 4th Series, vol. cxxix, pp. 494–5). The following day the Unionist Press was up in arms. See *The Times*, February 6, 1904: '. . . The Opposition cannot first obstruct the reinforcement of our Army and then pose as censors of the Government for not reinforcing it.'

[3] For the work which Haldane accomplished at the War Office see the interesting details given by himself, *Before the War*, 1920, pp. 156 sqq.; *An Autobiography*, 1929, pp. 168 sqq.

[4] *Army Order constituting a General Staff*. The text will be found together with a summary of Haldane's memorandum accompanying it in *The Times* of September 13, 1906.

strategy. They followed in rotation and were obliged to return to active service when their time on the General Staff had expired. Such was the new institution with which Haldane equipped the War Office to provide, as he said, the British army with a 'brain'. In consequence the organization of the War Office, so long inferior to that of the Admiralty, became superior to it. The army was indebted to Arnold-Forster for an Army Council, a copy of the Board of Admiralty. Haldane provided the Army Council with a General Staff of which the Board of Admiralty possessed no counterpart. From what source did he get the idea of his new institution? From Germany as he frankly admitted. Moreover, his institution of the General Staff had been immediately preceded by a journey to Berlin to study German methods, which had caused keen anxiety in Paris and alarmed the Foreign Office itself.[1] Haldane thus began to play the ambiguous role he would maintain till 1914. An admirer, indeed a devotee of Germany, by his constant declarations of affection for the Germans, his friendship with the ambassador Metternich and his frequent visits to Germany, he reassured the advanced Liberals and the partisans of an Anglo-German *entente*. On the other hand, knowing Germany too well not to admire the genius for organization, military organization in particular, which rendered her England's most dangerous rival, and entertaining nothing but contempt for pacifist idealism, though at times to flatter Liberal opinion he used its phraseology, he prepared by German methods to wage war with Germany. This creation of a General Staff, however cleverly he may have staged it, was not however his personal work. As early as 1890 Lord Hartington's Commission had asked for it;[2] and Lord Esher's Committee again in 1904.[3] Arnold-Forster on the very eve of the fall of the Unionist Government had drawn up a complete scheme,[4] which except for a few modifications of detail

---

[1] R. B. Haldane, *Before the War*, pp. 22 sqq.; *An Autobiography*, pp. 89 sqq., 202 sqq.; *British Documents . . .* vol. iii, pp. 357–69, 372–3: see especially on p. 373 a minute by Sir Eric Barrington attached as a note to despatch sent from Berlin on August 30 by Lord Granville to Sir Edward Grey: 'We have done all we could short of preventing Mr. Haldane from going to Berlin at all.'

[2] *Preliminary and Further Report (with Appendices) of the Royal Commissioners appointed to inquire into the Civil and Professional Administration of the Naval and Military Departments and the Relation of those Departments to each other and to the Treasury*, 1890, pp. xxii–xxiii.

[3] *War Office (Reconstitution) Committee First Report*, pp. 3–4. *Second Report*, pp. 21 sqq.

[4] *Memorandum by the Secretary of State for War on the General Staff of the Army*, November 21, 1905; for the origin of this Memorandum, which was in fact the work of Sir Henry Wilson, see Major-General Sir C. B. Callwell, *Field-Marshal Sir Henry Wilson, His Life and Diaries*, vol. i, pp. 56 sqq. (especially pp. 63–4).

Haldane had copied. Moreover, had not Arnold-Forster on the recommendation of Lord Esher and Sir John Fisher appointed as his private secretary Colonel Ellison, who had drawn up the Esher Committee's report? Had he not on Colonel Ellison's recommendation placed on the Army Council as Quarter-Master-General Sir William Nicolson who, under Brodrick, had occupied a position amounting to that of Chief of Staff without the title? And had there not been in existence from the beginning of 1904 a President of the Army Council who was entitled Chief of General Staff and who could not exercise his functions adequately until a General Staff had been completely organized? An irresistible force was pushing the Secretary for War, whoever he might be, to take a step which he fondly imagined his personal initiative. That old Gladstonian, Campbell-Bannerman, had been able to speak a very different language when he was a member of Lord Hartington's Commission. 'We have no designs against our European neighbours. Indian "military policy" will be settled in India itself, and not in Pall Mall. In any of the smaller troubles into which we may be drawn by the interests of some of our dependencies, the plan of campaign must be governed by the particular circumstances, and would be left (I presume and hope) to be determined by the officer appointed to direct operations.'[1] And at the beginning of the Boer War Lord Wolseley appears to have shared Campbell-Bannerman's opinion that it was not for officials in London to restrict by strategic orders the commander's free initiative.[2] Such views were now thoroughly out of date. And it was a triumph indeed for an imperialist and a champion of 'efficiency' like Haldane to put the finishing touches to a military reorganization inspired by principles wholly different from those of the older school. The creed of scientific preparation and organization was sweeping before it the philosophy of instinct, improvization, and liberty.

7

But the ease with which on this point Haldane overcame old Liberal prejudices and succeeded where Arnold-Forster had succeeded before him in reorganizing the headquarters staff was

[1] *Lord Hartington's Commission's Reports*, p. xxix.
[2] See my *History of the English People*, vol. v, pp. 81–3.

matched by the difficulty of reorganizing the army itself. Here Forster had failed and Haldane was likely to find the problem even more difficult. For the new Parliament was more eager than the Unionists had been to reduce expenditure on the army, and a reduction was harder to effect than it had been at the close of the Boer War, when on the one hand the return to a peace footing had automatically diminished expenditure and on the other hand a vast accumulation of unused material had made it possible to reduce purchases on a large scale. Paul Cambon doubted Haldane's success. 'To create an army money and men are required. The Liberal Cabinet will not provide the money, the nation will not provide the men. Haldane will not succeed.'[1] Haldane however did succeed, not only in effecting economies without detriment to the efficiency of the service, but actually in improving its efficiency and that not by round-about methods but by introducing in 1907 a comprehensive measure, for which he secured from the Premier the promise of ample time for its discussion and from the Leader of the Opposition a pledge that no systematic obstruction would make it impossible to pass the Bill before the end of the session.[2]

As regards the regular army (this had nothing to do with the Army Bill of 1907: it was a work of reorganization completed before the Bill was introduced[3]). Haldane's method was very similar to that which Forster had favoured, one which might be fittingly called a concentration of forces. Thanks to a host of economies effected in the general expenditure, the army would be less expensive, but at the same time it would be stronger, because its organization was more compact. Anticipating the wishes of the Liberal majority and thus obtaining forgiveness for his reputation as an imperialist, Haldane effected economies which exposed him to violent attacks by the Unionist opposition, in

[1] Conversation reported by Colonel Repington, *The Times*, July 16, 1916.

[2] 7 Edw. 7, Cap. 9: An Act to provide for the reorganization of His Majesty's military forces and for that purpose to authorize the establishment of County Associations and the raising and maintenance of a Territorial Force and for amending the Acts relating to the Reserve Forces (*Territorial and Reserve Forces Act*, 1907). For Haldane's system see the preliminary outlines of 1906 explained in his speeches in the House on March 8 and July 12, 1906 (reproduced in his book entitled *Army Reform and Other Addresses*, pp. 3 sqq., 40 sqq.); the *Memorandum by the Secretary of State for War on Army Reorganization*, July 30, 1906; also the important speech delivered on February 25, 1907 introducing the Army Bill (*Army Reforms and other Addresses*, pp. 94 sqq.).

[3] Haldane's speech at Glasgow, January 11, 1907; *The Army Order* of January 1, 1907, also the *Memorandum on the Organisation for War of the Troops forming the Field Army for Service Abroad*, same date.

particular by Arnold-Forster, who had become the bitter and
untiring critic of his successor's actions.[1] The army estimates,
which had fallen from £92,500,000 in 1901 to £69,400,000 in
1902, £36,700,000 in 1903 (the first years of complete peace),
£29,200,000 in 1904, and £28,800,000 in 1905 continued to fall
to £27,800,000 in 1906, £27,100,000 in 1907 and £26,800,000
in 1908.

Haldane's procedure was to abolish a number of units, and
instead of discharging the men who had filled them to employ
them in other branches of the service, thus strengthening the
army while reducing expenditure and without increasing the total
number of troops. He decided to dissolve eight battalions of the
line, and two battalions of Guards. He handed over the defence of
the coast to the Admiralty, thus freeing two thousand soldiers for
other service. The defence of the coast also employed some twelve
thousand militiamen. These could now be used in other employ-
ments of a semi-civilian character, to take the place of regulars
who could be employed in other ways. Moreover, profiting by
the mistakes of his two predecessors, Haldane substituted for
Brodrick's enlistments (three years in the regular army, nine in
the reserve), which unduly inflated the reserve at the cost of the
regular army, and Arnold-Forster's enlistments (nine years in the
regular army, three in the reserve), which incurred the opposite
fault and made impossible any other shorter term of enlistment
which would compete with the longer-term enlistments, an intermediate system, seven years in the regular army and five in the
reserve. The men secured by these various means he grouped in
an organization which was a return to the system of linked battalions, seventy-two battalions of infantry at home and an equal
number in the Colonies. Moreover, he abandoned the system
Brodrick had inaugurated of dividing these battalions into army
corps. Forster had intended to do this but had not had time to
carry out his intention. Haldane was content to group them in
divisions of fifteen thousand men, on the model of the divisions
in the Indian army. Six divisions with four brigades of cavalry

---

[1] H. of C., March 8, July 12, 1906 (*Parliamentary Debates*, 4th Series, vol. cliii, pp. 686
sqq.; vol. clx, pp. 1119 sqq.). Letter to *The Times* under the title 'Mr. Haldane's Scheme'
(*The Times*, March 5, 1907). H. of C., June 5, 19, 1907, March 4, 1909 (*Parl. Deb.*, 4th Ser.,
vol. clxxv, pp. 702 sqq., 761 sqq.; vol. clxxvi, pp. 492 sqq.; Commons, 1909, 5th Ser.,
vol. i, pp. 1626 sqq.); also his work entitled *Military Needs and Military Policy: With an
Introduction by Field-Marshal Earl Roberts*, 1909.

and all the artillery and engineers necessary to support them were kept in constant readiness, either to supply the men needed to relieve the garrisons abroad, or to be despatched after the reserves had been mobilized to make war outside the United Kingdom. There was a total force, with the reserves, of about a hundred and sixty thousand. This 'expeditionary force' was, though on a much vaster scale, the striking-force Arnold-Forster had in vain attempted to form during his two years' tenure of office.

Behind this army of the first line, but in close association with it, Haldane created (this was one of the provisions of the Act of 1907) a 'special reserve' which would differ from the militia by the fact that its officers and non-commissioned officers would be regulars and its recruits would take an engagement to serve abroad in case of war. But it would be recruited from the same sources as the militia had been. The enlistments, which would be for six years, would involve six months' training at the outset followed by periods of a fortnight a year, with the same pay as the soldiers in the regular army received. There was no need for the hundred and twenty-four battalions of which the militia had consisted. A number of battalions equal to those of the regular army would suffice and they could be attached to the latter as reserve battalions in the proportion of one, two, or three battalions to every regiment of two battalions in the regular army. The battalions of the special reserve would not be allowed to fall below a strength of five or six hundred. Arnold-Forster protested that Haldane was simply reviving his own scheme for reforming the militia. His protest was justified and it was apparently to give him satisfaction that the Bill of 1907 was amended on this point. In its original form the Bill presented the 'special reserve' as a new force, created *in toto* by Haldane, something entirely apart from the militia and volunteers. In the statute as it emerged from the debates the 'special reserve' was presented as a transformation of the militia. But was Arnold-Forster equally right when he went further, accused Haldane of wantonly ruining his system, and argued that the periods of training prescribed by the new measure were too short to turn out genuine soldiers? Haldane could reply that these short periods were inevitable if a sufficient number of recruits was to be secured and that their training could be completed, either when they were incorporated into the regular army or, on the outbreak of war, were organized in battalions and subjected to a lengthy training, and further that for men placed under regular military discipline and brought into close contact with professional soldiers the brevity of their training would have the advantage of forging a closer link between the regular army and the civil population.

8

It was in the matter of a second-line force in the strict sense that Haldane departed from Arnold-Forster. The latter, faithful to his method of concentrating the organization of the army, wanted to reduce the number of volunteers, and make of the remainder a nucleus, better trained than had been the case hitherto and more capable of fighting an army entirely trained in barracks. Haldane on the contrary bore in mind the principle laid down by Lord Elgin's Commission: 'That no military system will be satisfactory which does not contain powers of expansion outside the limit of the regular forces of the Crown, whatever that limit may be.'[1] And it was to the volunteers that he looked to ensure this power of expansion. Unlike Forster he did not want their numbers reduced. On the contrary he wanted them more numerous. Not indeed to repel an invasion. For that task a small body would be sufficient, and the guard kept by the navy rendered the eventuality doubtful. But to reinforce the expeditionary force when the latter, having faced on the Continent the enemy's initial attack, would need to make up its losses and receive reinforcements. This volunteer force need not be completely trained, but all its members, while acquiring without interruption of their normal life a modicum of military training and some experience of camp life, were invited to take an engagement that on the outbreak of war they would undergo the lengthy training necessary to transform them into competent soldiers.

Haldane therefore completely reorganized the second-line force, incorporating into a new army, to which he gave the name Territorial Force, whatever was left of the militia after its bulk had been formed into the Special Reserve, the Yeomanry which required little change, and the Volunteers.[2] The latter were res-

[1] *Report of Royal Commission on the War in South Africa*, p. 83.
[2] For the origins and history of the Territorial Army see three articles in *The Times*, April 1 and 2, and May 7, 1929, entitled 'A Citizen Army'.

cued from the state of disorganization in which they had stagnated for half a century. He abolished, thus effecting a reform Forster had proposed, the capitation grant, a government bounty given to the officers commanding volunteer battalions whose amount was calculated by the number of men under their command. For it was an encouragement to enlist the largest possible number of men without regard to capacity or training, 'a premium on the enlistment of inefficients'.[1] In future the volunteers would receive pay fixed by the Government, and their officers would have no interest in their enlistment, their duties being confined to commanding and training the men. The system imposed upon the soldiers of the new territorial army was not however very severe. They would be enlisted between the ages of eighteen and twenty-four and be obliged to undergo for four years periods of training in camp which might extend to a fortnight but might be no longer than a week. A new provision made them liable to a light fine—only five pounds—if they wished to leave the force before the four years had expired. Moreover, they were encouraged but not compelled to join the rifle clubs, already very numerous, whose development the Government assisted by augmented grants, to practise shooting in the interval between their periods of training.

Above all, the new army differed from the old volunteer force in being organized. In the volunteers there had been above the battalions only a confused and incoherent grouping into brigades. Haldane organized his new Territorial Army in fourteen divisions, corresponding to the administrative districts created by Arnold-Forster with two additional Scottish divisions, one for the Lowlands, the other for the Highlands. It was easy to divide the Yeomanry into fourteen cavalry brigades. Under the conditions of enlistment in the Territorials there would be no difficulty in finding the material of an excellent body of engineers, equal, if not superior, to the corps attached to the regular army. It would not be so easy to provide the Territorial Army with the equipment and personnel of a good artillery, but the effort must be made. It must also be provided with a commissariat and a sanitary corps, in short must be made at least 'the skeleton'[2] of a real army.

---

[1] H. of C., 25 February, 1907, Haldane's speech (*Parliamentary Debates*, 4th Series, vol. clxix, p. 1293).

[2] 'A skeleton organization. . . . You will, I think, have to resort to something of the

For this army Haldane wanted a force of three hundred thousand. If war broke out there could be no doubt that in the patriotic enthusiasm its declaration would arouse, the figure could be easily tripled by the influx of recruits eager to undergo as Territorials a six months' training. It was even likely that the Government would introduce conscription. The organization of the Territorial Army would be ready to receive the conscripts; in case of need, all the fit young men of Great Britain.[1]

9

His scheme once adopted, Haldane organized the propaganda necessary to win recruits for his new army. He made use of the press. A special department at the War Office supplied the papers with whatever news favoured his military policy.[2] The *Daily Mail* constituted itself his chief publicity agent and Haldane publicly thanked that great organ of popular imperialism for assistance which he had perhaps himself inspired.[3] He gained the confidence of *The Times* military correspondent, Colonel Repington, who without giving up his post on *The Times* accepted the semi-official position of editor of the *Army Review*. He also asked employers to encourage their workmen to enlist.[4] He took advantage of the industrial crisis which began about the end of 1907 and lasted over a year to call their attention to the value of the Territorial Army and still more the special reserve as employment for

kind if you are to have behind your striking force the certainty of a power of expansion.' (Ibid., vol. cliii, p. 678.)

[1] R. B. Haldane, address to the London Rifle Brigade, February 10, 1909: 'The question increasingly put to him was: "Why don't you ask Parliament to impose an obligation on all to serve for home defence?" He had sympathy with that question. He thought most people agree that as for the slacker, who simply amused himself and did nothing, the country would no doubt show what they thought of him. In all probability he would find a short and sharp Act of Parliament passed, if war broke out, compelling him to train himself, and do it in some inconvenient and unpleasant part of the country, when he would not have the prominence of the undoubted popular esteem which was given to the man who trained himself as a volunteer for the defence of his native land.' General Sir John French, speech at West Bromwich, March 22, 1913: 'He advised all those in favour of compulsory service to support the Territorial Army because, if ever their views came to prevail, compulsory service could be brought about with the present force by a mere stroke of the pen.'

[2] Arnold-Forster, *Military Needs and Military Policy*, p. 32 *n.*

[3] H. of C., March 7, 1910 (*Parliamentary Debates*, Commons 1910, 5th Series, vol. xiv, p. 1162).

[4] H. of C., October 21, 1908, Asquith's speech (ibid., 4th Ser., vol. cxciv, p. 1169).

the men thrown out of work.[1] He met indeed with discomfitures. For instance, when the historian, Fortescue, whom he had commissioned to study in the archives of the Foreign Office the military policy England had followed during her wars with republican and imperial France,[2] published a book which concluded with a panegyric of conscription[3] Haldane had recourse to a very unusual step for which he was severely criticized. He commissioned an officer of the high command, a member of the Army Council, General Sir Ian Hamilton, to refute the advocates of conscription and wrote the preface himself.[4] But his principal method of securing for his system the national support indispensable to its success was the Statute of 1907 itself and the administrative measures which accompanied it. It may be briefly described as the establishment of the governing classes in the very centre of his new organization, to act as its mainspring.

The Territorial Army, though divided into fourteen large divisions, was nevertheless organized on a county basis to appeal to the local patriotism so strong among the English. Forster had already contemplated such a county organization for his 'territorial militia'. Haldane carried it out for his Territorial Army. It is curious however to notice in what an ambiguous form he presented his plan in 1906.[5] 'There is', he declared, 'one school of thought which says that what you should do with our old constitutional forces is to extend them enormously, so that they shall be not merely a support to but an extension of the Regular Army. This school', he added, 'looks to the Lords-Lieutenant to give a new

---

[1] *War Office Advertisement for Recruiting for the Regular Army*, October 1908. See Arnold-Forster's protests, *Morning Post*, October 28, 1908, also *Military Needs and Military Policy*, p. 120. The Secretary for War resorted to even more blatant methods of advertisement. The Lord Mayor's Show on November 9, 1907, included a car filled with Territorials and Boy Scouts besides regulars.

[2] Lord Roberts, *Fallacies and Facts*, p. 29.

[3] *The County Lieutenancies and the Army, 1803–1814* p. 290. Fortescue after maintaining that England could not keep up her army in wartime without recourse to conscription added: 'Compulsion cannot be applied for service outside the British Isles.' Lord Roberts, however, quotes the phrase in a slightly different form and makes it read: 'Compulsion cannot *in peace* be applied for service outside the British Isles' (*Fallacies and Facts*, p. 30).

[4] *Compulsory Service: A Study of the Question in the Light of Experience*, by General Sir Ian Hamilton. With an introduction by the Rt. Hon. R. B. Haldane, Edition 1, November 1910; 2nd Edition with notes on the Admiralty view of the risk of invasion, January 1911. For the book and the circumstances under which it was published see the debates H. of C., March 13, 1911, Arthur Balfour's speech; March 14, 1911, Haldane's speech (*Parliamentary Debates*, Commons, 1911, 5th Series, vol. xxii, pp. 1972–4, 2073 sqq.).

[5] H. of C., July 12, 1906 (ibid., 4th Ser., vol. clx, pp. 1112, 1116; *Army Reform and other Addresses*, p. 85. Cf. H. of C., February 25, 1907 (ibid., vol. clxix, p. 1304; *Army Reform and other Addresses*, pp. 124–5).

life to the Militia.' It was the school to which he himself belonged, and of which indeed he was in many respects the head. But he proceeded immediately to repudiate its principles, at least as regards the functions to be assigned to the Lords-Lieutenant. 'The Lords-Lieutenant', he stated, 'cannot discharge that function. For such a purpose they are as dead as the dodo.' This reassured the Radicals and Labour members. Haldane clearly did not contemplate placing the old county aristocracy at the head of his new army. But the declaration had no sooner been uttered, when, without any transition, the speech of the Secretary for War once more took an unexpected turn. He expressed his conviction that those whom he had a moment before treated as fossils could be resuscitated and military functions entrusted to the Lords-Lieutenant provided they were surrounded by a more democratic framework. Actually the first five clauses of the Act of 1907 set up in every county a 'county association' which should contain representatives of the County Councils and secretaries of trade unions and were empowered to offer the presidency to the Lord-Lieutenant. In fact, they always did offer it and the Lord-Lieutenant always accepted.

The scheme aroused some protests from the Radical and Labour benches. Sir Charles Dilke gave it an ironical welcome and refused to regard it as anything but a masterpiece of organized snobbery.[1] Ramsay MacDonald said it reminded him of a new edition of Disraeli's novels.[2] Was it befitting secretaries of trade unions to become, by joining these associations, recruiters for the army under the patronage of the aristocracy? Conservatives also

[1] H. of C., July 12, 1906, Sir Charles Dilke's speech: 'Lords-Lieutenant did not command implicit obedience on the other side of the House, and on his side they commanded none at all. The suggestion that it was necessary to have their patronage brought to his mind Miss Barrett Browning's description in *Aurora Leigh* of how upon some occasions Lords-Lieutenant cast down on those who lived in a lower sphere a kind of beaming influence which crushed out the tendency to vulgarity.' (Everything following the words 'none at all' has been suppressed in the official report. *Parliamentary Debates*, 4th Series, vol. clx, p. 1136.)

[2] H. of C., April 23, 1907, J. R. MacDonald's speech: '. . . the county associations . . . would change the political and social centre of gravity in the country, and when in working order they would form a new nucleus of political and social influence. The right honourable gentleman seemed to have faced this modern problem with mediaeval ideas in his mind. Modern developments must be based on modern means; and the military scheme of the right honourable gentleman must have an industrial basis and not a basis which assumed the existence of the relations between the village and the hall. . . . The plan of county associations indeed was like an introduction or footnote to Beaconsfield's novels.' The jesting allusion to Lord Beaconsfield's novels has been omitted from the official report (*Parliamentary Debates*, 4th Series, vol. clxxii, p. 1592).

expressed apprehension. Surrounded as they would be by *nouveaux riches* to whom the old traditions of the gentry meant nothing, would it be wise of the Lords-Lieutenant to undertake functions which perhaps they might find themselves unable to fulfil honourably?[1] Nevertheless, his plan was adopted, and was more aristocratic in its final than in its original form: the County Councillors in the county associations were not the elected representatives of the County Councils but nominees of the Army Council. Nevertheless it proved a success. Throughout the country the associations were formed, flourished and even combined to form a vast national federation with its semi-official organ.[2] For more than half a century the landed gentry had been progressively dispossessed of local government and the Radical victory at the polls in 1906 had seemed likely to accelerate the process. Now however at one point Haldane's initiative had not merely slackened but reversed it. The landed gentry were invested with new functions of military local government.

When he instituted the County Associations and placed the Lords-Lieutenant at their head it was Haldane's intention to make use of the moral influence exercised by the landowners to attract into the Territorial Army and keep in it as many recruits as possible. How would these recruits, drawn from the lower classes, be provided with the officers they required? To provide officers for the reserve England had not at her disposal the sources of supply possessed by countries with a conscript army. It was to the upper middle class that she must look for volunteers to officer her territorial army. Why not appeal to the patriotism or, as Haldane dared to call it, the 'militarism', of the public schools?[3] For many

---

[1] William le Queux, *The Invasion of London*, 1906, Preface, p. xi: 'Under our twentieth-century social system, which has unfortunately displaced so many influencial and respected county families—everyone of which had military or naval members, relations or ancestors —by wealthy tradesmen, speculators and the like, any efficient county association will be very hard to create. Mr. Haldane's scheme is a bold and masterly sketch, but he will find it very hard to fill in the details satisfactorily.' So far as the Lords-Lieutenant are concerned, this social transformation had not yet been effected when Haldane prepared his Bill. After 1906 the Liberals began to make nominations calculated to change rapidly their social origins. (Lord Shuttleworth in Lancashire, Major-General H. F. Brocklehurst in Rutland, Sir William Brompton Gordon in Suffolk, Colonel Henry Cubitt in Surrey, Lord Nunburnholme in the East Riding of Yorkshire, Sir Hugh Bell in the North Riding.) But such nominations were still few, and since both parties had until 1906 respected the old traditions, on the eve of the Great War, members of old families were still at the head of almost all the counties.

[2] *National Defence*, the Organ of the National Defence Association, first number, November 1908.

[3] H. of C., February 25, 1907, Haldane's speech: '. . . We saw that there was only one

years games had been compulsory in these schools, and this not only because the masters wished to improve the boys' physique, but to foster that team spirit which in children is the germ of public spirit. But did public spirit thus understood differ very much from the military spirit?[1] Certain imperialists had appealed to these compulsory games as a proof that England was not so hostile to conscription as was commonly stated and believed.[2] Before imposing conscription on adults, they asked, why not at least introduce into the schools compulsory military training? Or

source from which we could hope to get young men of the upper middle class, who are the usual source from which this element is drawn, and that was the Universities and the big public schools, like Eton and Harrow, and other public schools of that character, which at present have large cadet corps. You are not in danger of increasing the spirit of militarism there because the spirit of militarism already runs fairly high both there and at the Universities' (*Parliamentary Debates*, 4th Series, vol. clxix, p. 1321). It would seem that Sir Edward Grey speaking six weeks later in defence of the Bill wished to undo the effect produced by this gratuitously provocative language. He was at pains to dissipate 'the apprehensions that the scheme may create too much of a military spirit in the country . . . I do not believe it will . . . I would much rather use the phrase "public spirit" than "military spirit" ' (H. of C., April 9, 1907; ibid., vol. clxxii, p. 108).

[1] H. of C., July 12, 1906, Haldane's speech: 'The people of this country will not be dragooned into giving military service. Lord Cardwell used to say that, so far from being a nation of shopkeepers, the British were the most fighting nation on earth. I think that the interest of our people in military matters is probably more profound, more real and spontaneous than that of any other nation in the world. The keenness and the willingness of our people to give up time to volunteering and to the study of military organization is one of the striking features we have to deal with' (*Parliamentary Debates*, 4th Series, vol. clx, p. 1082).

[2] Rudyard Kipling's letter to *The Times*, December 11, 1903: 'What someone ought to point out now is that there exists in the average English public school a highly efficient system of conscription (for games) based: 1. On physical coercion of the young conscript. 2. On carefully educated public opinion of the conscripts' equals. Under this system the conscript is compelled between the ages of twelve and seventeen to put in some 2,500 hours of drill. If he comes up at ten and stays till he is eighteen, the total is nearer 4,000 hours. . . . By the time he is fourteen or sixteen the conscript under this system is set and keen; and if he isn't keen he is at any rate moderately efficient. Of course, this system could not be applied to the youth of all England without raising a horrible outcry. But we find it actually and smoothly at work in a minute section of the community, and it turns out annually, let us say, between seven and ten thousand boys trained to its standard.' He continues, 'Now, suppose that even 10 per cent. of the hours devoted to cricket and footer drills could be taken up for military drill and target work, wouldn't it be for gain? It couldn't come to much more than an hour and a half a week for thirty-six weeks, but in five or six years that would go far towards making a trained man' (*National Service Journal*, January 1904). Ten years later Kipling's suggestion was taken up by Lord Willoughby de Broke, who introduced a Territorial Force (Amendment) Bill which must be noticed, if only as a curiosity. It proposed to render national service compulsory for boys attending public schools; in other words, make conscription the privilege of young men of the upper classes (H. of L., March 12, 1914; *Parl. Deb.*, 5th Ser., Lords 1914, vol. xv, pp. 461 sqq.). On this point we may remark an agreement queer enough in all conscience between the views of Conservatives like Willoughby de Broke and those of the Labour party. Haldane had at first intended to organize military training in elementary as well as in secondary schools. It was due to pressure from the Labour members that he abandoned the former part of his scheme (H. of C., June 19, 1907, A. Henderson's speech, ibid., 4th Ser., vol. clxxvi, p. 532).

without going so far, why not encourage the development of voluntary associations already in existence for the military training of children and youths? We are not alluding to the Boy Scouts, a flourishing institution, which certainly tended to instil into children habits of military discipline but whose character was ambiguous and which denied that it was inspired by a military spirit in the strict sense of the term.[1] Nor do we refer to the Boys' Brigades founded by philanthropists for boys of the lower classes to train private soldiers, regular or territorial, rather than officers.[2] We are thinking of those cadet corps which came into existence for the first time in 1859 and 1860, a product of that violent explosion of gallophobia to which the modern volunteer movement owed its birth. Why should not the War Office give official recognition to these bodies, or at any rate to some of them? The idea had been considered before Haldane's arrival at the War Office but it would seem had been opposed by the departments and the professional soldiers. He took it up again and made a success of it. He formed an Officers' Training Corps for the public schools and Universities.[3] To every school and University a contingent of cadets was attached of a definite size which would be regularly affiliated to the Territorial force of the county and for which the War Office would provide, in addition to a fixed payment of five pounds per company, the necessary arms, ammunition, and instructors. The experiment succeeded. There were schools, Eton for example, which provided such a number of cadets that they assumed the appearance of preparatory schools for Sandhurst, nurseries of professional officers. And everywhere young amateur officers sprang up, ready to serve as regular officers, if the country were ever in danger. It is not easy in relating the moral history of a nation to estimate the strength of successive currents of ideas. There can be no doubt that after the end of the Boer War a very pronounced movement of anti-militarism arose in England. But

---

[1] We should notice the institution by the education committees of 'classes for Boy Scouts' in the elementary schools of certain counties, Lancashire first, then Surrey, then Kent (*Times Educational Supplement*, June 4, July 2, 1912).

[2] For certain attempts made before 1906 to attach the Boys' Brigades to the regular army by granting special privileges to members of a Brigade who enlisted see Arnold-Forster, *The Army in 1906*, 1906, pp. 157–8.

[3] See *The Special Army Order* of March 16, 1908, which put into execution the recommendation of a Committee of which Sir Edward Ward was chairman. The clause of the Act of 1907 which authorized Government grants to the cadet corps had been vigorously opposed by the Labour members. To satisfy them it had been necessary to provide that only boys above sixteen could benefit by a grant.

we must not forget that, on the one hand, the number of volunteers, continued under a new form as the Territorials, remained higher than it had ever been before that war, and that, on the other hand, the youth of the middle class displayed a knowledge of things military and a taste for them which had not been witnessed before. May not we conclude that pacifist opinion, though often more vocal, was also more superficial, and that the militarization of the nation and particularly of the governing classes,[1] if more silent, was more profound?

10

'We are a first-class Power, and we are apparently looking out for a first-class war. The Cardwell system was inaugurated at a time when our chief military problem was India. That is no longer the case. It is now in Europe.' These words were spoken in January 1909 by an English general in the course of a debate on the future of the army opened by Lieutenant-Colonel Repington.[2] In Europe—more precisely in Western Europe—on the frontier which divided Germany from France and Belgium. But nothing had been achieved if the Government were content to maintain its expeditionary force in England in a state of preparation without taking the necessary measures for its embarkation, the protection of its transports, its disembarkation, and immediate concentration at particular points arranged beforehand with the army of a prospective ally. Haldane had scarcely reached the War Office when he took the necessary steps.[3]

[1] See Haldane's remarks to Sir Almeric Fitzroy, March 14, 1910: 'As for his work at the War Office, he looks upon it as complete, and would be glad to hand the system he has created over to the Opposition, which, he believes, in combination with the County Associations, would at this stage do more to develop the Territorial organization than it is in his power to do. He spoke with great gratitude of the assistance he had received from his political foes, and regretted that it was not possible to do more State business by co-operation between the two parties' (*Memoirs of Sir Almeric Fitzroy*, vol. i, p. 395). A month earlier George Wyndham in a conversation with Wilfrid Blunt used language which justified Haldane's comments: 'The strength of the Tory position is that they and the King together command the whole material force of the country, besides half its voting strength. They have the money and the Army and the Navy and the Territorials, all down to the Boy Scouts' (Wilfrid Scawen Blunt, *My Diaries*, February 5, 1910, vol. ii, p. 299).

[2] *Aldershot Military Society: The Future of Army Organization*, by Lieut.-Col. C. A'Court Repington, January 27, 1909, p. 27.

[3] *British Documents . . .* vol. iii, pp. 170 sqq. Lieut.-Col. A'Court Repington, *The First World War*, 1920, vol. i, pp. 2 sqq.; D. S. MacDiarmid, *Life of Lieutenant-General Sir James Moncrieff Grierson*, 1923, pp. 213–29; Général Huguet, *L'Intervention militaire*

It would seem that the Anglo-French agreement of 1904 had hardly been concluded when the Committee of Imperial Defence studied the possibility of co-operation by the British army with a French army on the Continent. However guarded in form Lord Lansdowne's overtures to the French Government in April and May 1905, at the time of the Tangier crisis, undoubtedly the French statesmen interpreted them as opening the door to a military understanding between the two nations and it was for that reason that they aroused at Paris the panic of which we have spoken already. It is probable also that Admiral Fisher discussed the question during the following months with some Frenchman in high position. The project of an armed landing on the coast of Hanover under the protection of the British fleet, whose revelation in the *Matin* created such a stir, presumably originated with him. And finally it is probable that Lieutenant-Colonel Repington, a staff officer who on retiring from the army had become military correspondent of *The Times*, was an unofficial agent between the military authorities of the two countries during the concluding months of Unionist Government. But it was not until December after the fall of the Unionist Cabinet, when the German Government, possibly encouraged by the political crisis in England following as it did the revolution in Russia, seemed to be adopting a decidedly bellicose attitude that a *rapprochement* between the two armies was effected, outside the Cabinet to begin with. Commandant Huguet, the French military attaché, happened to meet General Grierson, the director of military operations, who informed him in confidence that the War Office was studying the measures which must be taken to despatch rapidly to the Continent an expeditionary force of more than a hundred thousand men. A few days later, Huguet repeated what he had heard to the journalist Repington, while expressing his fear that the new Cabinet might be less favourable to French interests than its predecessor. Repington questioned Grey on this point by letter and obtained a sufficiently reassuring answer to take it on himself in concert with two important members of the Imperial Defence Committee to open unofficial communications with Rouvier's

britannique en 1914, 1928, pp. 13 sqq.; Viscount Grey of Fallodon, *Twenty-five Years, 1892–1916*, vol. i, pp. 71 sqq.; Viscount Haldane, *Before the War*, 1920, pp. 28 sqq.; *An Autobiography*, 1929, pp. 189 sqq.; J. A. Spender, *The Life of the Right Hon. Sir Henry Campbell-Bannerman*, 1923, vol. i, pp. 248 sqq.; Lucien Wolf, *Life of the First Marquess of Ripon*, 1921, vol. ii, pp. 292–3.

Cabinet through the intermediary of Huguet. Rouvier, who had been terrified the previous spring by the offer of military assistance, now asked for it. Paul Cambon, who was on leave, was sent to London. On January 10 he asked Grey what would be the attitude of the British Government in the event of a war between France and Germany. Grey replied that he was not in a position to pledge the country to more than neutrality—a benevolent neutrality, if such a thing existed. Would Grey at least authorize unofficial conversations between the military and naval commands in readiness for an eventual alliance between the two Governments? He did not refuse, and if Cambon concluded that he did not disapprove of the suggestion, it was only because he put a favourable interpretation upon his silence.

The electoral campaign was in full swing and Grey passed half the week in his constituency. The Government did not yet know how large its majority would be, or even if it would secure a clear majority. It was presenting itself to the electorate with a programme of peace. For such a government the signature of a military convention with France would be a strange beginning. On the other hand, if unfortunately Germany declared war on France and England remained neutral, what an outburst of French wrath it would mean against '*la perfide Albion*', what a triumph for German policy! Grey did not know how to answer Cambon's request which he believed to come from Paris, whereas it originated ultimately with certain British officers and members of the Committee of Imperial Defence. After a public meeting in his constituency he took the opportunity to discuss the matter with Haldane, an imperialist like himself, and they agreed upon the reply to make to Cambon. Conversations between the general staffs would be authorized on the clear understanding that they would remain strictly technical and not commit the two Governments. The Prime Minister, who was in Scotland, and with whom Sir Edward Grey was obliged to correspond by post, showed little enthusiasm for the solution. 'It comes', he wrote to Lord Ripon, 'very close to an honourable undertaking. I do not like the stress laid upon joint preparations.' Nevertheless, he gave way. The elections were over and on January 31 Grey, fortified by the consent of the Premier and without taking the trouble to obtain the approval of the entire Cabinet, made known his acceptance, hedged round with elaborate restrictions, of Cambon's proposal.

Conversations, equally unofficial, were begun with the approval of the Foreign Office between the War Office and the Belgian War Office. For a German violation of Belgian neutrality was already expected to be the first act of a war perhaps imminent.[1] Thus on the very morrow of the advent of the Liberal Government the system of relations took shape between England and France which would continue until 1914. There was no treaty or alliance between the two Governments. Nor was there any military convention. But there was an *entente* which amounted, or almost amounted, to an alliance between Downing Street and the Quai d'Orsay, and an understanding between the War Offices of London and Paris of a more detailed character than many military conventions.

II

To realize this vast scheme of preparation for war required plenty of guile, but it was a quality of which Haldane had no lack. The organization of an expeditionary force whose destination was obvious to anyone who took the trouble to reflect, was calculated to alarm the pacifists in the Cabinet and the party. But it was accompanied by a number of measures, reductions of certain

[1] See in *The Times* of January 23 the article entitled 'The Low Countries'. It is, however, interesting to notice how fluctuating was the language of speakers in Parliament, at the very time when under Haldane's patronage co-operation between the three general staffs of England, France, and Belgium was being arranged. When on March 8, 1906, Haldane had explained for the first time in the Commons his plans for army reorganization, Arnold-Forster intervened to declare that the reserve was completely incapable of conducting on the Continent the war he obviously foresaw. 'Were we to fight for the neutrality of Belgium, if that should be our fate, outside these islands and take with us these bands of irregular troops?' (*Parliamentary Debates*, 4th Series, vol. cliii, p. 690). Immediately, a Liberal member protested: 'He hoped that it would never be suggested in this House, as it was sometimes suggested outside, that the friendly relations with France rendered us liable, if hostilities broke out between that Power and any other, to take any part in the operations which might ensue' (H. of C., March 8, 1906: ibid., vol. cliii, p. 745). And some months later Balfour's language was calculated to banish the supposition, envisaged by Forster and rejected by Guest, and recall the attention of the British public to India: 'The right hon. gentleman talked as if there was to be an expedition beyond the sea in which 154,000 men were to be straightaway embarked and transported off to some distant theatre of operations. The contingency requiring such an expedition might occur, but it is not very easy to imagine that it would. . . . We might be asked to land 150,000 men on the coast of Europe, but I do not know that I should sacrifice much money or take enormous pains so to organize my force that that could be done straightaway and immediately. What is required, so far as I am able to see, is the power of sending continuous reinforcements off to India in a great emergency. That does not mean sending 150,000 men straight off in a few weeks to Bombay' (H. of C., July 12, 1906, *Parliamentary Debates*, 4th Series, vol. clx, pp. 1161–2).

categories of troops, and financial economies which aroused loud protests from the speakers and journalists of the Opposition and thus distracted the attention of the advanced Liberals. To the advocates of conscription on the one hand Haldane contrived to present his new Territorial Army as the utmost advance on the road to the organization of the 'nation in arms' to which the Parliament and country could be induced to consent. Therefore, though in 1906 they had given Haldane's policy an unfavourable reception, they became reconciled to it the moment it appeared in its true light, a policy not of excessive economies but of an indefinite development of the reserve forces under the patronage of the old aristocracy. In the words of Lord Roberts, who, however, did not discontinue his zealous campaign on behalf of compulsory military service, it was 'the greatest step forward in the direction of a great national army that had ever been made officially'.[1] To sincere Liberals, radical pacifists, and representatives of the working class on the other hand Haldane presented his system as an insurmountable barrier against conscription and the members of Parliament who from that quarter spoke and voted against the Bill were half-hearted in their opposition. After all, it was a force of volunteers. The individual was free to enlist or refuse to enlist. When we read the debates in the House of Commons on the army estimates during these years we receive the impression that the only questions which really interested the Labour members were whether the wages of the men employed in the national workshops would be raised, or whether on the plea of economy the number of men employed at Woolwich would be reduced.

Assured of the neutrality of the working class and the co-operation of the Conservative sections of the nation Haldane lost no time in carrying out his plan. On April 1, 1908, the statute was to come into operation as regards the Territorial Army. Six months earlier the King had received in public audience the Lords-Lieutenant of Great Britain, had expressed his satisfaction that duties they had once performed had been restored to them, and his conviction that they would fulfil their new responsibilities to the general satisfaction. A slump in industry favoured the recruiting of the regular army which had become the accepted refuge of the unemployed. A wave of indignation against Germany swept crowds of young men into the ranks of the Territorials. By the

[1] Speech at Birmingham, April 4, 1907.

end of 1908 their number had reached 188,000 officers and men The following summer, the King reviewed at Windsor after distributing their colours detachments from 108 units from every district in the country, industrial as well as agricultural. Of all the English counties Lancashire had given the best response to Haldane's appeal and in July 1909 King Edward presented its colours to the West Lancashire division which consisted of 16,000 men. At the beginning of 1910 the number of territorials had reached the figure of 276,000, nine-tenths of the maximum for which Haldane asked. Two years had then passed since Sir Henry Campbell-Bannerman's death, but by the beginning of 1908 Sir Henry's eyes had been opened to the truth that when he sent Haldane to the War Office it was not Haldane who had fallen into a trap. He had proved a most active and successful Secretary for War, indeed the only Secretary for War worthy of the name which England had possessed since Cardwell.

About the end of 1906 the rumour spread in Germany of the intimate discussions which had taken place between the English and French staffs. In the Senate Clémenceau replied to these rumours by a declaration whose form was so strange that it might well seem an avowal.[1] But not a single member of the House of Commons attempted to extract from the Government a denial or admission. Haldane and, after him, Campbell-Bannerman, reassured Metternich by stating categorically—which was true in the letter, if not in the spirit—that no military convention between England and France was in existence.[2] The German Government would appear to have accepted these declarations. Why was it satisfied so easily? Was it the presence at the War Office of Hal-

[1] 'How could I answer yes or no? . . . I have only been President of the Council for three weeks and . . . I have never heard anything of any document of the nature of that Anglo-French military convention you speak of. There are questions so framed that it is the first duty of a Government with any sense of responsibility to refuse to answer them (Senate, November 20, 1906). The British Press without distinction of parties seemed to have received orders to say as little as possible of what the *Daily News* of the 21st calls 'a curious expression' and the *Morning Post* of the 22nd Clémenceau's 'curiously lame' declaration.

[2] Count von Metternich to the Minister for Foreign Affairs, February 17, 1907 (*Die Grosse Politik* . . . vol. xxii[1], p. 125). This was the formula which Government speakers regularly used until the Great War. It may be thought however that Haldane exceeded the limits of permissible equivocation when speaking in the House of Lords on May 15, 1912, he stated that the 'friendship' between England and France had nothing to do with military questions, and repeated once more two years before the war the well-worn assurance which would have been true in 1900 that the object of the expeditionary force was not to fight near home on the Continent but to defend the distant possessions of the Empire (*Parliamentary Debates*, Lords, 1912, 5th Series, vol. xi, pp. 1037-8).

dane, 'a warm friend',[1] 'our only true friend',[2] that calmed German apprehensions? Up to a point yes; but the German attitude, and it is essential to understand this, was primarily determined by the fact that, if these disquieting rumours alarmed the diplomatists, they did not disturb the military experts. Bismarck was reported to have said that if a British army landed on the Continent he would send the police to arrest it.[3] And in the interval the Boer War had done nothing to restore the prestige of the British soldier in Germany. The German ambassador in Washington, reporting to Bülow a conversation he had just had with Roosevelt, represented the President as dismayed by his inability to discipline the American troops—'they desert sooner than obey'. 'Typically Anglo-Saxon,' was the Emperor's marginal comment, 'things are just the same in England.'[4] No doubt the German officers were convinced, like Lord Roberts, that without conscription the English could not think of challenging the German army, and equally convinced—and history down to 1914 would prove them right—that the English would turn a deaf ear to Lord Roberts's appeals.

---

[1] Count Metternich to Prince von Bülow, May 4, 1906: '. . . We have a warm friend in the English Minister for War, Mr. Haldane. He wrote to me a short while ago in a private letter what he has since repeated in conversation: "I hope the time has now come to establish the very best relations between our two countries. You know my attachment to yours." ' William II wrote on the margin: 'I don't believe it' (*Die Grosse Politik . . .* vol. xxi[11], p. 426).

[2] Anonymous letter from London, February 15, 1907: '. . . In fact . . . the mass of the population here . . . wants war. The only true friend Germany possesses here and who is an outspoken opponent of war—Mr. Haldane cannot swim alone against the stream' (*Die Grosse Politik . . .* vol. xxi[11], p. 487).

[3] Sir Ian Hamilton, *Compulsory Service*, p. 95.

[4] Baron Speck von Sternberg to Prince von Bülow, September 9, 1907 (*Die Grosse Politik . . .* vol. xxvi, p. 73). Cf. A report on the Territorial Army by (the) Captain (of a corvette) Seebolm, May 12, 1910: '. . . The young men lack the training given by compulsory service. The Territorial Army is a joke. When the men should have gone into camp, they struck and went home' (Tirpitz, *Politische Dokumente*, vol. i, p. 176). For the regular army see a report by the military attaché, Von Winterfeldt, who believed in the genuine existence of an agreement between the two staffs, written on February 7, 1911: 'On the question whether and when they would actually undertake this expedition across the Channel they have presumably not committed themselves. At present two important considerations militate against such a daring step on the part of the British army. In the first place their expeditionary force is still far behind other armies in its military training. This very year the English manœuvres produced an unfavourable impression upon my colleagues. The tactics, the handling of the troops, the staff arrangements, all betrayed an astonishing inefficiency, and the planning and execution of the manœuvres were wholly inadequate to modern requirements (*Die Grosse Politik . . .* vol. xxix, p. 66 *n*). On the other hand one must not forget the opinion of General von Falkenhayn who opposed his compatriots' prejudice. 'We must not underestimate the British army: it is an army of subalterns' (Conrad von Hötzendorf, *Aus Meiner Dienstzeit*, vol. v, p. 819). Falkenhayn said this, it is true, on December 19, 1914, five months after the beginning of the war.

Were the Germans then not afraid of the martial power of Great Britain? And did the refusal of the English to listen to Lord Roberts prove that they did not take the German peril seriously? No. But on both sides the issue was not regarded as a military one. The English permitted their general staff to contemplate in readiness for all eventualities the despatch of an army to the Continent, but they cherished the hope that it would never come to this. In a moment of panic they might swell the enlistment of their Territorial Army to provide against the danger of a German invasion, as if that had been Haldane's intention in forming it. But the navy would ensure their safety, if only the necessary money were spent upon it and not wasted on a useless army, and whenever on a technical question of this kind an Englishman listened to a debate between a soldier and a sailor, he instinctively supported the latter. Once the first enthusiasm had ebbed, the numbers of the Territorial Army decreased every year, and the 'special reserve' yielded disappointing results.[1] We are thus led to study the essential problem, which was naval not military. If for some years England had been morally at war with Germany, the cause must not be sought in the War Offices of the two nations, nor yet, where many are inclined to look for it, in the intrigues of diplomatists. It must be sought in their admiralties and naval command. The true architects of the new balance of power at sea, and in consequence of the breach between England and Germany and the Triple Entente against the latter, were Tirpitz, Pelletan, and Togo.

III FISHER AND NAVY REORGANIZATION

I

The year 1905, though it witnessed the substitution of a Liberal for a Unionist Cabinet, marked no cleavage in the history of British naval policy.[2] In the early years of the new century it was

---

[1] Duke of Bedford, 'The Collapse of the Special Infantry Reserve' (*Nineteenth Century* January 1913, vol. lxxii, p. 199).

[2] For the history of the British navy during the years we are studying two excellent year books are available: (1) *The Naval Annual*, 1886 (and onwards) edited by Lord Brassey (afterwards by Lord Hythe). Besides chapters giving the comparative statistics for all the navies of the world it contains a number of special studies of particular problems relating to

determined by two factors. The first was the construction of a powerful German navy. This dated from the law of 1898, but more particularly from the law of 1900. The second was the violent reaction which followed in England at the conclusion of the Boer War, against an imperialist policy and the swollen navy and army estimates it had involved. Both these factors began to operate before the fall of the Unionists and both influenced the naval policy of the Unionist Government during its closing years. From now onwards, the Admiralty's new policy is embodied in a single individual, namely Sir John Fisher, to whom we cannot deny genius of a sort, even when we have read his strange memoirs.[1]

Born in Ceylon in 1841 of a family of soldiers—his enemies said he was not a genuine Englishman and that Asiatic blood flowed in his veins—and therefore already in his sixtieth year when the new century opened, he had behind him a long and brilliant career. After taking part in the Crimean War as a cadet, and in the Chinese campaign of 1869 as a midshipman, he had been responsible during the seventies for the establishment of a separate school of torpedo gunnery, at the head of which he was placed. In command for the first time of a man-of-war he had taken an important part in the bombardment of Alexandria and when placed at the head of the landing force his invention of the armoured train attracted the attention of the press and the public. On his return from Egypt, severely invalided, his work for years lay on dry land. But he continued to rise. He became Director of Ordnance and Torpedoes and Admiral Superintendent of Portsmouth Dock-

the navy, the work of British, and sometimes of foreign, experts. (2) *The Navy League Annual*—founded and edited by Allan H. Burgoyne, 1907 onwards, follows similar lines. For a comparison between the British and foreign navies see further the official document published annually since 1896, entitled *Fleets (Great Britain and Foreign Countries) Return to an Order of the Honourable the House of Commons for Return showing the Fleets of Great Britain, France, Russia, Germany, Italy, United States of America and Japan, distinguishing Battleships built and building; Cruisers built and building; Coast Defence . . . Vessels built and building; Torpedo Vessels; Torpedo Boat Destroyers and Torpedo Boats, built and building. Return to show Date of Launch, Displacement and Armaments reduced to one Common Scale.* Volume ii of Fred T. Jane's *The British Battle Fleet, its inception and growth throughout the Centuries to the Present Day* is easy to consult and well documented especially as regards the material of the fleet. See further: *England in deutscher Beleuchtung, Einzelabhandlungen herausgegeban von B. Thomas Lenschav,* Berlin 5. Heft. und Graf. E. Reventlow *Die englische Seemacht,* 1906. For the period immediately preceding that with which we are dealing see Sir William Laird Clowes, *The Royal Navy: A History from the earliest Times to the Death of Queen Victoria,* 1897–1901, vol. vii, 1903. H. W. Wilson, *Ironclads in Action: A Sketch of Naval Warfare from 1855 to 1895 with some account of the development of the Battleship in England,* with an introduction by Captain A. T. Mahan, 2 vols., 1st Edition, 1896, 5th Edition, 1897.

[1] *Memories* 1919; *Records* 1919. See further, for Lord Fisher's life and policy, Admiral Sir R. H. Bacon, *The Life of Lord Fisher of Kilverstone,* 2 vols., 1929.

yard. In 1892 he was made one of the Naval or Sea Lords, the four official expert advisers to the First Lord of the Admiralty, the Minister responsible to Parliament. He was the Third Naval Lord, naval construction was his province, and he won further laurels.

He then returned to sea and took command first of the British North American station, then after representing the Admiralty at the first Hague Conference—where we have already seen the spirit which inspired his attitude—he was placed in command of the Mediterranean fleet. His fame steadily grew, the achievement, in part of the demonic zeal he displayed in the performance of his duties, in part of the skill with which he contrived to create a body of supporters among the sailors. In the Mediterranean he arbitrarily formed a committee of those captains and commanders of his squadron whom he considered more intelligent than the others and readier to welcome innovations, giving them regular instruction in strategy, tactics, and seamanship and in turn asking them for the advice their experience could give. He thus made himself very unpopular with those excluded from this circle of confidants but won a corresponding devotion from the small number of the chosen, applying unflinchingly the maxim 'that favouritism is the essence of successful command'. Further he invited journalists to his table and for years had counted among his intimate friends publicists of such world-wide repute as W. T. Stead[1] and Arnold White. At the head of his circle of friends was no less a personage than King Edward, whose confidence he had contrived to gain and whom he amused by his extraordinary conversation, smoking-room stories interlarded with texts from the Bible, and from whom he secured the position of 'first naval aide-de-camp', despite the King's occasional alarm at Fisher's indiscreet advertisement of the very genuine friendship which united them.

While in command of the Mediterranean fleet he received a visit from Lord Selborne, the First Lord of the Admiralty, who falling a victim to his spell made him an Admiral and Second Sea Lord, a position which enabled him to dispose of the personnel of the navy. Then, after a brief interval during which he was Commander-in-Chief at Portsmouth and, as we have already seen, assisted Lord Esher and Sir George Clarke to work out their

---

[1] It was Fisher who had inspired W. T. Stead's campaign in the *Pall Mall Gazette* which led to the introduction by the Government and the enactment of the Navy Defence Act of 1889 (Fred T. Jane, *The British Battle Fleet*, vol. ii, p. 61 *n.*).

scheme for reorganizing the War Office on the model of the Admiralty, he became First Sea Lord towards the end of 1904 on the anniversary, as his admirers liked to point out, of the Battle of Trafalgar. For seven years—if we reckon from his appointment, already a very important one, as Second Sea Lord, or five, if we reckon from November 1904, under three successive Prime Ministers, one Unionist and two Liberal—he was in fact the dictator of the Admiralty. By the new division of powers which he effected between the four naval members of the Board of Admiralty, by his dominating personality, and by cleverly organized advertisement, he secured a supremacy over this three colleagues which was alien to the traditions of the Admiralty and resembled the supremacy exercised at the War Office by the Commander-in-Chief, until on the advice of Fisher himself and because of the dangers that supremacy involved, the post had been abolished.[1]

[1] Lord Sydenham, *My Working Life*, p. 207. H. of C., March 6, 1905, Sir John Colomb's speech (*Parliamentary Debates*, 4th Series, vol. cxlii, p. 478 sqq.): the speaker calls for the publication of the Order in Council supposed to have altered the division of powers at the Board of Admiralty. When on the following day, March 7, Gibson Bowles hinted that the reason why Lord Selbourne had left the Admiralty to become Governor of South Africa was that he could no longer tolerate Fisher's dictatorship (*Parliamentary Debates*, 4th Series, vol. cxlii, p. 609) Lord Selborne published the document (*Board of Admiralty . . . Copy of Orders in Council, dated 10th of August 1904, showing designation of the various members of, and Secretaries to the Board of Admiralty and the business assigned to them*, 1905), and speaking in the House of Lords on the 21st undertook to prove, supporting his contention with ample evidence, that the Order in Council was not calculated to increase the authority of the First Sea Lord. Actually, the discipline of the navy and the promotion of officers below the rank of Commander were removed from his jurisdiction. His functions were restricted to examining special questions of naval policy. As to the final note which declared that 'in any matter of great importance the First Sea Lord is always to be consulted by the other Sea Lords, the Civil Lord and the Parliamentary or Permanent Secretary' and that it was the prerogative of the First Sea Lord to lay the matter before the First Lord of the Admiralty, Lord Selborne maintained that it did no more than put into writing the accepted practice of the Board. He denied that it amounted to a declaration that the First Lord had no right to submit a question to the Board without the approval of the First Sea Lord. The first argument is plausible but Lord Selborne omitted to state that the Order in Council gave the First Sea Lord authority to make decisions concerning 'the fighting and sea-going efficiency of the Fleet' which gave him an extraordinarily strict control over the Third Sea Lord, who had charge of the material of the navy. The second argument is also plausible. But on the one hand, to transform a custom into a written rule was certainly to give it new weight, a dangerous step, if it were not intended to increase the functions of the First Sea Lord, at a moment when the position was held by a man of such powerful personality as Admiral Fisher. And is it so certain that when Lord Selborne denied that it had been his intention when he signed the note to deprive the First Lord of all power or initiative, he was not protesting against the interpretation Fisher actually gave to the Order in Council of August 10, 1904? (Lord Tweedmouth, H. of C., July 4, 1907 (*Parl. Deb.*, 4th Ser., vol. clxxvii, p. 834). A. Lawrence Lowell (*The Government of England*, vol. i, pp. 92–3), though writing three years after the Order in Council of August 10, 1904, describes the respective functions of the four 'Naval Lords'; he does not employ the new terminology 'Sea Lords', as though they were still defined by the Orders in Council of 1872 and 1882.

The statements of principle which appeared over the signature of the responsible ministers had been presented to them by Fisher and drawn up previously under his direct supervision. He made himself chairman of the Commissions whose advice he pretended to ask and dictated their reports. In what did the 'naval revolution' consist of which he boasted himself the author? In three things: rejuvenation of methods, redistribution of squadrons, and the creation of the Dreadnought.[1]

2

It was when occupying the position of Second Sea Lord from the summer of 1902 to the autumn of 1903 that Fisher tackled the problem of bringing methods up to date. During the last half century the navy had undergone a revolution, which was the counterpart of the Industrial Revolution effected by the introduction of machinery. About the middle of the nineteenth century the British navy, the model of other navies, was still what it had been in the days of Nelson. The object in view, when a decision was sought, was a combat at close quarters. All the guns on one side of the man-of-war were directed upon the enemy's ship and if its rigging was successfully smashed and its bridge set on fire, the ship, thus reduced to a state of inferiority, was boarded. The seaman's entire art, whether he sought or evaded a grapple, consisted in such skilful handling of the sails that the wind which he could not control brought him as near as possible to the goal in view. Now there were no longer masts or sails on men-of-war, which depended no longer on the wind but on steam power to overtake or elude the foe. And, on the other hand, the artillery had become a scientific piece of mechanism which the gunners

---

[1] For a general account of Sir John Fisher's reforms see the panegyric by Archibald S. Hurd, *British War Fleets, The New Scheme of Reorganization and Mobilization with Special Reference to the Growth of the German Navy . . . with Full List of the Fleets and Squadrons at Sea and their Strategical Disposition; the Ships in Commission and in Reserve; and Details of Vessels struck off the War List*, 1905. See also the equally enthusiastic articles by Arnold White: 'Can we trust the Admiralty?' (*National Review*, March 1906, vol. xlvii, pp. 68 sqq.) and Archibald S. Hurd: 'Progress or Reaction in the Navy' (*Fortnightly Review*, April 15, 1906; vol. lxxix n.s, pp. 707 sqq.), also the critical article 'Admiralty Policy and the Manning of the Fleet' by 'Apex' (*United Service Magazine*, February 1906, vol. xxxii, pp. 516 sqq.), and Admiral Lord Charles Beresford's violent attack, *The Betrayal. Being a Record of Facts concerning Naval Policy and Administration from the Year 1902 to the Present Time*, 1912.

must know how to handle so that shots discharged from a moving platform might reach, at a range of several miles, an adversary equally mobile. Nor was machinery necessary only to navigate the vessels and bring the guns into position. Steam engines were also required to operate the steering apparatus and the dynamos, and electrical engines to work the ammunition loaders and transmit the commander's orders, hydraulic machines for the watertight chambers, machines of compressed air to work the torpedoes and for other purposes and refrigerators to keep the temperature of the store rooms cool. A competent witness writing in 1910 estimated at a hundred at least the pieces of machinery installed on a battleship of the most recent type.[1] The man-of-war had become a gigantic factory whose first need was a large number of trained mechanics.

But this 'revolution' whose results were so striking had taken place without the vessels thus transformed being subjected to the test of action. The Crimean War which had occurred too early and moreover had involved no fighting on a large scale, had provided an opportunity only for the first experiments with iron and steam. A few years later, still in the early days of the new equipment, the American War of Secession had been the occasion of a number of mechanical experiments which had made a considerable impression on public opinion. But it had been a flash in the pan. On the restoration of peace the American navy relapsed into insignificance. After this the important struggles were fought on land and the decisive event of the succeeding half century was the rise of a great land power which possessed no fleet. Under these circumstances it is not surprising that England, faced with such navies as the French and Russian against which she judged it prudent to arm but which at bottom she despised, delayed to face the question whether this revolution in the construction of men-of-war did not demand an equally thoroughgoing revolution in the professional training of their crews.

In high quarters the belief prevailed that, for officers and men alike, the old method of instruction employed during the 'great war' which opened the century and which consisted essentially in the manipulation of sails was the training required to turn out a sailor. Any other method was suspect, as in the schools any

---

[1] Frank Fox, *Ramparts of Empire: A View of the Navy from the Imperial Standpoint*, 1910, p. 122.

attempt to modernize the curriculum was suspect to the defenders of the classical tradition.[1] It required the new naval policy of Germany and in particular the law of 1900 to provoke a sudden reaction of British public opinion. Taken by surprise, England suddenly awoke to the fact that here too she must copy the German model. No one was better fitted than Fisher to become the mouthpiece of the movement. In the instruction he gave to his subordinates in the Mediterranean he emphasized the two factors on which in his opinion victory depended, the speed of the ship and the accuracy of her gunnery, and it was this instruction which had impressed Lord Selborne so favourably and placed Fisher in 1902 at the Admiralty.

A serious problem preoccupied the officers of the fleet. As the men-of-war were mechanized the number of engineers and the importance of their functions continued to increase. But they were not in the strict sense of the term officers. They formed a category apart, with a special organization, and distinguished externally by details of uniform. Not only did they form a distinct branch of the service, they entered it from a special school which drew its boys from an inferior social class. And the career of a naval engineer was not only a distinct career from that of a naval officer but it was comparatively without prospects, since its highest rank was on a level with that of a captain. However important their functions might be the engineers were not regarded as 'executive officers'. They belonged to the civil not the executive branch of the service and were incapable of holding a command. However great the personal merit of an engineer, however long his period of service, he had no hope of seeing himself an officer. The genuine officer was the man who controlled the conduct of an engagement by his orders given in the open air, on the poop. In the old days of sailing ships the captain had fraternized with all the members of his crew, whatever their rank. Now the engineers were nothing but automata, invisible and blind instruments of his will. But the engineer, the Caliban of the officers' corps, began to revolt against the Prospero of the upper deck. He observed that many officers, those for instance in the gunnery department, were scarcely less mechanics than himself and passed their lives

---

[1] See the debates on this subject in the House of Commons, June 26, 1900 (*Parliamentary Debates*, 4th Series, vol. lxxxiv, pp. 1128–9), and the discussions at the Royal United Services Institution on June 20 and 28 following an address by J. R. Thursley entitled 'The Training of Seamen' (*The Times*, June 21, July 2, 1900).

on board under conditions very similar to his own. He demanded the privileges and standing of the executive officer. And the problem of status was further complicated by the presence in the British navy of a body of marines, who formed an element apart. The marines composed landing parties, were responsible for a portion of the gunnery on board ship, and fulfilled a further function, not calculated to make them popular, the maintenance of discipline on board. They made the composition of a naval crew still more heterogeneous. If it were thought desirable to weld the crews into a homogeneous body, why not—since the problem of the engineers pressed urgently for solution—settle at the same time the problem of the marines? This was what Fisher attempted within six months of his arrival at Whitehall, in his capacity at Second Sea Lord in charge of the personnel.[1]

He revolutionized the entire system by which officers were recruited and trained. To make the recruiting of officers easier was an urgent necessity when the number of sailors had risen in fifteen years from 60,000 to 120,000. The need for officers had in fact become so acute that it had been found necessary to supply it by giving commissions wholesale to reserve officers from the merchant service. The experiment which had been made of raising the age for joining the navy in the hope of getting young men on leaving their public schools had not proved a success and Fisher reduced from sixteen to twelve the age at which a future naval officer began his career. But if they were taken at such an early

[1] For this reform of Sir John Fisher's see *Navy (Personnel) Memorandum dealing with the Entry, Training and Employment of Officers of the Royal Navy and the Royal Marines*, December 16, 1902; *New Scheme of Naval Training: Selection of Candidates for Nomination as Naval Cadets, Further Report of Members of the Interview Committee*, March 20, 1905. For the results obtained in three years see *A Statement of Admiralty Policy*, November 30, 1905. A lecture given by Commander H. Orpen on November 28, 1902—that is to say, some weeks before the publication of Lord Selborne's memorandum, published in *The Times* of November 29, 1902, under the title 'The Origin, Evolution and Future of the British Navy' amounts to an excellent sketch of Fisher's plan. For the criticism which the plan provoked in the navy see Dubitator, 'The Admiralty Scheme' (*United Service Magazine*, February 1903, vol. xxvi, New Series, pp. 466 sqq.), and Vice-Admiral C. C. Penrose Fitzgerald, 'The Admiralty Scheme': the new Regulations for the Entry and Training of Naval Officers (*United Service Magazine*, February 1903, vol. xxvi, n.s. pp. 586 sqq.). For the career of an English naval officer at the end of the nineteenth century see the interesting article 'The Navy as a Profession,' by Captain R.N. (*National Review*, January 1899; vol. xxxii, pp. 700 sqq.), and after the reform Frank Fox, *Ramparts of the Empire: A View of the Navy from an Imperial Standpoint*, 1910, pp. 179 sqq. See further two interesting articles, one dealing with the engineers by Sir William H. White, 'The Education and Training of Engineers: Civil and Naval' (*Nineteenth Century*, June 1906; vol. lix, pp. 1022 sqq.), the other with the marines, S.P.Q.R., 'The Past and Future of the Royal Marines; as indicated in "A Statement of Admiralty Policy" ' (*United Service Magazine*, February 1906, vol. xxxii n.s, pp. 524 sqq.).

age how could the navy be sure of obtaining the most suitable boys? Must the choice be left to the arbitrary decisions of the higher command, in other words to favouritism and personal influence? At the opening of the twentieth century it was impossible to advocate such a system openly. Must they then institute a competitive examination? The method surely of pedantic mandarins, and almost barbarous in its intellectual rigour if applied to these children. A compromise was devised. A Committee was set up on which a representative of the teaching profession had a seat with the admirals, the bigwigs of the navy, whose task it was to 'interview' candidates, the object of these interviews, which were to be as informal as possible, being to make sure of their moral and mental fitness. The Committee drew up a list of the most suitable from which the First Lord of the Admiralty made his choice.

For four years the boys were to be given the same education, whatever branch of the service they would join later. Promoted to the rank of midshipmen they would continue in that capacity this common education, but on board ship instead of on land. At the end of three years, on passing an examination, they would become acting sub-lieutenants and receive in common special courses of instruction, at Greenwich for three months, at Portsmouth for six. Only then at about the age of twenty would they be divided—as far as possible in accordance with personal preference—into distinct groups and receive special training as executive officers, engineers or marines. The 'new system' of training officers was marked by the following features. In the first place the instruction was extremely technical, and so urgent was the need for technical training that this aroused no protest. Already, a year before the new programme had been worked out, instruction in the handling of sails and rigging had been abolished and the officers who directed the firing of the guns and the launching of the torpedoes had been made responsible for the mechanism of the weapons they employed. Secondly, and this was a bolder step in an age of specialization, the same instruction was given as long as possible to all the pupils. This made it possible later on to employ engineers, gunners and executive officers as torpedo gunners. And all alike, once they had reached the rank of commander, had the same opportunities of promotion in the hierarchy of officers of the executive branch and were equally eligible for all posts including command at sea. The policy of the Board of Admiralty—in other words Fisher's—was to create 'a body of young officers who at the moment of mobilization for war will be equally available for all the general duties of the Fleet and to consolidate into one harmonious whole the fighting officers of the Navy'.[1]

Less than nine months after the publication of the new scheme the Crown put a mansion in the Isle of Wight at the temporary disposal of the Admiralty for the education of the new cadets until the building in course of construction at Dartmouth could be opened. The experiment so vigorously begun was tenaciously pursued, at least as regards the executive officers and the engineers. For in the case of the marines *esprit de corps* prevented the application of the 'new system'. What are we to think of the results? There were critics who, judging the scheme from the point of view of technical efficiency, while they recognized the advantages which would accrue to officers from knowledge of the machinery amid which their entire professional career would be spent, were afraid that the engineers whose special training was delayed would be less efficient than they had been under the old system.[2] There were others who, adopting the social standpoint, doubted whether the scheme was so democratic as its authors made out.[3] What guarantee was there that the choice of the Interview Committee which declared candidates eligible for Dartmouth was determined by their personal merit and that the Committee did not instinctively select boys who belonged by

---

[1] Memorandum of December 16, 1902 *sub finem*. The final sentences which follow read like the professional expert's challenge to Parliament: 'Difficulties there doubtless will be in carrying this part of the scheme into full effect, but those difficulties have been foreseen and they will be met. The advantage to the Navy of the realization of the scheme will be inestimable and permanent; the difficulties will be secondary and transient. *The Board are conscious that on them alone rests the responsibility, and they alone have the advantage of knowing all the conditions which govern the problem.*'

[2] H. of C., May 24, 1906, Bellairs' speech and replies by Arthur Lee and E. Robertson (*Parliamentary Debates*, 4th Series, vol. clvii, pp. 1461 sqq., 1471 sqq., 1747 sqq.). 'Whatever good effects the new plan may have in other directions, it can hardly increase materially the scientific education of the cadet' (A. Lawrence Lowell, *The Government of England*, vol. i, p. 104 *n*.).

[3] For Fisher's intentions see his *Memories*, p. 201: '. . . This democratic country won't stand 99 per cent *at least* of her Naval Officers being drawn from the Upper Ten. . . . It's amazing to me that anyone should persuade himself that an Aristocratic Service can be maintained in a Democratic State. The true democratic principle is Napoleon's "*La carrière ouverte aux talents.*" The Democracy will shortly realize this, and there will be a dangerous and mischievous agitation. The secret of successful administration is the intelligent anticipation of agitation.' But this was written in his old age, after the Great War of 1914, and is an admission that the reform of 1902 had not when he wrote made the officers of the British navy a democratic body.

birth to the wealthy and governing class? The training, at Dartmouth first, then during those later years when the young man served as a midshipman, alone cost his parents a hundred, perhaps a hundred and fifty pounds a year.[1] There were no scholarships for boys of humble origin. They spoke of democratizing the naval officers by breaking down the barrier which divided them from the engineers. The barrier was indeed broken down but it was by making the engineers an aristocratic body.

3

This reform excited such interest that less attention was paid to others which concerned not the officers but the crews. But they had their importance. Here also the navy had to be adapted to the new demands of a century not even of steam but of electricity.

Indeed, a year before Fisher's influence had begun to be felt at the Admiralty instruction 'in the rigging' had been abolished for the sailors as well as the officers. The South African War had provided a pretext for replacing the four sailing vessels which served as training ships by four cruisers. In default of training ships it became necessary to organize a new system of training for future sailors. In future all would receive elementary instruction in mechanics, and be given some knowledge of stoking. And all could be taught the rudiments of gunnery. Since this instruction did not, like the older training, promote the physical development of its subjects, gymnastic exercises were instituted. In this case a method was followed in some respects the reverse of that pursued in training the officers. Specialization from childhood was considered beneficial and a body of boy artificers was formed who would be trained in mechanics from the age of fourteen, four years that is to say before their admission into the navy. And the examinations, which after two years on board made an ordinary seaman an able seaman, would no longer be, as they had been hitherto, a mere formality. The good effects of this modernization were quickly felt. When the twentieth century opened the low standard of its gunnery was a disgrace to the British navy. Within a few years, it would seem, the defect had been made good. In 1909 Admiral Fisher mentioned with pride the example

---

[1] H. of C., May 24, 1906, Bellairs' speech (*Parliamentary Debates*, 4th Series, vol. clvii, p. 1463).

of a large ironclad which during some gunning practices hit fifteen times out of eighteen a target fourteen times smaller than itself and at a distance of five miles, the vessel moving at a rate of twenty knots, the target at an unknown speed.[1]

At the same time, even before Fisher reached the Admiralty, far-reaching alterations were made in the system of enlistment. Since the abolition of the press gang in 1852 the necessary number of men had been obtained by enlistments termed 'continuous', nominally for twelve years, actually for thirteen or fourteen. For the twelve years' enlistment was commenced at the age of eighteen, when the young sailors had already been serving for two or even two and a half years as 'boys'. When the twelve years had expired, the sailor was urged to re-enlist for a further period of ten years. That the Admiralty should abandon this system of enlistment for a very lengthy term was obviously out of the question; for it secured men in sufficient numbers and of excellent quality. But doubts had begun to be felt whether, in view of the constant increase in the number of sailors, sufficient men would always be found and the example of the German navy proved that first rate crews could be secured in which the majority of the seamen were enlisted or actually served for a shorter period.[2] And all the posts on board need not be filled by perfectly trained seamen. It was therefore decided in 1900 to institute a new class of enlistment, nominally for twelve years but providing that at the end of seven years the men should enter the reserve. In a navy entirely manned by 'volunteers' and where, when the term of enlistment had expired, the sailor could not be legally compelled to re-enlist, the new system offered the advantage of forming a body of reservists whose numbers were thus kept up automatic-

---

[1] Letter to Lord Esher, August 27, 1907 (*Memories*, p. 192).

[2] See the curious anecdotes collected by Tirpitz to show the astonishment inspired by the 'military' discipline of the German crews. 'When in the year 1873 an English lady at Gibraltar saw on board the *Friedrich Karl* our sailors already, as still at the opening of the World War, superior, I am convinced, to the British she exclaimed in surprise "Don't they look just like sailors?" and when I asked what ever else they should look like, replied firmly: "But you are not a seagoing nation" ' (*Erinnerungen*, p. 10). And again: 'I remember the astonishment expressed by English officers when in Malta in 1890 we lay in our old hulks close to the modern vessels of the British and our men were working like slaves, hard at it the entire day. If, they said, their own men were asked to work so hard, they would mutiny. They simply couldn't understand such hard labour, especially since, owing to the short term for which a German sailor serves, it could not be fully utilized. In the park at Osborne last year a detachment of our marines paraded before the Queen. British naval officers remarked in astonishment, "The men are soldiers." Their impression was not altogether correct but it was significant' (ibid., p. 16).

ally.[1] It was called the Royal Fleet Reserve and it supplemented the Royal Naval Reserve already forty years old, which was recruited by the voluntary enlistment of sailors in the merchant service and which could not guarantee under all circumstances the supply of men necessary to keep the crews at full strength during war. The institution of this new type of enlistment had the additional advantage of making it possible to effect considerable economies. The high rates of pay which must be given to the men enlisted for a long term and to those who renewed their enlistment need not be given to such a large number. On the other hand, the additional expenditure on the Royal Naval Reserve which would become necessary, if its numbers were increased, was avoided.

Once again, this last reform was not Fisher's work. But he was its convinced advocate and did his utmost to strengthen the Royal Fleet Reserve by extending the system of Non-continuous Service. For the new method of enlistments suited his system admirably and facilitated decisions of a sensational character taken about this time by the First Lord of the Admiralty, the Board of Admiralty, and in particular after the close of 1904 by its autocrat. They concerned not the personnel but the material of the navy.

4

When we were relating the history of British imperialism at the close of the Boer War we saw how the first Navy Estimates of the post-war period reached an enormous figure: £35,476,000, an increase of £4,306,000 over the preceding year. Three ironclads and four armoured cruisers were laid down. But the current of public opinion was flowing in a direction which soon convinced the Unionist Government that its position had not been strengthened but weakened by the conclusion of a victorious peace in South Africa, that the country considered that the war had cost

[1] In conformity with the report of a Committee of inquiry *Naval Reserves, Report of the Naval Reserves Committee*, January 20, 1903 (Sir Edward Grey's Committee); cf. *A Statement of Admiralty Policy*, November 30, 1905, pp. 20-1. See also on the problem of reserves H. of C. March 21-2, 1901 (*Parliamentary Debates*, 4th Series, vol. xci, pp. 806 sqq., 934 sqq.), and the excellent article signed 'Apex' and entitled 'Admiralty Policy and the Manning of the Fleet' (*United Service Magazine*, February 1906; vol. xxxii, New Series, pp. 516 sqq.). For the Royal Naval Reserve which was also reorganized by Fisher see Frank C. Bowen, *History of the Royal Naval Reserve*, 1926.

too dear, and would not be placated by a victory which resulted in a further increase of armaments. If the Navy Estimates in 1904 were higher than in the previous year—£36,830,000, an increase of £1,354,000, it was because two completed ironclads had been bought from the Government of Chile to prevent their purchase by Russia, then at war with England's ally Japan. As a result of the purchase, two cruisers only would be laid down instead of three, which encouraged the hope of considerable economies in future years. Actually, the Navy Estimates in 1905 amounted only to £33,389,000, a reduction of £3,500,000 on the previous year. Only one cruiser was laid down. Then Lord Cawdor succeeded Lord Selborne at the Admiralty and while continuing a policy of economy—the estimates he prepared at the close of 1905 effected a reduction of £1,500,000 as compared with 1904—proposed to incur further expenditure during the following years by laying down four ironclads. The Liberals who took office at this juncture deleted from the programme one of the four ironclads and protested against the attempt of a falling Government to force their hands. Moreover Campbell-Bannerman declared himself authorized to state that in reducing the programme of naval construction contemplated by Lord Cawdor, far from overruling the Board of Admiralty he acted with their assent.[1] The Board therefore possessed a definite policy, which for a little over a year had been the policy of the First Sea Lord, and which sought to increase the 'efficiency' of the British navy while reducing expenditure. What had been Fisher's object ever since he reached high command? To impress upon his superiors and subordinates alike the absurd situation of the British navy, loath to abandon its traditions and therefore clinging to the methods of the sailing vessel when there was no longer a single sailing ship in the fleet, a single sail in the new men-of-war. But what ideal should an Admiral, a Sea Lord, pursue in an industrialized navy? The ideal always pursued by the inventor of a machine, to obtain the same or better results at a lower cost. It was obvious in particular that the enormous increase in the speed of warships due to the invention and progress of steam navigation, and the marvellous and growing ease of communication, by telegraph first, then by wireless telegraphy, were reducing the size of the earth. It was natural that Britain to protect her vast mercantile marine and to link up the different parts

[1] H. of C., July 27, 1906 (*Parliamentary Debates*, 4th Series, vol. clxii, p. 115).

of the immense empire had multiplied her naval stations and amply furnished them with ships. But was it any longer necessary to maintain so many ships when faster vessels to which, moreover, it was easier to give the alarm, could be despatched more freely at a signal to any point on the globe? Fewer ships and fewer naval stations would suffice. As soon as Fisher became First Sea Lord he used the broom vigorously, and his success in sweeping away sources of unnecessary expenditure was the true reason why the Navy Estimates declined in 1905 and the succeeding years.[1] In the first line alone no less than 130 were given up within a few months.

Fisher proposed to confront foreign nations with a navy formidable rather by the quality than by the number of its ships. What then became of the standard, strictly quantitative, which for the last fifteen years had determined the supposed needs of the British Admiralty, the 'Two-Power Standard'? For the last fifteen years, for during the greater part, indeed almost the whole of the nineteenth century, the Admiralty had applied a different standard. Then only one other navy counted for anything, namely, the French, and England was therefore content in peacetime with a fleet one-third larger than the French. It was not until 1889 that the First Lord of the Admiralty, Lord George Hamilton, had asked for a navy equal to, if not slightly larger than, the two strongest foreign navies. Which were they?[2] At a moment when Russia was developing her navy and the Franco-Russian alliance was taking shape, no one had any doubt. Four years later when the Unionists vociferously demanded that the Liberal Government of the day should undertake a new programme of naval construction on a large scale their speakers put forward plainly the Franco-Russian peril and the Secretary to the Admiralty agreed that the minimum strength of the British navy must be equal to the combined navies of France and Russia.[3]

[1] For this policy of cleansing the navy see Pretyman's speech, H. of C., March 6, 1905 (*Parliamentary Debates*, 4th Series, vol. cxlii, pp. 438 sqq.).

[2] H. of C., March 7, 1889: Lord George Hamilton indeed presented the principle as that which the Government had already been applying for several years. 'I have endeavoured during the past year to study the speeches of those who in previous years have held my position, and that of Prime Minister, so as to ascertain what was the permanent idea underlying their utterances when they spoke of the standard of strength on which our naval establishment should be maintained. I think I am correct in saying that that idea has been that an establishment should be on such a scale that it should at least be equal to the naval strength of any other two countries' (*Parliamentary Debates*, 3rd Series, vol. cccxxxiii, p. 1171). Cf. H. of C., same sitting, Lord Charles Beresford's speech (ibid., p. 1203).

[3] H. of C., December 19, 1893, speeches by Lord George Hamilton, Arthur Balfour, Admiral Field, Macfarlane, Gibson Bowles, and Joseph Chamberlain and the statement by

We must however inquire how the Admiralty interpreted the Two-Power Standard. The British fleet had to fulfil three purposes—to fight a hostile navy, protect the mercantile marine, safeguard communications between the various parts of the empire. But it was only the first of these which the Two-Power Standard had in view. It was applied only to the ironclads, the battleships. The cruisers intended to serve the two other purposes might be built in unlimited numbers. But could this distinction between the battleship and the cruiser be maintained any longer now that the armoured cruiser had been invented? It was in the estimates for 1897 that there appeared for the first time six armoured cruisers of the Cressy type replacing the large cruisers simply 'protected' for which the budgets immediately preceding made provision. Their displacement was 12,000 tons, their length 440 feet, they carried two 9.2 inch B.L. guns, twelve 6 inch Q.F. guns. the armour plating attained in the middle of the vessel a thickness of six inches, their horse-power was 21,000 and their speed 21 knots. It was a speed equal to that of protected cruisers of the 'Powerful' type, but the new cruisers were armoured and their armouring was superior to that of the oldest ironclads the Admiralty still kept in commission. In short they were cruisers in their speed but the protected cruisers were powerless against them. They were not simple cruisers but real men-of-war. The Cressys were followed by the Drakes, and these by the Counties. Then after these two experiments came the Devonshires which hardly differed in speed, armour or armament from the Cressys.[1] In four years a revolution had taken place. The British fleet in 1900 did not contain a single armoured cruiser. At the end of 1905 it possessed twenty-six. All the calculations of the Two-Power Standard were thus falsified. Many Liberal members of Parliament argued, and their contention was never satisfactorily refuted,

the representative of the Government, Sir U. Kaye Shuttleworth (*Parliamentary Debates*, 4th Series, vol. xix, pp. 1775, 1810, 1822, 1828, 1837, 1856, 1873). See especially Lord George Hamilton's and Arthur Balfour's speeches and Lord Charles Beresford's memorandum of November 18. Some years later, when the *entente* in the Far East between France, Germany and Russia suggested more dangerous eventualities than a Franco-Russian alliance it was even questioned whether the Two-Power Standard would suffice to ensure the safety of the country (H. of C., March 5, 1897, Sir Charles Dilke's speech; ibid., vol. xlvii, pp. 68–9).

[1] Fred T. Jane, *The British Battle Fleet*, vol. ii, pp. 1101 sqq. The Drakes were larger (14,000 tons) and faster (23 knots), the Counties smaller (9,800 tons) and of much the same speed as the Drakes. The Devonshires, slightly smaller (10,850 tons) than the Cressys were not quite so strongly armed (their largest guns were 7.5 inches) and their speed was distinctly less than that of the Drakes and Counties.

that the British navy was numerically superior not only to two but to the three most powerful foreign navies.[1] But in fact when we read the lengthy debates which took place in the House of Commons in 1904 and 1905 on the question of the Two-Power Standard we receive the impression that the politicians at the Admiralty had lost their bearings and were uncertain whether to defend the standard or represent it as obsolete. 'I think', stated Lord Selborne in the House of Lords, 'I shall carry your Lordships with me when I say that you cannot compare with any reason or fairness the naval expenditure of this country with that of any two or more Powers, because what our navy has to do is totally different from what the navies of any one, two or three other Powers have to do.'[2] Also Lord Goschen: 'The Two-Power Standard is gone. It is no longer applicable to the state of Europe. ... As long as changes continue in the balance of naval power and in the fleets of other countries, it is impossible for the Admiralty to lay down any fixed standard.'[3] What in truth was left about 1905 of the Franco-Russian peril?

The French navy was still the most powerful in Europe after the British. But if it was numerically the strongest, its prestige did not stand high. The inventive genius of its engineers was universally recognized. But the caprices of Parliamentary committees and the effects of Cabinet crises had made it a navy built on no uniform plan, what was called in jest a fleet of samples, and since 1902 under the Pelletan government it had still further deteriorated. Not only did the French Admiralty anticipate the wishes of the British by giving up the construction of great ironclads and

---

[1] H. of C., August 4, 1904, Edmund Robertson's speech: '... At the present time, from the report in his hand, he saw that we had battleships of the first class, 49; the next three Naval Powers—France, Germany, and Russia—had 50 and all the other navies of the world 80. That was a Three-Power Standard. We had five-sixths of the battleship strength of all the rest of the world. In armed cruisers we had 28; France, Germany, and Russia 27; and the rest of the world 55. Here again there was a Three-Power Standard. In protected cruisers of the first class we had 21; France, Germany, and Russia 13; and the other navies of the world, 16. In second-class cruisers we had 49, as against 27 for France, Germany, and Russia; and 59 for all the other navies. In third-class cruisers we had 32; France, Germany, and Russia 32; and the rest of the world 55. So that in the case of the fleet in being we were maintaining a Three-Power Standard. It was the same story with regard to fleets on paper. In battleships and armed cruisers we were building 39 as against 35 by France, Germany, and Russia, and 68 by all the other navies of the world.' And Robertson remarks that the British navy built faster than any other (*Parliamentary Debates*, 4th Series, vol. cxxxix, p. 1054). Cf. March 6, 1905, speeches by Herbert Roberts, Reginald Lucas, T. Lough (ibid., vol. cxlii, pp. 456 sqq., 459 sqq., 463 sqq.).
[2] H. of L., August 9, 1904 (*Parliamentary Debates*, 4th Series, vol. cxxxix, p. 1529).
[3] H. of L., March 21, 1905 (ibid., vol. cxliv, p. 610).

concentrating on the formation of a fleet of submarines and torpedo boats, but its haphazard methods and undisciplined crews had made the French navy the laughing-stock of the world. The Russian fleet left the Baltic and, after its command had given in the North Sea a pitiful display of brutality and bad nerves, had confronted the Japanese fleet which had already proved its worth in 1904 and had been annihilated at Tshushima. But other navies were coming to the fore, the Japanese in the first place, but also the American and the German. The British Admiralty had decided to make an ally of the Japanese fleet. With the American navy it was impossible to compete. The United States were wealthy enough to build as many warships as they pleased. London accordingly decided to proclaim the principle that war would never be waged against a nation of kindred race and language so that in applying the Two-Power Standard the American fleet need not be taken into account. But what two navies could the British take into account, if they were thinking all the time of only one: the German?

For the past five years the Emperor William assisted by Admiral Tirpitz had been engaged in the task of providing himself with a fleet so powerful that to use the official formula 'if the strongest naval power engaged it, it would endanger its own supremacy'. No one could mistake the allusion when a memorandum inspired by Fisher drew the attention of Parliament and the nation to a navy 'of the most efficient type and so fortunately circumstanced that it is able to concentrate almost the whole of its fleet at its home fronts'.[1]

The days had therefore returned when before the adoption of the Two-Power Standard Britain had only one foreign navy to consider. But that navy was no longer the French and there was this further difference from the earlier period that the German navy was not, as the French had been in the middle of the nineteenth century, the sole foreign navy which counted. There were others whose friendship it was prudent to gain by a system of *ententes* and alliances. For the time there was no longer any question of the Two-Power Standard and when after a short interval it would make its reappearance it would possess, as we shall see later, a totally different significance.

---

[1] *Navy: Distribution and Mobilisation of the Fleet*, December 6, 1904, p. 2.

5

In the meanwhile the Admiralty under the inspiration of Sir John Fisher effected a significant redistribution of the squadrons.[1] In the East only one squadron of cruisers would in future be stationed, entirely concentrated, after the abolition of the station at Esquimault on the Canadian coast and the Pacific station, in the three stations of China, Australia, and the East Indies and placed under the command of the Commander-in-Chief of the Chinese station. After this nothing until the Cape, where a squadron was stationed consisting of second- and third-class cruisers to guard communications between the east and west—that is to say, in these distant seas England yielded supremacy to the rival navies of the United States and Japan and accepted the second place, because she was obliged to concentrate her attention on European waters. In the Atlantic the same homeward movement was effected. The north Atlantic squadron was abolished and the squadron in the south Atlantic, charged with the protection and policing of the West Indies, was profoundly modified. The number of ships was considerably reduced and the squadron would henceforward be confined to five vessels called the 'Particular Service' Squadron to which—this was another of Fisher's innovations—cadets and boys would be sent to be trained by actual service at sea. These ships would make three cruises yearly, one of them to the West Indies, but would always return to their base which was not on the American but on the British coast, at Devonport.

Where then would the battleships be concentrated? The Mediterranean squadron was reduced to eight ironclads and an adequate complement of cruisers. The day had gone by when a war with France and Russia was expected and the Mediterranean seemed likely to be the principal theatre of naval warfare. The Channel fleet, on the other hand, was transferred to Gibraltar under the new name of the Atlantic fleet. Like the Mediterranean fleet it was composed of eight battleships with an adequate num-

[1] For this aspect of Fisher's policy see the memorandum signed by Lord Selborne entitled: *Navy: Distribution and Mobilisation of the Fleet*, December 6, 1904, which is completed by the *Circular Letter to Commanders-in-Chief at Home and Abroad*, signed Evan MacGregor and dated December 10, 1904, and Lord Selborne's memorandum entitled: *Redistribution of the Fleet: Arrangements consequent on the Redistribution of the Fleet*, March 15, 1905.

ber of cruisers. It took over a small part of the area formerly assigned to the Mediterranean fleet, but must be prepared to sail to whatever point in western waters the exigencies of war might require its despatch. What did this point seem likely to be? The extensive preparation made by the Admiralty in the waters surrounding the British coast enables us to guess. The Home Fleet under the new title of Channel fleet comprised, in accordance with the programme laid down by Fisher in December 1904, the large number of twelve battleships, not to mention the cruisers. A year later it consisted of seventeen battleships besides six armoured cruisers of the most recent type. The scrapping of so many antiquated vessels placed enough men at the disposal of the Admiralty to maintain all three squadrons at full strength. Each was to be permanently concentrated under the command of its admiral, though to prevent the captains losing all personal initiative a few units would be detached from time to time for isolated manœuvres. Measures were also taken to ensure the homogeneous composition of the crews. Hitherto ships stationed in home waters had been 'in commission' for an indefinite period, a quarter of the crews being renewed annually, those stationed in distant waters 'in commission' for three years, a period so long that it had been necessary to detach from time to time a number of sailors and send them ashore to undergo a course of special training and send on others to take their place. In future all ships, whatever their station, would be 'in commission' only for two years during which, except for some very exceptional reason, no officer or sailor would be allowed to leave the ship to which he had been assigned.[1]

Other measures of equal importance were adopted to provide for the defence of the British coast by employing the reserve. According to the system hitherto in force, it consisted of vessels older than the others and slightly out of date, which lay up empty in the home ports. If it became necessary to mobilize them, what a time it would take to fit them out, provide them with crews and train men, unaccustomed to active service, to take part in naval

---

[1] Very strict measures were adopted at the same time to prevent the squadrons being depleted of too large a number of vessels on the ground of repairs. No ship might be laid up for repairs for more than thirty days a year and repairs must always be carried out in such a way that in case of necessity the ship could be ready for sea in four days. No more than two ships might be detached for repair from the Channel Fleet, not more than one from the Atlantic and Mediterranean fleets (*Circular Letter to Commanders-in-Chief*, December 10, 1904).

warfare! All this Fisher changed within a few weeks, one is tempted to say within a few days.[1] Thanks to the policy of reducing the number of units hitherto dispersed by the Admiralty in distant oceans, he had at his disposal a fleet of twelve ironclads, fourteen armoured cruisers, and eight large protected cruisers which he could station in home waters 'in commission'. And thanks to the purge he had effected he disposed of sufficient sailors to man these vessels with what he termed nucleus crews, about two-fifths of the full complement, composed of men whom we might term 'skilled labourers' in those large factories which modern men-of-war have become. At regular intervals reservists joined them for training, who would then be competent in case of war to play the part of unskilled labourers and enable the reserve squadron to reinforce the Channel fleet in a few hours. Behind these vessels, there were other ships exempted from the condemnation passed upon all the worthless material of the British navy. If not sufficiently good to be kept armed, they were not bad enough to be sold as scrap iron. But it was the creation of a large reserve fleet permanently 'in commission' which together with the redistribution of squadrons constituted the original features of the new naval policy. It made possible 'the complete and instantaneous' mobilization of a formidable fleet in home waters. And the need for 'efficiency' was reconciled with the need for economy. But once again were not the two things at bottom synonymous? True economy is to obtain the maximum of results with a minimum of expenditure. A policy of concentration of forces was thus carried out, aimed at a new enemy. It was the German navy.

These innovations made by the British Admiralty aroused in Germany feelings not of alarm or annoyance but rather of gratified pride. Not only were the Germans proud of the fact that it was their example which had induced the British Admiralty to throw off its lethargy and modernize its methods, so that even in a sphere where Britain had so long been regarded as supreme, the

[1] 'The test which is to be made to-day of the readiness for immediate service of a portion of the recently reconstituted naval reserve in the home ports makes the beginning of what may almost be regarded as a new epoch in the history of the British Fleet.... It is possible that the British public may not realize at once all that this new departure means in terms of naval efficiency; but that it will be patent to every foreign professional critic is beyond doubt. It is, indeed, a remarkable fact that within a few weeks of what many people regard as a revolution in the system of our organization for war, we are able to witness a perfectly equipped squadron of ships in reserve proceeding to sea for a week's cruise, organized and prepared for instant battle, and this without withdrawing an officer or man from duties or studies he may be engaged in elsewhere' (*The Times*, February 9, 1905).

German Empire had become the model nation, but the redistribution of squadrons could be legitimately regarded at Berlin as the first victory won by the partisans of a strong navy.[1] Only four years after the passing of the law of 1900 Germany had compelled England to reduce her fleet in the Pacific and withdraw it from North American waters. Her high-seas fleet stationed between Heligoland and Kiel, still in its infancy but thoroughly up to date, which could count a dozen ironclads and for the next fifteen years would be increased in the regular proportion provided by law, had reason to be proud of the strange influence, the attraction, which we might almost call a suction, that it exercised upon the British navy. In England Fisher had skilfully contrived to win the support of the Liberals, who on the verge of taking office were delighted that a great sailor, an expert in the art of war, should declare it possible to reduce the navy estimates without weakening the navy. But he abolished too high-handedly too many posts not to make many enemies among those in high command. With the officers of the fleet and the Unionist politicians he was as unpopular as he was popular with the Liberals and for the same reason. This no doubt annoyed him and it was probably the desire to put an end to his unpopularity which led him to proclaim sooner than he had wished and with an imprudent flourish of trumpets the creation of the Dreadnought.

6

Immediately on his arrival at the Admiralty Fisher had appointed a Committee on Designs composed of naval officers and engineers to assist the director of naval construction to prepare plans for men-of-war in accordance with the instructions of the Board, in other words of the First Sea Lord. At the same time he

[1] 'It was certainly our example which compelled the English also to set to work and master once more the methods of naval warfare. Germany's position in the world set a standard which was methodically pursued by a navy which was still practically without vessels. We had no alternative but to build ships or make foreigners a present of our ideas. We built and when the world war broke out were still superior to the English in the quality and handling of our vessels though not in their number, although the days when their tactics were a traditional routine and their manœuvres chaotic had long passed' (Von Tirpitz, *Erinnerungen*, p. 47). It will be seen that Tirpitz regarded the German navy as superior in quality to the British even before the laws of 1898 and 1900 had been passed. In 1892 the German navy had, according to him, invented a new system of naval tactics which all the other navies beginning with the British subsequently copied (ibid., p. 46).

gave orders to speed up work in all the dockyards so as to turn out ships more quickly and meet the competition of the German fleet. A year had not passed before the results of his initiative became visible. In September the papers proclaimed to the world that a man-of-war was being built in the utmost secrecy, whose launching would mark an epoch in the history of the British fleet. On October 2, 1905, the first plate of her keel was laid and she was launched on February 10, 1906. It had been expected that she would not be ready for service until sixteen months after the construction began. In December 1906, the Dreadnought left the docks and received the official visit of the First Lord of the Admiralty and the First Sea Lord. The most advanced methods of organizing labour had been employed to expedite the construction of the ironclad with the avowed object of laying down rules to speed up normal construction.[1] But this extraordinary speed was to a large extent deceptive. The necessary material had been got together in advance, and material and guns intended for other vessels had been diverted to the Dreadnought, their construction being correspondingly delayed.[2]

What then was this masterpiece of the British Admiralty? The Dreadnought was a monster vessel, larger than any ironclad previously built—17,900 tons as against 16,000—more powerfully armed and swifter. Instead of four twelve-inch guns and ten six-inch, she possessed ten twelve-inch guns so arranged that six could be pointed together in all positions, eight in almost all. Her speed was twenty-one knots instead of the eighteen and a half of ironclads of the Lord Nelson type, almost equalling the twenty-two and a half knots of the armoured cruisers of the Devonshire type. The employment for the first time of the turbine had made this last improvement possible. At the same time in a more genuine secrecy the three armoured cruisers laid down as provided in the estimates for 1905 constituted an innovation as sensational as the Dreadnought. The Invincibles had a displacement of 17,250 tons, whereas the displacement of the Devonshires had not exceeded 10,850. They had an armament of eight twelve-inch guns; the Devonshires carried no guns of more than 7.5 inches. Their armour plating at its thickest measured seven inches instead of six. Their speed was twenty-five knots. They were genuine men-of-

---

[1] *The Times*, October 13, 1905.
[2] Fred T. Jane, *The British Battle Fleet*, vol. ii, p. 126 *n*.

war scarcely less powerfully armed than the Dreadnoughts and markedly swifter.

The immediate advantages which accrued to England from the invention of the Dreadnought[1] were incontestable.

In the first place the innovation took all the rival navies by surprise. While England blazoned so dramatically in the face of the world her increased speed of naval construction and the greater strength of her vessels, the other Powers found themselves compelled, if they wanted to launch men-of-war, not below the standard of the Dreadnoughts, to alter their programmes of naval construction, possibly even to stop the building of certain ships and recommence it on new lines. England gained time.

And time was also gained in another way. The German coastline was cut in two by the Danish peninsula. No communication could be established in wartime between the Baltic coast and the coast of the North Sea except by forcing a passage through the straights which divide the Danish islands from Sweden, and the British fleet would have to be faced before junction with the North Sea fleet could be established. It was to establish direct naval communications between the two portions of the German coast that the Kiel Canal had been cut. But the Dreadnoughts drew too much water and were too huge to pass through the Canal. If in her turn Germany were to build Dreadnoughts, either her fleet of Dreadnoughts must be divided into two or concentrated entirely on one side of the Kiel Canal, leaving the other coast devoid of Dreadnoughts which in no circumstances could take refuge from one sea in the other. The invention of the English Dreadnought confronted Germany with the urgent task of making the Kiel Canal wider and deeper so that it would be navigable by Dreadnoughts.[2] It was a task which would require many years to complete.

[1] For the Dreadnought its merits and dangers see, in addition to the general works already mentioned, two articles signed 'Captain R.N.' and entitled respectively '1881–1906: The Inflexible and the Dreadnought' and 'Food for Thought' which appeared at an interval of two months in the *United Service Magazine* for November 1906 (vol. xxxiv, New Series, pp. 121 sqq.), and January 1907 (vol. xxxiv, New Series, pp. 350 sqq.) and Archibald Hurd's reply to this writer's criticisms in an article entitled 'Uneasiness. Is it justified?' which appeared in the same number, January 1907, of the *United Service Magazine*. See further Arthur Lee, 'A Plea for maintaining our Battleship Programme' (*National Review*, August 1906, vol. xlvii, pp. 914 sqq.); and against the Dreadnought W. H. White, 'The Navy Estimates and Naval Debate' (*Nineteenth Century*, April 1908, vol. lxiii, pp. 517 sqq.).

[2] The question of the Kiel Canal and the difficulties it presented to the increase in the size of warships had already caused anxiety to the German Admiralty before the Dread-

But Fisher's dramatic surprise had its drawbacks.

In the first place, England lost a moral advantage. In modern times her naval policy had hitherto presented a defensive aspect. To possess a navy stronger than the French, as strong, even a little stronger, than the French and Russian navies combined, never to take the initiative in inventing engines of war but to leave that responsibility to some other nation, France for example, whose engineers had created the torpedo boat, the armed cruiser, and submarine, to wait until the experiment had been made abroad and then build torpedo-destroyers and torpedo boats, submarines, and armoured cruisers in reply to those already invented by the enemy nation—such hitherto had been the British method. Now all this was changed. The Admiralty seemed to be proclaiming to the world that in the armament competition it would henceforward take the initiative and challenge rival navies to overtake the British. At bottom to be sure it regarded itself as on the defensive against the threat of German attack. But it gave this defensive the air of an offensive, and moreover an offensive theatrically staged.

And did this invention of the Dreadnought, so loudly advertised by Fisher and his friends, really give the British navy such a lead over the others that it could not be caught up in four or five years? This ostentatious advertisement was calculated to alarm the other nations unnecessarily and hasten their reply. The Dreadnought had not left the dock before Germany laid down a ship whose dimensions were to rival those of this yet mysterious monster. And when later on Germany would build Dreadnoughts

nought made its appearance. See Von Müller's letter to Tirpitz of February 5, 1905: 'It is obvious that our main strength must lie in vessels of the line and in torpedo boats. It is equally clear that in so far as natural difficulties do not prevent it the gigantic battleship must be the type of our future men-of-war, indeed, that we shall do well to anticipate in this direction the latest types of vessels contructed by our opponent. But we have to face a natural obstacle, the size of the canal between the Baltic and North Sea. It might indeed be argued that to concentrate our naval power on vessels of 17,000 or 18,000 tons is so important that it would be better to give up the use of the canal than the giant man-of-war. I, however, do not set so high a value on the latter. To my mind the strategical concentration of our fleet by the canal is more important than its tactical concentration in these monster men-of-war and I would therefore not adopt the latter until domestic conditions permit the canal to be reconstructed' (Tirpitz, *Politische Dokumente*, vol. i, p. 15). It was, we must add, not only the Kiel Canal but the waters around the North Sea ports which the German naval authorities would be obliged to deepen by extensive dredging operations to enable monster battleships to move freely. Another unexpected advantage for the British Dreadnoughts. 'The German Admiralty is going, is indeed obliged, to spend 12½ million sterling in dredging so as to allow these existing ships of ours to go and fight them in their own waters, when before they could not do so. It was, indeed, a Machiavellian enterprise of Providence on our own behalf that brought about the evolution of the Dreadnought' (Letter from Admiral Fisher to King Edward, 1907, *Memories*, p. 15).

every year, she in turn would enjoy an unexpected advantage over England. The British fleet was an old fleet containing many antiquated vessels. If the Dreadnought really possessed all the value Fisher claimed for it, these old ships would be rendered worthless as soon as the German Admiralty began building Dreadnoughts and confronted England with a navy consisting entirely of modern vessels. The fact that her navy was only a few years old, hitherto a disadvantage for Germany, would, Fisher's critics maintained, prove an advantage, if the superiority of the Dreadnought over previous types of vessels were really so great. For in that case the invention amounted to scrapping at a stroke the entire British fleet built before 1905.

But it was not so certain after all that the Dreadnought was the marvellous innovation it was declared to be. All navies about 1905 were tending to adopt this type of monster vessel. The idea would seem to have been borrowed by the British Admiralty from the Italian navy which perhaps would have been the first to launch a Dreadnought if the nation had been sufficiently wealthy.[1] Already Japan and Germany were considering and the United States had actually begun the construction of new types of ironclad strikingly similar to the Dreadnought. And it might well be asked whether when the construction of larger and still larger vessels better armed, better armoured, and swifter was the fashion in naval quarters, the invention of the torpedo and the development of heavy artillery were not changing the entire conditions of naval warfare? Of what use would be a sea monster, which cost £1,800,000 to build, if a single torpedo or shell could sink it in a few minutes? A war without precedent in history was expected to prove these criticisms sound. But for the moment the Russo-Japanese War, the first real naval war the world had witnessed since the days of Trafalgar and Aboukir, seemed to justify the champions of monster vessels. The torpedo had played a very minor part and the war had been decided by a battle between ironclads, a Trafalgar of the Far East.[2] And even if there had been

[1] F. T. Jane, *The British Battle Fleet*, vol. ii, pp. 134 sqq.
[2] 'Lessons of the Japanese War' (*The Times*, January 6, 1905). Admiral the Hon. E. R. Fremantle 'The Japanese Trafalgar' (*United Service Magazine*, July 1905; vol. xxi, New Series, pp. 349 sqq.). Cyprian A. G. Bridge, 'The Russo-Japanese Naval Campaign of 1904' (*Naval Annual*, 1905, pp. 97 sqq.). Captain A. T. Mahan, *Naval Administration and Warfare, Some General Principles with other Essays*, 1908, p. 165. The French Minister of Marine, Camille Pelletan, had adopted the ideas of the new school which regarded the epoch of large ironclads as ended by the advent of torpedo boats and submarines; and the

no Russo-Japanese War to justify the Dreadnought, the same impulse, the same instinct of megalomania, would undoubtedly have produced the same effect. Fisher, who prided himself on his modernity and was determined to introduce into the British navy the methods of large-scale industry, was perhaps in his patronage of the Dreadnought the victim of industrialism. Of its very nature the machine signifies first and foremost an economy of energy in the pursuit of a given object. But it also signifies production on a large scale, fabrication of the colossal, and in this aspect often produces a waste of energy in the pursuit of an aim sentimental rather than rational. The invention of the Dreadnought may be regarded as a challenge launched by particular shipbuilders against their rivals. The builders of German liners said to the builders of British: 'You are building transatlantic giants, your Olympics, we shall build Imperators.' And the builders of British men-of-war spoke the same language. 'You are building large ironclads, we shall construct giant ironclads, Dreadnoughts, and if you in turn build Dreadnoughts, we shall reply by building super-Dreadnoughts.'[1] On balance when war broke out the advantage of one nation over another as regards the dimensions of its ships would be the very trifling advantage of a few months. But we shall understand the nature of the conflict better if we regard it as a war already being waged in peacetime. It was not simply that preparations were being made for a future battle of Dreadnoughts. The battle had been joined. The question was, which of the two nations would admit ruin first?

7

At the end of 1906 a mutiny of serious proportions in which civilians participated broke out in the Royal Naval Barracks at Portsmouth. It was of course quickly suppressed, but though a

deterioration of the French navy under his administration seemed to confirm the lessons of the 'Japanese Trafalgar' (*Naval Annual*, 1909, pp. 15 sqq.).

[1] For a comparison between the giants of the mercantile marine and the giants of the navy see Frank Fox, *Ramparts of the Empire: A View of the Navy from an Imperial Standpoint*, 1910, p. 14: 'The *Lusitania* is 785 feet long, the Dreadnought 490 feet. But whilst in breadth the *Lusitania* has 88 feet, not much more than a tenth of her length, the Dreadnought has 82 feet, over a sixth of her length. The indicated H.P. of the Atlantic liner is 68,000, giving a speed of 26 knots; of the Dreadnought 27,500, giving a speed of nearly 22 knots.'

number of the mutineers were sentenced, some of the sentences were reduced and Campbell-Bannerman speaking in the House of Commons let it be understood that all might be reduced before their expiration. On the other hand, several of the officers against whom the mutiny had been made were deprived of their command, one was reprimanded, and the officer who, in consequence of these changes, took command of the barracks, offended supporters of the old traditions by the tone of democratic good fellowship with which he spoke to his men on his first introduction to them. At the same time rumours began to circulate, which would shortly assume serious proportions, of a dissension in the high command. Everywhere two hostile parties were in existence, Fisher's supporters and his enemies. The Commander-in-Chief of the Channel fleet who in case of war would presumably become Commander-in-Chief of the entire navy was said to be at daggers drawn, on the one hand with the officer in command of the squadron of cruisers attached to his fleet, on the other with the First Sea Lord, a condition of affairs which gave rise to unfortunate incidents at the manœuvres of 1908. In 1904 the report of the Esher Committee had contrasted, with the spirit of faction which poisoned army headquarters, the harmonious co-operation traditional in the high command of the navy. Had the three years of Fisher's dictatorship put an end to it? These rumours and episodes must have been solid comfort for German statesmen.

The German Government however was not having an easy task. Algeciras had not been a success for its diplomats. Then Holstein who had been recalled had avenged himself by spreading in the press infamous accusations against the Emperor's most intimate friends. Meanwhile, alleged scandals in the Colonial Administration were the object of violent debates in the Reichstag, and a rising of some negro tribes in South-West Africa was suppressed only with considerable difficulty. But the Reichstag's refusal in December 1906 to vote the credits demanded by the Chancellor for its suppression provided William II and his Prime Minister with the opportunity to re-establish their authority. It was dissolved in conformity with the tradition of Bismarck and at the following election in February 1907 the Opposition suffered a severe defeat: the Social Democrats lost about half their seats. It was a contrast with the British and French elections of the previous year. In France three years' government by a Bohemian had lowered the French fleet several degrees in the naval hierarchy of Europe. What was happening in every rank of the British navy gave some ground for fearing that England had caught the infection from France. In Germany alone the Government was able to maintain its authority against the attacks of democratic anarchy. This encouraged the German Government to approach in a spirit of insolent cynicism the sessions of the Hague Conference which met at the beginning of the summer after three years of laborious negotiation between the Great Powers. The programme of the Conference as drawn up by the Russian Government in April 1906 was confined to the development of the Hague Court of Arbitration, the reform of international law governing warfare on land and sea and the extension of the Geneva convention to the latter. But the British Government insisted that the limitation of armaments should be discussed and to announce its intention to the world made use of a novel method.

The *Speaker*, a small weekly review which ever since the Boer War had conducted a violent campaign against imperialism and militarism, appeared in a new form in the early part of 1907, not to change its policy but better equipped with funds to pursue it with even greater vigour under a new editor, the eminent journalist, H. W. Massingham. The first number of the remodelled review, now called *The Nation*, opened with an important article on 'the Hague Conference' written by Campbell-Bannerman, evidently with the approval of his Cabinet. It began by recalling that the object for which the Conference had been originally summoned in 1898 was precisely to discuss the problem of limiting armaments; if since that date the burden of armaments had considerably increased, pacific ideals had made equal progress. Surely the time had come to satisfy their devotees by some practical limitation of armaments. England, Sir Henry pointed out— and here we see what a valuable support for his plea were the reforms carried out by Haldane at the War Office and by Fisher at the Admiralty—had already set the example by reducing her military and naval expenditure. She would go further in that direction if the other powers would follow her lead. Moreover, such a policy would not endanger her supremacy at sea. For 'the sea power of this country implies no challenge to any single State or group of States. I am persuaded that throughout the world that power is recognized as non-aggressive and innocent of designs against the independence, the commercial freedom, and the legitimate development of other States. . . . Our fleets . . . carry with them no menace across the waters of the world but a message of the most cordial goodwill, based on a belief in the community of interests between the nations.'

This quaint manifesto which began with a pacifist[1] act of faith to conclude by subscription to the creed of Mahan created a bad impression in every Continental country. When it confused in this way the freedom of mankind with the naval supremacy of England, was the British Government deceiving itself or with an even greater simplicity trying to deceive other nations? The French fleet was deteriorating, the Russian had been almost wiped out and the German fleet, which promised to be more dangerous, had not had time to become sufficiently large to threaten the safety of the British coast. A general limitation of armaments on the basis of the *status quo* would be the cheapest way for Britain to perpetuate her naval supremacy.

We must, however, bear in mind the difficult position in which the Liberal Cabinet was placed at the opening of the second Hague Conference. Disarmament was part of its programme. On the eve of the General Election the Prime Minister had formally pledged himself to it.[2] After the Election, when the programme submitted to the powers by the Russian Government had just been made public, a Liberal member of the House of Commons had moved a resolution demanding a drastic reduction of armaments and the insertion of the question in the agenda of the Conference. Replying for the Government Sir Edward Grey was compelled to accept the motion.[3] But a Unionist member proposed an amendment declaring that the naval supremacy of Great

---

[1] It was in 1907 during the discussions which preceded and accompanied the second Hague Conference that the word 'pacifist' first became current. See *Speaker*, March 30, 1907, *Economist*, July 6, 1907. It makes its first appearance in the *Grosse Politik* . . . on February 18, its second on March 12 under the pen of Von Schön. Hatzfeld uses it on May 8, Marschall on October 21. The French origin of the word (see my *History*, vol. v, p. 66 *n*. is shown by the following quotation from the *National Review* (October 1907, vol. I, p. 154): 'From that moment commenced the education of French governments and the awakening of the French nation to the sterner aspects of national existence, and the abandonment of those amiable illusions which, under the influence of *pacifistes*, and other perilous charlatans, the Republic had begun to cherish.' But its use did not become fixed as quickly as one might imagine: as late as July 31, 1914, Sir Francis Bertie writes to his government: 'M. Jaurès has been killed in a restaurant by a young man on the ground that he was a pacifist and a traitor' (*British Documents* . . . vol. xi, p. 233).

[2] Speech at the Albert Hall, December 21, 1905.

[3] H. of C., May 9, 1906, Vivian's motion (*Parliamentary Debates*, 4th Series, vol. clvi, pp. 1383 sqq.).

Britain must be maintained and Grey, while asking the mover to withdraw it so as not to hamper the Government's action, said that he felt as much as any man the force of his argument. The Admiralty felt it even more strongly. The following winter Fisher asked for the construction in 1907 of three new Dreadnoughts. If it gave him the ships, the Liberal Government, only a year after taking office, would return to the old path of large naval estimates and competition in armaments; if it refused, he threatened to retire and with him three other members of the Board of Admiralty. How could the Cabinet escape the impasse? By developing a plea which appears to have originated with the Unionist leader of the Opposition, Balfour,[1] and maintaining that the British navy, unlike the armies and navies of other powers, was exclusively a weapon of defence. The powers had therefore no reason to object to the supremacy of the British fleet, since it policed the seas without detriment to the liberty of any nation. The contention was ludicrous. Obviously a maritime blockade violated the independence of the nation blockaded as gravely as an invasion.[2] And at that very moment the Admiralty was contemplating the day when by transporting an expeditionary force to the coast of France, Belgium, or even Germany, it would take a direct part in an offensive. But the argument was seductive. It became a commonplace of the Press and Parliament.

The manifesto therefore which the Government published in the *Nation* was not a masterpiece of Machiavellian cunning but an attempt to compromise between two conflicting forces which confronted each other in England or perhaps, to speak more

---

[1] H. of C., May 9, 1906: '. . . We ought . . . to have . . . a Fleet which would make us absolutely secure against any possible combination against our shores. Is there anything aggressive in that policy? . . . Our Fleet is for defensive purposes and their fleet, (the navy of certain foreign powers) is not for defensive purposes alone—[Why not?]—Because their shores are unassailable, partly for geographical reasons and partly for the reason that they have great land armies which would make invasion by any Maritime Power absolutely ludicrous and futile' (ibid., vol. clvi, p. 410). Even an organ of such strong pacifist convictions as the *Nation* was compelled to write, if it would keep its readers' sympathies: 'Nothing could be more damaging to our influence as a Liberal Power or *more threatening to our naval supremacy* than to associate that supremacy with abuses like the destruction of innocent merchant ships and the bombardment of defenceless towns' (July 6, 1907).

[2] See the instructions given by Grey himself to Sir Edward Fry, the head of the British delegation at The Hague: '. . . The proportion between the British Army and the Great Continental Armies has come to be such that the British Army, if operating alone, could not be regarded as a means of offence against the mainland of a Great Continental Power. For her ability to bring pressure to bear upon her enemies in war Great Britain has therefore to rely on the navy alone. The Government cannot agree to any resolution which would diminish the effective means which the navy has of bringing pressure to bear upon an enemy.'

accurately, in the minds of many Englishmen. To satisfy one of these the Government said: 'We will ask at the Hague for measures of disarmament.' To satisfy the other it added immediately: 'But they must not endanger the nation's safety or sea power.' The Sea Lords were told: 'Give up your demand for three Dreadnoughts, be content with only two.' But the Government added: 'The concession we are asking you to make is after all, conditional. If the Conference does not produce practical measures of general disarmament you shall have your third Dreadnought.' And the Sea Lords could accept the compromise the more readily because they were certain the Conference would fail. But what Englishman expected it to succeed? What Englishman witnessed its opening or followed its proceedings without marked dissatisfaction? The advanced Liberals, partisans of a reconciliation between England and Germany, were quick to perceive that the English proposals were diametrically opposed to their desires and calculated to lead directly to a conflict between the two nations. And the Foreign Office reached the same unfavourable conclusion though for different reasons. For many years it had worked hard to establish good relations between England and all the foreign nations in order to defeat the opposite policy pursued by the German Emperor, who had hoped to lead Europe against England. By raising the question of disarmament, indeed by simply going to the Hague, England ran the risk of once more reuniting Europe against her and enabling German policy to score a success.

8

At the Hague the same ritual was observed as in 1898. The international propagandists of the pacifist creed flocked to the Conference. W. T. Stead—a friend, moreover, of Admiral Fisher—was at their head. He passed to and fro between London and the Hague, visiting London to rouse the English Government from its lethargy, and returning to the Hague to edit the *Courrier de la Conférence*, the unofficial organ of the Conference throughout its sessions. We can judge of the spirit which animated the various delegations from our knowledge of the attitude of the rulers and statesmen who sent them to the Hague. The three

Emperors were opposed even to the meeting of the Conference and their hostility increased when they saw on its programme the disarmament which they regarded as a craze of Jews, Socialists, and hysterical women.[1] The King of England had confided to William II that he regarded the Conference as 'a humbug'.[2] President Roosevelt was sceptical[3] and brought forward a scheme for disarmament—it limited neither the expenditure on navies nor the number of vessels, but merely their size[4]—which seemed devised as a counterblast to the plans of the British Admiralty. And the French Government had waited, before publicly declaring itself opposed to the discussion of disarmament, only until Prince von Bülow in measured but vigorous language had defended the German Government's opposition to the proposal. Baron Marschall, the head of the German delegation, felt himself therefore on this crucial point in agreement with every foreign office in the world, not even perhaps excepting the British. For in his interviews with Metternich, Grey seems to have had no other purpose than to minimize, as far as he could, the bad impression produced in Germany and throughout the entire Continent by a proposal for which he was responsible only as a member of the Cabinet.[5] The German delegates intended to withdraw if the

---

[1] Isvolsky's words reported by Von Schön in a telegram of March 18, 1907 (*Die Grosse Politik*, vol. xxiii[1], p. 163).

[2] Letter from the Emperor William to President Roosevelt, communicated by Von Bülow to the German Ambassador at Washington, January 5, 1907 (ibid., vol. xxiii[1], p. 93).

[3] Roosevelt to Henry White, August 14, 1906 (Allan Nevins, *Henry White: Thirty Years of American Diplomacy*, 1930, p. 498). See further Roosevelt's words reported to Edward VII by Count Gleichen, August 31, 1906: '. . . Tell Lord Grey and Haldane [he meant of course Sir Edward Grey] not to let themselves be carried away by sentimental ideas at the Hague Conference. Wars are not to be conducted on sentimental principles, and I'm afraid from what I see and hear, they may let themselves be swayed by their party in that direction against their own conviction . . . but don't let them do it' (Sir Sidney Lee, *King Edward VII* . . . vol. ii, p. 437).

[4] Von Tschirschky to Von Tirpitz, September 7, 1906 (*Die Grosse Politik*, vol. xxiii, pp. 88–9). Baron Speck von Sternburg to the Minister for Foreign Affairs, January 4, 1907 (ibid., vol. xxiii[1], pp. 91–2) the same to the same, January 6, 1907 (ibid., pp. 94–5).

[5] Von Stumm to Prince von Bülow, March 8, 1907: '. . . "Count Bosdari" (who had submitted to Grey a proposal by Tittoni) received the impression . . . that he did not intend to examine it and he does not believe that the British Government is in earnest with its policy of disarmament. On the contrary, in his opinion the Government only desires to make a good impression on Parliament and the nation and has no intention of bringing forward any concrete proposals. . . . Sir Charles Hardinge told me a little while ago in the course of a conversation in which we touched upon the question of disarmament that he had repeatedly impressed upon the Liberal idealists who attach such weight to it that under present circumstances the discussion of the question would achieve no practical results. He expressed the opinion that the subject was arousing too much excitement, that divergent standpoints should be given a calm hearing and if no agreement were reached, the failure should not be taken too much to heart' (*Die Grosse Politik*, vol. xxiii[1], pp. 206–7).

question of disarmament was discussed. But the Conference was content to adopt unanimously and without debate a colourless resolution affirming the desirability of disarmament which simply reiterated in slightly stronger terms the resolution adopted in 1908.

The matter was disposed of at a single sitting. The real work of the Conference, which lasted from June 15 to October 18, dealt with a number of questions of a more legal character. In the first place there was the development of international arbitration, possibly the institution of compulsory arbitration. For the past year the English Conservatives had urged that this should be the leading issue at the Conference. The Government, after some hesitation it would seem, adopted their point of view. It was in harmony with the views of the French delegation which already at the first Conference had pursued the same policy. But here the opposition of Germany stood in the way and nothing came of the attempt except a lengthy declaration of principle which the Germans had no difficulty in accepting for, as the head of their delegation said, it would be 'difficult to say less in more words'.

The important question remained of belligerents' rights at sea. Neutrals continued to demand, as they had always demanded, the abolition of the right of capture, freedom of the seas; and the United States of America, which had no conception that the day would come when its navy would take part in a European war, espoused their cause. The American delegation proposed to place very severe restrictions upon the right to capture neutral vessels in time of war, and the German Government, brushing aside Tirpitz's opposition, cleverly declared in favour of the proposal. It was indeed rejected. But it made it easier for Germany to join with America and France in opposing an English resolution of a plainly pacifist character demanding the complete abolition of contraband of war. Though the proposal was accompanied by reserva-

The same to the same, April 20, 1907, report of a conversation with Grey: '. . . I was (I told him) fully convinced that the English idealists who champion disarmament were inspired by the best and most honourable intentions. They were not however practical politicians and I asked him to tell me whether it was his personal belief that on this question the Conference would achieve any positive result. It testifies to his honour and frankness that he shrank from an affirmative answer and refused to reply. . . .' And he concludes: 'I have no doubt that the Government itself does not believe that in this matter the Conference can achieve any practical result. That in spite of this it persists in its intention is to be explained by reasons of domestic policy. There is in my humble opinion no reason to believe that the British Government entertains any sinister designs, in particular against Germany' (*Die Grosse Politik*, vol. xxiii[1], pp. 215-16).

tions which rendered it suspect in certain quarters, England had all the small powers on her side that day. But when she raised the question of floating mines and championed what was obviously the humanitarian point of view, she again seemed to the weak nations, for whom the floating mine was their only weapon against British domination at sea, to be defending brazenly her own interests. Finally, a complicated resolution was adopted which in theory slightly restricted the use of floating mines. On the question of the right of capture it was Germany that took the initiative by proposing that an international court should be set up to decide all disputed questions of contraband in time of war. On the main issues, the final decisions were left to a committee of experts which met in London at the beginning of 1908 and whose work led to the declaration of London of February 26, 1909, which restricted severely the right of blockade and the application of the doctrine of 'continuous voyage' and limited contraband of war to a small category of merchandise of an obviously military character. Throughout the discussions, too incoherent and vague to hold the attention of the public, the British press without distinction of party protested against the combination of timidity and bungling displayed by the British delegation. Lord Reay, an eminent lawyer and a member of the delegation, bombarded the Prime Minister with his complaints. He protested against the instructions he received from the Admiralty which compelled him to speak against his conscience.[1] The vagueness and incoherence of the discussions turned to the advantage of Germany. At the Hague she was no longer an isolated country against which the entire world was conspiring. By proposing an international prize court the nation whose delegates cynically paraded their contempt for the illusions of pacifism contrived to take control of the proceedings. This success compensated the Emperor William for the blow to his prestige he had suffered by the conclusion of the Anglo-Russian agreement. Three weeks after the Conference closed he arrived at Windsor. His visit in October 1902 had been his last visit during the period of friendship. This was the first during the period of enmity.

[1] J. A. Spender, *The Life of the Right Hon. Sir Henry Campbell-Bannerman*, vol. ii, p. 333.

9

The visit had been preceded by complicated negotiations. King Edward's invitation had been given as early as June 14. It had at first been coldly received, following as it did the conclusion of the Mediterranean agreement. Fisher had made the situation worse by offering to put himself personally at the Emperor's service while he was the guest of the British nation. This offer of the English Admiral aroused suspicion at Berlin. What if the invitation had originated with Fisher, who wished to humiliate the Emperor by making him visit the King of England before the King visited him? To reassure the German Government on this point King Edward during his stay at Carlsbad paid a visit to his nephew, who was in the neighbourhood. Then the Emperor announced his intention to come escorted by a squadron, and when persuaded to abandon his intention refused to come at all. Then he wanted to bring his Chancellor with him. A violent attack on Bülow's policy which appeared in *The Times* of October 10 may have contributed to make him abandon the idea. He was accompanied only by his Minister for Foreign Affairs, Von Schön. The Liberal press gave him an enthusiastic welcome, the attitude of the Unionist press, in obedience to the wishes of the Court, was correct and even courteous. He was cheered in the London streets and at the Guildhall where he made a pacific speech. When his visit to Windsor was over he spent a few weeks on an unofficial visit to a friend, and did not leave for Germany until December 11 after spending a month in England.[1]

While the Emperor was his uncle's guest many British statesmen who had never met him were delighted at this opportunity to see and converse with a man whom the accident of birth had placed in so formidable a position, and he won their good opinion by his jovial and easy manner. The Bagdad railway was discussed and his attitude seemed conciliatory. But the question of the navy, the only burning question, was carefully avoided, and while the

---

[1] For the incidents connected with the preparations for this visit and the visit itself see from the English side, *British Documents*, vol. vi, pp. 78 sqq.; from the German, *Die Grosse Politik*, vol. xxiv, pp. 15 sqq. See also R. B. Haldane, *Before the War*, 1920, pp. 42 sqq.; *An Autobiography*, 1929, pp. 289 sqq.; John Viscount Morley, *Recollections*, vol. ii, pp. 237–8; and John Morley to Bryce (H. A. L. Fisher, *James Bryce, Viscount Bryce of Dechmont*, vol. ii, p. 92).

Emperor was actually in England the German Government laid before the Reichstag its naval estimates for the coming year. Apparently they did not exceed the provisions laid down by the law of 1900. But it was decided to reduce the life of vessels of the line from twenty-five to twenty years. This would hasten by one-fifth the rate of replacement and therefore the tempo of naval construction. Every year from 1908 to 1911 four large ironclads were to be laid down. And at the same time it was provided that all vessels of the line to be built in future would possess a larger tonnage than in the past, in other words would be Dreadnoughts —that is to say, the British Admiralty was already ceasing to profit by the confusion into which other navies had been thrown by the launching of the first of these giants. From now onwards both nations were doomed to fight and ruin each other in the battle of Dreadnoughts. After two years of Liberal government England had taken a step forward not towards peace but towards war.

Three months later an incident unimportant in itself but serious on account of the violent feeling it aroused revealed how intense was the hatred of Germany which prevailed in political circles.

On March 6, 1908, a short letter appeared in *The Times* headed 'Under Which King?' that is to say 'Under which monarch are we living? The King of England? or the King of Prussia?' The letter informed its readers that the German Emperor had sent a letter to Lord Tweedmouth, the First Lord of the Admiralty, which amounted to 'an endeavour to influence, in the interests of Germany, the Minister responsible for the navy estimates'. It appeared that the Emperor had in fact written a long letter to Lord Tweedmouth, couched in familiar and even bantering terms, intended to allay the alarm caused in England by the growth of the German fleet and that he had sent a courteous reply in which he communicated to the Emperor as a token of confidence and friendship the details of the forthcoming estimates, as yet unknown to Parliament. What was the source of the leakage? The War Office? The letter in *The Times* bore the signature of its military correspondent, Colonel Repington, whose relations with the War Office we already know. The Admiralty? It was a hot-bed of intrigue. The Court, King Edward's entourage? The Emperor's letter contained sarcastic remarks about Lord Esher, the King's intimate friend, which made its publication impossible, and we now know that William II received at the same time as Lord Tweedmouth's reply a very strongly worded letter from King Edward protesting against the breach of diplomatic usage committed by addressing the letter to one of his ministers and not to himself. In fact, from the explanations given in Parliament it transpired that immediately on the receipt of the imperial letter Lord Tweedmouth had communicated it to his colleagues and drawn up his reply with their approval. And finally it is possible that in giving the Emperor this information he was acting in accordance with Grey's wishes. For the British Government had suggested the previous summer that a mutual exchange between the powers of information as to their respective estimates might be a means of bridging over the naval conflict between the two nations and had empowered Sir Edward to make a proposal to that effect at the Hague, which however gained little support.[1] The press with few exceptions did nothing to inflame public feeling, the leaders of the Opposition in both Houses made no use of the incident against the Government, and Lord Rosebery even took the opportunity to congratulate himself publicly on having foreseen the dangerous consequences of the *entente cordiale*.[2] But Colonel Repington's blow had gone home. Lord Tweedmouth's position had been too severely shaken. It was obvious that he would be obliged to leave the Admiralty at the first opportunity.

10

It was not long delayed. When Colonel Repington's article appeared, for a month past the Prime Minister had ceased to take part in the debates in the House of Commons. Seventy-two years old, suffering from a severe disease of the heart, and deeply afflicted by the recent death of a wife whom he fondly loved, the old Parliamentarian could no longer cope with his crushing task. A nation naturally kindly and courteous sympathized with his sufferings without distinction of political views and they increased

---

[1] August 17, 1907. The *Manchester Guardian* (August 19) regretted the failure of a proposal whose adoption would have made possible private negotiations between the Powers, for example, between Germany and England.
[2] H. of L., March 9, 1908 (*Parliamentary Debates*, 4th Series, vol. clxxxv, pp. 1075–7).

his popularity. But it had indeed increased steadily since that day at the end of 1905 when he had insisted on being Prime Minister, and not in name alone. The members of the Labour party liked him. They did not forget how on the question of the Trade Disputes Bill of 1906 he had had the courage to outstrip his party which otherwise would probably have been compelled to yield their demands with a bad grace, and make them his own, their victory his. The Irish did not forget that after the defeat of the Irish Council Bill he had made it clear that he bore them no grudge for their refusal to accept a compromise, and so far as he was concerned was desirous to grant them far more extensive concessions as soon as circumstances permitted. To the advanced Liberals, the pro-Boers of yesterday, he had given their revenge, which surely was at the same time his personal revenge, by granting representative government to the Transvaal and Orange River Colony. The moderate Liberals and the imperialists might well have taken offence at this thoroughgoing Liberalism. This was not the case. The moderates felt that he was at bottom one of themselves and on the question of the Education Bill his sceptical attitude had brought him close to the Archbishop of Canterbury, another man of moderation, and enabled them to work together in a sincere attempt to discover a compromise. And the imperialists were grateful for an indolence which enabled the Foreign Office, the War Office, and the Admiralty to pursue their policy under the cloak of a kindliness which reassured the Premier's pacifist friends. And lastly King Edward, who had never liked Balfour, who, he felt, despised him, had soon learnt to appreciate his successor's geniality. 'C-B'—it was the name by which the Premier was customarily spoken of in Parliament and the familiar designation proved at once the extent and character of his popularity—had come to be widely regarded as the only leader capable of holding together that bundle of conflicting tendencies which now constituted the Liberal party.

When the term had been originally created, 'Liberal' had meant 'hostile to the state in every form, to the Socialist state and the militarist state alike'. Now, however, a Liberal was obliged to pose as the champion, more or less advanced, of social democracy, and at the same time, if he wished to govern the country, could not escape the necessity of piling up armaments both by land and sea. Confronted with two tendencies, neither of which was distinctively 'Liberal', the party which had obtained office under that label was faced with the problem of choosing between them or harmonizing both. It was a difficult but urgent task and the venerable 'C-B' did not preside over its fulfilment. On April 6, only a fortnight before his death, he resigned to make way for the Chancellor of the Exchequer, Henry Asquith, whom public opinion designated as his successor.

PART II
FOUR YEARS OF CRISIS

Winston Churchill and Lloyd George

I CHURCHILL AT THE BOARD OF TRADE

I

HENRY ASQUITH succeeded Sir Henry Campbell-Bannerman as Prime Minister. It was a victory for the Liberal imperialists. Already at the end of 1905 they had attempted to secure the leadership of the Commons for Asquith and force Campbell-Bannerman to enter the Lords. Now an accident had achieved their object. Asquith held the coveted post and Campbell-Bannerman had been got rid of more completely than they had dared to hope. The Conservatives were delighted: Grey's anti-German policy was assured in future of the Prime Minister's support. On the other hand, Asquith's promotion does not seem to have aroused much protest from the Radical pacifists. By his tact and conciliatory temper he had won the confidence of the entire party. Even with Campbell-Bannerman after the original disagreement he was soon on excellent terms. And in any case what was the use of resisting the inevitable? Asquith had hardly entered Parliament when his talents pointed him out to everyone as a future minister; he had hardly become a minister, when everyone hailed in him a future premier. His early education and his temperament had invested him with the indispensable gravity. His second marriage, when his first wife had left him the father of several children, to a young and brilliant madcap had introduced him to fashionable society and made his talents human. He was a man of sound judgment who lacked the flame—heavenly or demonic—of genius.[1] Were not other qualities required if the Liberal party after its almost portentous victory at the polls in January 1906 was to retain the ardour which alone could win new victories? And was it not obvious at the beginning of 1908 that the Liberal Government would be exposed to serious dangers,

---

[1] Biographies of Asquith: J. P. Alderson, *Mr. Asquith*, 1906. Frank Elias, *The Right Hon. H. H. Asquith: A Biography and Appreciation*, 1909. And more particularly: J. A. Spender and Cyril Asquith, *Life of Herbert Henry Asquith, Lord Oxford and Asquith*, 1932. His own works: *The Genesis of the War*, 1923; *Fifty Years of Parliament*, 1926; *Memories and Reflections*, 1928, are of poor quality, hastily put together and (especially the two latter) very uninforming. Contemporary French portraits: Jacques Bardoux, *Silhouettes d'Outre-Manche*, 1909, pp. 82 sqq.; Augustin Filon, *L'Angleterre d'Edouard VII*, 1911, pp. 97 sqq.; Princess Bibesco, *Portraits d'Hommes*, 1929, pp. 91 sqq.

unless it could find by the side of Asquith and in his Cabinet an eager and enterprising spirit to play the part Canning had once played beside Lord Liverpool and more recently Chamberlain beside Lord Salisbury, one day perhaps to supplant him and become Prime Minister in his stead?

The changes which were effected in the Cabinet after Campbell-Bannerman's death will perhaps help us to guess the quarter in which he was to be sought. If at the Board of Education Walter Runciman replaced Reginald McKenna and McKenna in turn took the place at the Admiralty of Lord Tweedmouth, who could no longer remain there after the incident of his correspondence with William II, and Lord Crewe succeeded Lord Elgin at the Colonial Office, these changes did not interest the public. But Asquith, now First Lord of the Treasury and Prime Minister, was no longer Chancellor of the Exchequer and Lloyd George took his place. He therefore left the Board of Trade, where he was succeeded by Winston Churchill, hitherto Under-Secretary of State for the Colonies. It was on these two men that the eyes of the public were fixed. Asquith, Premier at fifty-six, embodied the present; Lloyd George and Churchill, respectively forty-five and thirty-four, were the men of to-morrow.[1] They were united by close ties of friendship. Both were opposed to a policy of heavy expenditure on the army and navy, both advocates of a policy of social reform which, they maintained, the Liberal party

---

[1] Biographies of Lloyd George: John Hugh Edwards and Spencer Leigh Hughes, *From Village Green to Downing Street: The Life of the Right Hon. D. Lloyd George, M.P.*, 1908; John Hugh Edwards, *The Life of David Lloyd George, with a short History of the Welsh People*, 4 vols, 1913–1918 (with a supplementary volume by J. Saxon Mills, entitled: *David Lloyd George, War Minister*) (the writer was a Welsh M.P. who composed a panegyric, but a panegyric which is well documented); J. Hugh Edwards, *David Lloyd George—the Man and the Statesman*, 2 vols., 1925 (an abridgment of the previous work); Hubert Du Parcq, *Life of David Lloyd George*, 4 vols. (the fourth is a collection of speeches), 1912, well documented, since the author makes use of the diary and notes of Lloyd George's brother; Harold Spender, *The Prime Minister*, 1920 (the work of a political and personal friend); W. F. Rook, *Mr. Lloyd George and the War*, 1920; also E. T. Raymond, *Mr. Lloyd George: A Biography*, 1922 (more critical than the preceding works and of considerable interest. For impressions of his personality see the French contemporary portraits by Jacques Bardoux, *Silhouettes d'Outre-Manche*, 1909, pp. 58 sqq.; and Augustin Filon, *L'Angleterre d'Edouard VII*, 1911, pp. 199 sqq.

Biographies of Winston Churchill. See in the first place for his childhood and youth his own autobiography entitled *My Early Life, a Roving Commission*, 1930; his work entitled *The World Crisis, 1911–14*, to a great extent autobiographical, is practically confined to the preparations for war. The two excellent works by A. MacCullum Scott, *Winston Spencer Churchill*, 1905, and *Winston Churchill in Peace and War*, 1916, say nothing of Churchill's activities in the interval between his youth and his years at the War Office. There is the same lacuna in Ephesian's *Winston Churchill, being an account of the life of*, 1927. For a contemporary sketch, see the above-mentioned work of Jacques Bardoux, pp. 137 sqq.

must pursue with an unprecedented daring, if the Labour party were not to grow stronger on its left. They came forward as the two leaders of the Radical group of pacifists and advanced social reformers as opposed to the three imperialists Asquith, Grey, and Haldane—that is to say, they were two friends professing the same political creed but for that very reason rivals as well as friends. They were obviously too ambitious to be satisfied for ever with a second place. Which of the two would reach the first?

Churchill had the advantage of youth. If Lloyd George was eleven years younger than Asquith, he was eleven years younger than Lloyd George. He had the further advantage of aristocratic birth. He was the son of a junior member of a noble family, and grandson of a Duke of Marlborough. That surely still counted for something in England. In turn soldier, journalist, and politician, he won admiration not only by the diversity of his interests but by his biting eloquence and genuine gift of oratory. He had honoured the memory of his father Lord Randolph Churchill by an excellent biography which was almost a masterpiece, and it was the dream formed for him by an ambitious mother and his own to succeed where his father had failed and since his father had been unable to regenerate the Tory party by making it democratic, one day perhaps to lead the democratic party against the Tories.

But, on the other hand, it was to the advantage of Lloyd George at this juncture when the Liberal party was seeking a new leader that he was not quite so young as Churchill. Since he was in his forties he had reached that maturity which is ripe for great performance while as yet untouched by fatigue and old age. He lacked Winston's culture but his genius was at least equal, and possibly it was beginning to be realized that in one respect the election of 1906 had marked an epoch in the social history of England. She had dismissed her ancient aristocracy. It might continue to exercise its ceremonial functions, but the country no longer wished to be governed by it and Lloyd George's bourgeois career and plebeian origin were a point in his favour. And he possessed yet another advantage. Churchill was the object of all the bitterness and hostility which are the lot of a deserter from the aristocracy. Some refused to forgive his defection. Others felt uneasy in the company of this new friend, who styled himself a pacifist though he had sought fame on the battlefields of South

Africa and who at bottom seemed to have given up his true career, that of a soldier, only because even a military career was too commonplace, too monotonous to satisfy his craving for adventure. Lloyd George on the contrary, ever since he entered Parliament, had pledged himself so deeply to Radicalism that his elevation to the Exchequer could not fail to delight all the enemies of Imperialism. Moreover at the Board of Trade he had reassured the world of business and the employers generally by the spirit of conciliation he displayed on so many occasions. Therefore when Churchill and Lloyd George went respectively to the Board of Trade and the Exchequer, everyone distrusted the former, everyone entertained hopes of the latter.

2

When Churchill took over the Board of Trade he is reported to have said: 'This cake has been given me too late; Lloyd George has taken all the plums.' If the story is true, he was no doubt thinking of the two Statutes on Merchant Shipping and Patents which had won the unanimous approval of the public, and those clever arbitrations which had presented Lloyd George as the peacemaker who saved the country from social war. What was there left for Churchill to do? The Cabinet had not indeed waited for the April changes to perceive the necessity of doing something to satisfy the claims of Labour and had introduced in February a Bill establishing an eight-hours' day in the coal mines. But the mines were under the jurisdiction of the Home Office, not the Board of Trade, and it was Herbert Gladstone, the Home Secretary, who took charge of the Bill. As it is one of the three important measures of social reform passed by Parliament during the two sessions of 1908 and 1909 we must say something about it. Moreover Churchill played his part in the chequered incidents which attended its passing and application.

The demand for the legal restriction of the day's work in mines to eight hours went back not only in England but in the Continental countries to the closing years of the nineteenth century. Why in the mines rather than in any other branch of industry? Was it that humanitarian sentiment pitied more than the lot of other workers the miner's hard life in subterranean darkness?

It may have been so. But the labour of metal workers and glass makers is certainly as hard and unpleasant as the miners' underground labour, and the real reason why public opinion began to entertain the notion of limiting the hours of adult miners was that they were in a better position to make themselves heard. Around the mines—particularly the collieries—vast settlements had grown up, extremely homogeneous in their population, veritable republics which soon discovered their power to send representatives of their class to Parliament to defend their interests there.[1] When in 1874 the first two members of the working class entered Parliament, they were two miners. The great Keir Hardie was a miner elected in 1906 by a mining constituency. At the same election two other miners had been returned as candidates of the Labour Representation Committee. Thirteen others had entered Westminster with no other aid than that of their trade union and two years had passed before they amalgamated with the Labour party.

Already, before the Imperialists came into office in 1895, the House of Commons under a Liberal Government had twice affirmed the principle of an eight-hours' day in the mines.[2] But it was not until 1906 that the question could be considered ripe for solution. Till then the eight-hours' day had not received the miners' unanimous support. In Durham and Northumberland the work was so arranged that adults worked only six and a half hours, children over eight hours. The miners were afraid that if the children's day was reduced to eight hours the adults' day might be lengthened. Moreover, the miners' claim seemed exclusively and selfishly professional. If the reduction of hours led to a decrease in output and in consequence to a rise in the price of coal it was a prospect which the miners appeared to contemplate with equanimity, even perhaps with pleasure, provided their wages were increased, but a prospect calculated to alarm the general

[1] 'There is hardly another industry in which the actual conditions of production so readily provide the basis for a democratic trade union machine. The miner not only works in the pit; he lives in the pit village, and all his immediate interests are thus concentrated at one point. . . . The miners' intense solidarity and loyalty to their Unions is undoubtedly the result of the conditions under which they work and live. They are isolated from the rest of the world—even the rest of the Trade Union world; but their isolation ministers to their own self-sufficiency and loyalty one to another. They are narrow, and slow to understand others, or to feel the influence of outside public opinion. They have little skill in arguing their case before others; but they stick together' (G. D. M. Cole, *Labour on the Coal Mining Industry, 1914–1921*, 1923, p. 7).
[2] H. of C., May 3, 1893 (*Parliamentary Debates*, 4th Series, vol. xi, pp. 1841 sqq.); April 25, 1894 (ibid., vol. xxiii, pp. 1329 sqq.).

public and the great mass of labour. But these conflicts of interest which divided different branches of industry were, so to speak, swallowed up in the great movement of working-class solidarity which in January 1906 won so many victories for Labour. The miners of Northumberland and Durham accepted the programme of the eight-hours' day, and in 1908 joined the great Miners' Federation. And all the workers without distinction of trade supported the miners' claims. In their eyes the enactment of the eight-hours' day meant the acceptance by the British law of the principle, hitherto unrecognized, of legal limitation of adult labour, and would involve at no great distance of time a statutory limitation of hours for all adult workers in accordance with the programme of the Second International in support of which all the workers of Western Europe demonstrated every first of May.

In 1906 the Cabinet, still timid, refused to commit itself until the question had been examined by a Committee of Inquiry. In 1907 it introduced a Bill establishing the eight-hours' day in the mines but was unwilling to carry it any further. The report of the Committee had been published and no doubt the Government hoped it would discourage the advocates of the Reform, for without explicitly condemning the principle of the eight-hours' day, it pointed out the numerous difficulties in the way of its application. The average actual length of the working day in Great Britain was nine hours and three minutes. To reduce it to eight hours would reduce the output by 10.27 per cent—that is to say, there would be a decrease of 25,783,000 tons on the output of 1906. The experts, it is true, admitted that by increasing the number of men, reducing the number of holidays, and improving the machinery, the loss could be partly made good. But they doubted whether the change would be as beneficial as was supposed to the miner's health. It was excellent already. In their opinion, the length of the working day and the nature of the work performed varied so much according to locality that it would be impossible to apply a uniform rule. In any case the output would be diminished, and the price of coal would rise. Those countries in which the working day had been already reduced—France, Holland, and Austria—were not serious competitors with England, but the experts doubted whether under the system of the eight-hours' day the French collieries would be able to overcome the competition of Germany and America, two countries in which there was no legal restriction of hours and in which the working day, at present shorter than in Great Britain, would be longer if the eight-hours' day were adopted. Moreover the effect of a rise in the cost of coal, difficult to estimate but undoubtedly very considerable, upon all branches of national industry must be taken into account.[1]

What of this? The pressure of labour was irresistible. Neither the Liberals, afraid of strengthening the Labour party, nor the Unionists, afraid of strengthening the Liberals, could resist it. It was in vain that a 'League of Coal Consumers' was formed to organize opposition to the change. For these 'consumers' were not the host of small buyers, but a small group of large purchasers, railway companies and industrial magnates. The opposite side disposed of more formidable weapons. 'If this Bill is not to be passed,' declared Herbert Samuel, 'and if the miners are to be left to their own devices and to the strength of their own organization, it means a coal strike, and nothing else.'[2] It was all very well for Opposition speakers to declare it scandalous for a member of the Government to make such a statement; Lord Lansdowne in language slightly more veiled[3] said the same thing when he urged the Lords to pass the Bill which the Commons had sent up to it and which actually became law on December 21.[4] The Bill did not indeed give full satisfaction to the workers' claims. Even in its original form not only did it empower the Government to suspend its operation in the event of war or of imminent national danger, or in the 'event of any grave economic disturbance due to the demand for coal exceeding the supply available', and exclude from its scope certain classes of workmen (whose working day might extend to nine hours and a half), but it also excluded from the reckoning of the eight hours one of the two journeys made by the miners between the surface and the bottom of the pit and gave the coalowners the right to impose on their men an hour's extra work for a maximum period of sixty days a year.

---

[1] *Miners' Eight-Hour Day Committee. First Report of the Departmental Committee appointed to inquire into the probable Economic Effect of a limit of Eight Hours to the Working Day of Coal Miners, March 23, 1907. Minutes of Evidence—Final Report—Report (May 15, 1907) and Appendices. Minutes of Evidence and Index.*

[2] H. of C., July 6, 1908 (*Parliamentary Debates*, 4th Series, vol. cxci, p. 1279).

[3] H. of L., December 15, 1908 (ibid., vol. cxcviii, p. 1461).

[4] 8 Edw., 7 Cap. 57: An Act to amend the Coal Mines Regulation Acts 1887 to 1905, for the purpose of limiting hours of work below the ground (*Coal Mines Regulation Act*, 1908).

And other concessions were made in the course of debate. Though the new law was to come into operation on July 1, 1909, in the mines of Northumberland and Durham the date would be postponed for another six months. And both journeys, from the surface to the bottom of the pit and back to the surface, were excluded from the reckoning of the eight hours—originally for a period of five years, finally, in virtue of an amendment introduced in the Lords, in perpetuity. But all this did not alter the fact that for the first time an important principle had been accepted by British legislation, the principle of legal restriction of the working day for all workers and not, as hitherto, only for women and children.

The Act passed, it remained to put it into operation and the difficulties involved immediately became evident. South Wales was one of the coalfields in which the hours of work had been particularly long and the Committee of Inquiry had pointed out that it would be difficult to introduce the eight-hours' day in the Welsh collieries without dislocating the entire industry. And the difficulty was even greater in 1909, a year of industrial depression, than it had been in the early part of 1907 when the Committee drew up its report. The mineowners declared that they regarded the wages agreement as automatically cancelled by the legal institution of the eight-hours' day and attempted to take immediate advantage of the clause permitting sixty nine-hour days a year and to introduce the system of double shifts. On all these points they were faced by the opposition of the miners, supported by the Miners' Federation of Great Britain. The Federation threatened to call a general strike of miners if the Welsh coalowners did not give way. At the last moment the dispute was settled by shelving the points at issue and the eight-hours' day came peaceably into operation on July 1st.

3

It was in Scotland that further difficulties arose. Here, as in South Wales, the coalowners considered the wages agreement cancelled by their obligation to reduce the hours of work. The miners on their part refused to accept any reduction of their wages below the minimum fixed by existing agreements. As in

Wales they had the support of the National Federation, which secured a vote from its members in favour of a general strike in the mines to support the Scottish miners' claims. Now that the question of a maximum working day had been settled by law, the question of a minimum wage was raised. Churchill intervened and confronted at the Board of Trade the representatives of the owners and men, 'saying that if nothing else could be done, the Government would have to pass an Act of Parliament in twenty-four hours referring the dispute to compulsory arbitration. "Mr. Churchill," replied one of the miners, "you cannot put 600,000 men into prison." '[1] A compromise was arranged. The owners conceded the minimum wage for which the men were asking, the miners a modification of the sliding scale to the owners' advantage.

This was by no means the end of the conflicts occasioned by the introduction into the mines of the eight-hours' day. We shall have to follow later on the course of a very serious struggle. But for the moment everything passed without a hitch. And the new President of the Board of Trade could congratulate himself on having, like his predecessor, had his own labour dispute to settle and having settled it with equal success. In fact the disputes which had broken out among the engineers of the north and which Lloyd George had apparently smoothed out continued and it was Churchill who in June and again in September had the honour of effecting the final settlement. But his ambition was not content with the role of an arbitrator. It aimed higher, as he made clear to Parliament in the speech he delivered in the Commons on the Eight-Hours' Bill, the only speech by a member of the Cabinet which aroused the enthusiasm of the House and of the Labour members in particular. What the workers demand, he said, is not less work but more leisure. They would no longer be content with an existence which condemned them day after day to go from bed to the mill, from the mill back to bed. They wanted time to think and read 'and cultivate their gardens'. The claim did not surprise him; what filled him with amazement was the gentlemen 'in the silk hat and white waistcoat' who had 'the coolness, the calmness, the composure, and the complacency' to ignore the existence of the need. . . . Why, it was asked, stop at the mines? But who had ever said that they ought to stop at the

[1] Lord Askwith, *Industrial Problems and Disputes*, p. 131.

mines? For himself, he regarded the Bill as 'simply the precursor of the general movement which is in progress all over the world, and in other industries besides this, towards a reconciling of the conditions of labour with the well ascertained laws of science and health.'[1] When he uttered these words he was no doubt already thinking of the Bill he would introduce the following year to fix legally no longer hours of work but wages.

4

Within the working class a species of hierarchy could be distinguished, consisting of three classes. At the top was a class of skilled labourers whose skill required a long apprenticeship. Their labour was fixed and they were congregated in large factories and urban centres. They naturally tended to form powerful unions capable of offering a permanent opposition to the employers' claims. The miners and textile workers belonged to this category. Below these was a class of workers whose trade required little or no apprenticeship and whose labour was fluctuating, but who when grouped into large masses were able, if not to form such solid unions as the miners or cotton spinners, at any rate to organize spasmodic strikes on a large scale which sometimes proved successful. Such were the dockers. Lower still was a class of unskilled labourers, exposed to all the vicissitudes of supply and demand, but, since they worked dispersed in small workshops or in their own homes, incapable of combination, and therefore rendered defenceless to a shameless exploitation, which it had become customary to call the sweating system. Karl Marx in an analysis which has become classical has explained how this system was an inevitable product of developing capitalism.[2] The introduction of machinery, since it intensifies production with a reduced number of hands, must constantly throw more and more

---

[1] H. of C., July 6, 1908 (*Parliamentary Debates*, 4th Series, vol. cxci, pp. 1330 sqq.).

[2] Karl Marx, *Das Kapital*, vol. Band I. Cap. xiii, 8: 'Revolutionirung von Manufaktur, Handwerk und Hausarbeit durch die Grosse Industrie' ('Transformation of Manufacture, Handicraft and Domestic Labour by Large-Scale Industry'). S. and B. Webb's chapter 'Parasitic Trades' (*Industrial Democracy*, Part iii, Chap. iii) is directly inspired by Marx's thesis. Cf. on the sweating system and causes John A. Hobson, *Problems of Poverty; an Inquiry into the Industrial Condition of the Poor*, pp. 64 sqq.; David Schloss, *Methods of Industrial Remuneration*, Ed. 3, 1898 (Chaps. xi, xiv and xv); also in Charles Booth's comprehensive investigation, *Life and Labour of the People in London*, the chapter by Beatrice Potter entitled 'The Tailoring Trade' (First Series, vol. iv, 1902, pp. 33 sqq.).

labourers out of work. These labourers no longer needed to produce are of use to the capitalists as a 'reserve' from which they
can draw the necessary supplies of labour when their workers
make too exacting demands. Meanwhile these men are faced with
starvation. Rather than starve they are willing to accept any wage
and work in any slum.

Thus there sprang up at the base of capitalism an entire growth
of small workshops not equipped with machinery and homes
where the entire family slaved from morning till night for a
miserable pittance. That is to say, in the very midst of capitalism
types of production belonging to the era before the industrial
revolution persisted, displaying all the evils of capitalist exploitation without the compensating advantages of machinery, and in
which there was no factory owner whom the legislature could
make responsible for his workmen's welfare. This was the condition of the clothing trade in London. Thousands of workers,
usually Jews from Eastern Europe, packed in the Whitechapel
slums, worked for the large tailoring and dressmaking firms of
the metropolis. It was in this trade that Beatrice Potter, the
future Mrs. Webb, the daughter of a wealthy capitalist, breaking away from the upper middle-class surroundings in which
she had been brought up, had worked as a seamstress, had
graduated in Socialism, had explored the land of grinding want
and toil.

For a long time the indignation of British philanthropists had
been stirred by this spectacle of suffering. But almost half a century had passed since Hood wrote his *Song of the Shirt*, before
Parliament, ten or fifteen years before the close of the century,
saw the need of providing a remedy. In the late 'eighties Socialism
had reappeared in England and the London dockers were engaged
in an agitation almost revolutionary in character. A Conservative
member of the House of Lords, Lord Dunraven, obtained from
his colleagues in 1888 the appointment of a Committee to inquire
into the sweating system.[1] Opposition was not long delayed. The
Lords had voted in a fit of enthusiasm, and the Committee had
no sooner begun its labours when they took fright. Lord Dunraven retired, his place as chairman was taken by Lord Derby, a
man of more moderate views; and the Committee's recommen-

[1] H. of L., February 28, 1888 (*Parliamentary Debates*, 3rd Series, vol. cccxxii, pp. 1598
sqq.).

dations[1] were certainly very timid. But they were not wholly ineffective. How did the Committee of the House of Lords define the sweating system? Sweating exists, according to the report, when wages are inadequate, the work is excessively long, and the buildings in which it is done are insanitary. But why were these abuses so prevalent? The definition explained nothing, and the report did no more than reject certain current explanations with which public opinion was too easily satisfied.[2] Sweating was not specifically due to the existence of the middleman who contracted to supply certain goods and therefore gained the more on his contracts the worse he paid the domestic workers among whom he distributed the order.[3] For the worst cases of sweating, the sweating of seamstresses for example, took place in London where the large firms gave out the work directly to the home workers. To make the contract system illegal would put an end to a glaring abuse but would not go to the root of the evil. Nor were the foreign workers, the Jews of the East End, wholly responsible. Possibly they contributed to lower the general level of wages, but they were only a minority and a small minority of the sweated workers. Therefore to prohibit or restrict the immigration of foreign workers[4] would not effect very much. In consequence, unless like the Committee we prefer to leave the phenomenon unexplained, we are thrown back on the explanation given by Marx. And this was in fact the conclusion reached by Sidney and Beatrice Webb, who at that time were beginning their career as writers and social reformers.[5] What remedies then should be applied? Those Marx had pointed out, suggested by the inevitable economic development. Sooner or later the competition of the machine must put an end to the workshop without machinery and to domestic industry, even under the

[1] *First Report from the Select Committee of the House of Lords on the Sweating System; together with the Proceedings of the Committee; Minutes of Evidence and Appendix*, 1888; *Second Report*, 1888; *Third Report*, 1889; *Fourth Report*, 1889; *Fifth Report, together with an Appendix and Proceedings of the Committee*, 1890.

[2] *Fifth Report*, pp. xiii, sqq.

[3] David Schloss (*Methods of Industrial Remuneration*, chaps. xiv and xv) while recognizing that the contract system does not cover all the species of sweating is content with defining and analysing it.

[4] This was the purpose of the Aliens Act of 1905 (see my *History of the English People*, vol. v, pp. 371–5).

[5] Beatrice Potter (Mrs. S. Webb) 'The Lords and the Sweating System' (*Nineteenth Century*, No. clx, June 1890; vol. xxvii, p. 885). *Fabian Tract No. 50. Sweating; its Causes and Remedy*, Published by the Fabian Society, April 1895. Cf. J. A. Hobson, *Problems of Poverty. An Inquiry into the Industrial Condition of the Poor*, 1891.

novel forms they had assumed as an unexpected by-product of the first introduction of machinery. The atrocious conditions of such labour were sufficient to make their survival impossible. The legislator therefore should facilitate the transition from domestic labour to the factory equipped with machines in which since the employer was in actual contact with his workers the law could make him responsible for their welfare,[1] and this was in fact the tendency of measures adopted by Parliament from 1890 onwards as a result of the labours of the Lords Committee.

The Factory and Workshops' Acts Amendment Act of 1891[2] empowered the Government to require every owner of a factory or workshop to supply a list of the persons employed by him, as workmen or as contractors 'outside his factory or workshop' and the places where they were employed. This was the first legislative interference with domestic labour—and how timid it was! The statute was merely permissive and even so allowed the minister to do nothing more than gather information. An Act passed in 1895,[3] shortly before the fall of the Liberal Cabinet, imposed a fine not exceeding ten pounds upon any employer guilty of employing workmen in a building which had been condemned as insanitary by the Home Office inspector 'even if it were not a workshop' and inflicted the same penalty on an employer convicted of having given out pieces of clothing to be made up, cleaned or repaired in a 'dwelling house' where to his knowledge anyone was suffering from an infectious disease. But the statute remained a dead letter, principally because it imposed too heavy a task of supervision on the officials of the central Government. The comprehensive Factory Act of 1901[4] sought to remedy the defect by transferring from the Home Office to the County Councils the

[1] Sedgwick, a shoemaker, had already expressed the same point of view during the discussions of a Conference on Industrial Remuneration at which Sir Charles Dilke took the chair and which examined the social problem in its various aspects '. . . He described the moral evils resulting from working in the men's homes and suggested that the whole of them should be employed in factories and be subjected to the Factories Act.'

[2] 54 & 55 Vict., Cap. 75: An Act to amend the Law relating to Factories and Workshops (*Factory and Workshop Act*, 1891) Section 27, 11.

[3] 58 & 59 Vict., Cap. 37: An Act to amend and extend the Law relating to Factories and Workshops (*Factory and Workshop Act*, 1895) Section 5, 6.

[4] 1 Edw. 7, Cap. 22: An Act to consolidate with Amendments the Factory and Workshop Acts (*Factory and Workshop Act*, 1901) Section 111–115: a 'domestic factory', a 'domestic workshop' are defined as 'a private house, room or place which, though used as a dwelling, is by means of the work carried on there a factory or a workshop, as the case may be, within the meaning of this Act, and in which neither steam, water, nor other mechanical power is used in aid of the manufacturing process carried on there and in which the only persons employed are members of the same family dwelling there'.

task of prohibiting the giving out of work in buildings they deemed 'dangerous or injurious to the health'. For the first time the Act of 1901 defined what it termed a 'domestic factory' and 'domestic workshop', restricted the hours of labour for children even at home and attempted to prevent the employer deceiving the home worker as to the real amount of the payment he sent him. But all these provisions seem to have effected very little. If the Act of 1895 by making the Home Office responsible for its execution had placed the controlling authority at such a distance from its subjects that no effective supervision was possible, the Act of 1901 by transferring the task to the local authorities had put its enforcement into the hands of men who could not be trusted to enforce it. For these local authorities were under the influence of those whose interest it was that the Act should not be carried out. A Parliamentary Committee reported that in 1906 there had been 1,201 breaches of the law but only three prosecutions.[1] And the same year official statistics proved that no less than a quarter of the medical officers failed to send the Home Office the reports on the sanitary condition of workshops which they were obliged by law to draw up.[2]

5

What procedure then should be adopted? A group of women who had taken the name of the *Women's Industrial Council* and of whom Mrs. Ramsay MacDonald was the leading spirit had devoted many years to the study of the problem. For women were the principal victims of sweating. The Council had carried out an important inquiry into domestic labour in London,[3] and to secure further information had sent investigators to the English-speaking countries overseas. In America it had become acquainted with a legislative remedy which found favour with its members. On receiving the report of the women sent to investigate, Ramsay MacDonald and his wife made a personal visit to the United

[1] *Report from the . . . Select Committee on Home-Work*, 1908, p. vii.
[2] *Factory and Workshop Act*, 1901 (*Homework*) *Return to an Address of the Honourable House of Commons dated 27 March, 1906—for Return as to the Administration, in each County and County Borough during 1904, by the Local Authorities of the Homework Provisions of the Factory and Workshop Act, 1901, as shown by the reports of the Medical Officers of Health sent to the Home Office under Section 132 of the Act*, June 25, 1906, p. 3.
[3] *Home Industries in London*, 1st Report 1897; *Interim Report* 1906; *Third Report* 1908.

States and were converted.[1] In the states of New York and Massachusetts, and in some others, the law forbade any work to be given out unless the places where the workers did their work had been previously inspected and received a 'licence'. No employer might employ any domestic worker who had not presented this licence. It was for the workers to obtain the licence. Whereas under the system at present in force the factory inspectors and sanitary inspectors sought out or were supposed to seek out the workers, if the American system were adopted, the workers would be obliged to apply to the inspectors, if they wished to enjoy the right to work. In 1898 the Women's Industrial Council got a Member of Parliament to introduce a Bill on these lines in the Commons. But the system presented many difficulties. To carry out such a law would require an army of inspectors. And it would be inhuman to condemn to unemployment wretches whose poverty compelled them to work in a slum dwelling. There was no escape from a vicious circle. They wanted to subject domestic workshops to the same regulations as factories, but the difference between the domestic workshop and the factory consisted precisely in the circumstance that the Factory Acts could not be applied to the former.

It was then suggested that the problem should be approached from another angle. Instead of attempting to secure for the victims of the Sweating System a maximum working day, and a minimum of sanitary conditions in the places where they worked, why not, since the problem of supervision seemed insoluble, evade it by attempting to enforce a minimum wage? For some years past it had become customary for the state or the local authorities to insert into every contract contemplated or concluded with a contractor a fair-wages clause guaranteeing the workers the wage usually paid by the particular corporation or current in the locality.[2] But the first statesman to conceive in its full

---

[1] J. R. MacDonald, *Margaret Ethel MacDonald*, 1912, pp. 142 sqq.

[2] See the text of the *Fair Wages Resolution* adopted by the House of Commons on February 13, 1891: 'That in the opinion of this House it is the duty of the Government in all Government contracts to make provision against the evil recently disclosed before the Sweating Committee, to insert such conditions as may prevent the abuse arising from sub-letting, and to make every effort to secure the payment of such wages as are generally accepted and current in every trade for corporation works.' *Fair Wages Committee, Report of the Fair Wages Committee with Appendices, 1908—Minutes of Evidence taken before the Departmental Committee appointed to consider the Working of the Fair Wages Resolution of the House of Commons of 1891, 1908.* Cf. the resolution passed by the House of Commons on March 10, 1909, which differs from the former only by its more elaborate terminology

extent the plan of controlling sweating by fixing wages was the Australian Deakin, the Prime Minister of Victoria. Therefore, in the present instance, as in the suggestion to institute a system of licences, England was finding her models beyond her shores, though within the English-speaking world. Deakin had observed that employers, to evade the legislation which protected their workmen, closed their factories and gave out the work to home workers. In 1893 the Melbourne Government following the example set by the British House of Lords appointed a Committee of inquiry, and after the publication of two reports which dealt with two trades in which sweating was prevalent had passed the important Act of 1896, which laid down the principle of an apprenticeship in which the apprentices would be paid a minimum legal wage and set up special boards, whose members were elected, and which consisted half of workers, half of employers, to fix in every trade the number of apprentices, who were to be at least eighteen years old, and the minimum wage whether payable by time or by the piece. These boards were to be set up by a departmental order in every trade which seemed threatened with sweating. To begin with they were set up in four.[1]

On the benches of the House of Commons a politician sat who had once been universally regarded as marked out for the highest offices in the state but who had been debarred for ever from the ministerial bench by a scandal which was brought into the courts. Sir Charles Dilke remained, nevertheless, an influential Member of Parliament, an imperialist with Socialist leanings. He was a speaker heard with attention on questions of foreign policy,

and provides penalties for the contractor who infringes the conditions it prescribes. Charles Watney and James A. Little (*Industrial Warfare. The Aims and Claims of Capital and Labour*, p. 38) add that only powerful unions—for example, the Boot and Shoemakers', could secure the enforcement of the resolution: that is to say, it was a dead letter in those branches of industry where sweating prevailed just because the workers were unorganized.

[1] By 1908 they had been set up in fifty-two by-extensions of the law which far exceeded the domain of sweating. A special amendment was found necessary to prevent the boards fixing not minimum but normal wages. For this legislation see Albert Métin *Le Socialisme sans doctrine: La question agraire et la question ouvrière en Australie et Nouvelle-Zélande*, 1901, pp. 134 sqq.; V. S. Clark, *The Labour Movement in Australasia: A Study in Social Democracy* 1907, pp. 138 sqq.; also the important official report published under the title: *Home Office, Report to the Secretary of State for the Home Department on the Wages Board and Industrial Conciliation and Arbitration Acts of Australia and New Zealand* by Ernest Aves, 1908. We should notice—as belonging to the same order of ideas, the clause of the New Zealand Factory Act of 1901 which laid down the principle of the minimum wage for children and adolescents of both sexes, five shillings a week below sixteen, with an annual increase until the age of twenty. (Ernest Aves, *Report on . . . Australia and New Zealand*, 1908, p. 88.)

imperial organization, army reform, and labour legislation. His imperialism brought him into contact with the Colonial statesmen. His Socialist sympathies made him keenly interested in the experiments in state Socialism conducted by the Australian Governments. If we are to believe him, he had discussed with Deakin in 1887 the principle of a fixed legal wage. However that may be, in 1895 we find him still attracted by the system of licences.[1] It was not until 1900 that he began to introduce annually in the Commons a Wages' Boards Bill copied from the Victorian Act of 1896.[2]

At first it was a formality and the debate between the respective champions of licences and wage boards presented for a long time a purely academic interest. The attention of the public was engaged elsewhere, occupied by questions which had nothing to do with labour legislation. The situation was entirely changed by the powerful movement of public opinion which preceded the Election of 1906. Some dressmakers who had been fined for having made their workgirls work more than the legal hours pleaded in justification that they had been obliged to finish in time a valuable dress to be worn at Ascot, or at a charity ball. The papers expressed their indignation and aroused the indignation of their readers at the exploitation to which these unfortunate sempstresses were subject and a lady of position introduced a scandal of this kind into a play she wrote.[3] In 1906 the *Daily News* arranged an exhibition to bring home to the fashionable and middle-class public the horrors of sweating. Another was held in 1907 and was opened by Lord Milner.

6

What should be done to satisfy the obvious desire of the public? The Government appointed a Committee of Inquiry and sent one of its members to investigate the working of the Australian wages boards. The MacDonalds, opponents of the system, were

[1] H. of C., April 22, 1895 (*Parliamentary Debates*, 4th Series, vol. xxxii, p. 1465).
[2] For Sir Charles Dilke's initiative in this sphere see his evidence before the Committee of 1907 (Minutes of Evidence taken before the Select Committee on Home Work, May 13, 1908, pp. 173–4.)
[3] *Warp and Woof*, by Mrs. Alfred Lyttelton, 1904.

not converted.[1] After their visit to America they had visited Australia and did not approve of the Australian experiment. It had been conducted on too small a scale to be convincing. And in Australia society was constructed on lines so simple that it was impossible to be certain that a piece of social legislation which had proved successful there could be applied successfully to the complicated social structure of England. Nor was the problem the same in a country where there was a scarcity of women, and a country where because there were too many women, they were shamelessly exploited. The report of the Government commissioner confirmed their views. The Australian law, he reported, dealt only with one symptom of the social disease instead of attacking its root. Old age pensions and a system of universal state insurance were the reforms which should be adopted. Possibly, but in that case why persist in advocating the system of licences to which these criticisms were equally indeed even more applicable? Some immediate action must be taken against sweating and it was evident that it was not Ramsay MacDonald's but Sir Charles Dilke's remedy which had the favour of the public.

When on February 21, 1908, a Wages Boards Bill on the lines of Dilke's was read the second time and debated in the House of Commons it was clear that its principle was approved by the entire House without distinction of party or class. The only protests came from a few irreconcilable opponents of all state interference in the economic sphere. The Tariff Reformers were content to urge that the British market should be protected against the dumping of cheap goods produced by foreign sweating. The Home Secretary, Herbert Gladstone, in a speech which betrayed his embarrassment, explained that the Government could in no case accept the principle of the minimum legal wage, and that the Home Office was already too overburdened with work to assume any new functions. He asked the House to wait until the Committee had reported. Its report, published in the summer of 1908, was favourable to the system of boards,[2] and it was

[1] See Mrs. J. Ramsay MacDonald's evidence before the Committee (*Report from the Select Committee on Home Work*, 1907: Min. of Ev., pp. 211 sqq.); also J. Ramsay MacDonald, 'Sweating and Wages Boards' (*Nineteenth Century*, November 1908, vol. lxiv, pp. 748 sqq.).

[2] *Report from the Select Committee on Home Work: together with the proceedings of the Committee*, Minutes of Evidence and Appendix, 1907—also under the same title 1908. The Committee had been appointed 'to consider and report upon the conditions of labour in trades in which home labour is prevalent and the proposals, including those for the estab-

Churchill who when the session of 1909 opened took charge of the Government Bill dealing with the question. Like Herbert Gladstone he was the heir of a great name, but his inheritance was not the same. Under his control the Board of Trade did not hesitate to assume the responsibilities which frightened Gladstone at the Home Office.

The Bill[1] passed by both Houses without serious opposition set up in those trades in which wages were deemed 'exceptionally' low, Trade Boards to consist in equal numbers of representatives, elected or nominated according to circumstances, of employers and employed, and members nominated by the State, whose number must always be less than half that of the elected members. At the head of the Board were placed a chairman and a secretary appointed by the President of the Board of Trade. His choice was subject to only one restriction: he could not be himself a member of the Board. It would be the duty of the Trade Board to fix a minimum wage both for piecework and work paid by time. The Act was made applicable at first to four trades: ready-made and wholesale tailoring (branches of the dressmaking industry in which sweating was particularly rife), the making of paper or chip boxes, machine lace-making and chain-making. Altogether they employed some 200,000 workers, of whom 140,000 were women and girls. But the Act provided for its extension to other trades by an order of the Board of Trade subject to the veto of Parliament. In 1913 it was extended to five more trades, that is to some hundred and fifty to two hundred thousand additional workers.[2] Twelve years earlier the Webbs had not dared to contemplate such a measure. Nevertheless, it was a first attempt to introduce into the Labour code of Great Britain the principle of the minimum wage, which formed part of their formula the 'National Minimum'.

lishment of Wages Boards and the licensing of Work Places, which have been made for the remedying of existing abuses'. Its report, hostile to the system of licences, pronounced in favour of the system of boards. But it was not the same with the Commissioner's report. Ernest Aves had visited Australia. His conclusions are sceptical and on the whole unfavourable.

[1] 9 Edw. 7, Cap. 22: An Act to provide for the Establishment of Trade Boards for certain Trades (*Trade Boards Act*, 1909).

[2] *Trade Boards Act*, 1909. *Memoranda in reference to the Working of the Trade Boards Act*, 1913.

7

If the fundamental cause of sweating was indeed, as we have seen reason to believe, the existence of a large surplus of labour, constantly thrown onto the streets by large-scale industry and constituting a 'reserve' always ready to take the place of rebel workers, the problem of sweating formed part of the larger problem of unemployment which in 1908 once more began to engage public attention more seriously than three years before. We have already spoken of the origin of this new crisis which began in the United States towards the close of 1907, to spread immediately to England and which increased in gravity throughout the year 1908. At the end of October 1907 out of a hundred members of a union there were not five unemployed, a year later there were almost ten, and during the six months following never less than eight.[1] There was hardly a district unaffected. On the Clyde and Tyne the evil was aggravated by the strikes of which we have spoken, and this was also the case in Lancashire where there was a prolonged dispute in the cotton industry. But above all it was the East End of London, 'the Mecca of social reformers',[2] as John Burns ironically called it, and Glasgow which were the headquarters of an agitation provoked by the unemployment and systematically directed against the Labour Party as well as the two old bourgeois parties. At Glasgow at the beginning of September, riots broke out—they had been expected to be even more serious—on the occasion of Prince Arthur of Connaught's visit to the city. Throughout the country an agitator named Grey collected bodies of 'hunger marchers' who made their way, begging as they went, towards their 'Mecca', the East End of London. In London itself, bands of starving workmen setting out from the East End marched to Hyde Park and Belgravia and as near to Westminster as the police allowed, to parade their poverty under the eyes of the wealthy bourgeoisie. Their leaders spoke the language of revolution. 'If we cannot get bread for our starving wives and children, then let us rob and plunder all round.'[3] Grayson, the revolutionary member for Colne Valley, reminded his

[1] *Abstract of Labour Statistics. Board of Trade (Labour Department). Fourteenth Abstract of Labour Statistics of the United Kingdom, 1908–9*, 1911, p. 5.
[2] H. of C., October 26, 1908 (*Parliamentary Debates*, 4th Series, vol. cxliv, p. 1674).
[3] Williams at Tower Hill, October 28.

hearers, when his behaviour had led to his expulsion from the House,[1] that 'Parliament all along had passed measures for the good of the people only when dragged from their hands by riot and bloodshed.[2] 'Brush them aside like smoke,' said Cunninghame Graham,[3] a survivor of the revolutionary movement of 1889. Another orator was more pointed: 'Go to Westminster with bombs and make them jump!'[4] But all this unrest was in fact simply an echo of contemporary movements in Russia, where the Czar was within an ace of losing his throne, and in France where the syndicalists were spreading the idea of a general revolutionary strike and disorder tended to become chronic. We shall watch the infection spread in the following years. But these malcontents were extremely feeble revolutionaries. They did no more damage than a few broken windows. They were beggars who sought to inspire pity rather than fear. On Sunday morning the hunger marchers invaded the churches, listened quietly to the sermon the preacher delivered for their benefit and after the service took tea in his garden.

The Liberals, and still more the Labour party, were obliged to take these grievances seriously; to do otherwise would be to admit to the working-class electorate that the victory of January 1906 had been empty because the Liberals and Labour members were as powerless as the Conservatives to deal with the problem of unemployment. In the House of Commons on October 21 Asquith, addressing crowded benches in a speech[5] which was loudly applauded, enumerated all the measures actually taken or in contemplation. They were the undertaking of public works by the State, authorization of the local authorities to raise loans to the value of a million, and government grants. The Imperialists in the Cabinet took the opportunity to increase by a recruiting campaign the numbers of the Special Reserve, and lay down torpedo-boat destroyers and cruisers before the date fixed. Moreover, the Government undertook to double the Central Unemployed Fund and make its distribution more elastic. It also promised new legislation in 1909.

---

[1] H. of C., October 15-16, 1908 (*Parliamentary Debates*, 4th Series, vol. cxciv, pp. 495 sqq., 631 sqq.).
[2] Keighley, October 24.
[3] Glasgow, December 12.
[4] Hyde Park, October 16.
[5] *Parl. Deb.*, 4th Ser., vol. cxciv, pp. 1160 sqq.

What would be its character? Would it follow the lines of the Unemployed Workmen Bill, drawn up a year earlier by the Independent Labour party and which the Labour party headed by Ramsay MacDonald had been compelled willy-nilly to support in March 1908.[1] The Bill, intended to replace the Act of 1905 and bearing the same title, consisted of no less than fourteen clauses—was in fact rather a manifesto than a Bill in the strict sense. In substance it amounted to the demand that the local authorities instead of being merely empowered, as in the Act of 1905, to form Distress Committees, should be compelled to form them and that these Committees for dealing with unemployment in place of the very indefinite functions assigned to them in 1905 should be obliged to compile lists of all the unemployed and find them employment, or if that were impossible, relieve the men and their families. The Bill would introduce into English law the double principle of the right to live and the right to work. A committee was formed, at the head of which were Grayson, Blatchford, and Hyndman, by those Socialists who considered not only the Labour party but even the Independent Labour party too timid, to put pressure upon the Houses of Parliament to pass what had become known as the Right to Work Bill.

8

It was John Burns, the president of the Local Government Board, who in March 1908 speaking on behalf of the Government had asked the House to throw out the Unemployed Workmen Bill. Far from approving of this extension of the Act of 1905, he pronounced that measure itself mistaken, passed too hastily. It was a strange speech on the lips of the man who by the agitation he had once conducted had done more than anybody to hasten the introduction and passing of the statute. He denied however that since taking office he had done anything to hamper its execution; on the contrary he had given larger credits to the local authorities than they were in a position to make use of, and he attempted to prove by actual figures that the agricultural colonies,

[1] A Bill to provide Work through Public Authorities for Unemployed Persons; and for other Purposes connected therewith. H. of C., March 13, 1908 (*Parliamentary Debates*, 4th Series, vol. clxxxvi, pp. 10 sqq.).

founded in pursuance of the Act to bring back the workers to the land, had been costly failures. The Unionist benches applauded, the Labour members received his speech in icy silence. Now in the meetings of unemployed he was the object of violent attacks: he was 'Ananias', 'Judas', 'who had pledged himself to the people and had sold them for two thousand pieces of gold'.[1] The unfortunate man was indignant and from one point of view his indignation was justified. He had not been bought. He was scrupulously honest. But how could he have failed to see what a ridiculous figure he cut when he sang the praises of a social order which he found after all not so ill-constructed since it had allowed such a whole-hearted Socialist as John Burns to climb so high? The Cabinet however kept its pledge to attempt a legislative remedy. If it were not to be the Right to Work Bill what should it be? They were waiting for the report of the Royal Commission appointed to examine the problem by the Unionist Government at the time of the last industrial crisis. It reported in February 1909 just as the Session of Parliament opened. The time had come to act.

The Commission which had just reported had been appointed on December 4, 1905, the very day when the Unionist Cabinet resigned, to study on the one hand the working of the Poor Laws, on the other the different methods employed outside the Poor Laws 'for meeting distress arising from want of employment, particularly during periods of severe industrial depression'. That is to say, the same year in which for the first time by setting up the Distress Committees it attempted to tackle the problem of unemployment, Balfour's Cabinet was contemplating the possibility of more ambitious measures, to consist of a general reform of the Poor Laws. The Commission was composed of eighteen members, among them Beatrice Webb. Two years before, Balfour had put Sidney Webb on the Commission appointed to inquire into the best means of amending the laws relating to disputes between employers and workmen. But whereas Sidney Webb had seriously compromised his popularity with the working class by his views on the responsibility of the Unions, Beatrice made a very different use of the Commission of 1905. She persuaded three members of the Commission to join her in signing an excellent and voluminous minority report which recommen-

---

[1] Victor Grayson, speech at Glasgow, October 17, 1908.

ded a number of measures bearing a strong imprint of state Socialism—everything in fact contained in the Labour Right to Work Bill which could possibly be applied in practice. Printed at the Government expense, then reprinted in a handier form[1] and circulated among the public with considerable energy and skill, it finally became almost as important as the 'majority report', and appeared to represent almost equally the opinion of the Commission. We must examine both reports together.

On one point the majority and the minority were agreed. Both recommended the abolition of the Boards of Guardians directly elected which had administered the Poor Law since 1834. Now that there were county and borough councils, charged with the general administration of the counties and boroughs, why not hand over to them the functions formerly entrusted to bodies specially elected? In 1902 the directly elected school boards had been abolished and replaced by education committees elected by the County Councils. The Boards of Guardians must be also abolished and replaced by committees elected by the Councils for the special purpose of poor relief. But the majority report was content with transferring to these committees the functions formerly exercized by the Boards of Guardians. The signatories obviously hoped, though they did not say so, that the Poor Law would be more economically administered by a committee not in direct contact with the electors.[2] The Webbs, on the other hand, the real authors of the minority report, proposed to break up the entire machinery of the Poor Law. On one point in particular, among many others, it had not fulfilled its authors' hopes. They had intended in 1834 that different treatment should be applied to infants and adults, the aged and those still capable of work, the healthy and the infirm. In fact, all had been herded together in the workhouse. Why, asked the Webbs, should it be left to the masters of the workhouses to give a free education to

---

[1] S. and B. Webb, *The Break-Up of the Poor Law: being Part One of the Minority Report of the Poor Law Commission*, edited with Introduction by, 1909; *The Public Organization of the Labour Market: being Part Two of the Minority Report of the Poor Law Commission*, edited with Introduction by, 1909. For the problem of the causes of unemployment and the remedies to be applied, see the vigorous observations, trenchant and uncompromising as is the way of youth, by a disciple of the Webbs, W. H. (now Sir William) Beveridge (*Sociological Papers*, vol. iii, 1907, pp. 323 sqq., and also by the same author: *Unemployment: A Problem of Industry*, Ed. I, 1909).

[2] For criticisms of the proposed abolition of the Boards of Guardians by the orthodox Socialists see *Poor Law Minority Report.—Report of Debate between George Lansbury and H. Quelch on September 20 and 21, 1910*.

the pauper children when all children now had in principle the right to a free education? It was the business of the education authorities, as it was the business of the health committees to take care of the sick and of the asylum committees to look after lunatics and mental defectives. As for the aged, all that was necessary was to extend the application of the principle laid down by Parliament a few months earlier and provide them with old age pensions at the cost of the State. There remained the healthy adults. For their relief the minority proposed a new system which would have no connection with the old Poor Law, and lay entirely outside the scope of the majority report, a national system for abolishing unemployment by 'the organization of the labour market'.

The Webbs asked for the institution of a National Labour Exchange with branches throughout the country which would keep a regular and exact record of all the unemployed.[1] Employers would inform these Exchanges of the number of hands they required. Thus everything possible would be done, since supply and demand would be brought together throughout the country, to get rid of those 'stagnant pools' of unemployment of which the employers took advantage in particular localities to lower wages unduly. When the surplus of unemployed labour had thus been reduced very considerably, it would be reduced still further by making less use of child labour, prohibiting the employment of mothers of very small children, and reducing the railwaymen's working day to eight hours. Since, however, they could not hope to abolish unemployment completely, whatever surplus of unemployed still remained should be relieved by adopting within limits a system of compulsory insurance against unemployment. And special relief work should also be found for the unemployed, work of a useful nature and at the same time such as would re-educate them for regular employment at a trade. To perform all these new functions while taking over the administration of labour legislation hitherto confided to other departments a special Ministry of Labour should be created. Organization of the labour market, amounting in practice to organization

---

[1] It was a method which Germany had employed on a fairly large scale for the last ten or fifteen years as a cure for unemployment. But the German Labour Exchanges (*Arbeitsnachweise*) were either maintained by private associations, or organized by municipalities (W. H. Beveridge, *Unemployment: A Problem of Industry*, 1910, pp. 239 sqq.). England was therefore preparing to outstrip Germany on the path of state control.

of labour—Saint Simon's old watchword; the right to work—
Fourier's old slogan. They had made much stir in France about
1848. Now they were crossing the Channel. How many Englishmen who in 1909 were speaking the language spoken by the disciples of Fourier and Saint Simon knew the origin of the formulas
which came so readily to their lips?

9

Winston Churchill took the question of unemployment out of
the hands of John Burns, as at the same time he took the question
of sweating out of Herbert Gladstone's. The Bill he submitted
to the Commons on May 20 after explaining the day before the
main lines of the Cabinet's policy on the subject[1] adopted in a
modified form the recommendations of the minority report. It
was therefore, as Arthur Henderson speaking on behalf of the
Labour party jestingly remarked, nothing but 'the Right to
Work Bill in penny numbers'.[2] Churchill, who promised in the
near future a system of unemployment insurance with contributions from the workers, proposed to set up Labour Exchanges
throughout the United Kingdom. The country would be divided
into ten districts. In each of these the Labour Exchanges would
be grouped around a clearing house for the entire area, and the
work of the ten regional clearing houses similarly co-ordinated
by a central clearing house in London. It was intended to establish
some thirty or forty Exchanges in the large cities, forty-five in
towns of lesser size, and a hundred and fifty offices of the third
class in still smaller centres.

In all the large centres there would be a 'mixed consultative
committee' composed in equal numbers of the workers' and employers' representatives, with a permanent official chairman. The
object of this vast organization was to find employment for the
workmen available, workmen for the employment available. It
was understood that the officials of the Exchanges would observe
a strict neutrality in the case of labour disputes. In other words the
employers must not hope to make use of them to obtain 'black-

[1] H. of C., May 19, 1909 (*Parliamentary Debates*, Commons 1909, 5th Series, vol. v,
pp. 499 sqq.). For a more detailed defence of the Bill see H. of C., June 16, 1909, Winston
Churchill's speech (ibid., vol. pp. 1035 sqq.).
[2] H. of C., May 19, 1909; ibid., vol. v, p. 519.

legs'. In the same spirit it was laid down that a workman might always refuse the work offered him, if a union rate of wages was in operation in the district and he were offered a wage less than that rate. The economic philosophy which found expression in the reform must be clearly understood. Just as a certain type of collectivism does not contest the principle, dear to Liberal economists, that a worker's remuneration should be proportionate to the value of his work, but claims that if the principle is to be made effective state interference is necessary to establish what was called 'equality of starting point', so the 'organization of the labour market', to use Beatrice Webb's phraseology, does not contradict the principle, equally dear to the Liberal economists, which demands the utmost possible fluidity of supply and demand. But whereas the Liberal economist believes that it is sufficient to remove the artificial obstacles to this fluidity set up by particular statutes, according to the new Socialism the obstacles are natural, difficulties of movement, the ignorance of those concerned. To remove them the State must intervene. Actually, its intervention was rapid and vigorous. The two Houses passed the Bill without serious debate[1] and on January 31, 1910, eighty Labour Exchanges were opened. In London Churchill opened them in person amid the cheers of the crowd.

Responsible for introducing in a single session these two Bills, one intended to stamp out sweating, the other to get rid of unemployment, Churchill at the end of 1909 presented the appearance of a great social reformer. By the extension of its functions, as a result of which it was becoming in effect a ministry of labour as well as of trade, the Board of Trade was rising in the ministerial hierarchy, an advance recognized by the Act passed this year which permitted the salary of the President to be raised from £2,000 to £5,000.[2] What were these new functions which justified this increase of salary? In the first place, the work of arbitration and conciliation. We have already seen what an important

---

[1] 9 Edw. 7, Cap. 7: An Act to provide for the Establishment of Labour Exchanges and for other Purposes Incidental thereto (*Labour Exchanges Act*, 1909).

[2] 9 Edw. 7, Cap. 23: An Act to remove the Statutory Limitation on the Salary of the President of the Board of Trade (*Board of Trade Act*, 1909). It began by repealing an Act of 1829 which limited the salary to £2,000 so as to make it possible to raise the salary of the President of the Board of Trade, together with the salary of the President of the Local Government Board, to the same level as that of the Secretaries of State. A second clause added at Churchill's request provided that the actual holder of the office should not benefit by the increase (H. of C., April 20, 1909; *Parliamentary Debates*, Commons 1909, 5th Series, vol. iii, p. 1493).

part the numerous meetings between representatives of the workers' and employers' organizations, held under the aegis first of Lloyd George, then of Churchill, had come to play in the social history of the country. In September 1908 to make this work easier Churchill had three panels set up by his department, a panel of chairmen, a panel of employers, a panel of workmen so that a tribunal of arbitration composed of three suitable persons would be in readiness to intervene at the first sign of any dispute that might threaten.[1] The importance of this function may be judged by the fact that the machinery provided by the Conciliation Act of 1896, which had been utilized only 209 times in a period of ten years, was employed in thirty-nine instances in 1907, in sixty in 1908 and in fifty-nine in 1909, that is 158 times in three years.[2] But the Board of Trade had a further office to fulfil, to enforce the social legislation. And these statutes, ever more numerous and more complicated—particularly the Labour Exchanges Act—required for their execution a host of officials. A very serious change was taking place and for the first time attracting notice. England was becoming bureaucratic.

According to the Census of 1911 the Civil Service employed 162,000 officials as compared with 116,413 in 1901, 79,449 in 1891, 50,485 in 1881. According to the same census the local government employed 20,985 persons in 1881, 24,930 in 1891, 36,870 in 1901, 64,087 in 1911. The increase during the last decade had exceeded 100 per cent. It was a body of officials formidable by their numbers, formidable also for the delicate nature of their functions, for the performance of which they were invested with powers almost discretionary. For it was impossible for Parliament to draw up statutes in such minute detail that the text provided for every concrete case to which they were applicable. A statute was in current parlance only a 'skeleton'. It was for the official to clothe the skeleton with flesh,[3] by administrative rules

---

[1] *Board of Trade Memorandum*, September 15, 1908.
[2] Lord Askwith, *Industrial Problems and Disputes*, 1920, p. 126.
[3] H. of C., June 16, 1909, G. P. Gooch's speech: 'This Bill as it is before us is a mere skeleton. The flesh and blood will be put on it by means of the Regulations which will be issued by the Board of Trade (*Parliamentary Debates*, Commons 1909, 5th Series, vol. vi, p. 1028). Cf. Lloyd George's interesting observations when he introduced his Merchant Shipping Amendment Bill: 'It is very difficult to carry Acts of Parliament nowadays, under any scheme, with its present congestion of business. . . . It is inconvenient to require an Amending Act of Parliament whenever a new regulation seems to be necessary to meet the changing circumstances of our mercantile marine such as have taken place during the last twenty years. Who can foresee what may happen? There may be a totally different

or 'orders'. The number of these orders had become so great and the need that the public should be informed of them so urgent that from 1893 onwards an official collection was published more bulky from the outset than the annual collection of statutes and increasingly voluminous every year.[1] Moreover, it very soon became impossible in practice to allow anybody who wished to appeal to the ordinary courts from any administrative decision whatever. The courts would have been unable to cope with the work and the administrative machine would have been broken down. Therefore, since in England, unlike the Continent, there exists no special judicature to settle disputes between the state and the individual, the custom grew up—to be sanctioned within a few years by a decision of the Lord Chancellor[2]—of regarding the officials as free to decide, without recourse to the courts, specific cases submitted to them concerning the detailed application of Acts of Parliament.[3]

state of things, and what we want is to be able by means of an Order in Council, if necessary, to introduce regulations applicable to the changing circumstances of the hour, without having to have constant resort to the House of Commons to obtain sanction for every change that may be required' (H. of C., *Parl. Deb.*, 4th Ser., vol. cliv, p. 251).

[1] *Statutory Rules and Orders other than those of a Local, Personal or Temporary Character, issued in the year 1893* [and onwards]: *with a list of the more important statutory orders of a local character, arranged in classes and an index. Published by Authority.* The publication was made in obedience to the Rule Publication Act (55 Vict., Cap. 66) 1893. 'Something of the extent of this subordinate legislation may be indicated by comparing its volume with that of the parliamentary statutes. The annual volume of published general statutes contains from 80 to 100 Acts of Parliament, and from 500 to 600 pages. In addition to the public general statutes there are each year several volumes of local and private acts, including provisional orders and confirming acts which, while formally passed by Parliament, are the result of the actions of government departments and small private bill committees. But beyond this the annual volumes of Statutory Rules and Orders of a general character issued without parliamentary action, contain about ten times as many measures as the public general acts and run from 1,500 to 3,000 pages. Besides these there are each year several hundreds of rules and orders of local application, listed only by title in the annual volume' (Cecil T. Carr, Delegated Legislation 1926: *University of Illinois, Studies in the Social Sciences*, September 1925, vol. xiii, No. 30, p. 8).

[2] Board of Education v. Rae and others (1911); Local Government Board v. Arlidge (1915). Cf. W. A. Robson, *Justice and Administrative Law*, pp. 141–2, 143 sqq.

[3] These administrative regulations which amount to genuine laws constitute what Sir Frederick Pollock (*Encyclopædia of the Laws of England, being a new abridgment of the eminent legal Authorities*, vol. i, 1897, General Introduction, p. 6) proposed to term 'delegated legislation'. The name caught on. It serves as the title of three lectures given at Cambridge in 1921 by Cecil T. Carr which he published in book form the same year. He attributes it however to Sir Courtenay Ilbert. For the nature not only quasi-legislative but quasi-judicial of the administrative decisions see the recent work by William A. Robson, *Justice and Administrative Law: A Study of the British Constitution*, 1928. But the first writer before the war who seems to have been struck by the importance of the problem is the German D. Otto Koelreuther, *Verwaltungsrecht und Verwaltungsrechtssprechung im modernen England*, 1912. See in particular p. 223: 'If we consider the unsystematic fashion in which English law has regulated the power of government officials to make decisions, we cannot escape the feeling that it is not considered desirable that the public should realize that a powerful

The English system of entrance examinations for all branches of the Civil Service, for which moreover candidates were extremely plentiful, ensured an excellent body of civil servants. Was it a fair ground for complaint that the subjects set in these examinations were such as to favour the graduates of the two great universities, so that the government departments in London were staffed by members of the ruling aristocracy? Or if this were an exaggeration that at any rate this favoured class constituted in every department an all-powerful clique and since there were no examinations for promotion monopolized all the high positions.[1] Even if this were true, was it to be lamented? Was it not rather a matter for congratulation that an aristocracy which throughout the nineteenth century had occupied itself so zealously in Parliament with the conduct of national business should now put itself at the head of the administrative departments? Was there not rather genuine ground for anxiety in the new system adopted by the Liberal Cabinet of appointing the officials of the Labour Exchanges without holding an examination? Competitive examination, it was argued by those who advocated its abandonment, could not furnish the necessary guarantees for the proper exercise

bureaucracy has gradually grown up in its midst whose action is to a large extent exempt from parliamentary control. And if we adopt the point of view that the monopoly which the Courts asserted as guardian of the constitution during the eighteenth century expressed in the clearest and most mature form the principle of a state founded on law, we must regard the latest development in England, if not as a retrogression, at least as a deflection of the straight path which the development of English constitutional law has taken hitherto.' We shall gauge better the importance of the change undergone in this respect by British institutions and public opinion, if we compare with the earlier editions of A. V. Dicey's, *Introduction to the Study of the Law of the Constitution*, the introduction to the 8th edition written in 1915.

[1] A. Lawrence Lowell, *The Government of England*, vol. i, p. 163: '. . . By far the larger part of the successful candidates come from one or the other of (the) two great universities.' But the composition of the universities had undergone a profound change during the last few years and this did not mean that these Oxford and Cambridge graduates had all come from the seven great Public Schools. See the figures given by A. Ponsonby (*The Decline of Aristocracy*, 1912, pp. 295–6). The number of successful candidates from the seven great Public Schools was 16 out of 97 in 1906, 18 out of 92 in 1907, 13 out of 82 in 1908, 17 out of 89 in 1909, 17 out of 113 in 1910. Nevertheless the same author can write (pp. 117-18): 'The permanent Civil Service, partly recruited from this upper class, in close contact with it, and blindly on the side of law, authority and tradition, extends its influence and tightens the supremacy of the executive with bureaucratic bonds.' It is of interest to note how the decline of imperialism in conjunction with the growing influence of state socialism seems to have favoured the recruiting of the Home Civil Service. See Lord Selbourne's speech at Oxford, October 27, 1911: 'When I was at Oxford the best brains of Oxford, when they had a chance, went to the Indian Civil Service. It was only the second best as a rule who went to the Home Civil Service. Now all the best men put "H" first, "I" second, and "C" third. The best men are all prepared to take the least risks. Do you think what it means when an Oxford man, the pick of his year, says: "I would rather be a clerk in the Home Civil Service than go to India or the Colonies"?'

of these novel and delicate functions. What was wanted was not so much special knowledge or a high standard of general education as acquaintance with industrial and labour circles. No doubt, but the door was thrown open all the same to favouritism, personal influence and political preferences.

When all is said, it is beyond doubt that the excellence of British social manners, the courteous tolerance of those in command, and the obedience of their subordinates confer on the British Civil Service, as on other British institutions, qualities which distinguish it from similar institutions on the Continent. It is nevertheless indubitable that it was acquiring an importance altogether new in the life of the nation. At the Board of Education there was Sir Robert Morant's policy; in Ireland Sir Antony MacDonnell's, at the Admiralty Sir John Fisher's. And it was this policy of the head of the department which alone counted; the successive Ministers had been simply the Parliamentary mouthpieces of these great men of action. Parliament, it is true, revolted against the three, and it was indeed this revolt which made the names of Fisher, MacDonnell, and Morant so well known. But there were other secret dictators whose action was the more powerful because no one spoke of them. Askwith, the Comptroller-General, chief arbitrator of the Board of Trade, made it a rule, each time an industrial dispute was submitted to him, to secure the signature by the parties concerned of a permanent collective contract in such terms as would obviate future disputes. He thus built up piece by piece throughout the United Kingdom a vast written code governing the relations between employers and employed,[1] which if not strictly speaking law nevertheless possessed a very real binding force. Sir Herbert Llewellyn Smith prepared and organized the system of Labour exchanges. Sir Ernest Aves did the same for the Trade Boards. Who outside England ever heard of these men? And how many Englishmen even heard of them? Nevertheless, in the background of political life they played a part probably more important than the great political figures who occupied the stage while they worked in the wings.

Thus under a Liberal Cabinet the social creed of the Webbs—though they did not show the least gratitude to the Government for this—triumphed, a doctrine of very different colour from the official doctrine of the Labour party. The small apartment occu-

[1] Lord Askwith, *Industrial Problems and Disputes*, 1920, p. 137.

pied by the MacDonalds in Lincoln's Inn Fields was crowded at their evening receptions by a gathering typical of so-called 'advanced' circles. There were Utopians and philanthropists of every description, friends of the negro and the Hindu, anti-vivisectionists and vegetarians, militant labour leaders, revolutionaries from the Continent. In Grosvenor Road at the Webbs' the sort of people of whom we have just spoken did not feel altogether at home. There you would meet mingling with intellectual Fabians, high officials, politicians belonging to the most moderate sections of the House and representatives of fashionable society. The Webbs had their enemies who accused them of snobbery. It was a calumny without the slightest foundation. The uncompromising purity of their doctrine led to the resignation of one of the most important of the industrial magnates who had consented to join the governing body of the London School of Economics.[1] Of all English people they were at bottom the most remote from snobbery, and the most contemptuous of it. They pursued methodically and fanatically the end they had proposed to themselves, to transform the old England of individualism and *laissez faire* into an England organized from above. And this School of Economics which they had founded and of which they were the guiding spirits was intended by them to train the bureaucracy of a future collectivist England.[2] Every ambitious young man knew that if he got into touch with them and convinced them of his ability, they would be in a better position than anybody else to assist his career and place him where in their opinion he was best fitted to serve the state.[3] Listen to one of their circle, the young Keeling, who had asked them to put him on the right path. When the Webbs advised him to take up his residence in a working-class constituency, and there undertake political and above all administrative work, he enthusiastically obeyed, settled in a suburb of South London, and dreamed of persuading all his

[1] We refer to Lord Claud Hamilton whose resignation was a protest against a speech delivered by Sidney Webb at the opening by the Amalgamated Society of Railway Servants of its central offices in London. For the entire incident see Sidney Webb's letter to Lord Claud Hamilton of October 22, 1910 (*The Times*, October 23, 1910).

[2] For the function attributed to the School of Economics by the Webb group see Haldane's speech at Reading on October 27, 1906, in which he announced his intention to make the institution a training college in the art of administration for soldiers as well as for civilians.

[3] For the Webb's salon see the picture painted by H. G. Wells in his 'New Machiavelli' (Beatrice Webb appears under the name Altiora), a picture which, though intended as a satire, constitutes nevertheless an involuntary tribute to this remarkable woman.

friends, the Socialist intellectuals of Cambridge, to follow his example. 'By God! if we could capture a Borough Council or a Board of Guardians we would shift something.'[1] And in his youthful fervour he gave his thoughts a lyrical note foreign to the prose of his matter-of-fact teachers. 'I was wondering yesterday why the devil the world didn't found a religion on Cæsar instead of on Christ. Of course, one feels instinctively that it couldn't be done. But to me it also seems that Cæsar was a far greater personality . . . Perhaps it wasn't so incongruous as it was made to appear by damned Christian scholars. Worship isn't the same thing as prayer.'[2]

II LLOYD GEORGE AT THE EXCHEQUER

I

For all that has been said of the almost revolutionary importance of the legislation passed on Churchill's initiative—the introduction of the principle of the minimum legal wage, the institution of a general system of Labour Exchanges—it would be a mistake to suppose that at the end of 1909 he occupied the centre of the stage. The very calm with which his two Bills were debated in both Houses proves that neither the Unionist minority in the Commons, nor the Unionist majority in the Lords dreamt of giving battle on this ground. They were occupied in fighting on a wider front a more dangerous foe. When at the end of 1909 Churchill collected in one volume the speeches he had delivered on the social question during the past four years he asked the Radical journalist Massingham for a preface, and the outstanding passage of that preface is perhaps that in which Massingham sang the praises not of Churchill's statutes but of the Budget which Lloyd George, the Chancellor of the Exchequer, had just carried through the Commons. 'If it prospers, the social policy for which it provides prospers too. If it fails, the policy falls to the ground.'[3] In fact, at this date not Churchill but Lloyd George was the popular hero, the mouthpiece of British Radicalism. In his hands the

---

[1] Letter to Mrs. Townsend, July 21, 1908 (Keeling, *Letters and Recollections*, 1918, p. 31).
[2] Letter to Mrs. Townsend, July 6, 1912 (ibid., pp. 125–6).
[3] *Liberalism and the Social Problem* by the Right Hon. Winston Spencer Churchill, 1909; Preface, pp. xiii–xiv. (The Preface is dated October 26, 1909.)

Budget of 1909 became the ram for which the Liberals had been looking ever since 1906 to batter down the walls of the Upper House. To grasp the antecedents of this fiscal innovation we must trace the history of successive Budgets from the point where we left it in the last volume when we analysed the first Budget which followed the peace of Vereeniging.

Between the beginning of 1904 and Sir Henry Campbell-Bannerman's death, the Budget had been twice presented by Austen Chamberlain before the Election of 1906, twice by Henry Asquith after it. But it would be a mistake to conclude that a sharp line divided Austen Chamberlain's Budgets from Asquith's. The first Budget drawn up by Asquith on the very morrow of the General Election merely continued Chamberlain's. But the Budget of 1907 is already paving the way for Lloyd George's great Budget of 1909. Austen Chamberlain had been appointed, we remember, Chancellor of the Exchequer at the remodelling of the Cabinet which followed his father's retirement in October 1903. His appointment to this important post was a visible proof to the world that there was no rupture between Balfour and the apostle of protection. On the other hand, a species of compact had been concluded between the Unionist leaders and Joseph Chamberlain when the latter left the Cabinet. It was agreed that no departure should be made from the fiscal traditions of the country until his independent propaganda had eventually converted it to protection. During his two years at the Exchequer, Austen Chamberlain observed the agreement faithfully. He practised economy, reducing the naval and military expenditure while the increase of the civil estimates was slow. The reduction of the navy estimates in 1905 was sensational, amounting to £3,530,000, that is about a tenth of the navy estimates for the previous year. Moreover, he continued to apply strictly the policy of debt reduction. Even when in 1904 the industrial crisis produced a deficit he did not touch the sinking fund. The following year he increased it by a million pounds to pay off within ten years ten million of the floating debt. Since he refused to touch the sinking fund he was obliged to have recourse to taxation to make up the deficit, but the increases of taxation he submitted to Parliament were such as to win the approval of all parties. An increase in the duties on tobacco had an intentionally protectionist aspect and for that reason caused warm debates in the Commons.

But it was a tax which produced very little revenue. Apart from this Chamberlain sought to raise two sums of two million from two different sources. On the one hand he put twopence on to the tea duty. There was nothing protectionist in this; for the duty did not protect any home producer and damaged the colonial producer. On the other hand he put a penny on to the income-tax, which returned to the figure of a shilling in the pound which it had reached for the first time during the Boer War. In peacetime the increase was an application of the fiscal policy advocated by the Liberals. The following year when the economic position had improved and the Budget showed a large surplus, it was the tea duties which were reduced to their former figure. The income-tax remained at a shilling.

In 1906 Asquith followed the same policy. He reduced the army estimates, which at the close of the financial year had fallen by a million and the navy estimates which fell by almost two million. He added a further million to the sinking fund, and though an additional three million was placed at his disposal by the fact that certain bonds of the floating debt were due for redemption, instead of reducing taxation accordingly, he placed the sum at the disposition of the Treasury to pay off whatever portion of the debt it seemed desirable to pay off. He also pledged himself to combat the practice which had become usual in the Government departments for many years past of borrowing money for the execution within a fixed term of years of urgent public works. From the administrative standpoint it offered the great advantage of making it possible to carry out these works by methods more akin than usual to those employed in private enterprise. But it shocked the financial purists, eager to safeguard the principle of a consolidated Budget. It also shocked the champions of the sinking fund, who saw a host of private debts accumulating against the state, at the very time that the sinking fund was paying off the public debt. Finally, and this was perhaps the gravest objection, the practice, when employed by the War Office and the Admiralty, was regarded by the Radicals as a contrivance for withdrawing their expenditure from Parliamentary control. Asquith satisfied these critics by promising that so far as the military and naval expenditure was concerned, no more loans of this kind would be raised. The income-tax remained at the figure, henceforward regarded as normal, of a shilling, but the taxpayer was relieved by abolishing the tax imposed in 1901 on the importation of coal, taking a penny off the tea duty, and almost entirely abolishing the new duties on tobacco imposed two years before—three measures of free trade.

The heavy increase of expenditure involved by the Boer War had caused serious dissatisfaction in the country and it was only to be expected that the Unionist Cabinet on the eve of the Election should do its utmost to show that this inevitable burden had been temporary, and prove itself capable of reducing the Budget to its legitimate size. It was equally natural that the new Cabinet on the morrow of its victory at the polls when it had just denounced at countless public meetings the extravagances of its predecessor should concentrate its entire attention when it drew up its first Budget, on economy, which it carried to the utmost possible extent. And Asquith promised to do even more in future 'in the reduction of expenditure, in the repayment of debt'. He added, however, 'and in the readjustment of the incidence of taxation'.[1] By these words he raised a further problem, which the Unionist Cabinet had refused to consider, but which a Radical Cabinet was obliged to face, the problem of effecting such a reform of taxation as would relieve the poor taxpayer at the cost of the wealthy. At once another question arose. Was it to be the simple readjustment of a burden whose total amount would not be increased? Could they hope to effect sufficient economies in the army and navy estimates to provide for the new costs of a democratic Budget without increasing, possibly even decreasing, the amount of taxation? The Opposition speakers expressed their doubts. 'The House of Commons', said one of them,[2] 'has committed itself to the principles of old age pensions, of the supplying of free meals to school children, of a large increase in the cost of education, and the payment of Members of Parliament. These schemes all require money'. We must attempt to determine a little more exactly how the problem of direct taxation presented itself to British statesmen in 1906, before we describe the action they took to solve it in the years which followed.

[1] H. of C., April 30, 1906 (*Parliamentary Debates,* 4th Series, vol. clvi, p. 307).
[2] H. of C., May 1, 1906, W. H. Cowan's speech (*Parl. Deb.,* 4th Ser., vol. clvi, pp. 438–9).

2

Direct taxation in England was based on the income-tax. The income-tax was not progressively graduated but bore a fixed proportion to the amount of income taxed, with reductions for very small incomes. Incomes below £160 were entirely free of tax, below £400, £500, £600 and £700 they were subject to reductions which became smaller as the income increased. Above £700 the full tax was paid and its rate, which had exceeded a shilling in the pound during the Boer War and was a shilling when the Liberals took office, remained the same however large the income. Nor did the collection of the tax present an inquisitorial character. Two-thirds of it were deducted at the source in such a way that verification was easy and did not involve a full declaration of the taxpayer's income, unless the latter wished to make one to prove his title to the reductions allowed for small incomes. Nevertheless, the tax constantly increased. Its produce had exactly doubled during the ten years of Unionist Government rising from £15,600,000 in 1894 to £31,350,000 in 1905. Further, in addition to this proportional levy large fortunes were subject to the steeply graduated succession duties which the Liberal Government had introduced in 1894, the year before it was replaced by a Unionist Cabinet. Since that date the produce of these succession duties had almost doubled. A French financial expert writing in 1905 expressed his admiration for 'the self-sacrifice' with which 'the privileged class, a minority increasingly restricted in numbers on whose shoulders alone the burden of income-tax falls submits—in the public interest—to painful and inevitable ruin, an example which few other aristocracies could display'.[1]

Throughout the greater part of the nineteenth century the income-tax, subject as it was to a regular and finally to an annual vote of the Commons, had been regarded as a temporary expedient. Its rate was moderate and it was employed as an exceptional resource to defray the cost of a war or solve a temporary financial difficulty. Its reduction was promised, it was actually reduced and it was hoped that one day it might be possible to abolish it entirely. When Austen Chamberlain introduced the Budget of 1904 he

[1] René Stourm, *Systèmes généraux d'impôts*, Edition 2, 1905, p. 147.

was faithful to this tradition, and held out the hope of future reductions. But at the same time he raised the rate from elevenpence to one shilling in the pound, and this proportion of a twentieth began, it would seem, to be considered normal. But if the income-tax were to be a permanent burden of such heavy weight on the taxpayer it was no longer possible to be content with the careless method of collection and the rough and ready assessment which had been tolerated in the past. Problems with which the legislature had hitherto shown practically no concern became urgent on the eve of the Election of 1906.

The first of these was the evasion of payment. Though as the result of measures adopted in 1885 and in 1900 the abuse had apparently diminished, it still existed on a large scale. Ritchie, the Chancellor of the Exchequer in 1903, deplored its extent and suggested that its diminution would be perhaps the best means by which the rate of the income-tax could be lowered without loss of revenue.[1] A committee appointed to inquire into the reforms which might be effected in the system of collecting the income-tax explained in detail how this evasion of payment was practised. Of 600,000 declaration forms sent to taxpayers, 200,000 were not returned, and the assessment was made by the Commissioners. By what method? The Commissioners proceeded gradually raising the assessment annually until the taxpayer protested and the number of times they could increase the assessment without protest measured the distance between the original assessment and the taxpayer's actual income.[2] When a private business was turned into a public company and a strict account had to be given of the profits made, the glaring extent of the previous frauds was revealed. Foreign companies operating in England practised with English assistance a host of tricks which enabled them to evade payment entirely.[3] According to a contemporary estimate the

---

[1] H. of C., April 19, 1904 (*Parliamentary Debates*, 4th Series, vol. cxxxiii, p. 560).

[2] H. of C., April 23, 1903, speech by the Chancellor of the Exchequer, Ritchie: 'One of the most successful modes of evasion is to make no return of income, the income-tax payer preferring to be assessed by the Commissioners. In this particular case my friend saw that the particular firm, of which he knew something, had adopted this plan and the Commissioners had assessed them, I think it was at something like £3,000 or £4,000. My friend said: "What! £3,000 or £4,000; that is preposterous! These people are making gigantic profits." The Commissioner replied: "Then, we will make it £5,000." "£5,000," my friend said, "put it up to £55,000." The Commissioners acted upon the advice and they paid it.' (*Parli. Deb.*, 4th Ser., vol. cxxi, p. 254).

[3] For these ingenious devices see an excellent article in the *Economist* entitled 'Can Income Tax be avaded?' (*Economist*, October 8, 1915.) The article discusses the extremely inconsistent judgments of English and Scottish Courts in this respect and the debates on

loss to the revenue from these frauds in respect of commercial profits amounted to a fifth of the amount due.[1] To invest money abroad, let the income accumulate, invest that income abroad and eventually bring back the income transformed into capital was another method employed to cheat the revenue. The committee suggested remedies. Declaration of income should, they proposed, be made compulsory, the forms be drawn up in clearer terms and the penalties imposed better adjusted, rendered more severe, and published.[2] In 1907, 1914, and 1915 the legislature would act upon these recommendations and even devise additional measures to enforce payment.

These were not the only problems raised by the income-tax. In 1905 all incomes were taxed at the uniform rate of a twentieth. This was all very well. But was it in accordance with equity, in other words with genuine 'equality' that incomes which were the fruit of the taxpayer's personal work and those which were not should pay the same tax? This was the problem of the 'differentiation' of incomes. And how could it be maintained that the principle of equality was observed because the tax bore the same proportion to the income whatever its size? A tax of £50 on an income of £1,000 was certainly heavier than a tax of £500 on an income of £10,000. If there was to be genuine equality the tax must be increased in a proportion in excess of the increase in the income taxed. This was the principle of 'graduation'. As regards the income-tax the reductions for small incomes already constituted an indirect and timid application of the principle. Why not apply it more consistently? Attempts had been made to solve these problems of differentiation and graduation as regards the succession duties, why not do the same thing for the

the latest Finance Bill, 1915, which included provisions designed to render these frauds impossible, H. of C., November 4 and 17, 1915 (*Parliamentary Debates*, Commons, 1915, 5th Series, vol. lxxv, pp. 1856 sqq.). 5 & 6 Geo., 5 Cap. 89: An Act to grant certain Duties of Customs and Inland Revenue (including Excise), to alter other duties and to amend the law relating to Customs and Inland Revenue (including Excise) and the National Debt and to make further provision in connection with Finance (*Finance [No. 2] Bill 1915*) Section 31.

[1] L. G. Chiozza Money, *Riches and Poverty*, 1905, p. 13.

[2] *Income-Tax Committee: Report of the Departmental Committee on Income-Tax*, 1905, pp. v sqq. See also J. C. Stamp, who, writing a little later, sought to prove by solid arguments that the abuse did not exist on a very large scale (*British Incomes and Property: The Application of Official Statistics to Economic Problems*, 1916, pp. 315 sqq.). To these evasions of the income-tax we must add the evasion of death duties by gifts between the living. For this form of evading taxation see Galsworthy's novel, *The Forsyte Saga*. Measures were adopted in the Budget of 1909 to make the practice more difficult.

income-tax? Already in 1904 when Austen Chamberlain set up his committee to inquire into the evasion of taxation, Herbert Samuel and Richard Haldane wanted its scope extended to these further questions.[1] They were not successful. Chamberlain, hostile to the Gladstonian tradition in finance, in so far as it involved the maintenance of complete free trade, became its champion when it was proposed to introduce into British fiscal policy what seemed a first instalment of Socialism.[2] But after the Election of 1906, when Haldane and Samuel were both members of the Government, a committee was appointed to inquire into the problem and Samuel was its chairman. Set up on May 4 it worked quickly and reported on November 29.[3] The report recommended that the limit of reductions at the lower end of the scale should be raised from £700 to £1,000 and that a 'differentiation' between earned and unearned incomes should only be applied to incomes above £3,000. By combining this 'degression' and 'differentiation' the first step would be taken to satisfy the advocates of a democratic reform of the income-tax. At the same time the report recommended that the taxpayer should be compelled to disclose his income, that is to say that the system of a compulsory declaration of total income should be introduced into British legislation.

[1] H. of C., March 1, 1904, Herbert Samuel's speech (*Parliamentary Debates*, 4th Series, vol. cxxx, p. 1360). H. of C., April 19, 1904, R. B. Haldane's speech (ibid., vol. cxxxiii, p. 582).

[2] H. of C., April 19, 1904 (ibid., vol. cxxx, pp. 560 sqq.). Austen Chamberlain agreed however in reply to two questions by Herbert Samuel to obtain information as to what steps had been taken abroad or in the Colonies to graduate the income-tax. *Graduated Income-Tax (Colonies) Return to an Address of the Hon. the House of Commons, dated 11 August, 1904—for Return showing which of the Colonies have established systems of graduated Income-Tax,* or *of Income-Tax levied at different rates on earned or unearned incomes, or both, with particulars in each case of the rates of tax and the system of assessment and collection,* June 20, 1905. *Further Return—* August 1, 1905. *Miscellaneous, No. 2* (1905) *Reports from H.M.'s representatives abroad respecting graduated Income-Taxes in Foreign States,* April 1905. The report is preceded by an introductory report written by Bernard Mallet, Commissioner of Inland Revenue. The impression received from reading these two collections is that very little had been done in this direction by the Colonies and that, if the English Radicals desired to carry out this reform of the Income-Tax, they must seek their models on the continent of Europe.

[3] *Report from the Select Committee on Income-Tax, together with the proceedings of the Committee, minutes of evidence, and an Appendix.* The Committee's terms of reference were 'to inquire into and report upon the practicability of graduating the Income-Tax and of differentiating for the purpose of the Tax, between Permanent and Precarious Incomes'.

3

Such were the very moderate conclusions reached by the Committee, but its final suggestion was meaningless unless it contemplated the eventual adoption of a radical reform. Actually the report pointed out that once its recommendations had been adopted it would be easy to raise later on the rate of tax without affecting any taxpayer whose income was below £3,000 a year. Only the small minority of wealthy persons would have to bear the burden of the increase and it was this minority which must therefore be compelled to disclose their total income. This left the door open to those members of the committee who had formed an entirely novel conception of what a Budget should be. It should not, they held, be content with compelling every citizen to contribute to the needs of the state in accordance with his means on a basis of genuine equality. The financial machinery of the state must be employed to remedy the inequality of wealth, to make the burden upon the rich heavier, and lighten the burden upon the poor or more drastically to impoverish the rich and enrich the poor. It was perhaps prudent not to pronounce categorically against these Radical measures. For if it seemed inadvisable to attempt their immediate application, the fact could not be ignored that those members of the committee who advocated them represented a powerful current of public opinion which might become formidable. We have already seen the effect produced by Bernard Shaw's attacks on the hypocrisy of a Liberalism which accepted poverty as inevitable. We have witnessed the campaign of emotional appeal conducted by philanthropists against the horrors of sweating. And every play or novel Galsworthy wrote attempted to shake the confidence of the middle-class in what it called its morality, a morality whose mainspring seemed to be the desire for wealth and the instinct of property. Whence did this Socialistic demand for equality derive its new impetus? Had Marx proved a true prophet, and was society actually witnessing a steady decrease in the number of the wealthy, the increasing pauperization of the masses? The evidence gives no support to this view.[1] Or was it that a phase of economic

---

[1] According to the extremely detailed calculations of A. L. Bowley (*The Change in the Distribution of the National Income 1880-1913*, 1920, pp. 16 sqq.) the number of taxpayers

life in which the prices of all commodities were rising, and the price of labour alone lagging behind, inevitably aroused the discontent of the working classes? But though such an explanation would account for the disaffection among the workers, it does not explain why the middle-class intellectuals and philanthropists made common cause with the malcontents. The causes of the revolt which was now gathering strength were of the moral order. We are witnessing the decay of that Puritan asceticism which made the proletariat ashamed of its poverty as of a crime for which it was responsible and the rich regard their own enrichment by work and saving as the fulfilment of a duty. The rich man now wanted to enjoy himself, to display his luxury, to make a splash, and the revolt of the intelligentsia and the workers was the reply to this ostentation.

The economists supported by statistics these denunciations of the men of letters. The figures showing the revenue produced by the Estate Duty, the new tax on inheritances introduced in 1894, had revealed for the first time the extreme inequality in the distribution of the national wealth.[1] And the revelation was made the more striking by the fact that the introduction about the same time of a similar reform into the French system of inheritance made possible an instructive comparison between the two countries in this respect. There were twice as many small estates (of a value between £500 and £1,000) in France as in the United

with an income of over £160 a year remained during the thirty-three years under consideration proportionately the same, the number of manual labourers decreased, the increase was in the number of small taxpayers whose income was below £160, in other words, members of the lower middle-class. For the producing power of this marginal figure of £160 see the evidence given by Chiozza Money who appeals to the opinions already expressed by Marshall before the Select Committee on Income-Tax of 1906 (p. 48). '£3 a week does enable a man to command a fair quantity of the necessary comforts of life and to properly educate his children and so on. I regard that as a sensible line on which to begin your income-tax scale.' Cf. Lloyd George, H. of C., April 29, 1909: '. . . Income-Tax in this country only begins when the margin of necessity has been crossed and the domain of comfort and even gentility has been reached. A man who enjoys an income of over £3 a week need not stint himself and his family of reasonable food or clothing or shelter. There may be an exception in the case of a man with a family whose gentility is part of his stock-in-trade or the uniform of his craft.—What a man bequeaths, after all, represents what is left after he has provided for all his wants in life. Beyond a certain figure it also represents all that is necessary to keep his family in the necessaries of life. The figure which the experience of seventy years has sanctified as being that which divides sufficiency from gentility is from £150 to £160 a year.' (Parliamentary Debates, Commons, 1909, 5th Series, vol. iv, p. 505.)

[1] See Statistical Abstract for the United Kingdom in each of the last fifteen years from 1894 to 1908. Fifty-sixth number, 1909, No. 20. Classification of the number of Estates and Capital Value of Estates or Portions of Estates liable to Estate Duty in each of the years ending 31st March, 1900 to 1909 (Extricated from the Annual Report of the Inland Revenue Department).

Kingdom. Estates exceeding £50,000 were three times as few. Estates whose value exceeded £200,000 or £250,000 were four times as few.[1] Socialist propaganda could not fail to make capital of such figures. Towards the end of 1905 a little book was published entitled *Riches and Poverty* which made a profound impression.[2] Though its figures have subsequently undergone corrections of detail[3] their substantial accuracy has never been seriously contested. The author, a Socialist named Chiozza Money, proved that almost half the total income of the United Kingdom was in the hands of a ninth of the population, more than a third in the hands of only a thirtieth part, and that over half the capital of the nation belonged to a seventieth part of the population. He concluded that the fundamental social problem was the distribution of wealth, that if the poor were to be enriched at the cost of the wealthy, a 'public maternity fund' established, popular education developed, workmen's dwellings built, and old age pensions introduced at the state expense the system of national finance must be completely transformed. He advocated the total abolition of duties on articles of consumption, with the exception of alcoholic drinks. He also advocated the ultimate nationalization of the railways and mines. But they must begin by reforming the Estate Duty and Income-Tax.[4] The highest rate of the graduated Succession Duties did not at present exceed 8 per cent. It must be raised to 16 per cent. As regards the income-tax, a distinction should be made for incomes under £1,000 between earned and unearned incomes, and above £1,000 the tax should be graduated until for incomes above £25,000 it reached a maximum of a twelfth, or

---

[1] Paul Leroy-Beaulieu, '*Les Fortunes en France, d'après les déclarations successorales*' (*Economiste Français Août 1903*, vol. ii, pp. 154 sqq.).

[2] L. G. Chiozza (now Sir Leo) Money, *Riches and Poverty*. The first edition appeared in October 1905 and the work reached its 10th edition in 1911. Consult also another work by the same author, *The Nation's Wealth: Will it Endure?* 1914.

[3] A. G. Pigou, *Wealth and Welfare*, 1912; Sir Josiah Stamp, *British Incomes and Property*, 'The Application of official statistics to Economic Problems, Ed. I, 1916; Arthur L. Bowley, *The Division of the Product of Industry: An Analysis of National Income; Before the War*, 1919, also *The Change in the Distribution of the National Income 1880–1913*, 1920.

[4] L. G. Chiozza Money, *Riches and Poverty*, chap. xx and xxi, pp. 277 sqq. See his evidence before the Committee of 1906, pp. 35 sqq., esp. pp. 46 sqq., also Appendix No. 12, pp. 257 sqq. Was there no danger of finally reducing the sum of national wealth and discouraging the producer? Chiozza Money did not think so and in a little book published in 1914 with the title *National Wealth, Will it Endure?* he attempted to prove that the only effect of the fiscal legislation he urged would be to change the character of production. The purchasing power of the wealthy would be diminished, that of the poor increased. The production of luxury articles would therefore decrease but the production of articles of utility would be correspondingly stimulated.

1s. 8d. in the pound. Philip Snowden, who gave evidence before the committee on behalf of the Labour party, proposed a different system, though inspired by the same spirit. The existing assessment of the income-tax should not be altered, but in addition to the ordinary tax a super-tax should be imposed on all incomes above £5,000, differentiated and graduated, which would in the case of very large incomes reach the figure of seven shillings in the pound—over a third. The reform, he pointed out, could not fail to be popular since only 10,000 taxpayers would be affected.[1]

4

Under these circumstances we can imagine the curiosity with which the public awaited the Budget of 1907. When Asquith presented it in the Commons on April 18, 1907, the House was crowded. Not only were the benches reserved for members full, but the public galleries were packed. The American Ambassador was present, and the Prince of Wales. Asquith's speech did not disappoint his audience; he was enthusiastically applauded. He began by announcing for the past financial year a surplus of £5,139,000. It was due in part to the economies which had been effected, chiefly on the army and navy, on which less had been spent than the estimates had provided for, in part to the excellent yield of taxation, partly due to the industrial boom. For the financial year 1907–1908, if the present taxes were retained, they might expect a surplus of £3,433,000. What should they do in view of this fact? Increase the sinking fund? Certainly. Reduce taxation? Not necessarily. For 'the whole territory of social reform' had still to be conquered. Large sums had been spent since 1870 on public education. It remained to provide for the aged poor by granting them pensions from the state. For this reform which would be undertaken in 1908 the necessary funds must be raised. Raise them by protective duties, said the advocates of Tariff Reform. The Government however while retaining

[1] See Philip Snowden's evidence before the Committee of 1906, pp. 1910 sqq. See especially p. 113, and Keir Hardie's similar scheme Appendix No. 5, p. 237. See further Philip Snowden, *The Socialists' Budget*, 1907 also *A Few Hints to Lloyd George. Where is the Money to come from? The Question Answered*, 1909.

the duties on sugar, tea, and coffee, for all classes must contribute to the national purse, intended to find the money without tampering with free trade, and the excellent financial position enabled them to do so without increasing the existing taxes or imposing any new ones. Asquith did indeed, in accordance with the recommendations of the committee of 1906, reform the income-tax, but only to distribute the burden better, not to increase it. Below £2,000 a distinction would be made between earned and unearned income, the tax on earned income being reduced by 3d. in the shilling, a reduction which would, according to Asquith's estimate, in an average year cost the treasury £1,250,000. The loss would be made good by a steeper graduation of the Estate Duty on estates of over £150,000 in value, and by a super-tax on estates whose value exceeded £1,000,000. Thus by a circuitous route the Government introduced the principle of a super-tax, which Philip Snowden had advocated before the committee, applying it for the moment to death duties not to income-tax. On balance there would be a surplus of £1,500,000 for the financial year 1907-8. It would be applied to the sinking fund. Next year the surplus would be used to constitute a fund with which to launch the new system of old age pensions.

The Budget of 1907 was criticized by the Tariff Reformers, who wanted the duties on sugar and tea reduced. It was a reform they had always promised the electors, to compensate for the establishment of duties on imported articles of manufacture.[1] And the Labour members made the same demand. Why not relieve in this way the working masses instead of the members of the professional classes, as was done by the 'differentiation' in the taxation of small incomes?[2] But both were heard without atten-

---

[1] H. of C., May 13, 14, 1907 (*Parliamentary Debates*, 4th Series, vol. clxxiv, pp. 651 sqq. 805 sqq.).

[2] H. of C., May 13, 1907. J. N. Barnes' speech: 'The free breakfast table had again been relegated to the dim and distant future ... in order that the man with £2,000 a year might be relieved of a contribution which would in each case have provided the old age pensions upon the scale they were asking for them. ... This Budget was a mere pandering to the City clerk and the small gentry, who thought themselves superior persons and took their politics from the *Daily Mail*.' (ibid., vol. clxxiv, pp. 680-1). Cf. H. of C., May 14, 1907, J. R. MacDonald's speech: 'At the present time, the working classes whose incomes averaged £70 were paying something like £48,000,000 to the National Exchequer. There was not a sensible man in the House who would not say that that basis ought to be narrowed. It worked out at 2s. in the pound income-tax. If they considered the final utility of 2s. in the pound to a man whose income was anything between 15s. or £1 a week, and

tion by apathetic benches. The protectionist amendment was rejected by three hundred and seventy-six votes to a hundred and eight, and only fifty-four Labour members voted against the second reading of the Budget. It was however plain that their arguments had not been without effect when the following year Asquith presented his third Budget.

The financial position remained excellent. The financial year 1907–8 produced a surplus of £4,723,000. For the financial year 1908–9 on the basis of the existing taxation a surplus of £4,901,000 might be expected. How should it be employed? Asquith traced the outline of a comprehensive system of old age pensions to be provided exclusively by taxation which his Cabinet intended to submit to Parliament and which would cost according to official estimates £6,000,000. It would not be put into operation until the last quarter of the financial year 1908–9; and the million and a half set apart for it in 1907 would be sufficient for that quarter. A round sum of £3,500,000 remained to be found. It was roughly the equivalent of the surplus at their disposal, when a number of minor alterations had been effected in next year's taxation. If Asquith had remained faithful to the principles he had laid down the previous year he would have applied his surplus for the current financial year to the sinking fund, while employing the following year's surplus to defray the cost of the old age pensions. But he stated that in his opinion since the conclusion of the Boer War the country had done enough towards paying off the national debt and he proposed to make use of the whole or almost the whole surplus to reduce the taxes on articles of consumption. The duty on sugar was accordingly reduced by 2s. 6d. a hundredweight. It was necessary therefore in 1909 to devise some new sources of revenue unless one could reckon in perpetuity on surpluses of several millions without increase of taxation. But would it be possible to continue much longer saving on the navy estimates? And would the industrial situation always remain so satisfactory? A slump had set in since the end of 1907.

worked that out, they got an equivalent in final utility to a man whose income was £5,000 of probably something like £2,000. At the present time the income-tax upon the working classes was a tax upon life, not upon property. . . . What the Chancellor had to discover was now to remove all taxes upon life and place them upon property.' (ibid., vol. clxxiv, pp. 825–6.)

It is at this point in the history of British finance that Lloyd George comes upon the scene. Out of courtesy the honour of presenting the Budget which he had drawn up had been left to Asquith. But now that he was Prime Minister he was no longer Chancellor of the Exchequer and it was the task of his successor Lloyd George to defend in detail the clauses of his Budget. Lloyd George had also to introduce the Bill dealing with old age pensions, which was as it were the counterpart of the Budget, since it was to come into operation on January 1, 1909, and therefore the cost must be defrayed for one quarter by the Budget passed in the spring of 1908. In the normal course this would have been the duty of John Burns, the President of the Local Government Board. But in 1907, though promising that the Cabinet would introduce a Bill dealing with the subject in the near future, he had accompanied the promise with so many adverse criticisms of the principle it would embody, that it would probably have been a gratuitous provocation to the Labour members if the Government had put him in charge of the Bill.[1] Lloyd George supplanted him, as a year later Churchill would supplant Herbert Gladstone and Burns himself when the Trade Board Bill and the Labour Exchanges Bill were introduced. Thus the Old Age Pensions Bill, though put into shape by the permanent officials at Asquith's orders before Lloyd George became Chancellor of the Exchequer, seemed to the nation and the entire world as in a sense his work.

The question of old age pensions, when in 1908 the Government took it in hand, was ripe and more than ripe for settlement. As we have already seen it had been the subject of lively debates before the Boer War.[2] Forgotten while the war lasted, from the moment peace was restored it had been one of the most insistent demands of the working class. Every year the Trade Union Congress passed a motion demanding a national system of pensions. In 1903 a parliamentary committee accepted with a few reserva-

---

[1] H. of C., May 10, 1907 (*Parliamentary Debates*, 4th Series, vol. clxxiv, pp. 523 sqq.). *The Times* in its account of the sitting put the following words into Burns' mouth: 'He hoped he would have the honour of working out the details.' But they are absent from the official report.

[2] See my *History of the English People*, vol. v, pp. 233–6.

tions the plan proposed by the committee of 1899.[1] The candidates at the election of 1906 who did not include old age pensions in their programme were very few, the Unionist candidates merely adding the reservation that for financial reasons the question could not be dealt with until the basis of taxation had been widened by the establishment of a tariff. On the morrow of its election the new House of Commons had passed unanimously a motion in favour of the scheme,[2] and in November a deputation from the trade unions urged Campbell-Bannerman and Asquith to give effect to their wishes. The Budget of 1907 promised a Bill for 1908. In September the Trade Union Congress expressed its dissatisfaction that the Bill had not been introduced in 1907 and demanded 'the payment, on January 1, 1909, of pensions of at least five shillings a week to all persons aged sixty or over'.

No further delay was possible. The publication in 1908 of a memorandum dealing with the German system of old age pensions provided by compulsory insurance and the system adopted by New Zealand of pensions provided by the State[3] was a mere formality. Everyone knew that the Government had already made its choice and that any system involving the payment of contributions by the workers was condemned in advance. A circular addressed in January to the friendly societies asking for their advice was equally an empty form. The Government had already laid its scheme before Parliament when on June 15 the replies of the friendly societies, two-thirds of which were unfavourable, were published.[4]

The system adopted by the Cabinet was not that advocated by Charles Booth and accepted by the trade unions—a pension paid by the State to all men and women without distinction who had

---

[1] See Report and Special Report from the Select Committee on the Aged Pensioners Bill together with the proceedings of the Committee, Minutes of Evidence, Appendix and Index, 1903.

[2] H. of C., March 14, 1906. O'Grady's motion (*Parliamentary Debates* 4th Series, vol. cliii, pp. 1330, sqq.).

[3] *Old Age Pensions (New Zealand and Germany) Return to an Order of the Honourable the House of Commons, dated 1 June, 1908, for Copy of a Memorandum of the Old Age Pensions scheme in force in New Zealand and the Scheme of Insurance against Invalidity and Old Age in force in the German Empire*, June 1908. See further for the preparation of the Bill, the official documents published in 1907 with the title *Old Age Pensions. Tables which have been prepared in connection with the question of Old Age Pensions, with a preliminary Memorandum* (the memorandum contains a useful historical sketch of the question). Cf. William Sutherland *Old Age Pensions in Theory and Practice, with some Foreign Examples*, 1907.

[4] *Circular Letter issued by the Chief Registrar to the Principal Friendly Societies with reference to the proposal Non-Contributory Scheme of Old Age Pensions, with an Abstract of their replies thereto*, 1908.

reached a certain age. It was the system in force in New Zealand, which granted pensions only to those who could prove that they did not possess an income in excess of a certain figure—that is to say, who could prove their poverty. Moreover, the Government scheme was more timid than the scheme in force in New Zealand. In New Zealand pensions were given from the age of sixty-five, in Britain they would not be given before seventy. In New Zealand to receive a pension of £18 a year a man must not have an annual income exceeding £34. In England he would receive only 5s. a week—that is to say, £13 a year—and to receive it he must not have an income exceeding £26. In New Zealand persons with an income of more than £34 were not totally excluded from the benefit of the scheme. For every pound of income above £34 they would lose a pound of the pension, so that it was only when an income of £52 was reached that a man lost all claim to a pension. The British Government gave nothing to anyone who had an income of over £26. Moreover, whereas in New Zealand an aged married couple received each a full pension, provided their total combined income including the pension did not exceed £78, the British scheme proposed to grant them a joint pension of 7s. 6d. instead of the 10s. they might have expected. In New Zealand, apart from restrictions of nationality and residence, the applicant for a pension must not be a lunatic or an habitual drunkard nor within a certain period have been sentenced to imprisonment. In all these points the English followed its Australasian model. But it added two further demands. To receive a pension the applicant must prove that his poverty was not due to the fact that he 'habitually failed to work according to his ability, opportunity, and need'. Nor was he allowed to add the pension to any Poor Law relief of which he might be in receipt. Indeed, he was excluded from the pension if he had received poor relief since January 1, 1908. As in New Zealand the Act would, to all intents and purposes, be administered by the national authorities. The pensions would be paid by the State not by the local authorities and though the examination of claims was entrusted to local committees elected by the borough, district and county councils, the central Government would have a representative, the pensions officer, on each of these.

By employing the closure, the instrument which for some years past had hastened legislation so considerably, the discussion of this

Bill of twelve clauses was rendered extremely rapid. Begun on June 13 the debates in both Houses occupied only thirteen sittings. The House of Commons was not even given time to discuss all the clauses. On July 31 the debates ended and the Old Age Pensions Act[1] became law on August 1.

But the rapidity of the debates was not due solely to the unflinching application of the closure. The Opposition put up no serious fight. It was feeble and timid. An amendment introduced by the House of Lords which restricted the operation of the statute to seven years deserves only a passing mention. It was an absurdity which the Commons swept aside. In the Commons Unionist speakers were content to reiterate, as they did on every possible occasion, their propaganda for tariff reform. The industrial crisis, then at its height, encouraged their hopes. Unless the funds were provided by a tariff, they argued, the cost of the new legislation could not be met. But they had themselves promised their constituents old age pensions. And Unionists and Liberals alike were afraid of the working-class electorate. The only amendments introduced into the Act, the effect of which was to extend its scope and therefore render it more costly, were made by the Government under pressure from private members, Unionist as well as Liberal. The clause which reduced the joint pension of a married couple was deleted. Were they to discourage matrimony? In imitation of New Zealand a 'sliding-scale' of pensions was introduced. It was unfair that the workman who saved and in return for his regular subscriptions received from his union or friendly society a pension slightly above 10s. a week—that is, £26 a year—should be penalized by the State for his economy by exclusion from the benefits of the Act. For an income of £21 a year the full pension of 5s. a week would be given, for an income below £23 12s. 6d., a pension of 4s.; below £26 5s. 0d., 3s.; below £28 17s. 6d., 2s.; below £31 10s. 0d., 1s. Finally, the clause which refused a pension to a recipient of poor relief was seriously modified in the course of debate. Only paupers lodged in the workhouses were excluded from the pension; persons in receipt of outdoor relief were entitled to the full pension, and even those in the former category were excluded only until

---

[1] 8 Edw. 7. Cap. 40: An Act to provide for the Old Age Pensions (*Old Age Pensions Act*, 1908). Modified in certain details by 1 & 2 Geo. 5, Cap. 16: An Act to amend the Old Age Pensions Act, 1908 (*Old Age Pensions Act*, 1911).

December 1910 unless Parliament should decide otherwise. In the interval the commission appointed to inquire into the Poor Law would have reported and might suggest a different solution. Thus, during the session of 1908 two social reforms of the first magnitude were carried by Asquith's Cabinet—the Act limiting the working day in mines, which for the first time laid down the principle of a legal limitation of hours for adult male workers, and the Old Age Pensions Act, which affirmed the principle of the right to live by recognizing the right of those too old to work to receive a pension from the community.[1]

6

But the ministerial account also showed a debit side. The House of Lords was wrecking a third Education Bill, the final attempt to reach a compromise between the conflicting claims of the Anglicans and Catholics on the one hand and of the sects on the other. It had also thrown out a Licensing Bill, which the Government had introduced to satisfy the temperance reformers and restrict the drink traffic, and a Land Valuation Bill for Scotland, which, by enabling the Government to ascertain the value of land, would have enabled it later on to tax increments of value. On these three questions the House of Lords had beaten the Government and the Government had taken the defeat lying down. The Unionist Press was jubilant. It glossed over the awkward fact that in the sphere of social reform concessions had been made to democratic opinion which more than counterbalanced these three victories. It sought to make its readers believe that the Liberal Cabinet owed its continued existence to the toleration of the Tories, who were willing to let it remain in office so long as Sir Edward Grey was at the Foreign Office and the imperialist members of the Cabinet took care that the national defences were not weakened. If the Government desired to appeal to the country on the Irish question, on the question of the denominational school, or on the question of temperance reform, let it do so by all

[1] To complete the enumeration we must mention the Act for the protection of children to which we have already referred, pp. 82-83 n. (8 Edw. 7, Cap. 67: An Act to consolidate and amend the Law relating to the Protection of Children and Young Persons, Reformatory and Industrial Schools, and otherwise to amend the Law with respect to Children and Young Persons [Children Act, 1908]).

means. The Unionists were certain of victory and it was evident that the Liberals were of the same opinion because they dared not join battle.

Was it tolerable that the Cabinet should continue to shrink from taking up the challenge thus flung in its face by the House of Lords, the Unionist party, and the Unionist Press? The more cautious Liberals, headed by Asquith, were perhaps disposed still to postpone the conflict, but the two leaders of the democratic wing of the Cabinet, Lloyd George and Churchill were impatient to take action. In September Churchill paid a long visit to Lloyd George at his country house at Criccieth.[1] They formed their plan of campaign which they partially disclosed to the public in two violent speeches, delivered, the one by Lloyd George at Liverpool on December 21, the other by Churchill at Birmingham on January 13. 'We cannot', declared Lloyd George, 'consent to accept the present humiliating conditions of legislating by the sufferance of Lord Lansdowne. This nobleman has arrogated to himself a position he has usurped—a sovereignty that no king has claimed since the ominous days of Charles I. Decrees are issued from Lansdowne House that Buckingham Palace would not dream of sending forth. We are not going to stand any longer the usurpation of King Lansdowne and his Royal consort in the Commons.' But the Liberals had the choice of the moment to deliver their attack, and Lloyd George let it be understood that it would be the presentation of the Budget. Three weeks later Churchill spoke even more plainly. 'I do not, of course, ignore the fact that the House of Lords has the power, though not, I think, the constitutional right, to bring the Government of the country to a standstill by rejecting the provision which the Commons made for the financial service of the year. That is a matter which does not rest with us, it rests with them. If they want a speedy dissolution, they know where to find one. . . . And, for my part, I should be quite content to see the battle joined as speedily as possible upon the plain simple issue of aristocratic rule against representative government, between the reversion to protection and the maintenance of free trade, between a tax on bread and a tax on—well, never mind.' Everyone was in expectation—everyone, Liberals and Unionists alike—and the more anxiously because the hand on which the young Chancellor of

---

[1] A. MacCallum Scott, *Winston Churchill in Peace and War*, 1916, p. 10.

the Exchequer was staking his career seemed at the opening of January 1909 particularly difficult to play. The day was past when the Liberals had only to denounce the extravagant policy of the late Government and blame the imperialism of Chamberlain and his followers for the fact that the Budget had increased by one half between 1895 and 1906 rising in ten years from £100,000,000 to £150,000,000. For two years Asquith had contrived to keep in the neighbourhood of the latter figure—but the speech he delivered when he presented his last Budget in 1908 was a warning to the taxpayer that the democratic neo-liberalism of the twentieth century had little in common with Gladstonian Liberalism, that the Cabinet did not intend to govern on the cheap and that a large increase in the amount and in the sources of expenditure was inevitable. A year later Lloyd George did but develop what his Premier had said in 1908 in more veiled language.

7

In the first place Admiral Fisher's methods had made it possible until 1908 to effect an annual reduction of the navy estimates without weakening the navy, possibly even increasing its strength. In 1908 the navy estimates for the first time had shown an increase. But it had been slight and signified merely that since every possible economy had been made, the estimates must automatically rise, even if no new expenditure were undertaken. Germany however was speeding up the construction of her navy. The Conservative Press redoubled its attacks on Fisher, and called upon the Government to recognize frankly the necessity for strengthening the fleet. The First Lord of the Admiralty, McKenna, was convinced. He was faced in the Cabinet by the opposition of Lloyd George and Churchill but he overcame it and it was agreed that he should be granted the necessary credits for a new programme of naval construction. Lloyd George took his revenge by making it clear that he would raise the money by direct and graduated taxation; in other words that he would make the wealthy pay for the new vessels. Even so, McKenna's demand was an initial difficulty which he had to face in drawing up his Budget. When the Navy Estimates were presented to Parliament in accordance with custom two months before the Budget as a whole, they amounted to £35,124,700, an increase of almost three million over the estimates of 1908. And it must be borne in mind that, if the demands of the imperialists were to be satisfied, they would continue to increase in subsequent years. For the four Dreadnoughts it was proposed to lay down would be far from completed when four others would be laid down in accordance with their programme. From that moment the country would have to bear a double cost, the cost of finishing the former and the cost of building the latter.

In the second place, the policy of social reform had proved by the beginning of 1909 far more costly than had been expected a year earlier when the Old Age Pensions Bill was drafted. It had been calculated that 500,000 persons would be entitled to a pension, but 480,000 had established their claim by January 1,[1] and 130,000 further claims were expected. In Ireland especially, the expected number of claims had been exceeded by an incredible figure. There, it would appear, one person out of every twenty-five was seventy years of age or over, as against one out of every eighty-eight in England, either because the immigration of the youthful element of the population did in fact leave an enormous proportion of aged people, or because it was more difficult to verify the age and income of applicants or because control was intentionally more lax.[2] In any case the old age pensions would prove far more costly than had been estimated. And there was more to come. When he introduced the Old Age Pensions Bill, Lloyd George had explained that in his intention the Bill was only 'a beginning'.[3] Immediately after the close of the session he had spent three weeks in Germany, where the attention he received was a flattering proof of the important position he already occupied in the eyes of the entire Continent. He had inquired into the practical working of the social legislation which was Bismarck's gift to his country, in particular of the laws of insurance against sickness and invalidity. Would it not be possible to en-

---

[1] The number of pensioners in the whole of the United Kingdom amounted to 669,352 in 1910, 907,461 in 1911, 942,319 in 1912, 967,721 in 1913 and 984,131 in 1914 (*Annual Reports of the Local Government Board, Part I, Administration of the Poor Law, the Unemployed Workmen Act, and the Old Age Pensions Act*). See further for the application of the Act *Old Age Pensioners and Aged Pauperism Memorandum*, 1913.

[2] For the Administration of the Statute in Ireland see the debate in the House of Commons occasioned by the complaints of two Irish members who maintained that the Statute was applied too stringently. (*Parliamentary Debates*, Commons, 1910, 5th Series, vol. xv, pp. 663, sqq.).

[3] H. of C., May 25, 1908 (ibid., 4th Ser. vol. clxxxix, p. 871).

graft a similar system with contributions from the workers into the system of non-contributory old age pensions now being set up in England? When he gave the Press an account of his visit he expressed his regret that nothing had yet been done in Germany to grapple with the problem of unemployment.[1] He evidently intended to grapple with it himself. At Criccieth he had discussed those questions in his conversations with Churchill. When he drew up the Budget of 1909, he was looking for sources of revenue sufficiently extensive and sufficiently elastic, to enable him to introduce, possibly in 1910, a system of insurance against all the risks incident to labour, not only the poverty of old age, but sickness, invalidity, and unemployment.

Nor was this all. He must contemplate further expenditure. Had we solved the problem of unemployment if we accepted it with resignation like a natural fatality and were content to compensate its victims? And was it a commendable method of dealing with the problem to provide even the unemployed with work whose utility was doubtful? Must not the State step in where private enterprise had failed and carry out a comprehensive plan of public works which would exploit the resources of the country? The automobile industry was making rapid strides. It had originated in France. But at present England with her 55,000 cars was proud to find herself at the head of Europe. During the previous half century the roads had been increasingly abandoned for the railways. Today the contrary process was taking place. The old road system of Great Britain required complete renovation. The existing roads were too narrow, their corners dangerous. They must be made to skirt the towns instead of traversing them. Their material was no longer suitable. And a number of entirely new roads must be made. Moreover, a Commission on afforestation appointed in 1906 had reported in January that in its opinion two million and a half acres in England and Wales were suitable for planting with trees, six million acres in Scotland, five hundred thousand in Ireland. This would involve heavy expenditure for forty years, but the benefit would then begin to be felt and meanwhile work would have been provided every year for almost forty thousand men. And once we had entered upon this path, why not go further? Why not solve the problem, so serious in Great Britain, of rural depopulation, by a number of different

[1] *The Times*, August 27, 1908.

undertakings—by creating experimental farms, improving the breed of livestock, developing agricultural education, and encouraging co-operation, providing better means of transport, splitting up large estates into small farms, draining marshes and cultivating waste land?

Such were the needs for which the Chancellor of the Exchequer had to make provision and which he explained to the Commons when he introduced his Budget on April 29, 1909, in a speech of formidable, even gargantuan proportions. He spoke for four hours and a half and towards the end his strength seemed on the point of giving way. He announced the introduction at the same time as the Finance Bill of a Development Bill, which would confer upon the Government the necessary powers to embark upon those practical and costly undertakings of which we have just spoken.[1] In all, he made provision for an expenditure of £164,350,000 instead of the £154,350,000 of Asquith's Budget the year before. The increase was a large one, and expenditure would certainly continue to increase. On the one hand he was proposing expenditure which according to his own programme must rise every year and a Budget of £2,000,000, double the Budgets before the Boer War, was in sight. On the other hand when Asquith drew up his three Budgets he had benefited by an industrial and commercial boom which produced a large surplus every year. It had therefore been an easy task in 1908 to reduce taxation while increasing expenditure. The situation was now very different. Since the end of 1907 the industrial situation had steadily deteriorated and in April 1909 there were no signs of recovery. The financial year, ending on March 31, had left a deficit of £1,502,000. And it would have been even greater, if the duties on alcoholic liquors had not risen enormously. For the importers, foreseeing a large increase in the duties in the 1909 Budget, had made haste to import before the new financial year opened sufficient stock to supply the entire demand of 1909. The Treasury estimate of the £550,000,000 thus received in advance would have to be deducted from the receipts for 1909–10.

In short to defray an expenditure which exceeded £164,000,000 the Treasury had in hand £148,390,000 of receipts. That is to say,

[1] An Act finally passed: 9 Edw. 7 Cap. 47: An Act to promote the Economic Development of the United Kingdom and the Improvement of Roads therein (*Development and Road Improvement Funds Act*, 1909).

there was a deficit of almost £16,000,000. How was it to be made up? And where would the Chancellor of the Exchequer discover sources of revenue whose yield would progressively increase to keep pace with the increased expenditure foreseen in future years. Must he 'enlarge the basis of taxation' by returning to protection? That was the Unionist solution. The Liberals boasted that they could solve the problem without abandoning free trade. Their solution was the new system of taxation proposed by Lloyd George.

8

In the first place, dealing with the direct taxes Lloyd George repeated Asquith's previous declaration that the income-tax must no longer be regarded as a temporary expedient but as the centre, the 'sheet-anchor' of British finance. And he announced his intention to graduate it more steeply. For incomes below £500, an allowance of 10s. would be granted for every child below sixteen years of age, and on all incomes below £2,000 the tax would be lowered to 9d. instead of 1s. On the other hand on incomes above £3,000, it would be raised to 1s. 2d. Finally, above £5,000 incomes would be liable to that super-tax which Philip Snowden had urged upon the committee of 1906 and which the committee, without actually recommending it, had recognized to be feasible. Its rate would be 6d. in the £ for all incomes above £5,000, with a further 3d. for incomes above £6,000, to be levied on the amount of income which exceeded £3,000. This meant a rate of 1s. 6d. in the £ for an income of £9,000, 1s. 7d. for an income of £18,000. A similar reform of the death duties was effected. The lower limit of the Estate Duty remained unaltered, 1 per cent on an estate above £100 in value. Nor was the maximum rate of 15 per cent raised but it was reached quicker, by a steeper ascent, at £1,500,000 instead of £3,000,000. The legacy and succession duties were raised from 3 to 5 per cent when the legatee was a brother or sister, or the descendant of a brother or sister, and to a uniform rate of 10 per cent when the legatee was a more remote relative. The exemption from the 1 per cent duty hitherto granted to heirs in the direct line was abolished. In future such heirs and even the husband or wife of the deceased would be exempt from legacy or succession duties only when the value of the property did not exceed £15,000. The duty on settled estates was raised from 1 to 2 per cent. To prevent evasion, gifts between the living were liable retrospectively to death duty, if they had been made less than five years before the testator's death. In the third place the stamp duties were raised very considerably on all sales and Stock Exchange transactions and in the latter case steeply graduated.

The reform of the income-tax would produce an additional £3,500,000, the reform of the succession duties an additional £2,850,000, the increase in the stamp duties an additional £650,000.

We now turn to the indirect taxes—duties on articles of consumption. Liberals and Unionists were agreed in demanding the reduction and eventual abolition of the duties on tea, cocoa, and coffee. For they increased the cost of living for the working man. Nor were they protectionist in character. But it was not an easy matter at a moment when such a large amount of additional revenue must be raised while preserving intact the system of free trade to push fiscal heroism so far as to deprive the State of a source of revenue to which it had been long accustomed. Lloyd George therefore did not reduce these duties though he refrained from raising them. But there were other indirect taxes—taxes on articles of consumption of which the zealots of a democratic Budget did not desire the reduction still less the abolition. The English Radical party supported by the leaders of Nonconformity was the party of temperance reform. It therefore wished in the moral interest of the lower classes to raise the duties on alcoholic drinks, both the customs and the excise duties. 'I am all for making it as easy as possible', Lloyd George had declared a few months earlier, 'for the people to get every commodity that is good for them. I am all for making as difficult as possible the access of the people to any commodity that injures them. That is the Liberal policy.'[1]

A 'liberal' policy? That we can hardly term it. In any case it was not a policy calculated to attract the masses. And the House of Lords felt that they were improving the prospects of the Unionist party at the polls when they opposed it. Dissatisfied with the results of the Unionist Licensing Act of 1904, the Liberal Cabinet had carried in the Commons in 1908 a new Licensing Bill, which obliged the Government at the expiration of fourteen

---

[1] Lloyd George. Speech at Liverpool, December 21, 1908.

years to reduce the number of licensed houses so that their number bore a fixed proportion to the population of the locality.[1] The Lords had thrown out the Bill. By the Budget of 1909 the Government would avenge its temporary humiliation at the hands of the Upper House. The licensing system was radically reformed and a general tax on licences imposed which when collected in full, for a relief was granted in certain cases, amounted to half the annual proceeds from the sale of drink. The duties on beer and spirits were raised. For these measures in the view of the Government would benefit at once the treasury and public health. They would produce, if the treasury estimates were correct, an additional revenue of £4,200,000. Smokers would help to make up the deficit by paying an increase of more than double on the tobacco duties—an additional revenue of £1,900,000; owners of motor-cars by an increase of the motor-tax and the duty on petrol would provide an additional £1,600,000, of which a fixed proportion would be spent on improving the roads. The total revenue raised from these various sources would amount to £6,700,000.

A third category of taxes remains—which we might be tempted to pass over lightly since this entire aspect of the great Budget of 1909 has proved in less than fifteen years a complete and dismal failure. We must however dwell upon it, for of all Lloyd George's proposals those we have now to relate aroused the most intense feeling at the time, kindled the anger of his opponents to its utmost pitch, and were received with the greatest enthusiasm by his supporters. When after explaining the new taxation he intended to impose upon the drink traffic, Lloyd George paused and then continued 'I now come to the question of the land' he was interrupted by a tempest of applause.

We must clearly understand in what respect his democratic finance differed from the doctrine of an orthodox Socialist. The year before, Philip Snowden had harassed the Government with speeches biting as *aqua fortis* in which he denounced its financial and social policy. Neither the Budget of 1908 nor the Old Age Pensions Act met with his approval. Neither answered his definition of good legislation, legislation which made 'the rich poorer

[1] For the details of this extremely complicated Bill see H. of C., February 27, 1908, Asquith's speech. (*Parliamentary Debates*, 4th Series, vol. clxxx, pp. 73 sqq.). For the effect, evidently slight, of the Act of 1904, see *Statistics as to the Operation and Administration of the Laws relating to the sale of Intoxicating Liquor in England and Wales for the year 1907.*

and the poor richer'.[1] The Budget of 1909 might well constitute, if not a measure of satisfaction to Snowden, for he was one of those men whom you can never satisfy, at least the first effort to satisfy him. It did not however amount to a declaration of war upon the rich, unqualified, and indiscriminate. It was indeed war against the extremely wealthy on whom it imposed the new burdens of the heavy supertax on income and the increase in the succession duties. Lloyd George explained however that he did not intend in the strict sense to supertax them—that is, to make them pay more than their fair proportion of the taxes but only to make them pay sufficient to satisfy the principle of genuine equality. It was but equitable that the wealthy should pay a premium for the security the State guaranteed their wealth. It was only fair that they should contribute a large share to the social expenditure of every kind undertaken by the democratic State. For a well-educated and well-fed populace was a more solid foundation on which to build the national wealth than a semi-barbarous proletariat. It was against the monopoly of the landowners that he summoned the rest of the nation to revolt. In the large towns and in the mining areas the landlord became wealthy without any action on his part at the cost of the workers and as a result of their work. In the mines the capitalist risked his capital, the miner only his life. The landlord was certain to gain. In the towns, all who needed land for factory, shop, or lodging, were his victims. A little later Lloyd George attempted to arouse the sympathy of a proletarian audience for the lot of the proprietor of one of the great fashionable West End shops exploited by his landlord, the Duke of Westminster.[2]

This denunciation of the great landed estates was no novelty. It was a tradition which dated from the birth of modern Radicalism. Ricardo had worked out a theory of ground rent according to which it increased automatically without any expenditure of labour whereas wages always remained at the same level, and

---

[1] H. of C., May 25, 1908: 'The condition of the people remained practically the same ... the old age pensions scheme would make no great change in the distribution of wealth. No rich man was going to be a penny poorer than he was to-day by this scheme' (*Parliamentary Debates*, 4th Series, vol. clxxxix, p. 828). May 4, 1909: 'The extreme Socialist School ... are charged with wanting to make the rich poorer and the poor richer. I have never denied that that is my purpose. My object is to make the rich poorer and the poor richer, because there is no other way under heaven by which you can make the poor better off except by making somebody poorer than they are.' (Ibid., 5th Ser., vol. iv, p. 1073.)

[2] Speech at Limehouse, July 31, 1909.

profits continually diminished. There was therefore no reason, he concluded, why the capitalist and the worker, comrades in misfortune, should not combine to tax the landlord for the benefit of society as a whole. His disciple, James Mill, had pushed the suggestion a little further, John Stuart Mill further still and the American, Henry George, had carried it to the furthest possible point. He wished to introduce a single tax on land alone equal to the value of landed property. It amounted to expropriation. Taxation of the landlord would thus provide a radical solution of the social problem by liberating the capitalist and the labourer at the same time. A quarter of a century earlier his formula had made a great stir in England. Lloyd George was beginning to apply it by introducing some new taxes. The first, the unearned increment value tax, was a tax of 20 per cent on an increase in the value of land, to be ascertained every time it changed hands. The second, the determination of lease tax, was a tax of 10 per cent on the increased value of property let out on lease, calculated at the renewal of the lease. The third, the undeveloped land and ungotten minerals tax, was roughly a tax of a halfpenny in the pound on the value of land which its owner did not cultivate or subsoil whose mineral wealth he did not exploit. These taxes, particularly the last, would not be a serious burden. And they would be further reduced by the fact that they could not produce their full return until a general valuation of the land and a revision of the survey had been carried out which would itself cost money. The treasury expected these taxes to bring in £500,000 during the year 1909–10. But Lloyd George probably regarded them as a mere beginning. They could be increased later until, in the course of time, they produced a revolutionary effect.

The additional receipts would amount therefore to a total of £14,200,000 to meet an expected deficit of £15,772,000. By taking £3,000,000 from the sinking fund the Budget would be balanced with a surplus of almost £500,000. A new era was opening in the history of British finance. It was admitted that expenditure must inevitably increase, constantly and normally. But the Government refused to meet it by adopting tariff reform. New land taxes were instituted which might later become an important source of revenue. Moreover they came under the heading of direct taxation which, together with the taxes on alcoholic liquors, remained as in the days of Gladstone, the foundation of the fiscal system. We have seen that at the end of the nineteenth century the moment was at hand when the yield of direct and indirect taxation would be equal. Now the balance inclined to the side of direct taxation.[1]

9

Lloyd George had expected the Budget to exasperate his opponents. Stunned for the moment as by the blow of a club, they soon recovered and a protracted and bitter struggle began. From April 30 until the beginning of November, Parliament was in almost continuous session. Other measures were indeed passed during this session of 1909—an Act which granted the native Indians genuine representation in the 'councils' of British India, an Act conferring an autonomous constitution upon a united South Africa, the two Statutes which set up the Trade Boards and Labour Exchanges, an Act extending the powers of the local authorities as regards the housing of workmen and town planning[2] and a Land Act for Ireland. But the Budget alone was the subject of embittered warfare between the parties. The Opposition secured only very inconsiderable amendments whose details it would be tedious to describe, the substitution for the tax on ungotten minerals of a tax on royalties (the change gave the treasury an additional revenue of £175,000), a reduction of the new duties on licences and stamps, and a larger reduction of the sinking fund, £3,500,000 instead of £3,000,000. But in spite of such modifications of detail it was Lloyd George's Budget which was passed in November. It could not well have been otherwise. The Government's majority in the Commons, though reduced by a number of unfavourable by-elections, was still too strong to

[1] In 1900–1 the direct taxation represented 49.4 per cent of the total revenue. In 1901–2 and 1902–3 the war Budgets made it increase faster than the indirect. It represented respectively 52.5 and 52.4 per cent of the total revenue. During the subsequent years it fell below 50 per cent, but that proportion was definitely exceeded in 1905–6: 50.3 per cent. In 1906–7 the proportion was 51.4, in 1907–8, 51.1, in 1908–9, 52.6 per cent. Lloyd George's great Budget brought it to 56.4 in 1909–10, and 1910–11. In 1911–12 it was 57.3, in 1912–13, 57.6. (Bernard Mallet, *British Budgets 1887–1913*, p. 493.)

[2] 9 Edw. 7, Cap. 44: An Act to amend the Law relating to the Housing of the Working Classes, to provide for the making of Town Planning Schemes, and to make further provision with respect to the appointment and duties of County Medical Officers of Health and to provide for the establishment of Public Health and Housing Committees of County Councils, 1909.

be destroyed even by a combined revolt of all the Irish and
Labour members. And there was no reason to fear such a combination. The Labour members liked a Budget in which they saw
the first fruits of a Socialist legislation. The Irish did not like it. On
the question of Protection they shared the views of the Unionist,
not the Liberal party. They were also very hostile to the clauses of
the Budget which imposed crushing duties on alcoholic drinks.
They voted against the Bill on the second reading. They abstained
from voting when on November 4 the Bill passed its third reading. But it was passed by 379 votes to 149. They knew that neither
their opposition nor their more cautious absention could endanger
the Bill. Neither did they wish to endanger it. Whatever they
might think of the measure itself, they understood what an excellent weapon it was against the House of Lords. And this was a
consideration which in their eyes eclipsed all others.

In fact, it is not upon these impassioned debates, noisy scenes,
and applications of the closure with the protests to which they
gave birth that we must fix our eyes. It was in the country that
the real battle was fought out. A league was formed against the
Budget and an opposition league to defend it. Campaigns of
oratory were conducted on a large scale. The offensive was
launched by the Unionists. But these meetings of business men
with a great landowner often in the chair were not calculated to
frighten the Government. Their organizers were playing into
Lloyd George's hands by proving to the entire country that the
Liberals were faced by a combination whose object was to defend,
not the interests of the nation, but those of a particular class.
The Government replied and with slashing onslaughts. Lloyd
George and Churchill, particularly the former, carried the war
into the enemy's camp. Lloyd George began by attacking Lord
Rothschild, who imprudently made himself a prominent figure
as a leader of the campaign. 'There are countries where they have
made it perfectly clear that they are not going to have their
policy dictated merely by great financiers, and if this sort of thing
goes on this country will join the rest of them.'[1] But soon, faithful
to his tactics, he portrayed the entire nation, artisans, men of
business, manufacturers, merchants, and engineers in alliance
against the intolerable yoke of the great landowners, the 'Dukes'
as he became accustomed to call them. 'The ownership of land

[1] Speech at Holborn Restaurant, June 24, 1909.

is not merely an enjoyment, it is a stewardship. It has been reckoned as such in the past, and if the landowners cease to discharge these functions, the time will come to reconsider the conditions under which land is held in this country. No country, however rich, can permanently afford to have quartered upon its revenue a class which declined to do the duty which it was called upon to perform.'[1] He was accused of driving capital from the country by the panic his Budget had provoked. A ridiculous lie! On the contrary, after the introduction of the Budget the position of trade was recovering from long months of depression. Every month the imports and exports were increasing. 'Only one stock has gone down badly; there has been a great slump in Dukes.'[2] 'A fully-equipped Duke', Lloyd George calculated, 'costs as much to keep up as two Dreadnoughts; and Dukes are just as great a terror and they last longer.'[3] Why this harping on the Dukes? It was not simply because the Duke of Westminster, the Duke of Rutland, and the Duke of Northumberland were taking part in too many public meetings. It was also because the Dukes were the heads of the peerage; and the entire House of Lords was the target of these insults, each one a challenge. If the Lords dared to throw out the Budget they would make a revolution and the people would soon take that revolution out of their hands. Their own folly had raised the question: 'Should five hundred men, ordinary men, chosen accidentally from among the unemployed, override the judgment—the deliberate judgment—of millions of people who are engaged in the industry which makes the wealth of the country?'[4]

We may well believe that at the beginning neither the Liberal nor the Unionist leaders desired to press the issue to such extremities. Asquith and Sir Edward Grey and Lord Lansdowne and Arthur Balfour were prudent men inclined to moderate courses. But a large number of their followers in both camps were of more warlike stuff. On the side of the Government were Lloyd George and Churchill. On the side of the Opposition was the host of Tariff Reformers: Joseph Chamberlain, crippled and invisible, penned from his retirement at Highbury a summons to resistance. The entire Unionist Press re-echoed his appeal. *The Times* alone

---

[1] Speech at Limehouse, July 30, 1909.
[2] Speech at Newcastle-on-Tyne, October 9, 1909.
[3] Ibid.
[4] Ibid.

for a time preached caution;[1] and there was even a moment when the great demagogue who directed both *The Times* and the *Daily Mail* seemed shaken by the force of Lloyd George's fervid eloquence and showed a disposition to support his policy.[2] Lord Rosebery attempted his favourite role of mediator.[3] It was too late. Already Lord Lansdowne—no doubt with reluctance—had bowed to the will of his party[4] and Balfour would shortly be persuaded to commit himself irrevocably.[5] The alternative he declared was the Budget or tariff reform. It was for the people to choose. And it was for the Lords to invite their choice by throwing out the Budget.

10

In what terms was the issue stated? The Liberals claimed that it was a question of constitutional law. The constitution, they argued, gave the House of Lords no right to reject the Budget. But England does not possess a written constitution. On what then was this alleged limitation of the Lords' prerogative founded? On a number of 'resolutions' passed by the Lower House in which the House of Lords had acquiesced and to which custom had accordingly given the force of law. Two of these passed under the Stuarts, the former in 1671, the second in 1678 declared in substance that it was the right of the Commons to initiate legislation granting supplies to the Crown, and that the Lords had no right to amend such Bills.

If, however, these resolutions denied that the House of Lords had the right to amend a Money Bill sent up from the Commons, they did not deny that the Lords had the right to reject it *en bloc*. On the contrary, a resolution passed by the Commons in 1689—

---

[1] *The Times*, July 5, September 11, 1909.
[2] *The Times*, August 4, *Daily Mail*, August 5, 1909.
[3] Speech at Glasgow, September 10, 1909.
[4] Speech at Bowood, August 7, 1909. With reluctance we have remarked. See the entry in Sir Almeric Fitzroy's diary for November 16, 1909: 'I sat next to him at luncheon at the Travellers' and thought him nervous and ill at ease; further, from some remarks he let fall about the Irish Land Bill and the Housing Bill, I could not fail to gather that he entertained grave misgivings upon the course he was about to take. There can be no doubt, in fact, that it has been forced upon him by the clamour of the Unionist Press, and the apprehensions of Tariff Reformers. He has not had a free choice in the matter; Whig scruples have been ruthlessly sacrificed to Tory passion and the petulance of wire-pulling demagogy.' (*Memoirs*, vol. i, p. 386.)
[5] Speech at Birmingham, September 24, 1909.

that is, on the morrow of the Revolution which had overthrown the Stuarts, expressly recognized their right to do so. The House of Lords had attempted to amend a Money Bill, the House of Commons had refused to give way. A conference had been held between representatives of the two Houses at which the representatives of the Commons declared that the Lords when presented with a Money Bill had only one option, 'that of adopting it or of rejecting it wholly, without alteration or amendment, if it might be to the relief of the taxpayers'. Subsequently the Lords had made frequent use of this right to reject Money Bills. Often, both before and after the Reform Bill of 1832, they had thrown out Money Bills sent up by the Commons, imposing customs or excise duties. But the day came when the Lords had the imprudence to carry too far the exercise of a right tolerated by the House of Commons and suffered or seemed to suffer a further curtailment of their prerogative.

Until that date it had been the custom to include in the Budget only those 'annual' taxes renewed every year by the Commons. When to balance the Budget it was necessary to alter a permanent tax, a special Act had to be passed, distinct from the annual Budget. This happened in 1860. The Government passed through the Commons a Bill abolishing the duties on paper. The Lords threw it out. This amounted undoubtedly to amending the Budget though it was by an indirect method. The Liberals protested vehemently. They denied that the Lords, because they were permitted to reject Money Bills which did not directly affect the composition of the Budget, could claim the right to interfere in any way whatsoever with the latter. The Liberal Government, postponing for a year the alteration of the excise duties for which it had asked, adopted the following year the novel procedure of incorporating into the Finance Bill every tax without exception and introduced into this complete Finance Bill the abolition of the excise duties on paper. The Lords were therefore faced with a dilemma. They must either adopt the daring course of rejecting the Budget as a whole, which was the only method by which they could protest against the abolition of the duties on paper. Or they must accept the entire Budget including the abolition of the duties on paper. In the former case the Government would appeal to the country and obtain its support against the Lords. In the latter case the conclusion would be drawn that the Lords re-nounced not only the right to amend the Budget but the right to reject it.

Actually, the Upper House never displayed subsequently any disposition to reject the Budget sent up by the Commons at the close of the session, not even in 1894 when the Liberal Cabinet effected by means of the Budget a reform of the succession duties nothing short of revolutionary and which the Government had decided to incorporate in the Budget for the very purpose of overcoming the opposition which the Lords offered to all their measures of reform. In consequence, it was taken for granted that in the sphere of finance the British constitution was not bicameral but unicameral. It became the custom to levy the new taxes set down in the Budget from the day when they were passed by the Commons without waiting for the assent of the Lords. Twice in 1907 and again in 1908 Arthur Balfour had expressly recognized that the House of Commons alone possessed authority in the sphere of finance.[1] Was the doctrine therefore beyond question? To Balfour's imprudent declarations, which he now found extremely embarrassing, the Unionists could oppose an equally imprudent declaration to the contrary made by Lord Spencer in 1904 when he was leader of the Liberal party in the House of Lords.[2] The fact of the matter was that for more than two centuries the House of Lords had never thrown out a Budget, and only circumstances of exceptional gravity could justify the breach of a custom so firmly established. It was a question of

---

[1] H. of C., June 24, 1907: '. . . We all know that the power of the House of Lords thus limited, and rightly limited as I think, in the sphere of legislation and administration, is still further limited by the fact that it cannot touch those Money Bills, which if it could deal with, no doubt it could bring the whole executive machinery of the country to a standstill.' (*Parliamentary Debates*, 4th Series, vol. clxxvi, pp. 929–30.) Speech at Dumfries, October 6, 1908: 'It is the House of Commons, not the House of Lords which settles uncontrolled our financial system.'

[2] H. of L., July 29, 1904: 'We all know that we in this House cannot amend a Money Bill, but we have a perfect right to discuss it and a full right to throw it out if we so will.' (*Parl. Deb.* 4th Ser., vol. cxxxix, p. 5.) When on July 20, 1908, the Old Age Pension Bill was read a second time in the Lords and Lord Wemyss had proposed to wait, before discussing it, for the report of the Commission which was inquiring into the Poor Law, Lord Rosebery pointed out that the Bill was a Money Bill, adopted almost unanimously by the other House and that an amendment at this point would amount to rejecting it. But if he advised against rejection, he did not regard rejection as unconstitutional, as is proved by the fact that in a speech delivered a week later he said that 'if he were to move the amendment which would commend itself most to his mind it would be to refer the Bill to the country at large. It was no part of the programme of the Government in the last election'. Lord Lansdowne also advised against the rejection of a Bill 'which was really a financial Bill, and which had been supported by colossal majorities in the other House'. He concluded that 'the wisest course' (he did not say the only constitutional course) was

expediency rather than of constitutional law, and weighty arguments could be pleaded in support of the more daring course.

For conditions had changed since the custom first arose. Could it be maintained that the position occupied by the House of Commons at the beginning of the twentieth century was the same as it had been in the seventeenth and eighteenth centuries, when it asserted the right to exercise an entire and unfettered control over a grant of supplies which the Sovereign might employ against itself and the country which it claimed to represent in its dealings with the Crown? The real sovereign, *de facto* if not *de jure*, was no longer the King but the electorate and the intention of the Commons when it asserted its financial omnipotence was to prevent any restriction being placed upon the revenue it desired to exact from the taxpayer to distribute it lavishly among the majority of the nation. And, on the other hand, was it possible any longer to differentiate among Money Bills between those which while having a financial aspect were concerned with objects outside the sphere of finance[1] and those—for example, the annual Budget—whose sole object was to provide the Government with the revenue it required for national purposes? Budgets whose authors inquired not 'how much money each taxpayer

---

to proceed to the discussion of the clauses. He was content to express the hope that 'the Government would not too severely press the privilege of the House of Commons'. What followed was this. When Lord Cromer brought forward an amendment restricting the operation of the Act to seven years, the Lord Chancellor observed that the amendment bore a financial character, and therefore violated the privileges of the Commons. In spite of this the amendment was carried, but when the Bill was returned to the Commons the Speaker pronounced it inadmissible for the same reason. The House of Lords finally submitted though not without protests. (H. of L., July 20, 1908; *Parliamentary Debates*, 4th Series, vol. cxcii, pp. 1379 sqq.; July 28, 1908, ibid., vol. cxciii, pp. 1073, 1077-8. H. of C., July 31, 1908, ibid., p. 1970.) We must however bear in mind that if the doctrine that Money Bills were unalterable was pushed very far, the Lords' right to reject them was not contested. See further H. of L., March 25, 1908, Lord Loreburn's speech (*Parl. Deb.*, 4th Ser., vol. clxxxvi, p. 1382) also the debate between Lord Loreburn and Lord Salisbury on the subject of this declaration. H. of L., May 24, 1909 (*Parl. Deb.*, Lords, 1909, 5th Ser., vol. iv, pp. 929 sqq.).

[1] See on this point the admissions made by John Morley himself, H. of L., November 29, 1909. 'The bare legal right (to reject the Budget) has not been denied. Some, no doubt, and I do not know that I would quarrel with them, would argue that the bare legal right may, on certain occasions, be appropriately transformed into a moral duty. Yes, but [*sic*] I can imagine a state of things—I can imagine it without difficulty—which would justify the transformation of a legal right into aspects of moral duty by reason of the wildest proposals of a demented House of Commons.' (*Parl Deb.*, Lords 1909, 5th Ser., vol. iv, pp. 1140-1.) The opposition speakers exhumed declarations made by Gladstone during the conflict of 1860 which admitted the Lords' right to 'amend the Budget if provisions not strictly financial were illegitimately embodied in it'. July 5, 1860, May 16, 1861 (*Parl. Deb.*, 3rd Ser., vol. clix, pp. 1433-4; vol. clxii, p. 2131).

had got, but how he had got it' and expressly proposed to 'make the rich poorer and the poor richer' were not Money Bills in the strict sense, but social legislation of the most far-reaching character whose object was to redistribute private wealth. The House of Lords might therefore with perfect fidelity to the logic of the constitution consider itself entitled to take the opportunity of declaring that under these novel circumstances, though it could not revive the claim to amend the Budget, since it had acquiesced in the formal resolutions of the Commons which deprived it of that prerogative, it was at least free to reject it as a whole, thereby making use of a right recognized by a resolution no less formal and which had not been revoked even in 1861.

We must therefore consider the House of Lords as placed, when presented with the Budget of 1909, in the same position in which it had been placed when presented with numerous Bills sent up to it by the Lower House since the Election of 1906. It had acted wisely—that is to say, it had not damaged its position— when it rejected the Education Bill of 1906 and the Licensing Bill of 1908. On the other hand, it had shown equal wisdom in accepting the Trade Disputes Bill of 1906 and the numerous measures of social reform which had followed it, the Workmen's Insurance Bill, the Eight-Hours' Day Bill, the Trade Boards Bill, and the Labour Exchanges Bill. Would it not be prudent to adopt the same attitude towards the far-reaching measure of social reform which called itself the Budget of 1909? If it threw out the Bill, a chamber in which the influence of the great landowners was regarded as predominant would be accused of doing so, to defend not the national welfare but the pecuniary interests of an order, a particular class. It would incur the responsibility of plunging the public finance into chaos, nine months after the financial year had opened. It would also expose itself to the charge, plausible in a country where the constitution was entirely customary, of attempting an almost revolutionary *coup d'état*. But, on the other hand, Lloyd George by his violent diatribes was doing his utmost to drive the House of Lords into a desperate course. He wished apparently to make it plain to the entire world that if the House of Lords passed the Budget it would accept a severe defeat, a marked humiliation. He was—deliberately perhaps—forcing the Lords to take an heroic decision. It was taken. A motion by Lord Lansdowne which declared that the House of Lords 'was not bound to give its adherence to the Finance Bill so long as it had not been submitted to the judgment of the country' was carried on November 30 after six days of serious and solid debate, by 350 to 75 votes. The House of Commons replied on December 2 with a declaration, carried by 349 votes to 134 that the action of the Upper House amounted to 'a breach of the Constitution and a usurpation of the rights of the Commons'.

The Constitutional Crisis and the House of Lords

I FROM THE DISSOLUTION OF 1909 TO THE DEATH OF EDWARD VII

I

THE course of events had caused King Edward considerable anxiety. By no means well disposed to the Budget of 1909 he was no less dissatisfied with the uncompromising attitude of the Unionists. By thus meeting intransigence with intransigence they were surely playing the Radicals' game? He was believed to have inspired Lord Rosebery's speech in September in which he had pressed caution upon the Lords.[1] It was known that in the beginning of October he had invited the Prime Minister to Balmoral and asked his permission to have an interview with the Unionist leaders to urge a compromise upon them. Asquith had given his consent, either because he was in favour of a compromise, or, knowing that the Unionists had already made up their mind to refuse an amicable solution, he wanted to make them shoulder the entire responsibility for the coming struggle. And in fact when the King on his return to London met Lord Lansdowne and Arthur Balfour, he could effect nothing.[2] When therefore after the vote of the Lords, Asquith asked him to dissolve Parliament, he was no doubt more annoyed with the Conservative statesmen who had hurt his vanity by refusing to let him play the part of peacemaker than he was with the authors of the objectionable Budget. He therefore made no objection to declaring Parliament dissolved on December 15. The General Election would follow in January. What under the circumstances was the choice before the voters? A Unionist victory would mean the rejection of the Budget. It would also mean what admittedly was the only alternative method of providing for the enormous in-

[1] Comte d'Haussonville 'Les élections et la situation politique en Angleterre' (Revue des Deux Mondes, February 1, 1911, vol. ccccxxxvii, p. 560).
[2] Sir William Angus. Speech at Newcastle-on-Tyne, October 9, 1907. Sir Almeric Fitzroy, Memoirs, October 11, 1907 (vol. i, pp. 384–5). Sir Sidney Lee, King Edward VII (vol. ii, pp. 667–8).

crease in the National expenditure, abandoning the tradition of free trade and applying the principles preached by the Tariff Reformers. A victory of the Liberals with their Labour and Irish allies would mean the approval of the Budget by the electorate. But it would involve more than this. For it would be necessary to prevent by an express enactment any further encroachment by the House of Lords upon the prerogative of the new House of Commons. 'We shall not assume office,' declared Asquith at a public meeting held on December 10, 'and we shall not hold office, unless we can secure the safeguards which experience shows to be necessary for the legislative utility and honour of the party of progress.'

If the Unionists expected a full swing of the pendulum, a complete reversal of the popular verdict and a striking revenge for their defeat in 1906, they were disappointed.[1] What actually occurred was a return after the abnormal Election of 1906 to a normal situation. But the Conservatives did not experience once more the triumphant days of 1895 and 1900. They reconquered the south-eastern counties, those Home Counties which they had always regarded as their province and which they had lost only by accident in 1906. It was a gain of 44 seats. But it was their sole victory. Their gains in London barely sufficed to give them a slight majority. The result was the same in the eastern, midland, and western counties. The industrial north remained faithful to the Liberals. Lancashire, which from hatred of Home Rule had gone over to the Conservatives in 1895 and 1900, had apparently, in its fear of Chamberlain's protection, returned permanently to its old allegiance. In these northern districts there was only a slight decline in the number of Liberal seats as compared with 1906: more than four-fifths were won by candidates supporting the Government. In Scotland the Liberal party, whose domination had been threatened at the close of the nineteenth century, was once more sovereign. With the exception of a solitary seat all the Welsh constituencies returned Liberal candidates. As always, Ireland returned a little over eighty Nationalists, inflexible enemies of the House of Lords. On balance, the Opposition secured only 273 seats as against 397 held by the supporters of the Govern-

---

[1] For the forecasts—very vague and often markedly divergent—of the forthcoming election see Sir Almeric Fitzroy, December 11, 14, 1909; January 4, 19, 1910 (*Memoirs*, vol. i, pp. 390, 391, 392).

ment—that is to say, the Government had a majority—possibly the more solid because it was smaller—of 124.[1]

But the Conservatives found consolation by analysing the composition of this majority. In England itself they had obtained a majority of seats, 239 as against 191 held by the Liberals, 34 by the Labour party and 1 by the Nationalists, that is to say a total of no more than 226 members on the Government side of the House. It was upon Scotland, Wales, and Separatist Ireland—that is to say, upon all those portions of the United Kingdom which were not English, that the Government's majority rested. A somewhat similar position had resulted from the General Election of 1835, two years after the overwhelming Whig triumph of 1833 which might be compared with the Liberal victory in 1906, and six years later the Conservatives had secured a decided majority in the Commons. And the situation presented another feature even more serious for the Government. In the new House the Unionists gained 100 seats, the Liberals lost 100, and in consequence the numbers of both parties were equal. The Government therefore had to depend for its majority upon two parties distinct from the Liberal though in alliance with it, the Labour party with roughly 40 seats and the Nationalists with some 80 seats. If the Nationalists were to abstain from voting the Government's majority would be reduced from 125 to 43. If they voted with the Unionists, its majority would be transformed into a minority—that is to say, in Parliament the Nationalists were masters of the situation.

It was a paradoxical state of affairs. The Irish, for the reason we have explained, disliked the Budget. It was only very reluctantly that they accepted it, for tactical reasons. It was their present to their friends the English Radicals, for which they in return would subsequently give them the Home Rule they desired and in the meanwhile would take the necessary steps to prevent the House of Lords from withholding it. They lost no time in pressing their demands home. The most urgent desire of the Government was to settle the question of the Budget, which had been hung up for months and on which it would seem the election had been held. They would then proceed to deal with the House of Lords. But it was the Budget which gave the Irish their hold over

---

[1] For a good analysis of the result of this Election of January 1910 see an article by Captain E. N. Mozley 'The Political Heptarchy. An Analysis of seven General Elections.' (*Contemporary Review*, April 1910; vol. xcvii, pp. 400 sqq.).

the Government. Once the Budget had been safely passed, it would have a freedom of action which the Irish did not desire it to possess. John Redmond indeed, a revolutionary well tamed by parliamentary methods, might possibly have proved more accommodating; but he felt his footsteps dogged not only by his own party but worse still by those dissidents who in Ireland were on the watch for the least sign of weakness on the part of the official Nationalists. The Irish therefore successfully demanded that before dealing with the Budget, Parliament should pronounce at least in principle on the question of the House of Lords. What form exactly did that question take? And in the first place what was this Chamber whose prerogatives or composition the Government proclaimed its intention to alter?

2

The House of Lords, we need hardly point out, did not represent, as did for example the Prussian *Herrenhaus*, a closed aristocracy, a noble caste. Nor is the difference sufficiently denoted by the fact that out of the British peerages of 1910 only thirty-two dated from the seventeenth century, eleven from the sixteenth, four from the fifteenth, five from the fourteenth and two from the thirteenth. For in every country in the world hereditary aristocracies speedily decay by the extinction of families. The distinctive feature of the British peerage was that the old families were swamped by an ever increasing flood of new peers. Throughout the greater part of the eighteenth century the increase had been slow, the number of peers rising only from 153 at the Revolution of 1688 to 174 at the accession of George III. But we have seen how for political reasons George III and above all his Minister, William Pitt, had lavished new peerages.[1] George IV had followed their example. At his death just before the crisis of the Reform Bill the number of peers had risen to 326. Once that crisis had passed a long halt followed, a period which witnessed no new constitutional developments. From 1837, the year of Queen Victoria's accession, to 1865, the year of Palmerston's death, the number of peers remained practically stationary. From

[1] See my *History of the English People*, vol. i, pp. 193–6.

385 it had risen to 400. It was after the latter date and especially after the passing of the Reform Bill of 1867, that creations of peers became more frequent as the constitution became more democratic. At the end of 1909 there were 544 hereditary peers.[1] At this rate within a few years, the House of Lords would have a larger membership than the Commons.

From what sources were these new peers drawn? Large numbers of them had been members of the Lower House who already belonged to the old gentle families and whose promotion to the peerage did not alter fundamentally its social composition. There were soldiers and sailors rewarded for distinguished service to their country—for example, Lord Wolseley, Lord Roberts, and Lord Kitchener. It is a curious fact that since for many years there had been no naval warfare, the navy in 1909 was practically unrepresented in the Lords. There were men who filled or had filled important administrative posts, ambassadors or Colonial governors. There was a small number of lawyers whose presence was indispensable when the House sat as a court of justice. On these occasions the other peers kept away and a few lawyers composed the entire assembly. Intellectual merit received little recognition. In 1909 there was not a single representative of literature, art or science. Lord Leighton, Lord Lister, and Lord Kelvin were dead and only the name of Lord Tennyson recalled the fact that his celebrated father had been a peer. But the really striking phenomenon was the invasion of the House of Lords, more marked every decade, by representatives of the business world, bankers, industrial magnates, and proprietors of newspapers.[2] We might

[1] To complete the membership of the House of Lords we must add 26 archbishops and bishops, 44 representative peers of Scotland and Ireland and 5 or 6 life peers. They bring the total to a figure exceeding 600. We must remember that the titles of Duke and Marquis had kept all their old value. (There were 22 dukes in 1909 in place of 20 in 1805, and 21 in 1837; 23 marquises in place of 19 in 1865 and in 1837.) It was the titles of Viscount and Baron which had been bestowed so lavishly. There were 42 Viscounts in 1909 as against 21 in 1865, 18 in 1837; 334 Barons as against 207 in 1865, 193 in 1837. (For all these figures see *Vacher's Parliamentary Companion* (from 1833).)

[2] For this invasion of the Peerage by business magnates see Labouchere's complaint in the House of Commons as early as 1888 (H. of C., March 9, 1888. *Parliamentary Debates*, 3rd Series, vol. cccxxiii, pp. 763 sqq.). Lord Salisbury's Government (1895–1902) created 50 peers, among them 6 business men (Baron de Worms created Baron Pirbright, the banker; H. H. Gibbs created Baron Aldenham, the Canadian railway director; Donald Alexander Smith created Baron Strathcona, the banker; Sir John Lubbock created Baron Avebury, the journalist; Sir Algernon Borthwick, director of the *Morning Post*, created Baron Glenesk; William Louis Jackson, leather and skin merchant later a railway director, created Baron Allerton. Balfour's Government (1902–1905) created 18 peers, among them 5 business men, a banker M. Biddulph created Baron Biddulph; an armament manufac-

have expected Conservative protests against such a debasement of the governing aristocracy, especially when these creations were the work of a Liberal Cabinet. And it was surely the strict duty of the Radical party to denounce this transformation of the Upper House into a frank plutocracy. But protests were in fact very few. A speech by Ramsay MacDonald[1] found little echo in the Press. From the opposite quarter the *Saturday Review* denounced in December 1905 the double elevation to the peerage of the eminent Jewish banker Herbert Stern and the popular journalist Sir Alfred Harmsworth.[2] But the Toryism of the *Saturday Review* was of an eccentric quality. Lord Northcliffe's peerage was calculated to please journalists of every camp. In 1906 King Edward revolted against the excessive number of peerages created by the new Liberal Cabinet, sixteen in six months not counting the Lord Chancellor's peerage, and attempted to veto the elevation to the peerage of Pirrie, the great Belfast shipbuilder. But Campbell-Bannerman held his ground. Three years later, Asquith made Pirrie a knight of Saint Patrick, and it was the turn of the nobility to revolt. The other knights of the order struck and refused to take part in the ceremony of inauguration which had therefore to

turer, W. H. A. F. Watson Armstrong, created Baron Armstrong; an ironmaster, Sir A. J. Forbes-Leith, created Baron Leith of Fyvie; the great Jewish financial magnate, Herbert Stern, created Baron Michelham (he had been made a baronet six months earlier), and the banker, E. B. Faber, created Baron Faber; also the journalists Edwin Levy-Lawson, director of the *Daily Telegraph*, created Baron Burnham, and Sir Alfred Harmsworth, director of the *Daily Mail*, created Baron Northcliffe. Campbell-Bannerman's Government was responsible for 21 new peerages, of which eight were given to business men. James Joicey, mine owner and newspaper proprietor, was created Baron Joicey. W. A. Wills, tobacco magnate, was created Baron Winterstoke; the Belfast shipbuilder W. J. Pirrie, created Baron Pirrie; J. J. Jenkins, Chairman of the Swansea Metal Exchange, created Baron Glantawe; G. Armitstead, a merchant, created Baron Armitstead; James Kitson, an ironmaster, created Baron Airedale; the Jewish banker, Montagu Samuel Montagu, created Baron Swaythling and Alexander Peckover, also a banker, created Baron Peckover.

[1] Speech at Longton, June 27, 1910: 'The seven new peers created by the Liberal Government were an awful warning of what would happen if they voted for the reform of the House of Lords. Let them look at the list. If he was going to have an aristocrat, he wanted a genuine aristocrat and not merely a plutocrat. If they were to have men of title holding even the limited power in the Constitution which the veto resolutions gave, he wanted men whom he could respect and not men who had bought their way into the Upper Chamber by liberally subscribing to party funds. . . . The Labour Party would not allow the new aristocracy to subvert the will of the people. . . .'

[2] *Saturday Review*, December 16, 1905: 'The Adulteration of the Peerage.' But after this violent outburst the *Review* was completely silent about the creations of January and June 1906. The *National Review*, in January 1906 very sarcastic about Sir Herbert Stern's elevation to the peerage, expressed its delight at seeing Sir Alfred Harmsworth made a peer. 'A man of supreme ability. . . . Now that he has become a Peer he may turn his attention to public life. He would be an interesting ingredient in a Cabinet and an admirable head of a department.'

be omitted.[1] But neither in 1906 nor in 1909 did these incidents reach the ears of the public. And in the end both the King and the nobility submitted.

3

For this capitulation two reasons can be given. The first of these on which we have already had occasion to remark,[2] is that the House of Lords was also being made plutocratic by another process, the reverse of the former, the fact namely that the members of the old aristocracy to repair fortunes damaged by a diminished rent roll, were engaging in business. Lloyd George was speaking the language of another age when in his campaign of 1909 he attempted to direct his hearers' indignation against the landlords alone. The wealthy landowners who lived on the rents of an urban estate or the royalties of a coal mine were a minority of their class. The others, owners of arable or meadow land, ruined under a system of uncompromising free trade by the fall of prices which had marked the last quarter of the nineteenth century and crushed by the enormous succession duties imposed upon them by Sir William Harcourt and lately increased by Asquith, would have been unable to meet the heavy cost of keeping up their estates, if they had not found new sources of wealth in the great joint-stock companies. A list drawn up in November 1909 by a leading Unionist journal, the *Standard*,[3] enumerated thirty-five bankers in the House of Lords. But among them were a Duke of Buccleuch, a Marquis of Ailesbury, a Lord Fitzwilliam and a Lord Harrowby. It enumerated thirty-nine 'captains of industry' but among the number were the Duke of Abercorn, chairman of the British South Africa Company, the Duke of Argyll, chairman of two steamship companies, and the Earl of Shrewsbury, chairman of the Brereton collieries—that is to say, while business men were becoming peers, peers were becoming business men, so that when the new rich reached the Upper House they found themselves on familiar ground.

The second reason why the new elevations to the peerage caused

[1] Sir Sidney Lee, *King Edward VII*, vol. ii, pp. 451–2.
[2] In my *History of the English People*, vol. v, pp. 15–18.
[3] November 22, 1909.

no scandal was their connection with the system of party organization. In older days two great opposing parties had indeed existed. But discipline was not very strict and both alike consisted of
a loose alliance of great families whose heads fought an election as
private individuals, some in agreement with the Government in
office, others opposed to it. The corruption that existed was practised either by these noble families who bid against each other for
the representation of 'county' seats or by *nouveaux riches* who
sought to snatch from the former representation of boroughs in
which the number of voters was sufficiently small for their votes
to be purchased *en bloc*. But little by little as the system of representation became democratic the parties had consolidated their
organization, had imposed on candidates a collective discipline,
and subjected the electorate to methods of corruption equally
collective. Henceforward politics was a battle between two
wealthy middle-class groups which whenever a costly measure
of social reform was passed submitted with equal resignation,
perhaps with equal lack of enthusiasm, to the demands of the
working class, and conducted their struggle, as though performing a ceremony, according to rules accepted by both parties.

The most fundamental of these rules was that either party had
the right to collect sufficient funds to face the next election with
some prospect of success. Wealthy candidates paid not only their
own expenses but the expenses of poor candidates and wealthy
members of the party contributed to the party funds in the hope
of securing not a seat in the Commons but a peerage or at the least
a baronetcy or knighthood[1] or one of those decorations whose
number had been multiplied of late years.[2] Possibly there was not

[1] H. of C., February 19, 1908. H. C. Lea's Speech: '. . . He left out the usual baronetcy
for the Lord Mayor of London and the two knighthoods to the sheriffs for entertaining
foreign potentates at their own expense. From November 1903 to December 1905 the
Tory Party were responsible for the creation of 13 Peers, 16 Privy Councillors, 33 Baronets, and 76 Knights: a total of 138 in two years, of which number 36 or 28.1 per cent were
Members of that House. From December 1905 to November 1907, two years of Liberal
régime, 20 Peers were created, 19 Privy Councillors, 33 Baronets, and 95 Knights; total
167, of which 37 or 22.1 per cent were Members of that House.' (*Parliamentary Debates*,
4th Series, vol. clxxxiv, p. 911.)

[2] Arthur Ponsonby, *The Decline of Aristocracy*, 1912, p. 124: 'The practice has never
reached the absurd extreme to which it has been pushed in foreign countries, where soldiers, courtiers, diplomatists, and officers are literally plastered over with decorations, but
they have already become common enough in this country to have lost all distinction.
Only within the last thirty years six new orders, two new decorations and several new
medals (not war medals) have been constituted. The large membership of these four orders
shows there is justification for saying that the craving for this really rather childish form
of public recognition is on the increase. The Victorian Order has some 870 members, the

in every case an express agreement to this effect. But when a wealthy manufacturer or merchant had contributed a large sum of money to the party funds, the Government could hardly refuse those who asked for some honour to be given him in return. And on the other hand when the insistent request of a financier who wanted to see himself a 'baron' had been granted, he could do no less than show his gratitude to the party which had made him a peer by contributing to the party funds in proportion to his wealth. The Home Secretary and the Patronage Secretary for the ministerialists, the Opposition leader and Whip for the opposite party, conducted these negotiations which, during the powerful wave of democratic feeling expressed by the Election of 1906, inevitably aroused protests. A certain Lancashire magnate whose elevation to the peerage had caused scandal in 1895 and who had loaded his native town with his interested benefactions, became on this account the object of such violent local attacks that he decided to leave the neighbourhood and transfer his gifts to some other district of England.[1] But if the incident is typical, still more typical is the fact that so little was said of it in the papers, and the equanimity with which on the whole the nation accepted this sale of honours carried on almost in public. In a country where the party organization is loose, extremists on the left or right may successfully agitate against an abuse of this kind; but in England they were faced by the solid mass of moderate members of both parties leagued against them to maintain practices equally indispensable to both. Lord Robert Cecil among the Tories, Hilaire Belloc and two or three other isolated individuals among the

---

Imperial Service Order 475, the Distinguished Service Order 1,650, and the Order of Merit 17.

Some of the old orders are restricted in their membership: the Garter, the Thistle, and Saint Patrick include altogether under 70 members but the Bath has been extended to 2,000 members, Saint Michael and Saint George to 1,000, and in addition to these are the Star of India (291 members) and the Indian Empire (414—not including natives of India). This makes a great total of nearly 6,800 decorated persons, not counting the recipients of war medals, the Victoria Cross, the order of St. John of Jerusalem, Volunteer and Territorial decorations, orders for Women, or the vast number who receive ceremonial medals.' A detailed analysis of all the honours (titles and decorations) bestowed from the beginning of Asquith's Government in April 1908 to the end of Lloyd George's Government is contained in an interesting article by Harold Laski entitled 'The Prime Ministers' Honour Lists' (*Nation*, July 15, 1922).

[1] James Williamson, manufacturer of linoleum in Lancashire created in 1895 Lord Ashton. This creation, together with that of Sidney Stern, made on its deathbed by the Liberal Cabinet which was resigning had aroused strong Unionist protests. 'Lord Linoleum' was accused of buying his title by a gift of £100,000 to the party funds. See the obituary notice of Lord Ashton in *The Times*, May 28, 1930.

Radicals, attempted in vain to rouse Press and Parliament from the apathy they had deliberately assumed on the subject. The Speaker, the umpire between the parties, acting in concert with Sir Henry Campbell-Bannerman and Arthur Balfour contrived to prevent the question even being raised. He claimed that since the grant of honours was part of the royal prerogative, to make the Prime Minister responsible was to derogate from the dignity of the Crown.[1] Silence fell and the Liberal party continued to replenish its funds by manufacturing noblemen with the tacit approval of the Unionist Opposition.

We must not then picture England in 1910 as on the verge of revolution and the House of Lords threatened with violent extinction for throwing out the Budget. The rejection did not provoke the riotous demonstrations against the peers responsible for it which had been provoked in 1832 by the rejection of the Reform Bill. After, all the majority of the population both in Great Britain and Ireland was opposed to the Budget on one point or another, and the House of Lords did not incur any real or profound unpopularity by rejecting it. If there were still old families whose uncompromising Conservatism protested indignantly against the growth of the democratic spirit and the debasement of the House of Lords, they were not numerous, and hidden in the depths of the country far from arousing indignation they inspired respect. Other noble families in touch with all the movements of London and cosmopolitan life might label themselves 'Tory'. But their drawing-rooms welcomed men of letters, artists, actors, and journalists of every political complexion. And the vast majority of the peers were men of fashion averse to serious thought who liked hunting, racing, sport of every description, and who, because they shared the taste for open air exercise and the love of

---

[1] The Parliamentary campaign against the traffic in titles was begun when the great shopkeeper Whiteley was created a peer, by Hugh Lea, a Radical M.P. who wrote a letter to *The Times* denouncing the sale of honours. (*The Times*, July 12, 1907. Cf. the letter signed M.P. in the *Morning Post* on July 13, 1907, and G. K. Chesterton's Letter in the *Daily News* July 15, 1907.) At the same time the question was raised in the House of Commons by Lord Robert Cecil (July 12, 15; *Parliamentary Debates*, 4th Series, vol. clxxviii, pp. 198, 346 sqq.), but the Leader of the House of Commons and the Leader of the Opposition asked the House to pass to the order of the day and the Speaker did as they requested. Cf. the debate provoked the following year by Hilaire Belloc (H. of C., February 19, 1908; *Parl. Deb.*, 4th Ser., vol. clxxxiv, pp. 899 sqq.) and Lord Knolly's letter to the *Glasgow Herald*, September 7, 1909. For a general discussion of the sale of titles see an interesting article entitled 'The New Corruption. The Commons and the Sale of Honours' in the *Candid Quarterly Review of Public Affairs* . . . conducted by Thomas Gibson Bowles, No. 1, February 1914 (vol. i, pp. 39 sqq.).

gambling common to all Englishmen, were perhaps more intimately in touch with popular feeling than many a Radical orator. In the political sphere they gave little trouble. Normally they never took part in the sittings of a House to which the Commons usually left little work and when an important debate was held, barely a fifth of the peerage was present. But the nation liked to see them preside over the amusements of the people.

And not only over the amusements of the populace but at the ceremonial functions of British public life. We have seen how Haldane, to enable the Lords-Lieutenant in the counties to patronize the reorganization of the reserve force, had succeeded in extending their functions on condition that they were assisted in the performance of these new duties by committees of democratic composition. About the same time violent Radical protests were raised against the appointments to the benches of magistrates made by the Lords-Lieutenant. Too many Unionists they complained were made Justices of the Peace, and only a handful of Liberals. But the Lords-Lieutenant had the good sense to recognize that the charge was well founded and asked to be released from an exclusive responsibility which was proving too invidious. Finally, a compromise was reached which resembled the provisions of the Territorial and Reserve Forces Act of 1907. Henceforward a local advisory committee composed of members of the different parties would assist the Lords-Lieutenant, who, however, would make the actual choice after consultation with the committee.[1] In one of his most violent diatribes Lloyd George

---

[1] One of the first measures passed under the Liberal Government had been a Statute which modified the institution of Justices of the Peace by 6 Edw. 7, Cap. 16: An Act to amend the law relating to Justices of the Peace (*Justices of the Peace Act*, 1906). The Act abolished all pecuniary and residential qualifications and the ineligibility of solicitors. It was immediately after this that the question of their nomination was raised. See the memorandum presented to the Chancellor by Mr. John Brunner in the name of 88 Liberal and Labour Members of Parliament and the Chancellor's reply (*The Times*, December 29, 1906). To understand the exact nature of the reform, it must be premised that hitherto the Chancellor had appointed the Justices of the Peace on the Lord-Lieutenant's recommendation. In future, the latter would recommend only candidates who had first been recommended to him by the newly appointed consultative committees. In November 1906 the Government appointed a Royal Commission on the Selection of Justices of the Peace which reported on July 6, 1910. Its recommendations were adopted, see H. of C., May 1, 1911, Asquith's speech (*Parliamentary Debates*, Commons 1911, 5th Series, vol. xxi, p. 103). The appointment of Justices of the Peace continued until 1912 to arouse serious protests. Since then no complaints have been raised. See the letters to *The Times* by Sir Hugh Bell, September 11, 1925, Lord Graham, September 22, 1925, the Chancellor, Lord Cave, October 1, 1925, and Lord Haldane's speech to the fourth annual conference of the

admitted implicitly the continued popularity of the peerage. 'As long as they were contented to be mere idols on their pedestals, preserving that stately silence which became their rank and their intelligence, all went well, and the average British citizen rather looked up to them.'[1] In 1909 they made a mistake; 'they stepped off their perch' and threw the country into a turmoil which might well have been avoided. Obviously, they must be taught a lesson. But how many people wanted that lesson to be a severe one?

From the moment of the Lords' rejection of the Budget, and the subsequent verdict of the electorate in favour of the Government, it was noticeable that Lloyd George abstained from those inflammatory speeches by which the year before he had done his utmost to intimidate, or rather to exasperate, the 'Dukes'. The Premier, Henry Asquith, assumed the leadership of a campaign in which the Chancellor of the Exchequer had no longer a direct interest. He gave it the strictly constitutional character of a debate between two parties equally anxious not to allow the country to slip into revolution and against whose powerful organization the free lances and extremists were powerless. A choice presented itself between two alternatives. Either the composition of the House of Lords could be left untouched and its control over the decisions of the Commons restricted, or its control could be left intact and its composition reformed.

4

Anxious to act as speedily as possible, the Cabinet did not touch the question of reforming the Lords but choosing the former alternative asked for a Statute which would expressly restrict their prerogative and make it impossible for them in future to violate constitutional usage, as they had violated it by rejecting the Budget. Asquith therefore adopted the attitude of a defender of the constitution threatened by revolutionaries. For a manifest error of judgment on the part of the Unionists enabled him to make the Liberal programme appear Conservative. 'The immediate cause, the actual irritant cause of what we may with reason

Magistrates' Association at the Guildhall, October 23, 1925. The appointment of the Lords-Lieutenant themselves was a source of friction between 1906 and 1910 between the King and his Liberal ministers. (Sir Sidney Lee, *King Edward VII*, vol. ii, p. 447.)

[1] Speech at Newcastle-on-Tyne, October 9, 1909.

call a constitutional crisis is the entirely novel pretension on the part of the House of Lords, not only to interfere in matters of public finance, but even to exercise a controlling right upon them and mould them to its liking . . . hence this paradoxical issue. It is we, the Progressive party, who are occupying today, before all else, a conservative and constitutional position. We are defending the liberties that the past has handed down to us against encroachments and usurpations which have for the first time received the official approbation of the Tory party.' When therefore on March 29, 1910, he invited the newly-elected House of Commons to pass three resolutions which embodied the Government's policy, the first of these declared it to be 'expedient that the House of Lords be disabled by law from rejecting or amending a Money Bill'. To avoid ambiguity, a Money Bill was defined as any Bill which in the judgment of the Speaker contained provisions relative to one or more of the following subjects: the imposition, abolition, reduction, alteration or modification of a tax, the charging of any item of expenditure to the Consolidated Fund, or the authorization of any item of expenditure by the Commons, the budget of receipts, the employment, control or regulation of the national revenue, the issue, guarantee, or repayment of a loan, or questions indirectly relating to any or all of these subjects.

But the Liberal Cabinet, secure of its parliamentary majority, was not satisfied with a defensive victory over the Unionists and the House of Lords. It met the Unionist offensive by a counter-offensive. In the speech from which we have just quoted Asquith denied not only the right claimed by the Upper House to limit the financial powers of the House of Commons, but even its right to compel a dissolution, since it was itself exempt from dissolution, and in this way to set up and overthrow Governments at its pleasure. This amounted to contesting the Lords' right to do what they had successfully done in 1886 by summoning the Liberal Government, if it dared, to appeal to the electorate. No one, however, at the time seems to have charged the House of Lords with a breach of the Constitution. The Cabinet's present design—an obvious innovation—was not simply to declare by an express Statute the Lords' impotence in financial questions, but to limit their powers in every sphere.

The method by which the Cabinet proposed to do this was no novelty. It was as old as Radicalism itself.

As early as 1835 when the two Houses joined issue over the Bill reforming Municipal Corporations, a young Radical member, Roebuck, had moved that the amendments introduced into the Bill by the Lords should be rejected *en bloc*. He had then proceeded to point out that as a result of the Reform of 1832 two Houses confronted each other divergent in origin and in the temper which inspired them, doomed therefore to conflict, and that this conflict might issue in revolution unless a constitutional procedure were devised for settling such crises. He therefore proposed that the House of Lords should be deprived of its absolute veto and should in future possess only a power to suspend Bills. It would still be able to send a Bill back to the House of Commons, but if the Commons passed it a second time during the same session and the King gave it his assent it would become law without being passed by the Lords.[1] A few months later James Mill, who since Bentham's death had been the philosopher and patriarch of British Radicalism, gave Roebuck's proposal his blessing.[2]

Half a century passed and the veto of the Lords was untouched. Then a crisis threatened. It was in 1884. The occasion was a third Reform Bill of an extremely democratic character, passed by a Radical House of Commons. An important speech was delivered at a public meeting by the Radical veteran John Bright.[3] He prescribed exactly the same remedy as Roebuck forty-nine years before. Its effect would, he said, be to get rid of the veto altogether except in a few very exceptional cases. Only genuine statesmen would take part in the debates of the Upper House. Peers who were indifferent to politics would enjoy their titles and their honours in the counties and would not trouble to come to Westminster, on a fool's errand, to reject a measure that was certain to be adopted the following year. These significant words reveal the reasons why the Radical party preferred limiting the powers of the House of Lords to altering its composition. It should be made harmless, but that once accomplished, there was no reason why it should not be left intact as a picturesque survival.

[1] H. of C., August 31, September 2, 1835 (*Parliamentary Debates*, 3rd Series, vol. xxx, pp. 1162 sqq., 1269–70).
[2] 'Let Bills be sent up from the Commons, so soon as the pressure from without shall have compelled them also to open their eyes, for unseating the thirty Prelates and suspending the definitive veto of the Peers—tacking them both to the supplies.' (*Westminster Review*, January 1836, vol. xxiv, p. 78.)
[3] Speech at Birmingham, August 4, 1884.

On this occasion a compromise was reached and a long period followed during which the electorate and the Lords agreed in preventing the Liberals from passing a Home Rule Bill. Before the General Election of 1895 the Liberal leaders were fond of saying that, if their party were returned, they would take measures to restrict the powers of the House of Lords and abolish its veto. But the Liberals were not returned and it was not until a decade later after the Election of 1906 that the problem of the relations between the two Chambers once more became acute. The Liberal Ministers at once revived the old programme of Roebuck and John Bright. At the beginning of 1907—when a serious conflict had just broken out between the two Houses on the subject of the Education Bill—the question was systematically examined. Obviously, a Government measure could not be content with the rough suggestions which had been enough for Roebuck and Bright. It was suggested at first that in case of conflict between the two Chambers, the House of Lords should elect a hundred delegates who sitting together with the House of Commons should constitute a joint body with which the final decision would rest.[1] It was an excessively simplified solution which Campbell-Bannerman modified by incorporating it into a system of very different inspiration. The resolution which he carried in the House of Commons on June 26, 1907, by a majority of 285 provided that in case of conflict both Houses should elect each an equal and limited number of delegates to arrange if possible a compromise. If they failed the House of Commons could pass the original Bill a second time with any amendment it thought desirable. If it were thrown out again, a joint conference would again meet to seek a compromise. If it failed again the Commons could pass the Bill a third time in which case it would become law without the assent of the Lords. To prevent the Commons abusing their new prerogative, the legal duration of Parliament would be reduced from seven to five years.[2]

What use would the Liberal Cabinet make of this resolution?

---

[1] J. A. Spender, *The Life of the Right Hon. Sir Henry Campbell-Bannerman*, vol. ii, p. 350. See also Sir Henry Campbell-Bannerman's criticisms, ibid., p. 351. James Mill had already considered the idea in the article mentioned above. (*Westminster Review*, January 1836; vol. xxiv, pp. 76–7.)

[2] See the debates H. of C., June 24, 25, 26, 1907 (*Parliamentary Debates*, 4th Series, vol. clxxvi, pp. 909 sqq., 1157 sqq., 1408 sqq.).

Take it for granted that the House of Lords would accept it as in the seventeenth century it had accepted the resolutions restricting its financial powers? Or would it immediately send up a measure which it knew beforehand that the Upper House would dislike and if it were thrown out embody the resolution in a Bill? In that case the problem would arise of the method by which the Lords could be compelled to pass the Bill.[1] As we know, no action was taken. The Government waited before joining battle until the House of Lords presumed to contest the financial sovereignty of the Lower House. Then the machinery held in reserve for the last three years was put in motion. The second and third resolutions submitted by Asquith to the House of Commons on March 24 resembled that of 1907 in two essential points. They made it impossible for the Lords to reject more than twice in the course of the same session a Bill passed by the Commons. And they restricted the duration of Parliament to five years. But on one point they were more radical. They made no provision either after the first or the second passing of a Bill by the Commons for the meeting of a 'conference', a committee of arbitration, to attempt a friendly settlement of the dispute.[2]

We must not mistake the significance of this second resolution, no longer Conservative but a manifest innovation. The Unionists' chief argument in favour of the prerogatives of the Upper House was the necessity for protecting the country against the autocratic rule of a legislature which it had no doubt elected but at a particular juncture and as the result of a movement of opinion from which a reaction might well have followed. Moreover, even if this were not the case, the election did not imply that the nation accepted every point of an extremely complicated programme. The House of Lords therefore fulfilled an extremely useful function when it distinguished between the different items of the Government's programme and accepted or rejected the Bills sent up from the Commons as in its opinion they did or did not express the permanent will of the nation. If the Nonconformists

---

[1] See the speech delivered at Edinburgh on January 24 by the Lord Advocate, Thomas Shaw.

[2] It is of interest however to observe that some politicians of the left groups depicted the proposal to establish a 'conference' as inspired by motives far from conciliatory. See J. R. MacDonald, speech at Bradford, October 13, 1907: '. . . The Liberal party were going to fight the House of Lords by the creation of a third Chamber, or joint committee of both Houses which would lord it with an iron hand over both the Lords and the Commons.' But his argument was perhaps only rhetorical.

demanded an alteration of the Education Bill of 1902, was it not evident, more evident each year, that the majority of the electorate, indeed the majority of the Liberal party itself, took no interest in the question? If the Irish Nationalists gave the Liberal Cabinet the indispensable support of their eighty votes was it not with the avowed intention of carrying by what amounted to a ruse their Home Rule Bill, which though it figured on the official programme of the party, could not be regarded with any certainty as representing the wishes of the Liberal electorate? The Lords allowed the Liberals, if they desired, to make a fresh appeal to the country and if the electorate still supported them the Bill in question would have received the sanction of the popular vote and the Upper House would give way, as it was doing at this very moment by passing Lloyd George's Budget. But this right to compel a dissolution of Parliament and the election of a new House of Commons was regarded by the Lords as the core of their prerogative.[1]

The Liberal reply to this argument was twofold. In the first place, they alleged that the Conservative peers abused their power by rejecting Bills passed by the Lower House to which it would be difficult to maintain that the country was hostile but whose nature was too special for it to be possible on such an issue to undertake the expense of consulting it. The country, for example, would not appreciate its opinion being asked on the plural vote or on Welsh Disestablishment. Yet it would be impossible to deny that the majority of the electors were in favour of abolishing the plural vote or that the entire body of Welsh Liberals—that is, the overwhelming majority of the Welsh people, wanted disestablishment, or to allege that their claim met with any strong opposition from the English and Scottish electorate. In the second place, they argued that a body whose composition was so aristocratic as the House of Lords could not exercise this right of control satisfactorily. Since it was exclusively hereditary and the new members who entered it were men whose class or caste interest would quickly imbue them with the prejudices of an hereditary nobility,

---

[1] There was a method of restricting by law the veto of the Lords which would actually have had the effect of strengthening its powers understood in this sense. W. E. H. Lecky (*Democracy and Liberty*, 1896, vol. i, pp. 386-7) proposed that no law could be passed in opposition to the Upper House which had not been passed by two successive Houses of Commons and by a majority of two-thirds. He adds: 'Such a change would, in theory, diminish the powers of the House of Lords. In practice it would, I believe, considerably increase them.'

it was inevitably an appanage of the Conservative party and the Liberals a small minority. The House of Lords therefore exercised its function of control only when the Cabinet was Liberal. Suppose a Liberal majority unexpectedly passed a Bill conferring a separate Parliament upon Ireland, the House of Lords would rise in revolt and demand an appeal to the country. But suppose a Unionist majority, though elected on a programme of opposition to Home Rule, unexpectedly passed a Bill in favour of tariff reform, would the House of Lords on the same principles compel the Government to consult the country before making such a serious decision? On the contrary, they would of course register automatically the decision of the Lower House. In short, the British Constitution, according to the Liberals, was bicameral only in appearance. In reality there was only one sovereign Chamber, the House of Lords when the Liberals had a majority in the Commons, the House of Commons when the Conservatives were in a majority.

In that case, why not adopt the programme of unmitigated democracy and abolish the House of Lords? The Labour members and a handful of Radicals were in favour of this course. But it was perhaps simply to discharge their consciences and without deep conviction. In any case that solution found no favour with the ministers and the vast majority of the Liberal party. Then why not reform the House of Lords and while keeping it in existence make its composition democratic? In principle the Government was in favour of reforming the House of Lords. It had been explicitly mentioned in the King's speech. But on the one hand it was a difficult problem which it would take time to settle, and the previous November had made it clear that a settlement of the relations between the two Houses could not be delayed. And on the other hand there was a danger that such a reform by making the constitution of the House of Lords less of an anachronism might strengthen its position in face of the Commons. Even after the House of Lords had been reformed it would therefore still be necessary to define strictly the relations between the two Houses and prevent a right to revise and suspend the Bills passed by the representatives of the people degenerating into a right of absolute veto. This in the eyes of the Liberals was the essential matter.

5

It was left therefore to the Conservatives to put forward as a practical issue the question of the Reform of the House of Lords, deliberately thrust into the background by the Liberals. In truth, the question was not new. Twice already within the last half century it had been raised, on both occasions after a democratic reform of the representative system which had convinced a number of peers that the House of Lords would do well to modernize itself if it were to continue to exercise its traditional functions in relation to the Lower House. On both occasions it was a Liberal who had taken the initiative, but a Liberal of independent views, who received little support from the leaders of his party and found many supporters among the Conservatives.

In 1869, two years after the passing of the important Reform Bill which in current parlance had given universal suffrage (or something approaching it) to the boroughs, Lord John Russell submitted to the House of Lords a Bill authorizing the Crown to create life peerages. They would not exceed twenty-eight in all and no more than four might be created in any one year. These life peers were to be chosen from persons who had occupied high judicial or administrative positions, or had sat in the Commons for ten years at least, or had achieved distinction in science, literature or art. His object was to strengthen the position of the House of Lords, and improve the quality of its debates 'by introducing there the talents of a Jenner or a Watt'. Lord John was a former Liberal Prime Minister who watched with uneasiness the progress of the new democratic England. The Liberal party, which under Gladstone's leadership occupied the majority of seats in the Commons, bore little likeness to that which he had himself led before the reform of 1867. Many Conservatives approved of his proposal. To confer an hereditary peerage on judges, on soldiers without private wealth, in a democratic age in which a Government could no longer lavish grants and sinecures on new peers and their descendants, would be to create a class of impoverished peers who would not enhance the prestige of the order. Lord Salisbury declared it advisable to widen the composition of the House of Lords by introducing representatives of the intellectual and industrial classes. Lord John's Bill nearly passed the House of Lords but at the last moment dislike of change proved too powerful. It was rejected on the third reading.[1]

On one point nevertheless everyone agreed that it met an urgent need. The House of Lords was not only a legislative body of the first rank, it was also a supreme court of justice. But it was ill constituted to perform this latter function. For such a task, the Lord Chancellor, one or two peers who had been former Lord Chancellors and had been raised to the peerage after filling other important judicial posts, men whose intellect had often been weakened by age, did not suffice. Already in 1856 the Government of the day had attempted to promote a lawyer to the Upper House as a life peer. But the attempt had aroused the wrath of the House of Lords and after lengthy debates in both Houses the Cabinet had given way and transformed Baron Wensleydale's life peerage into an hereditary peerage. After the failure of Lord John's Bill, which would have solved the problem, another method was adopted. In 1873 when the organization of the superior courts of justice was completely remodelled, the opportunity was taken to divest the House of Lords of all its judicial functions, which were given to a new body called the 'High Court of Appeal'. The Act was scarcely on the Statute Book when the Lords repented of having surrendered so easily the privileges of their order. The execution of the Statute was suspended and a compromise was finally reached. Above the new court of appeal the House of Lords remained the court of last instance. But when sitting in that capacity it would be assisted by Lords of Appeal in Ordinary, professional judges appointed by the executive. Two at first, their number would be raised later to four. So long as they exercised their functions they would possess all the rights of a member of the House of Lords. That meant very often that they would be peers for life. And this fact would be expressly recognized by a Statute of 1888 which declared all the Lords of Appeal were life peers. It was the first departure from the principle of an Upper Chamber exclusively hereditary.[2]

---

[1] H. of L., April 9, 27; June 3, 8; July 8, 1869 (*Parliamentary Debates*, 3rd Series, vol. cxcv, pp. 452 sqq.; 1648 sqq.; vol. cxcvi, pp. 1172 sqq.; 1370 sqq.; vol. cxcvii, pp. 1387 sqq.). From a speech made by Lord Lyndhurst in 1856 it would seem that the idea of creating life peers had already found favour during the struggle over the Reform Bill with certain members of Lord Grey's Cabinet. (H. of L., February 7, 1856; ibid., vol. cxl, pp. 275–6.)

[2] For all this legislation see 36 & 37 Vict., Cap. 66: An Act for the constitution of a Supreme Court and for other purposes relating to the better Administration of Justice in

In 1884 the representative basis of the House of Commons was rendered still more democratic. The new reform extended to the counties the franchise which the Act of 1867 had established in the boroughs. We now find the young Lord Rosebery playing the part played fifteen years earlier by the aged Lord John Russell, and bringing forward in the same spirit the problem of reforming the House of Lords.

While the Bill was being debated in the Commons and John Bright was raising the other question of restricting the Lords' prerogatives, Lord Rosebery moved in the Upper House that an 'enquiry' should be undertaken 'into the best means to employ for improving its effectualness'.[1] It was desirable, he urged, that medicine, science, art, literature, commerce, and even the working class should be represented, also India and the Colonies. It would also perhaps be advisable to create life peers and permit men who were not peers to take part as consultants in the work of the House. The motion was rejected. But Lord Rosebery did not abandon the idea and he found support among the Conservatives.

In 1886 the Conservative party, transformed in virtue of its coalition with those Liberals who disapproved of Home Rule into the Unionist party, returned to office. In 1888 a Radical member invited the House of Commons to pass a resolution condemning the principle of an hereditary legislature.[2] His motion was rejected as we should expect of an assembly with a Conservative majority. But it again drew public attention to the problem of the composition of the Upper House, and the Unionists, who felt their hold on office precarious, were the first to interest themselves in it. Lord Rosebery came forward again, once more asked for the appointment of a Committee to examine the question, and

England: and to authorize the transfer to the Appellate Division of such Supreme Court of the Jurisdiction of the Judicial Committee of Her Majesty's Privy Council (*Supreme Court of Judicature Act*, 1873). 37 & 38 Vict., Cap. 83: An Act for delaying the coming into operation of the Supreme Court of Judicature, 1873 (*Supreme Court of Judicature [commencement] Act*). 38 & 39 Vict., Cap. 97: An Act to amend and extend the Supreme Court of Judicature Act, 1873 (*Supreme Court of Judicature Act*, 1875). 39 & 40 Vict., Cap. 59: An Act for amending the Law in respect of the Appellate Jurisdiction of the House of Lords and for other purposes (*Appellate Jurisdiction Act*, 1876). 50 & 51 Vict., Cap. 70: An Act to amend the Appellate Jurisdiction Act 1876 (*Appellate Jurisdiction Act*, 1888). In another and more indirect way the principle of life peerages has found expression in the House of Lords. The Cabinet when conferring new peerages so lavishly, has often conferred them on bachelors or men without male heirs. In theory such a peerage is hereditary. In practice it is a life peerage. We cannot regard Viscount Morley, Viscount Haldane, and at the present time Viscount Snowden as anything but life peers.

[1] H. of L., June 1889 (*Parliamentary Debates*, 3rd Series, vol. cccxxxii, pp. 937 sqq.).
[2] H. of C., March 9, 1888. Labouchere's motion (ibid., vol. cccxxiii, pp. 763 sqq.).

suggested an Upper House composed in part of peers elected by their order, in part of members elected either by the new County Councils or by the House of Commons itself. Life peers might be created by the Government. The Self-Governing Colonies might send representatives. In case of conflict both Houses would sit and vote together in a joint sitting.[1] And, on the other hand, an independent Unionist, Lord Dunraven, brought in a Bill to reform the House of Lords, more carefully thought out than any of the earlier projects and in entire harmony with Lord Rosebery's views.[2] He proposed an Upper House consisting of two elements almost equal in number. There would be hereditary peers elected to represent the entire body of hereditary peers as was already the case for Scotland and Ireland, but there would also be representatives of the Colonies, the Church of England, the free Churches, and the Catholic Church, of literature and the sciences, above all representatives elected by the County Councils. Lord Salisbury, as we should expect, condemned the Bill, but he admitted that it contained acceptable suggestions and promised on behalf of the Government to introduce a Bill 'to facilitate the entry of life peers into the House of Lords'. He soon kept his word. He brought in a Bill very obviously inspired by Lord Russell's Bill of 1869.[3] The Crown would be empowered to create life peers chosen among the judges, soldiers, sailors, diplomatists, high officials who were members of the Privy Council and Colonial Governors. Under exceptional circumstances and by a special procedure intended to prevent any possibility of abuse the Crown might create a limited number of new peers, outside these categories—at the most five in one year. And the total number of life peers must never exceed fifty. We may add that by extending a measure adopted in 1871 to exclude bankrupts[4] Lord Salisbury's Bill permitted the Crown acting in concert with the House of Lords to expel a peer judged unworthy of a seat in the House.

But the Bill introduced by the Unionist Premier was soon dropped. The General Election of 1895 seemed to inaugurate in English history an epoch of Conservative supremacy which would

[1] H. of L., March 19, 1888 (*Parliamentary Debates*, 3rd Series, vol. cccxxiii, pp. 1538 sqq.).
[2] H. of L., April 26, 1888 (ibid., vol. cccxxv, pp. 518 sqq.). See also his article written some years before entitled 'The House of Lords. Its Reform.' (*Nineteenth Century*, No. 84, February 4, 1884, vol. xv, pp. 200 sqq.).
[3] H. of L., June 18, 1888 (*Parl. Deb.*, 3rd Ser., vol. cccxxvii, pp. 387 sqq.).
[4] 34 & 35 Vict., Cap. 50: An Act for disqualifying Bankrupts from sitting or voting in the House of Lords. (*Bankruptcy Disqualification Act*, 1871.)

be prolonged indefinitely. The sole echo of these projects was the occasional discussion in imperialist circles of a reform of the House of Lords which would solve at the same time the problem of Irish Home Rule. Separate local parliaments, it was suggested, should be set up for England, Scotland, and Ireland, possibly also for Wales. An Upper House, reformed and rendered elective, would represent not only the entire United Kingdom but the Empire. The discussion however remained academic. The scheme never enjoyed the least popular support either in England or Ireland or in the Self-Governing Colonies. But the situation was changed by the Election of 1906. It was not surprising that this dramatic reverse shook the Unionists from their slumbers, and that the reform of the House of Lords as well as the restriction of its prerogative, became once more a burning question.

6

In 1907 without waiting for Campbell-Bannerman's motion in favour of abolishing the veto of the House of Lords, Lord Newton introduced a Bill to reform it. The measure restricted the right to sit in the Upper Chamber to those hereditary peers who had occupied certain important positions in the State; the hereditary peers would elect representatives equal in number to a fourth of their entire body, and the Crown would be empowered to create a hundred life peers. But instead of debating the clauses, the Lords appointed a Committee to advise as to the best methods 'of reforming the work of the House of Lords'. Lord Crewe, speaking on behalf of the Government, refused even to express an opinion of Lord Newton's Bill. It was not a question of altering the composition of the House of Lords but of settling the relations between the two Houses.[1] The Committee was composed entirely of Unionists with the exception of Lord Rosebery, who could no longer be called a Liberal. It was on his motion that the Committee had been appointed. And it elected him its chairman.

It reported in December 1908.[2] About the principle on which reform should be based it had no hesitations. It declared it 'un-

---

[1] H. of L., May 6, 1907 (*Parliamentary Debates*, 4th Series, vol. clxxiii, pp. 1203 sqq.).
[2] Report from the Select Committee on the House of Lords together with the proceedings of the Committee and Appendix, 1908.

desirable that the possession of a peerage should give by itself the right of sitting and voting in the House of Lords'. To apply that principle it suggested a House of Lords composed of 200 peers elected by the entire order, like the existing representative peers of Scotland and Ireland, peers who had the right to membership because they held or had held a number of high offices; according to the report there were 130 of these in the contemporary peerage, and finally a maximum of forty life peers. But the plan, as the members of the Committee admitted, was open to a serious objection. When the 130 peers had been deducted, who retained their seats in virtue of the high offices they occupied or had occupied in the State, only nonentities would be left. Therefore, the 200 representative peers must in the very nature of things be nonentities. Moreover, being elected by a body of which the overwhelming majority was Conservative, they would be all Conservatives. There would not even be amongst their number that small majority of independent Liberals which a purely hereditary House contained. What then should be done? Admit representatives elected by the Borough and County Councils?[1] The suggestion was too bold for the members of the Committee, more timid in 1907 than Lord Rosebery and Lord Dunraven had been in 1888. Allow the government of the day with a majority in the Commons to nominate a certain number of its followers as members of the House of Lords for the duration of Parliament? It was a bizarre suggestion which the Committee rejected by a large majority.

It was once more left to Lord Rosebery to raise in 1910 this question of the reform of the House of Lords. Arthur Balfour, in his address to the electorate of December 10, had deliberately shirked the issue, careful even, as he has himself told us, not to declare against reform. Why indeed should he commit himself at a moment when he might still hope for a victory at the polls which would be the victory of the House of Lords as at present composed? The Unionists therefore who had indeed been defeated at the January Election but whose defeat had not been hopeless, while not going so far as to place reform of the Lords on their programme, welcomed the intervention of an independent states-

[1] Lord Saint Aldwyn to Lord Newton, February 8, 1907 (Lady Victoria Hicks-Beach, *Life of Sir Michael Hicks-Beach* (Earl Saint Aldwyn) 1932, vol. ii, pp. 255–6). Lord Saint Aldwyn suggested the election, at every General Election, of a number of peers not only by the County Councils but also by the Colonial legislatures.

man who though bitterly hostile to the Budget of 1909 had nevertheless advised the House of Lords—how wisely the event had
proved—against the tactical mistake of throwing it out. Lord
Rosebery's three resolutions of March 14, and his two more
detailed resolutions of April 13, embodied in substance the principles laid down in 1908 by the committee over which he had
presided. On March 14 he moved that 'the possession of a peerage
should no longer confer, by itself, the right of sitting and voting
in the House of Lords'. On April 13 he proposed a House of
Lords consisting in the first place of peers elected by the body of
hereditary peers, in the second place of peers sitting in virtue of
their official position, in the third place of peers 'chosen from
outside'. What are we to understand by these words? Life peers
created by the Crown? Or temporary peers chosen by a more or
less democratic electorate?[1] The formula was intentionally vague.

II FROM THE DEATH OF EDWARD VII TO THE PASSING OF THE PARLIAMENT BILL

I

Thus, about the end of April 1910 the plan of the Government
and Lord Rosebery's plan to which it would seem Lord Lansdowne had given his approval[2] confronted each other. The
Government had carried in the House of Commons their resolutions intended to weaken the check exercised by the Upper upon
the Lower House. Lord Rosebery had carried in the House of
Lords two resolutions intended to strengthen the Upper House
by modifying its composition. Asquith had just introduced a Bill
to give effect to his policy, Lord Rosebery promised to do the
same thing for his. What would happen if when the Commons
passed the Government's Bill, the Lords replied by passing Lord

---

[1] It would not have been in the least democratic if Lord Wemyss' suggestion had been
adopted that a fixed number of peers should be elected by a number of important bodies,
three by each. Lord Wemyss suggested twenty-one bodies on whom this right might be
conferred. For example the Royal Institute of British Architects, the Royal Academy of
Arts, the Society of Engineers, the Shipping Federation, the Employers' Parliamentary
Council, the Liberty and Property Defence League, etc. (H. of L., April 25, 1910. *Parliamentary Debates*, Lords 1910, 5th Series, vol. v, p. 683).

[2] Not it would seem without considerable reluctance and under pressure from the
agents of the party (Lord Newton, *Lord Lansdowne. A Biography*, pp. 385 sqq.).

Rosebery's? There was nothing to prevent the House of Commons rejecting a Bill not sufficiently democratic to satisfy the Liberal majority. Even those Ministers who were least disposed to destroy the House of Lords, were aware that the Radicals would accept nothing but a purely elective chamber.[1] But a Bill on these lines if it even passed the Commons, would certainly be rejected by the Lords. How was it possible under a bicameral system to escape an impasse of this kind unless the question of the relations between the two Houses were settled first? But how could they be settled by a Statute so long as the House of Lords retained an absolute veto on the legislation of the Lower House? By making use of the King's prerogative of creating on his ministers' advice a sufficient number of peers to change the majority in the House of Lords?[2] The increase in the number of peers had rendered this method extremely difficult. It would be necessary to create 500 new peers. And at first the Ministers themselves were sharply divided on the point. Finally, however, the Cabinet decided to ask the King to create them if the fear of seeing their order so cheapened did not make the more obstinate peers submit. 'If', Asquith declared, 'we do not find ourselves in a position to ensure that statutory effect shall be given to that policy in this Parliament, we shall then either resign our offices or recommend the dissolution of Parliament. Let me add this, that in no case will we recommend a dissolution except under such conditions as will secure that in the new Parliament the judgment of the people as expressed at the Elections will be carried into law.'[3] Reassured by this solemn pledge the Irish at last allowed the

[1] Sir Edward Grey, speech at the Hotel Cecil, March 14, 1910.

[2] We may mention as a curiosity another solution suggested by an Irish member. The actual issue of the writ of summons to the peers was part of the royal prerogative. What was there to prevent the King, on the advice of the Cabinet, from withholding writs from a sufficient number of peers to ensure a majority for the Government's Bill? (J. C. Swift MacNeill 'A Short Way with the House of Lords' *Fortnightly Review*, January 1, 1894, New Series, vol. lvii, pp. 1 sqq., especially pp. 6 sqq.), also a letter to Sir Henry Campbell-Bannerman, *The Times*, April 1, 1907. King Edward was attracted for a moment by the idea (J. A. Spender and Cyril Asquith, *Life of Lord Oxford and Asquith*, vol. i, pp. 261–2) and a few months later he put it forward again in a modified form. Only those peers would be allowed to vote who were chosen by the leaders of the two great parties, fifty for either party. To these alone the writ of summons would be sent. (See the King's Conversation with Lord Crewe at Windsor, January 30, 1910 as reported by Sir Sidney Lee (*King Edward VII* ... vol. ii, p. 695.) It would seem that in 1884 the Socialist Pankhurst contemplated the possibility that the House of Lords might be abolished by this indirect method. The Sovereign would no longer summon the peers and the House of Lords would therefore cease to exist. (E. Sylvia Pankhurst. *The Suffragette Movement*, pp. 81–2.)

[3] H. of C., April 14, 1910 (*Parliamentary Debates*, Commons 1910, 5th Series, vol. xvi, p. 1548).

Budget of 1909 to be passed with a few amendments of detail. By a ruthless use of the closure it was passed in ten days. By April 29 the business had been despatched and the recess began. It was when Parliament reassembled at the end of May that the dramatic struggle between the two Houses would reach its *dénouement*. If again the House of Lords refused to yield, it would be the King's turn to act.

But the unforeseen happened. The King, who had returned from Biarritz on the very day when the Commons passed the Budget, died on May 6. His health had been failing for many months and his entourage and himself were aware that the first illness might prove fatal. But the secret had been so well kept, and to the last moment he had performed his official duties with such zest that the public were taken by surprise. The English gave free rein to those feelings of national grief which always accompany an English monarch to his tomb. Journalists acclaimed in chorus with complete seriousness and without provoking a smile from their readers his political genius and even his private virtues. Had he not by his visits to all the rulers in Europe taken a prominent place in the history of his time? Was he not loved in France, hated in Germany, in both countries regarded as a great monarch? Had he not, moreover, possessed from his youth the reputation of a liberal prince, a friend of the popular cause? Unfortunately, much of this was legend. The part he had played in foreign policy had not perhaps been so important as was almost universally believed, and his Liberalism was certainly not as solid as it was said to be. As he grew older and became ill and tired his opinions became increasingly similar to those, sufficiently commonplace in all conscience, held by the clubmen among whom he lived, those people, we all know so well, who, completely ignorant of public affairs, lament every day as they puff at their fat cigars that the country is going to the dogs and declaim against what they are pleased to call the vulgar behaviour of the 'outsiders' who have forced their way into society.[1] As uncultivated as his mother, he

---

[1] In view of certain legends the judgment expressed by an important English review on the entourage of King Edward which appeared on the eve of his death is well worth quoting 'The King has many qualities, no one is more kind-hearted. He is a capital sportsman, and in foreign affairs he possesses a fine instinct which seldom leads him wrong. His very geniality and good fellowship deprives him of much of the awe with which the late Queen was regarded. His Majesty is a man of the world, going freely into society. But not even the most servile courtier could say that he has ever, whether as Prince or King, surrounded himself with men who are influential in either House of Parliament. Those who

did not possess, if the truth must be told, her grasp of political realities. And this had its good side. For the complaints with which he wearied his Ministers and of which they took little notice were less concerned with questions of general policy than with personal matters, appointments, and honours. For the rest, punctilious over points of etiquette and a past-master in the art of good fellowship, extremely conscientious in the performance of his ceremonial functions, delighted when his time-table was crowded with levees, openings, race meetings, dinners, visits to the opera or music hall, he was a model constitutional sovereign. But if all these things contributed to his popularity, here also there are reservations to be made. Though on the morrow of his death no one dare admit it publicly, he was too fond of the theatre and casino, too fond of travelling and visits abroad, too cosmopolitan, too 'European', to be the national monarch England would fain have possessed. In him the monarchy was honoured rather than the monarch. It would certainly not be very long before it was perceived how superficial his popularity had been.[1]

King George, who ascended the throne at the age of forty-five, had become heir unexpectedly in 1893 by the death of his elder brother. He had been brought up to be a sailor not a King. Like his father he was a great traveller, but he had not visited the watering-places and capitals of the Continent. He had opened the first Parliament of the Australian Commonwealth, had visited India, South Africa, and Canada. Because he had not been educated for the throne, he spoke foreign languages badly. English to

have shared his valuable counsels, may be the worst of men, as they are often among the pleasantest, but to the great political world they are unknown. With the doubtful exception of Lord Esher who has one of the sanest heads in Europe, none of those who constitute the entourage of the King count for anything in politics.' (*Contemporary Review*, May 1910, vol. xcvii, p. 517.)

[1] The authoritative work on King Edward is Sir Sidney Lee, *King Edward the Seventh. A Biography*, 2 vols., 1925–27. Edward Legge's two volumes *King Edward in his true Colours*, 1912 and *More about King Edward*, 1913 seem the work of a courtier dissatisfied with the tone, not sufficiently laudatory for his taste, of the article on King Edward in the *Dictionary of National Biography*, though it did not prevent the royal family entrusting its author, Sir Sidney Lee, with the task of writing the official biography of the dead monarch. They are a mere collection of anecdotes and give us little information. See also the study of King Edward by Lord Esher, who knew him intimately, in his book entitled, *The Influence of King Edward and Essays on other Subjects*, 1915 also H. E. Wortham, *The Delightful Profession: Edward VII. A Study in Kingship*, 1931. We may mention as a curiosity the speech delivered by Lord Haldane on December 14, 1907, in which in the course of a panegyric of King Edward he maintained that in England a constitutional monarch possessed a power of initiative not essentially different from that possessed by a so-called absolute monarch. The speech aroused the wrath of the Radical Press. But it seems to have been nothing but the fantastic expression of a metaphysician's dream.

the backbone and married to a Princess of the royal blood who was English by birth, he and his wife presented for the first time in England the spectacle of sovereigns who spoke English without a foreign accent, and in whose entourage more English was spoken than German. Strictly patriotic and strictly conservative, of middle-class tastes and habit, he was capable of decisive action. Whether, surrounded by his numerous children he were piously performing his religious duties, or reviewing with the competence of an old sailor the manœuvres of one of his fleets, or following amidst a huge crowd the fortunes of a football match, his unsophisticated feelings were shared by his people. He was in truth the imperial and insular monarch his subjects desired. He was better fitted than the late king to become one day the nation's darling.

2

When in October King Edward had held conversations with the leaders of the Opposition the Radical Press had suspected a desire to intervene in the conflict. Two months later when Asquith, stating his programme at a public meeting,[1] declared his resolve not to remain in office unless he could obtain the necessary assurances, the Unionist Press had accused him of putting pressure on the King to compel him, when the issue was joined, to support the Cabinet against the House of Lords. King Edward, there can be no doubt, dreaded the approach of that decisive moment, at a loss which course to adopt when faced with the choice between such formidable alternatives. Either he must refuse the request of a Cabinet supported by a majority of the Commons, and would be accused by the Radicals, as the House of Lords had been accused in December, of attempting a *coup d'état*. Or he would yield and be obliged to create such an enormous host of new peers to outvote the present majority in the Chamber that he would be accused and accused even by his own conscience of overthrowing and debasing the hereditary House and in the sequel perhaps of assisting the debasement and destruction of the hereditary monarchy itself. He died and his death barbed the denunciations of the Unionists. The insolence of the Radical Ministers, they said, had darkened his old age, perhaps even shortened his life. Were they

[1] Speech at the Albert Hall, December 10, 1909.

proposing to embarrass by conduct equally insolent the young sovereign who was a novice in the art of kingship? The Ministers seized this opportunity to postpone a crisis which some of them dreaded, Grey and Haldane and others besides. Every preparation had been made for the dissolution of Parliament in the event of a further conflict between the two Houses on the question of the House of Lords, its functions and prerogatives. The electoral campaign had practically begun. Funds had been collected, the list of candidates drawn up, and public meetings multiplied. Suddenly the Government suspended all these preparations and contented itself with raising to the peerage five great capitalists, in recompense apparently for the contributions they had just made to the Liberal party funds.[1] And the Ministers approached the leaders of the Opposition in the hope of discovering a compromise. When Parliament met again on June 8 Lord Rosebery announced in the Lords that he did not wish the House to proceed with the discussion of his resolutions. In scarcely-veiled language he gave it to be understood that he was taking this course at the request of the Government. It had been agreed that a conference should be formed, to consist of the principal representatives of the two opposing parties—four Unionists and four Liberals, the leaders of both parties in both Houses, with two other representatives of either party, among them Lloyd George. The Constitution just set up in South Africa had been the work of a conference sitting in private and containing representatives of the two hostile races so lately in arms against each other. To effect an amicable agreement between the two English political parties on the question of the relations between the two Houses would surely prove a less difficult feat. The Government's decision was in fact acclaimed by the mass of the nation. But the Labour members and the Irish Nationalists protested. They had been excluded from the Conference, which had therefore the appearance of an attempt by the two traditional parties to settle the crisis apart from the two groups whose recent appearance on the scene interfered with the normal operation of the Parliamentary machine. On June 30

[1] The printer Richard Knight Causton (Baron Southwark), the tea merchant Hudson Ewbanke Kearley (Baron Devonport), the cotton spinner William Henry Holland (Baron Rotherham), the shipbuilder Sir Christopher Furness (Baron Furness) and finally the king of Mexican petroleum, Sir Weetman Dickinson Pearson (Baron Cowdray of Midhurst). For the last of these see J. A. Spender, *Weetman Pearson First Viscount Cowdray 1856-1917*, 1930.

Lloyd George introduced after an inevitable delay, the Budget for the financial year 1910–11. The expenditure which it contemplated was enormous, almost reaching the figure of £200,000,000. But its new provisions were extremely simple so that the Irish had reason to fear that Parliament would pass it before the recess. In that case an autumn session might, if the Cabinet wished, be declared unnecessary. And since it soon became evident that the Conference was multiplying its sittings without any hope of reaching an immediate result, the Irish ran the risk that the Budget would be passed with the question of the House of Lords in suspense and they would therefore find themselves once more at the mercy of the Cabinet. But they were quickly reassured as to the Government's intentions. On July 29 before the Budget had passed its first reading the Prime Minister explained that since the Conference had not concluded its labours Parliament would suspend its sittings until November 12.

The Conference had held twelve meetings by this date. It met again on October 12 and held nine more, the last on October 21. They were private and the members were pledged to secrecy. But enough has been allowed to leak out to make it possible to guess the points on which the discussion turned.[1]

3

The first and most obvious suggestion which occurred to the members of the Conference was to employ for the permanent settlement of the question the same device to which the party leaders had recourse in holding it. Had not the resolution passed by the Commons in 1907 on the motion of Campbell-Bannerman provided for the election in the first instance by both Houses of a joint conference of ten or twenty members to attempt an amicable settlement of disputes? It is probable that the question of the composition of the 'Conference' or 'Joint Committee' gave rise to interminable discussion. If in the Conference the number of peers of either party were to be proportionate to its numbers in the House of Lords, the procedure would obviously give the Conservatives an unfair advantage, certain as they would be of a

---

[1] See *The Times*, November 16, 1910, February 28, 1911: Lord Newton, *Lord Lansdowne. A Biography*, pp. 395 sqq.—J. A. Spender and Cyril Asquith, *Life of Lord Oxford and Asquith*, vol. i, pp. 285 sqq.

majority in the Conference however overwhelming might be the Liberal majority in the Commons. If, on the contrary, the majority of Unionist peers in the Conference were reduced excessively, even eventually abolished, the Unionists would have reason to declare themselves duped. For a Government which had a majority in the Commons would be sure of a majority in the Conference.[1] It would seem however that it was on another point that the difficulties proved insurmountable. The representatives of the Opposition wanted a distinction made between three classes of Bills. The first of these would consist of Bills of the normal type, such as any Parliament is called upon to pass every year—Education Bills, Bills for the protection of labour. When Bills of this type were the subject of dispute between the two Houses the Conservative representatives were willing that the dispute should be submitted to the arbitration of a joint committee about whose composition an agreement would eventually be reached. As regards financial measures they agreed that the House of Lords should formally renounce the right to reject them, and were content to demand that the question whether or not a particular Bill was or was not exclusively financial should be decided by the committee. But there was another class of Bills for which, the Unionists claimed, a special procedure was necessary. They were measures which might be termed fundamental or constitutional laws—that is to say, laws which if Britain had possessed a written constitution would have formed part of it. At this point the question of a referendum was raised.

The referendum is an institution which originated and has flourished in Switzerland. When Switzerland had achieved its unification in the nineteenth century on a federal basis, some of its cantons were still faithful to the principle of pure democracy, the direct government of the people by the people. All the citizens met to discuss, reject, or accept the measures submitted to them. The other cantons which were governed by representative institutions progressively rendered them more democratic and devised an indirect method of returning to the system of direct democracy, by enacting that on the demand of a certain number of electors any measure passed by the legislative assembly of the

---

[1] See Charles Nicholson's plan (*The Times*, July 4, 22, 1910)—Of the hundred members of which the joint committee would consist fifty were to be elected by the House of Commons, to represent each party in proportion to its numerical strength, and fifty by the House of Lords of which one-half would be Unionists, the other Liberals.

canton must be submitted to the ratification of all the electors, and that the electors might even under certain prescribed conditions take the initiative and compel the assembly to discuss a particular measure; and the Federal Government followed the example of the cantons and adopted the referendum.[1] The institution had spread to the English-speaking countries. In the great republic of North America the procedure had been adopted in every State but one for the revision of constitutional laws. Two States had even granted the people the right to initiate legislation by petition.[2] And within the British Empire itself the new Constitution of the Australian Commonwealth had been based on the referendum. An alteration of the Constitution which had been passed by both Houses could not become law until it had been submitted to a referendum. And if it had been passed twice by one chamber and rejected twice by the other the Governor-General could settle the conflict by a direct appeal to the people.[3]

Advocated in 1907 by certain Radicals[4]—what institution had a more democratic appearance?—the referendum had been considered sympathetically in 1908 by Lord Rosebery's Committee of the House of Lords though in its report the Committee had refused to pronounce on a question 'which extended beyond the limits of its programme'. The suggestion had been put forward again in various quarters during the years 1907–1910.[5] It would

[1] *Miscellaneous No. 3* (1911) Reports from His Majesty's Representatives abroad respecting the Institution known as the *Referendum*, pp. 13 sqq., and *Miscellaneous No. 6* (1911) Report by His Majesty's Minister at Berne respecting the Institution known as the *Initiative* in Switzerland.

[2] See Bryce's Letter of April 18, 1910, printed in *Miscellaneous No. 3* (1911) Reports from His Majesty's Representatives abroad respecting the Institution known as the *Referendum*, pp. 3 sqq. Cf. S. R. Money, *The Referendum among the English. A Manual of Submissions to the People in the American States with an Introduction by M. St. Loe Strachey*, 1912.

[3] Commonwealth of Australia Constitution Act (*Imperial Act*, 63 & 64 Vict., Cap. 12, Sec. 128). For the application of the referendum not only in the Commonwealth but in the individual States see *Commonwealth of Australia. Papers with reference to the Referendum and its Working in Australia*, 1911 and *Commonwealth of Australia. Further Report with reference to the Referendum and its Working in Australia*, 1911. This very year Natal held a referendum on the question of entering the Union of South Africa (Natal—*Correspondence respecting an Act for a Referendum in Natal on the Draft South African Union Act*, 1910). And Queensland had just introduced the referendum under circumstances calculated to attract the attention of the English legislator (*Edinburgh Review*, No. 431, January 1910, Art. VII: 'The Referendum,' vol. ccxi, pp. 143–44).

[4] See in the *Speaker* for January 19, 1909, the scheme expounded by J. A. Nelson at the New Reform Club. See the same author's, *The Crisis of Liberalism. New Issues of Democracy*, 1909, pp. 32 sqq.

[5] On the Radical side by the *Nation* (February 26, 1910, Cf. G. Lowes Dickinson's letter in the issue of March 5). On the Unionist side by A. V. Dicey (The Referendum and its Critics. *Quarterly Review*, No. 423, April 1910, vol. ccxii, p. 538).

even appear that on the eve of the Lords' rejection of the Budget Asquith had played with the idea of introducing into Parliament a very short Bill, an emergency measure, which without making the referendum a permanent part of British constitutional machinery would submit the Budget of 1909 to the direct vote of the nation.[1] And again on April 28, 1910, in his last official letter to King Edward he informed the King that he was preparing a Bill to take in the last resort a referendum upon the proposed restriction of the Lords' prerogatives.[2] But it was undoubtedly the opposition of the Liberal members, headed by Asquith, which prevented the referendum being adopted by the Conference. Why did they object to it?

To understand their objection imagine that a Liberal Government had carried in the Commons a Bill which the Lords then threw out. What could the Government do under the existing system? Appeal to the country by dissolving Parliament and holding a General Election which amounted, no doubt, to a referendum on the particular Bill but at the same time, if the Government won at the polls, to a vote of confidence in the ministry, embracing its programme as a whole and the general character of its policy. What could the Government do under the same circumstances if the referendum existed? Invite the electorate not to return for their several constituencies the members of a new House of Commons but throughout the kingdom as a whole to decide for or against the measure in question. Suppose the referendum went against the Government. It would be still in office though definitely defeated. Not even a favourable General Election could make good the loss of authority it had sustained. The sovereignty of Parliament or rather of that executive committee of the Parliamentary majority which is the Cabinet would no longer be absolute. The government machine as the English had become accustomed to work it would be thrown completely out of gear.

But there was another and more immediate reason, a reason of

---

[1] *The Times*, October 12, 1909.

[2] Sir Sidney Lee, *King Edward VII* . . . vol. ii, p. 710. At the beginning of the following year when he introduced his Parliament Bill Asquith stated that he would not absolutely exclude the referendum which might be practicable in 'some exceptional case' but could not accept it as 'a normal part of our regular constitutional machine'. (H. of C., February 21, 1911. *Parliamentary Debates*, Commons 1911. 5th Series, vol. xxi, pp. 1750–51.) This amounted to an admission that he might have contemplated recourse to the referendum as an exceptional emergency measure.

political expediency rather than principle, which made it impossible for the Liberal ministers given the existing composition of Parliament to accept a referendum. The fundamental or constitutional law about which the Unionist Opposition felt certain that the mass of the electorate, however democratic on a host of other questions, would refuse to follow the demand of a democratic government for its repeal, was the law which at the opening of the nineteenth century effected a legislative union between Ireland and Great Britain. The eighty Nationalist members of the House of Commons were therefore inevitably hostile to the referendum. But since January they had been the cornerstone of the ministerial majority. They supported Government Bills in which they had no interest, to which indeed they were even strongly opposed, in return for the promise of a Home Rule Bill in the immediate future. But if that Bill even when passed by the House of Commons could be rejected by the direct vote of a hostile British electorate, their contract with the Government would be broken, and its majority would be destroyed by their secession. In the intention of those Unionists who advocated it, the referendum was simply a weapon to destroy that majority.

4

On November 10 an official communication informed the public that the Conference had failed to reach an agreement and on the following day Asquith visited King George at Sandringham. But the visit did not result in the expected announcement of an immediate dissolution. The King, it would seem, asked permission as his father had done the year before to approach first the Unionist leaders and Asquith had refused, whereupon the King refused Asquith's request for an immediate dissolution before Parliament reassembled, and the Parliament Bill was sent up to the Lords. In Unionist circles it was reported that Asquith, unable to carry his point, had tendered his resignation.

But he did not resign. On November 15, the day when Parliament reassembled, a Cabinet Council was held and Asquith had two interviews with Lord Knollys, one during, the other after the council. On the 16th the King, who had come up to London, received in audience the two leaders of the Liberal party and Lord

Knollys visited Asquith, while the King returned to Sandringham, fixing his final return to London for the 29th. The debates in Parliament throw sufficient light on what was happening. Lord Rosebery again moved his resolutions of the previous winter and the House of Lords announced its intention to proceed with their discussion, concurrently with the debate on the Parliament Bill which Lord Crewe reintroduced. But Lord Crewe let it be understood that he only did so for form's sake since after the failure of the Committee no compromise between the two parties seemed possible and the Government were resolved not to accept any amendment. Lord Lansdowne replied by embodying in a formal resolution the amendments to the Government Bill which the Opposition would propose. The Parliament Bill forbade the House of Lords to alter or amend a Money Bill and left it to the Speaker to decide whether or not a Bill belonged to this category. The Opposition wanted the question decided not by the Speaker but by a Joint Committee on which both Houses would be represented. The Parliament Bill provided that if in three successive sessions the House of Lords had thrice rejected a Bill passed by the Commons it would become law in spite of their rejection. The Opposition proposed that after two disagreements in the course of two successive sessions, the third time the two Houses should not vote separately but that, as was provided by the Constitution of several Colonies,[1] both Houses should hold a joint sitting to settle the question by a majority of votes and that in issues of exceptional gravity a referendum should be taken. But the Government allowed the House of Lords only an exceedingly brief period in which to pronounce upon these amendments. For even before Lord Lansdowne rose on November 16 to explain their character, Lord Crewe had announced a dissolution for the 28th 'acting on the supposition that the Lords would not accept the Parliament Bill'. That is to say, the King had given way and promised that if the electorate were consulted and the Election

---

[1] The Commonwealth of Australia in 1900, the Transvaal in 1906, the Orange River Colony in 1907, and the Union of South Africa whose constitution came into force at the very time when the British Parliament was discussing Lloyd George's Budget. In England where the Upper House was numerically almost equal to the Lower and almost wholly Conservative the system was obviously too favourable to the Conservative party. In the Dominions it produced no such effect. In Australia the Senate in virtue of its constitution was a less conservative body than the House of Representatives, and the operation of this particular piece of constitutional machinery produced results which seemed paradoxical. (Sir John A. Marriott, *The Mechanism of the Modern State*, vol. i, pp. 251-52.)

produced an adequate majority for the Government, he would carry out its wishes by putting pressure on the Lords.[1] The debates which ensued were lifeless, conducted before almost empty benches. No one thought of anything but the approaching Election. The essential portions of the Budget were passed and the remainder left over until the early months of the new Parliament before the financial year ended.

The Election was held in the first half of December only ten months after the last. The Unionist speakers everywhere brought Home Rule to the fore. Were the voters, they asked, prepared once again to place the majority in Parliament at the mercy of Redmond and his crew? Balfour, moreover, expressly declared that if the Unionists obtained a majority in the new House, they would not regard their victory as a mandate to restore Protection without having first submitted the question to a referendum. This piece of strategy won him a certain number of gains in Lancashire (a net gain of four seats in the borough and four in the county divisions). The Unionists also won two or three more seats in the South and West. But these gains were only just sufficient to balance the Liberal gains in the poorer districts of London and in the North of England. The Parliament returned in January had contained 273 Unionists. There were 272 in the Parliament elected in December. There had been 275 Liberal members in the late Parliament. There were 272 in the Parliament just elected. There were now 42 Labour members in place of 40; and 84 instead of 82 Nationalists. Obviously the parties had, after the abnormal Election of 1906, found their level in January 1910, for if the Liberals were, it would seem, mildly disappointed by these results (they had counted upon a gain of thirty seats),[2] the Unionists were equally disappointed by the stability of the ministerialist combination. And its solidity was the more remarkable because the Prime Minister had taken up the Unionist challenge, and placed Home Rule in the forefront of the programme which it would be the task of the new Parliament to carry out, once the question of the House of Lords had been settled.

---

[1] For the circumstances of this surrender see the debates H. of C., August 7 and 8, 1911, especially Asquith's speech of August 7. (*Parliamentary Debates*, Commons 1911, 5th Series, vol. xxix, pp. 810–11.) Also Sir John Marriott 'The Crown and the Crisis' (*Fortnightly Review*, September 1911 n.s., vol. xc, pp. 448 sqq.).

[2] *Round Table* No. 9, December 1912, vol. iii, p. 104.

5

By relating the lively and often violent debates which occupied the two Houses from February until August 1911, the historian might easily give the impression that the struggle between the two parties had brought the country to the brink of revolution. Nothing could be more false. The agitation was only on the surface. The December Election had been surprisingly peaceful and half a million voters who had taken the trouble to poll in January decided to stay at home in December. In the eyes of the electorate, of the country as a whole, the question was settled. Without interest or passion the nation witnessed the sturdy efforts of the Conservative stalwarts to keep their flag flying to the last. On February 21 Asquith introduced in the Commons the Government's Parliament Bill. It was exactly the same as the Bill of the previous year. It passed the first reading on February 22 after two days' debate by a majority of 124, its second on March 2 after three days' debate by a majority of 125. When the clauses were debated the obstruction was so persistent that it could be overcome only by the Speaker's constant application of the closure. The debates which began on April 3 did not end until May 15 when the final voting yielded a majority of 121 votes for the Bill out of 603. By way of rejoinder as soon as the session opened the Conservative leader in the House of Lords, Lord Lansdowne, announced his intention to introduce a Bill to alter the composition of the House. And Lord Balfour of Burleigh with Lord Lansdowne's approval brought in a Bill to give the referendum a place in the British Constitution. On March 31 before Parliament rose for the Easter recess Lord Lansdowne carried in the Lords an address to the King asking him to permit the introduction of a Bill 'limiting the prerogative and powers of the Crown is so far as they related to the creation of peerages and to writs of summons'. On May 5 after the recess he introduced his Bill. The reformed House of Lords would consist of a hundred Lords of Parliament to be elected by their peers but who would be eligible only if they fulfilled certain conditions laid down in a schedule, 120 elected by the members of the House of Commons, grouped in a number of electoral districts, a hundred appointed by the King on the advice of the Cabinet, in proportion to the respective strength of both parties in the Commons, seven spiritual Lords of Parliament, the two archbishops and five bishops elected by the episcopate, and finally sixteen peers who had occupied important judicial positions. With the exception of the archbishops, who would hold their seats so long as they occupied their sees, and the judges, who would hold their seats for life, every peer would hold his seat for twelve years. A quarter of the membership of the House would be elected every three years.

The Bill was certainly far more radical than the Bill Lord Rosebery had contemplated the year before, and far more than any of the Bills proposed by those who during the last forty years had sought to strengthen the House of Lords by rendering it more modern. So restricted was the field of choice that the hundred peers theoretically elected by their fellows would be of necessity those high officials, sailors, soldiers, Viceroys of India or retired Colonial Governors, for which former Bills had made a special place, and 220 of these new Lords of Parliament—that is to say, a large majority of their number, would be chosen more or less directly by the majority in the Commons. When Lord Lansdowne first spoke of introducing his Bill many Conservatives took alarm, and their alarm increased when its detailed provisions became known. One peer declared that he was willing to vote for the first reading but only on the understanding that he accepted nothing more than the general principle of a Bill whose clauses were open to such serious objections. Another declared that he could not even vote for the first reading. Why, asked Lord Rosebery, be so imprudent as to bring in a Bill instead of proceeding, as he had desired in 1910, by way of resolution? Dissension reigned in the Unionist camp between the diehards determined to defend at all costs the privileges of the Upper House as at present constituted, and those who to save it brought forward a measure more radical than the proposals of the Government. A Chamber which presented such a spectacle of internal strife was not in a favourable position to embark upon the discussion of the Parliament Bill.

But at the very moment when the final struggle seemed on the point of opening, the same thing occurred which had occurred the previous year. The warring parties concluded an armistice.

The Coronation was approaching. And an Imperial Conference was to meet in London. For a month the Houses of Parliament suspended their sittings and the parties their polemics. Much comment was aroused by a fancy dress ball given at one of the great London hotels during the Coronation festivities by F. E. Smith, the future Lord Birkenhead, a young Member of Parliament who for the past year both in the House and at public meetings had attracted attention by his brilliant rapier thrusts. The leading statesmen of both parties were invited. Asquith and Lord Lansdowne came and were chatting together when their host introduced another guest in the costume of a peer of the realm wearing a baron's mantle and coronet and on the coronet the number 499. He impersonated one of those 500 peers which the Government, it was said, intended, if necessary, to create to ensure the passing of its Bill. A peer wrote an anonymous letter to *The Times* protesting against such flippancy.[1] But we may wonder how many shared his indignation. In fact this fancy dress ball was a revelation. It brought home to the English themselves that the struggle between the parties was not after all so very serious and that the invective used by speakers in Parliament was often the violent language of barristers who, after abusing each other in court, walk down the street arm-in-arm. An Englishman excellently placed to observe the political drama from the wings was undoubtedly thinking of the ball at Claridges' when he noted in his diary on June 29 that 'both parties seem to be playing different parts in a carefully arranged masquerade'.[2]

---

[1] *The Times*, May 26, 1911. According to Jacques Bardoux the letter was written by Lord Rosebery: *L'Angleterre radicale. Essai de Psychologie Sociale (1906–1913)*, 1913, p. 207.

[2] Sir Almeric Fitzroy, June 29, 1911 (*Memoirs*, vol. ii, p. 451). *The Times* had published the anonymous peer's letter of protest under the title 'A Political Masquerade'. See to the same effect the following reflections of a French witness: 'Every day the outcry is keyed to a higher pitch, abuse is followed by threats. "This is nothing short of a Revolution" we hear it said. But there is universal calm, not the calm which sometimes marks the eve of a cataclysm but the genuine calm of everyday life. More than that there is even a gaiety in the air and from time to time outbursts of laughter which mock the forebodings of storm treat the English revolution of to-morrow or the day after as the tail of a stray comet caught in the earth's atmosphere, and envisage the lists so solemnly opened between the Lords and the People, heredity and popular election, as a game of cricket played between a famous eleven and a rival team. If it did not involve the possibility of another General Election in May with its labour and expense, so soon after the January Election, the nation would be inclined to regard the battle as the most exciting sport of the season of 1911.' (Augustin Filon, 'La Chambre des Lords dans le Passé et dans l'Avenir'. *Revue des Deux Mondes*, May 1, 1911, vol. cdxxxii, pp. 101 sqq.)

6

The House of Lords had begun to debate the Parliament Bill sent up to it by the House of Commons six weeks earlier and had already passed its second reading before the Coronation. It did not reject it but was content to mutilate it by various amendments. It would not be for the Speaker to decide whether a Bill were or were not a Money Bill over which the Lords had no control but for a Joint Committee so constituted that Conservative influence would preponderate. And the Joint Committee was empowered to demand a referendum when for the third time the Houses had disagreed. Finally, Irish Home Rule was excluded from the scope of the measure. There were certain amendments, Lord Lansdowne declared on July 20, the day when the Bill passed its second reading, which his friends and himself would never renounce, so long as their liberty of action remained to them. His meaning was not doubtful and the last words presaged imminent defeat. For that very day Balfour received a letter from Asquith informing him that the amendments which the Lords had inserted in the Bill were unacceptable, that it would be sent back to the Lords in its original form and that if they refused to bow to the will of the Commons twice expressed, he would ask the King, with the certainty that his request would be granted (he had been sure of this ever since November 15 and the royal pledge had just been explicitly renewed) to make use of his prerogative to create the necessary number of peers to force the Bill through the Upper House.[1] At a large Unionist meeting held next day at Lansdowne House, the leaders of the party informed their followers that the hour of surrender had struck. Lord Lansdowne and Balfour had an audience with the King at His Majesty's request in which it would seem he begged them not to compel him by their obstinacy to take a step he loathed, and on July 23, the former with the support of Balfour and Lord Rosebery publicly advised the acceptance of the Bill. For this there was no need actually to vote for the Bill on the division but simply to abstain from voting against it. Two hundred and thirty Unionist peers promised to adopt this attitude.

---

[1] See J. A. Spender and C. Asquith, *Life of Lord Oxford and Asquith*, vol. i, pp. 329 sqq. Chap. xxv. Appendix. A list of 249 whom Asquith regarded as suitable persons to receive a peerage on this eventuality.

It was therefore with every prospect of success that on August 9 when the Parliament Bill was returned to the House of Lords unaltered except for a few very slight retouches, Lord Lansdowne explained the uselessness of further resistance and contented himself with expressing the hope that at some future date another Statute might restore the balance of the constitution.

But if Lord Lansdowne and Balfour had the support of the Northcliffe Press, which like themselves had in 1909 thrown in their lot with the belligerents after considerable hesitation, they were not conscious of a well-disciplined army at their back ready to obey their signal of retreat. In the *Observer* Garvin continued his noisy protests and the *Morning Post* preached resistance to the last ditch. In the Commons on July 22, the extremists of the Opposition by keeping up a persistent uproar prevented Asquith from obtaining a hearing. In the Lords, Lord Halsbury, who for the past month had been leader of the group known as the diehards, became a hero in whose honour a banquet was given.[1] This opposition which divided the Opposition itself might prove formidable. If they mustered a hundred it would not be enough for Lord Lansdowne and his friends to abstain from voting if the Bill were to pass. Some of them would be obliged to go further and positively vote for a Bill they detested. This actually happened after scenes of tumult under the eyes of an indifferent nation. The Bill passed its third reading in the Lords on August 10 by 131 to 114 votes. This artificial majority rested on the votes of thirty-seven Unionist peers, the two archbishops, and eleven bishops.

7

Now that we must pass judgment on the reform, thus at last accomplished, we are conscious of a certain hesitation. We are too remote, we feel, from the event, yet too near it. For up to the present the Statute has never been put into operation and the Parliament Act, twenty years after it became law, cannot be regarded as a living element of the British Constitution. The British Parliament has passed an Act introducing universal suffrage (including the suffrage of women), an Act disestablishing the Church in

---

[1] For these final struggles see Alice Wilson Fox, *The Earl of Halsbury Lord High Chancellor (1823–1921)*, 1929, pp. 231 sqq.

Wales[1] and an Act granting Home Rule to Ireland without any need to make use of the provisions of this Act of 1911. Does this mean that the House of Lords suffered that year a more crushing defeat than was believed at the time and will never dare to employ the suspensory veto it was permitted to retain? It may be so. But on the other hand we know what exceptional events have during these twenty years diverted from its course the current of English history in common with that of the entire world. Who would dare to prophesy that the consequences of this upheaval will be permanent and that one day or another under circumstances we cannot anticipate, the Parliament Act will not recover its importance? In our uncertainty of the future we must endeavour to forget a past still too close in 1931 and by an effort of the imagination return in spirit to that summer of 1911 when the Parliament Bill had been passed at last by both Houses and enquire what impression the event produced at the time and what were its immediate results. It was obvious that, on one point at any rate, the British Constitution had ceased to be a Constitution resting on unwritten custom and had become a written Constitution, that the relations between the two Houses were henceforward defined, if not by a special 'constitutional' law which could be altered only by an exceptionally difficult process, at least by an express Statute whose terms were unambiguous, that this Statute established a supremacy of the House of Commons, absolute in matters of finance, almost absolute in all others and that the British political system was therefore on the way to become unicameral. But the Conservatives, the supporters of the Lords' check upon the Lower House were not slow to detect an advantage for themselves which no one it would seem had noticed.

In matters of finance, as we have just said, the Parliament Act seemed to render the Lower House omnipotent. The Opposition had in vain attempted to secure the reference to a joint Committee of both Houses of the question, whether or not a Bill passed by the Commons was strictly a Money Bill and as such exempt from the

---

[1] For greater accuracy we must add that, if it had not been for the war, the Act disestablishing the Church in Wales would have become law in 1914 against the will of the Upper House but that finally in 1919 an Act was passed in due form by both Houses postponing the date at which disestablishment should take effect and introducing certain amendments favourable to the Anglican clergy: 9 & 10 Geo. 5, Cap. 65: An Act to continue in office the Welsh Commissioners appointed under the Welsh Church Act, 1914, to postpone the date of disestablishment, and to make further provision with respect to the temporalities of, and marriages in, the Church in Wales (*Welsh Church [Temporalities] Act*, 1919).

control of the Lords. The Speaker elected by the House of Commons was to decide the question without appeal from his decision. The utmost that the Speaker, who was somewhat alarmed at the responsibility thus placed upon his shoulders, could obtain from the Government, when the Bill was discussed in the Commons for the last time at the end of July, was the annual appointment of two members of the House to act as his advisers.[1] But the position and functions of the Speaker in England, sanctioned as they were by the unanimous approval of public opinion, must not be confused with those of the president of a popular assembly on the Continent, a party member elected by a party. Once elected the Speaker, whatever the party to which he originally belonged and whatever party possesses the majority in the House, is always re-elected. In his constituency he will be returned unopposed. He is not a politician but a judge. In December 1911, when the Finance Bill passed by the Commons was about to be sent up to the Lords the Speaker decided with all the authority which attached to his decisions that in virtue of certain amendments which had been incorporated into it, the measure could no longer be regarded as a Money Bill within the meaning of the Parliament Act, in other words that the Lords were free to reject it.[2] Closely scanned, this decision affirmed by implication that the Budget of 1909 also had not been a Money Bill in the strict and legal sense, in other words that the House of Lords had not exceeded its competence in rejecting it.[3] To obviate the dangers the Government might incur as a result of this decision, the Chancellor of the Exchequer declared in 1913 that the Budget would consist of two portions, a Finance Bill which would simply renew, increase or reduce the annual taxes and a Revenue Bill containing all measures whose

---

[1] 1 & 2 Geo. 5, Cap. 13, Sec. 1(3): See on this point Lord Ullswater's reflections, *A Speaker's Commentaries*.

[2] In its original form the Parliament Bill forbade an amendment to be introduced into a Budget which in the Speaker's judgment would remove it from the category of a Money Bill. The prohibition was dropped in April (H. of C., April 11, 1911, *Parliamentary Debates*, Commons 1911, 5th Series, vol. xxiv, pp. 387 sqq.), and it was this trifling victory which the Speaker's decision enabled the Conservatives to exploit. (H. of C., December 15, 1911, ibid., vol. xxxii, p. 2707.)

[3] This is expressly recognized by Lord Ullswater (The Speaker of 1911) in his memoirs. (*A Speaker's Commentaries*, vol. i, p. 103.) On what clauses of the Budget did he base his decision? Probably on some involving the regulation of the drink traffic, possibly on one which concerned the valuation of landed property. (H. of L., December 15, 1911, Lord Morley's speech, *Parl. Deb.*, Lords 1911, 5th Ser., vol. x, p. 1137.) T. M. Healy, *Letters and Leaders of my Day*, vol. ii, p. 507, insists on the difficulties with which the Government was faced during the session of 1912 in consequence of the Speaker's decision.

fiscal provisions affected the general legislation of the United Kingdom.[1] The former the Lords could not touch, the latter they could amend or reject as they thought fit. When in 1914 the Government could not find the necessary time to complete the discussion of the Revenue Bill, Lloyd George attempted to insert certain fiscal reforms in the Finance Bill. But he was recalled to order by the Speaker and found himself involved in inextricable difficulties[2]—that is to say, counter to all expectation it seemed on the eve of the Great War that, so far as financial measures were concerned, the Parliament Act might after all, have diminished instead of increasing the powers of the House of Commons. There was reason to wonder whether in some respects there had not been a return not only to the period before 1911 but to the period before 1861.

There remained the other part of the Bill which had monopolized public attention, the provisions which transformed the Lords' absolute veto into a suspensory veto. The duration of Parliament was reduced from seven to five years. If the Government maintained the old custom of dissolving Parliament a year before the expiration of its legal term, the Parliament elected in December 1910 would be dissolved at the end of 1914 at latest. The session of 1912 must therefore be devoted by the House of Commons to passing all the Statutes it was determined to force

---

[1] H. of C., April 23, 1913 (*Parliamentary Debates*, Commons 1913, vol. ii, p. 280)—The necessity to free the Budget from these non-financial provisions was the more urgent because the Conservatives had devised another expedient for obstructing the radical policy of employing taxation for purposes of social reform. Custom allowed many taxes to be levied by anticipation before the provisions of the Budget had been actually passed. A Member of Parliament of independent views, T. Gibson Bowles, brought a case before the Courts to test the legality of the practice. The judges decided that it was illegal. And the Government was obliged to pass a Bill which, while it legalized the practice, strictly limited the period within which the House of Commons must pass the Budget after the anticipatory collection of its taxes had begun. 3 Geo. 5, Cap. 3: An Act to give statutory effect for a limited period to resolutions varying or renewing taxation, and to make provision with respect to payments and deductions made on account of any temporary tax between the dates of the expiration and renewal of the tax (*Provisional Collection of Taxes Act*, 1913).

[2] H. of C., June 22, 1914 (*Parl. Deb.*, Commons 1914, 5th Ser., vol. lxiii, pp. 567 sqq.). June 29, 1914 (ibid., vol. lxiv, pp. 175–6). Cf. Sir Almeric Fitzroy, June 23: 'Lloyd George seems never at a loss for expedients to humiliate the Government of which he is a member. Lord Morley described Asquith as "writhing" under the indignity of the position in which he was placed last night when the Finance Minister had to take back half the Budget. How the officials of the Treasury could have been parties to the blunder passed Lord Morley's understanding. He thinks Lloyd George confuses them with a torrent of reasoning, the readiness and plausibility of which obscure the radical unsoundness. Lloyd George's sin is lack of concentration: the time that should be given to thinking out these high problems is frittered away in interruptions, now from this person, now from that—anybody in short, to whom he is accessible and these are legion.' (*Memoirs*, vol. ii, p. 553.)

upon the Lords. After this, it would have only to wait and see whether three times, in 1912, 1913 and 1914, the House of Lords would throw out those Bills and in that case after the third rejection, give the Statutes rejected the force of law as though the Upper House had no existence.[1] But the question would still remain to what extent in the case of each of these Bills the House of Commons or the House of Lords represented the real opinion of the country, what risk therefore by thus deciding to brush aside the opposition of the Upper House, the former would incur, of arousing at the approaching Election a dangerous reaction of public opinion and how far it would shrink from running that risk. Time would show. A drama had begun whose *dénouement* was reserved for 1914.

III   LLOYD GEORGE AND THE NATIONAL INSURANCE ACT

I

For the moment victory lay with the Liberal party and within the party it was the Prime Minister who had carried off the honours of the battle. It was he who had successfully conducted the struggle as a lawyer not as a demagogue and leaving to the Conservatives such unpractical novelties as the Reform of the House of Lords and the referendum, had presented his solution as fundamentally conservative, nothing more than the formulation in a written law of what, up till 1909, had always been regarded as the constitutional usage of the country in regard to the relations between the two Houses. Throughout the contest Lloyd George had been relegated to the second place. It was even rumoured that in the Committee of eight he had opposed to Asquith's scepticism an unexpected trust in methods of conciliation and had believed it possible to settle the question by an amicable agreement with the Unionist leaders.[2] Indeed, he had gone further and actually discussed with Balfour the formation of a Coalition Cabinet, with

---

[1] See however for certain difficulties as to the interpretation of the clause in the Parliament Bill providing that a Bill twice passed by the House of Commons should become law even after the Lords had thrown it out for the third time. Lord Ullswater, *A Speaker's Commentaries*, 1925, vol. i, pp. 112–5.
[2] W. F. Spender, *The Prime Minister*, 1920, p. 171.

or without Asquith, to settle on a non-party basis not only the question of the House of Lords but even the question of Home Rule, and perhaps to introduce some form of compulsory military service.[1] In short, this man of genius had been no longer the demagogue whose fiery denunciations of the Boer War, the Education Bill of 1902, and the Lords' opposition to the Budget were notorious. He had been the conciliator, the arbitrator whose skill had disarmed Unionist hostility during his occupation of the Board of Trade between 1906 and 1908. He had indeed failed. None the less he continued to gain ground at the expense of his real rival in the Cabinet. There can be no doubt that the fact that he was the scion of a noble family was a disadvantage rather than an advantage to Winston Churchill in the new epoch of English history now opening. He was not given a place in 1910 among the four Liberal representatives on the Joint Committee. His vanity, it is said, was hurt,[2] and the manner in which in 1911 he made use of the troops during some serious labour troubles damaged his popularity with the working class. Meanwhile, Lloyd George, leaving to the Premier the task of delivering the final assault upon a citadel admittedly doomed, returned to his role of social reformer.

When he introduced the Budget of 1911 he could congratulate himself on the success of his fiscal reforms of 1909. Thanks—as he confessed—to the years of prosperity through which trade was passing, the new sources of revenue instituted by the Budget of 1909 made sufficient provision for the constantly increasing expense of the navy and the social services. The cost of the old age pensions had risen from £9,790,000 to £12,415,000, more than double the amount originally contemplated by Asquith. Nevertheless, not only was the additional expenditure met, but the national debt was reduced at a rate certainly less rapid than during the first three years of Liberal government, but very rapid nevertheless. And Lloyd George was convinced that the taxes imposed in 1907 would also enable him to meet the increased expenditure he must expect in the ensuing years. In the first place, there were the navy estimates. But it might be hoped that in view of the

[1] W. F. Roch (*Mr. Lloyd George and the War*, 1920, p. 51). *The Times*, March 20, 1930: *Obituary Notice of Lord Balfour*. J. A. Spender and Cyril Asquith, *Life of Lord Oxford and Asquith*, vol. i, p. 287.

[2] Comte d'Haussonville '*Les élections et la situation politique en Angleterre*' (*Revue des Deux Mondes*, February 1, 1911, vol. cdxxxvii, p. 561).

great effort the Government had decided to make in 1909, these would not increase after 1912. Then there was the expenditure on the social services. An Act was passed during this session of 1911 to extend the operation of the Old Age Pensions' Act. And most important of all, Lloyd George carried an important measure of national insurance against sickness and unemployment. To be sure, Llewellyn Smith at the Board of Trade had been given ample time to prepare it. As early as 1909 Lloyd George had promised it and Llewellyn Smith was free to begin to work upon it as soon as he had given the finishing touches to the scheme of Labour Exchanges. In normal circumstances it would have been passed by Parliament in 1910. It was not the unreal and abstract question of the rights of the House of Lords but this Bill which from the beginning of May 1911 till the middle of December held the attention of Parliament and country, which had been kept waiting for it for two years.

2

In the important speech he delivered in the House of Commons on May 4, Lloyd George explained the nature of the risks against which the worker would be insured—death, sickness, and unemployment. So far as life insurance was concerned sufficient, it might well be thought, had been accomplished by private enterprise and there was no need for State intervention. In fact, forty-two million life-insurance policies had been issued in the United Kingdom. But it was not the same with insurance against sickness and unemployment. Not more than six to seven million were insured against sickness, and even so the trade unions provided only sick pay, not medical treatment. And only one million four hundred thousand were insured against unemployment, barely a third or a quarter of the hands employed in industries in which it was a constant threat. If, therefore, the workers were to be effectively insured against the double risk the State must intervene. That intervention must not take the form of unconditional grants —the system which England had just adopted in imitation of New Zealand—for old age pensions. Nor on the other hand must the State be content to make insurance compulsory for employer and employee without granting any financial aid, as Bismarck's Germany had done in the case of insurance against sickness. They must adopt the system Bismarck had devised to insure the German worker against disablement and old age, the system of a triple contribution by the workers, the employers and the State. This general principle would be applied in the following fashion to provide insurance against sickness and invalidity on the one hand, and against unemployment on the other.

The German system of insurance against sickness distinguished five different classes of workers according to the rate of wages. In England there would be only one rate of contribution, 4d. a week for the employee, 3d. for the employer, and 2d. added by the State. The only distinction made would be to relieve of a part of the contribution workers whose daily wage did not exceed 2s. 6d. and that deduction would be greater when the wage was only 2s. or 1s. 6d.[1] The deduction would be charged to the employer and thus be an indirect penalty on underpayment. Medical treatment would be provided, the services of a midwife and maternity benefit, special treatment for tuberculosis, sick pay for a definite period beyond which insurance against sickness would be replaced by insurance against disablement, a species of anticipatory old age pension at the rate of 5s. a week. The contributions would be collected according to the German method, the employer being obliged, whenever he paid his wages to an employee, to attach to his book two stamps whose value was equal to his own and the employee's contribution. The administration of the Act, the management of the funds thus collected, and the disbursement of payments would be entrusted to the societies already in existence, sprung from private enterprise, which need only comply with certain prescribed conditions to be 'approved'. The benefits of the Act might but need not be extended to those who without working for a wage depended for a livelihood exclusively or principally upon their work and to those who having been subject to the provisions of the law ceased after a certain term of years to come within its scope, and who would be allowed to continue their contributions. But a measure intended to be universal must make provision for those who did not wish to be members of any approved society or whom none of these societies would admit

---

[1] For women the rate would be lower (8d. instead of 9d.). The employee would pay less, 3d. instead of 4d., the contributions by the employer and the State remaining the same.

to membership, an inferior class both in health and morals. For their benefit a special system was set up less advantageous to themselves, more completely a State service, and operated by the Post Office. According to the Government's estimate the total number of persons uninsured both compulsorily and optionally would amount to fifteen million. The first year the insurance would cost the employers £9,000,000 and the workers £11,000,000, a total of £20,000,000. The cost to the State, nothing in 1911–12, would be £1,743,000 in 1912–13, rise to £3,359,000 in 1913–14, and reach its maximum £4,563,000 in 1915–16.

This, so far as sickness and invalidity were concerned, was the system proposed. It was on a larger scale than the German. The numbers involved were larger, and the benefits given more considerable.[1] In dealing with unemployment they were tackling a question from which in spite of Bismarck's pledges the German legislature had recoiled, a problem indeed which no government on the face of the earth had hitherto grappled. There were no actuarial statistics on which legislation could be based, as in the case of sickness. It must therefore necessarily be experimental. The system proposed, at which the department had been at work for the last two years, would apply to begin with to certain industries described as the most 'precarious', those in which experience had proved that the periodical periods of unemployment were most acutely felt, the engineering trades on the one hand (engineering in the strict sense, shipbuilding, coachbuilding), the building trade on the other. In these two branches of industry the Bill provided for the compulsory payment of contributions by the employers and men (2½d. from either party), and a supplementary contribution by the State, to take the form of an annual payment of a sum equal to a third of the joint payment made by the employers and workmen. Relief would consist of a weekly payment to the unemployed man, 7s. a week in the engineering trades, 6s. in the building trade. The payment would begin from the second week of unemployment and could not be continued longer than fifteen weeks. The Labour Exchanges set up in 1909 would provide the machinery for operating the new law. The unemployed

[1] It was estimated that in the United Kingdom a third of the population would benefit by the new measure. In Germany not more than a fifth benefited by the provisions of Bismarck's legislation. (Alfred P. Hillier 'National Insurance and the Commonwealth' *Nineteenth Century*, No. 314, August 1911, vol. lxx, p. 342.)

workman must apply to the Labour Exchange which would offer him work. If he refused it, he must justify his refusal to the satisfaction of a committee of arbitration appointed for the purpose. If he made out a satisfactory case he would be entitled to receive benefit under the Act, which would include in its scope a sixth of the industrial population, some 2,400,000 workers.

It was estimated that the total cost of the new legislation during the first year, including the cost of building sanatoria for the treatment of consumption would amount to £24,500,000 of which £2,500,000 would come out of the taxes. In spite of this enormous outlay the Bill, as Lloyd George was careful to point out at the conclusion of his statement, must not be regarded as a complete cure for the evils against which they sought to insure the working class. To effect a radical cure they must, he said, cut deeper. The great merit of the Bill was 'to lay bare' a vast mass of social suffering and 'to force the State, as a State, to give its attention to it'. But as it stood, the Bill would alleviate a great deal of suffering. Nor did Lloyd George wish it to be regarded as the work of one party alone. Introduced as it was on the eve of the Coronation and the meeting of an Imperial Conference he expressed the hope that it would be passed by the unanimous vote of the House, though improved in the course of debate by the friendly collaboration of all parties. At the outset it seemed possible that his wish would be granted. At first sight the Bill appeared an imposing, a magnificent measure. And surely it would be to the interest of the Opposition to court the favour of the working-class voter by accepting with inevitable reservations a popular Bill? But it soon became clear that the Bill ran counter to many interests, disturbed many deep-rooted habits.

3

The workers, to whom all the earlier measures of social reform from the Education Act of 1870 to the Old Age Pensions Act of 1908 had consistently given something without asking for anything in exchange, were annoyed at the prospect of a tax imposed upon them by the State, and, except for the poorest, uniform in amount. Their annoyance found support from the theorists of

Socialism who asked for a measure which did not require any contribution from the worker. This was the position adopted by the indefatigable Philip Snowden, by Bernard Shaw, and by the entire Fabian group, which found itself for once in agreement with the exponents of orthodox Socialism against the moderates of the Labour party.[1] They pointed out that the new measure favoured those who because they were comparatively speaking well-to-do had already been able to insure themselves against sickness with the friendly societies. The others on the contrary, whose poverty entitled them to the Socialist's special sympathy, must content themselves with the ludicrously inadequate benefit given to the Post Office contributors. This group of critics also objected to the treatment the Bill accorded to women. Should they marry and cease to work outside their home, they would lose, unless they were left widows, the entire benefit of their contributions before marriage. Though they received the maternity benefit of thirty shillings, they could not receive in addition the sickness benefit, although the Bill forbade their employment for four weeks from the child's birth. In conclusion they blamed the measure for favouring unduly, in the administration of the insurance, the friendly societies at the expense of the trade unions. The former, or some of them at least, had been given a privileged position by that part of the Bill which dealt with unemployment. But what trade unions were in a position to fulfil the conditions necessary to become approved societies? In the first place out of 1,200 only twenty had a membership of over 10,000. And even these could not, without bringing their official activities to a standstill, accept the conditions prescribed by the Bill, the deposit with the Government of a sum equal to one pound per member, a pledge to devote all their funds to distributing benefit to their members, submission to the control of auditors appointed by the State, and even so, to be 'approved' only if they managed their finances on exactly the same lines as a friendly society pure and simple. Further, must the workers be treated by the doctors chosen by the 'approved societies'? This was indeed the intention of a measure which sought by that provision to prevent any fraudulent collusion

[1] H. of C., July 6, 1911. Philip Snowden's speech. Letter from Bernard Shaw to *The Times*. (*The Times*, October 22, 1911.) *The Fabian Society. The Insurance Bill and the Workers, Criticisms and Amendments of the National Insurance Bill. Prepared by the Executive Committee, June 1911. The Fabian Society. The National Insurance Bill, October 1911. The National Insurance Bill. A Criticism with a Preface by Mr. Bernard Shaw.*

between the insured and his doctor. But the workers revolted in advance against such bondage.

On this last point the grievances of the medical profession were the same as those of the working class. Doctors already employed by the friendly societies complained of unfair treatment at their hands. Would their position become the position of all doctors who attended working people under a measure which seemed to place the entire system of insurance against sickness under the societies' control. They wearied the nation with their complaints and finally drew up a statement of their demands which comprised the following six points. No insurance of persons in receipt of a wage of above £2 2s. a week. Free choice of doctor by the sick person. Medical assistance and midwifery to be withdrawn from the control of the friendly societies. The doctor's remuneration to be fixed in each area by the decision of the majority of doctors in that area. The profession to be represented on the bodies administering the law. The legal establishment in each locality of a distinct Committee composed entirely of doctors.

Both these oppositions, that of the workers and that of the medical profession, were formidable and it would be difficult to say which of the two caused the Government the more embarrassment. In their numerical strength the workers had indeed the advantage of the doctors. If they refused to pay their contributions, how could they be compelled to do so? But on the other hand their discontent failed to assume a definite shape. Their organizations both professional and political, the trade unions and the Labour party alike, when certain concessions had been made, declared their acceptance of the Government scheme, compulsory insurance, and contributions from the workers. The doctors' opposition seemed more dangerous and for months their powerful organization, the British Medical Association, threatened to sabotage the Bill. The Opposition in Parliament, at first friendly, could not resist making capital out of the discontent. At first Lloyd George seems to have hoped that the Bill could be passed in a few weeks. When at the beginning of June he perceived that a detailed discussion of the clauses was inevitable he clung to the hope that it might pass through all its stages before the end of August and that after eleven months of almost unbroken toil Parliament having passed the Parliament Bill, the Budget, and the

National Insurance Bill could be prorogued until January. The hope proved vain. When on August 18 the Parliament Bill became law, the Budget had not been passed and out of the eighty-seven clauses of which the National Insurance Bill consisted in its original form only seventeen had been carried and these not without serious amendment. An extraordinary session in the autumn was therefore inevitable. Meanwhile he would do his best to amend the Bill so as to satisfy all these divergent interests.

Laborious negotiations were therefore undertaken between the Chancellor of the Exchequer and the organizations concerned. Such negotiations, unlike Parliamentary debates, are not recorded in writing. Nevertheless, they constitute what amounts to a novel form of parliamentarianism beyond and above the official Parliamentary government. The friendly societies raised unexpected difficulties. From the outset indeed sporadic complaints had been made by certain important societies of a Bill which it was said would inevitably transform them from free institutions into instruments of the State, fettered by bureaucratic control. However, on the whole the friendly societies had been satisfied with a Bill which gave them a position of such importance. But the Government was now obliged to do justice to the criticisms brought by the trade unions and above all by the medical body against the excessive favour shown to the societies, and every concession made to the trade unions or doctors increased the discontent of the latter until it in turn became formidable. To be complete we must mention another agitation, more comic perhaps than dangerous, but extremely vocal, especially in London. In its original form the Bill did not include domestic servants. Later on, the Government decided to extend its benefits to them. But many servants, particularly those in the employment of the wealthy, found the attentions of the law more unwelcome than beneficial. They listened to the advice of their masters who encouraged them to protest. Crowded meetings of domestic servants were held with ladies of title in the chair, to denounce the intolerable tyranny of the Chancellor of the Exchequer. Were they—employers and servants alike, to be subjected to an odious system of red tape, doomed to pass their lives 'licking stamps'?

4

On October 21 Parliament reassembled. The Government declared that nineteen sittings should be sufficient to finish the discussion of the Bill. In the end two additional sittings were granted, twenty-one in all. That is to say the Bill was divided into a fixed number of 'compartments' and when the time allotted to the discussion of a particular compartment had been spent, all the clauses which the Commons had not had time to discuss would be passed automatically without debate. The Bill, now very considerably altered, comprised in its final form 115 clauses (not counting the schedules) instead of the eighty-seven of the original Bill. Not many changes were made in that portion of the Bill which dealt with unemployment. The amount of benefit was made uniform for both the branches of industry concerned and fixed at 7s. a week, and the age at which a worker might, under certain conditions, benefit by its provision was lowered from eighteen to sixteen. In the event Parliament had no time to debate these clauses, nor did the public raise any objection to this hasty procedure. The only portion of the Bill in which it was interested was that which dealt with sickness. On this point the Bill had been remodelled. Though on the one hand, to satisfy the farmers, the contributions due from employers and employees were reduced if the former continued to pay wages during illness, on the other hand the benefits given to the insured were increased. Insured women who subsequently married were enabled to benefit by the provisions of the law by entering the class of those optionally insured, and women in confinement might receive sickness allowance as well as maternity benefit, if they were insured individually as well as their husbands. The number of those eligible for benefit was increased. The wives and children of insured persons might use the sanatoria. And not only were domestic servants not excluded from the scope of the measure, but special provision was made for soldiers, sailors, and seamen in the merchant service. The conditions imposed on societies which desired to become 'approved' were modified so as no longer to exclude the trade unions,[1] and the friendly societies were obliged to accept still

---

[1] The unions however never gave their unqualified support. See on this point the views of an active trade unionist of extremely moderate opinion. 'Conferences were held and

further sacrifices to satisfy the grievances of the medical profession. To gauge the real importance of these concessions we must call attention to another aspect of the Insurance Bill, of fundamental importance.

It set up a small body of Insurance Commissioners furnished with very wide powers at once administrative, judicial, and legislative or, if you prefer, quasi-legislative. They were made responsible for the administration of the law, empowered to define its meaning by administrative regulations—which in very many instances must be regarded as supplementary laws—and judging, in most cases without appeal, infractions of the law. In strict logic the new service of sickness insurance should have been given to the local Government Board, but Lloyd George no doubt wished it to be an independent branch of administration in order to withdraw it from the influence, in his opinion sterilizing, of John Burns.[1] On November 28 the list of the first Commissioners was read in the House of Commons. At its head was Sir Robert Morant, who, driven from the Board of Education by a revolt of the elementary school teachers, exchanged one important administrative position for another. Subject to the Commissioners, the Bill set up Insurance Committees in every country and county borough. In the original form of the Bill as introduced in May they were called County Health Councils. Only a quarter of their members were appointed by the Government. The remaining three-quarters were to be elected, a third by the County Councils or County Borough Councils, a third by the 'approved societies' and a third by the Post Office Insurers, and in the original draft their sole function had been to do for those who paid their contributions into the Post Office what the approved societies did for the vast majority. But even then the Bill betrayed a tendency to extend their functions. With the assent of the friendly societies, they might take over the administration of medical assistance. This became compulsory in the remodelled text finally passed in November. The approved societies were to distribute the sickness allowance, the maternity benefit, and the disablement benefit, but

amendments tabled, some of which were carried. But ultimately there were embodied in the Bill, which was passed into an Act of Parliament, provisions which gave railway companies and other employers, as well as capitalistic insurance companies (whether of the "Friendly" type or otherwise) power to set up a society.' (G. W. Alcock, *Fifty Years of Railway Trade Unionism*, p. 419.)

[1] Sir Almeric Fitzroy, March 23, 1917 (*Memoirs*, vol. ii, p. 646).

the entire administration of the medical benefit was entrusted to these administrative bodies, the local Insurance Committees, who were to draw up panels of doctors amongst whom the insured might choose. The composition of these committees was also modified. Only a fifth would be elected by the County Councils. Others would be nominated by the Insurance Commissioners, others appointed to represent the insured, and others elected by the medical corporation. And the Insurance Committees were empowered, in conjunction with the central Commissioners, if in their opinion the public health was being endangered by the insanitary condition of dwellings, by a tainted water supply, or failure to apply strictly the provisions of the Factory Acts, to exact a species of fine from the local authorities, to cover the exceptional expenditure which these agents of national insurance were therefore obliged to incur.[1]

The history of British institutions had witnessed a singular reversal of outlook. Formerly the English had prided themselves on having created the representative system to control the agents of the executive and restrict their action. They were now setting up a new bureaucracy to control their representative assemblies and compel them to act.

5

The National Insurance Bill passed its third reading in the Commons on December 6, after an amendment delaying its operation brought forward by the Opposition had been rejected by 320 to 223 votes. In the House of Lords it passed its second reading without a debate, after a speech by Lord Lansdowne, on December 11. The House of Commons having accepted a further number of small technical amendments introduced by the Lords, the Bill received the royal assent on December 16.[2] The House of Lords, in fact, was employing the tactics it had adopted in 1906, not to oppose a popular measure of social reform. But why in that case had it taken the bold step in 1909 of throwing out Lloyd George's Budget? It had provoked a crisis which had lasted for two years, had thrown the public finances into disorder, and had

---

[1] 1 & 2 Geo. 5, Cap. 55, Sec. 63.

[2] 1 & 2 Geo. 5, Cap. 55: An Act to provide for Insurance against Loss of Health and for the Prevention and Cure of Sickness and for Insurance against Unemployment and for purposes incidental thereto (*National Insurance Act*, 1911).

brought the political life of the country to a standstill to no purpose, and the final result had been that the country had made the peerage realize its weakness without even the compliment of hatred. The Budget for the current financial year was also hurried through without debate several months late. And on the very day, December 16, when the Budget, the Insurance Bill and several other measures jointly received the royal assent, Parliament was at last prorogued. After all the noisy agitation a feeling of weariness was felt throughout the country. But at first sight it did not seem likely to damage the position of the Cabinet. The ministry had emerged from the crisis victorious. Asquith had defeated the House of Lords. And Lloyd George had accomplished the feat of carrying in a single session a measure so bold and so complicated.

When he introduced the Bill on May 6 he was recovering from a disease of the throat which had kept him away from Parliament for several months and he had asked the indulgence of his audience should his strength fail him while he was speaking. But it did not fail him either that day or during the following months. Six days every week until the winter he worked fifteen or sixteen hours a day, hours occupied by conferences with the experts of the Treasury or the Board of Trade, or with representatives of the various classes of persons affected by the Bill—the doctors, the friendly societies, the trade unions. Even his hours of rest were not wasted. Luncheons and dinners could be employed for useful interviews. When in September he took a semblance of holiday in his native Wales, at Criccieth, he took his expert advisers with him. Add to this excessive pressure of work the fatigue of parliamentary sittings and the important speeches delivered from time to time at a public meeting.[1] When as Christmas approached, it was certain that he had gained the victory, even his enemies paid tribute to his genius. Never had he appeared so great.

6

Thanks to Lloyd George even more than to Asquith the Liberal party was victorious. And its victory was first and foremost a victory over the new Labour party whose rapid growth had

[1] Speech at Birmingham, June 10; at Whitefield's Tabernacle in London, October 14; at Bath, November 26.

alarmed many Liberals a few years earlier. Two causes about this date, 1910, contributed to its temporary eclipse.

The first, with which Lloyd George had nothing to do, was a decision of the courts. The employers, elated by their victory in the Lords in 1900—the Taff Vale decision—lost no time in launching a further attack. For they saw the workers preparing to take their revenge by using the Committee for Labour Representation to form at Westminster a class party closely dependent on the unions. Was this tolerable? Was it indeed lawful? Were not the unions exceeding the competence prescribed by their technical objects when they raised by a compulsory levy from their members' subscriptions the funds necessary to support a political party? As early as the beginning of 1906, even before the new Labour party had secured the passing of the Trade Disputes Bill, a miner in South Wales called Steele, with the financial support of the local Conservatives, brought an action against his union for making the levy without his consent. Meanwhile, the Trade Disputes Bill was debated in the House and the Labour members believed that owing to their efforts the measure had been so worded as to bar Steele's action. But the lawyers who worked for the Cabinet took care that reservations should be inserted into the clause intended to make such actions impossible, which actually gave it the opposite effect.[1] Steele's action was allowed. It is true he lost his case.[2] The statutes of his union provided for the levy of which he complained and the union had therefore the right to make it. But very shortly another rebel came forward, Osborne, a member of the railwaymen's union.[3] In view of Steele's defeat the court in which he first brought his action non suited him. He appealed against the decision. In November 1908

---

[1] Clause 4 (1) laid down: 'An action against a trade union, whether of workmen or masters or against any members or officials thereof on behalf of themselves and all other members of the trade union in respect of any tortious act alleged to have been committed by or on behalf of the trade union, shall not be entertained by any court.' But Clause 4 (2) went on to add: 'Nothing in this section shall offset the liability of the trustees of a trade union to be sued in the events provided for by the Trade Union Act, 1871, Sec. 9 except in respect of any tortious act committed by or on behalf of the union in contemplation or in furtherance of a trade dispute.'

[2] Steele v. South Wales Miners' Federation King's Bench Division, January 12, 1907.—A previous decision against Steele had been given by the Cardiff County Court on March 9, 1906.

[3] 'Liberally financed from capitalist sources' (S. and B. Webb, *History of Trade Unionism* Revised Edition 1920, p. 608). See however on this point Osborne's categorical denial (*Morning Post*, October 8, 1910—also *My Case*—pp. 23, 28). Cf. G. S. Alcock, *Fifty Years of Railway Trade Unionism*, 1922, pp. 338–40.

the judges of the Appeal Court unanimously reversed the decision of the inferior court. It was the turn of the union to appeal to the House of Lords. On December 21, 1909, five judges (among them a declared Radical, Lord Shaw) decided unanimously in Osborne's favour.[1]

They all agreed in pronouncing that the trade unions were entitled to the special privileges conferred by the Act only in so far as they did not overstep the functions attributed to them by the Acts of 1871 and 1875 and that the constitution of a political party was not among these. Two of the judges further argued that the formation of a political body ruled by the trade unions was opposed to the spirit of the British Constitution and subverted the foundations of representative government. It was in vain that the unions attempted by all kinds of shifts to elude the force of this decision; the law had the last word. Therefore, to defray the cost of electioneering campaigns and provide a salary for the members it returned, the party was obliged to depend on voluntary subscriptions which produced a most inadequate revenue. Under these circumstances until the day when a ministerialist majority would consent to a Statute restoring the right of which the Osborne judgment had deprived them, they were financially dependent upon the Liberal party.

Nor was this the sole cause of the Labour party's weakness. Another and more potent cause was the active policy of social reform pursued since 1908 by the two Radical leaders, Winston Churchill and Lloyd George. The Trade Disputes Bill of 1906 had been passed under the direct pressure of the unions. But this was not the case with the legislation which followed it. With the possible exception of the Old Age Pensions Bill it was the work of energetic statesmen—Churchill first, then Lloyd George—whose policy it was to anticipate the demands of the working-class. How unenterprising and timid in comparison seemed those Labour

[1] Osborne v. The Amalgamated Society of Railway Servants of England, Ireland, and Wales, Chancery Division, July 21, 1908—Supreme Court of Judicature. Court of Appeal November 16, 1908—Amalgamated Society of Railway Servants v. Osborne, House of Lords, December 21, 1909—Walter Osborne (of the Osborne Judgement) *My Case. The Cause and Effects of the Osborne Judgement*, 1910—W. V. Osborne (of the Osborne Judgement) *Sane Trade Unionism* (1913). This last brochure prints as an appendix the five opinions of the judges in the House of Lords—M. Beer, *Geschichte des Sozialismus in England*, 1913, pp. 489 sqq.—S. and B. Webb, *The History of Trade Unionism*. Revised Ed. 1920, pp. 608 sqq. (an extremely thorough and exhaustive criticism of the judgement)—G. D. H. Cole, *A Short History of the British Working Class Movement 1789–1927*, vol. iii, 1927, pp. 55 sqq. (He summarises and follows closely S. and B. Webb).

members who were the typical parliamentary representatives of British trade unionism—Henderson, Bowerman, Shackleton, Hodge, and Abraham! Not one of them had the imagination to pursue a policy so bold and so far-reaching in its scope and not one no doubt who would not have been alarmed had he been told that in the near future he must shoulder the responsibility of office. Their party lacked prestige at a moment when Lloyd George was raising the prestige of the Liberal party. Between the representatives of Labour and Lloyd George there was all the difference that there is between sleep and wakefulness or, if you prefer, between health and fever.

The Government majority had emerged from the Election of January 1910 greatly reduced; the Labour members and the Irish constituted its mainstay. We should therefore be inclined at first to wonder why the Labour members did not profit by this state of things to increase their influence in Parliament. The foregoing considerations explain why, on the contrary, their power declined. At the January Election unlike the Irish they lost a number of seats. Before the dissolution there were 44 Labour members, in the new Parliament only 40. In only twenty-six of the seventy-eight constituencies in which Labour put forward a candidate, did he oppose a Liberal and in not one of these was he returned. On the morrow of the Election Ramsay MacDonald stated plainly his desire for a coalition with the Liberals.[1] The party dared not adopt this policy and chose the policy of independence advocated by the veteran Keir Hardie. But when the new members had to choose their places at Westminster it became obvious how unreal this independence was. In 1906 the Irish and Labour members had taken their seats on the Opposition side of the House. Indeed, they had had little choice in the matter; the Government benches were so crowded. But now when they could choose freely, the Irish remained on the Opposition benches, whereas the Labour members preferred to sit on the Speaker's right. In the December Election Labour did indeed win two seats from the Liberals. But this was a pure accident. Never had the alliance between Labour and the Liberals been so close, and at no previous Election had the Labour party displayed so little activity.

[1] Interview with Ramsay MacDonald, *Christian Commonwealth*, February 2, 1910. See also Keir Hardie's reply at Newport on February 8 when he opened a special conference of the Labour party, summoned to discuss the Osborne decision.

In all they put forward no more than 58 candidates, and of these only 11 opposed a Liberal. It might well seem as though the hopes of those who at the opening of the century had dreamed of forming an independent party had been disappointed and the Labour party had resigned itself to being no more than a professional group dependent upon the Liberals.

7

Lloyd George had also triumphed over the Unionist party. It was his great Budget of 1909 which had provoked the crisis and the combination, heterogeneous as it was, of moderate and radical Liberals, Labour members, and Irish Nationalists which had supported him, had proved sufficiently solid to survive the test of two successive Elections. There was therefore no need to have recourse to tariff reform, to 'widen the basis of taxation', it was sufficient to apply the principles of the neo-Gladstonian Budgets, to defray, without imposing or increasing tariffs, both the growing burden of naval expenditure—for which Lloyd George blamed the Unionists—and of the Social services whose cost he expected to increase still further. And the proof of his victory was the dissension which prevailed among the Unionists.

For the uncompromising tariff reformers blamed Balfour for the Unionist defeat. In January 1910, under the banner of Tariff Reform they had very considerably reduced the Liberal majority, in fact, in England itself had transformed it into a minority. Their success should have been pushed further. But Balfour had preferred in December to relegate tariff reform to the background and concentrate on the question of Home Rule. What had he gained by this policy? In Yorkshire he had still further decreased the Unionist minorities. In Lancashire he had not gained so many as ten seats. Taking the country as a whole the result had been the *status quo*, and the House of Lords had suffered a decisive and humiliating defeat. The outcry became so violent that on November 8, 1911, Balfour resigned the leadership of the party. Who would take his place? Should it be Austen Chamberlain or Walter Long, the representative of the Balfourian tradition? To avoid the spectacle of a disputed election both candidates agreed to retire in favour of Bonar Law, a new man, little known to the general public, a Canadian by birth and the son of a Presbyterian minister, who had made a fortune in the steel manufacture at Glasgow before he went into politics and had taken an active part in the propaganda for tariff reform. That a man of such antecedents could be unanimously chosen only nine years after Lord Salisbury's retirement to be the leader of the Conservative party is a proof, perhaps as significant in its way as the defeat of the House of Lords, of the speed with which British public life was becoming democratic. His difficulties began immediately. Should he ask for the taxation of foodstuffs? Should the composition of the British Budget be made subject to the decisions of an Imperial Conference? Was he bound by the pledge Balfour had given before the Election of December 1910 not to impose a protective tariff without a previous referendum? He could not answer any of these questions without offending either the stalwart disciples of Chamberlain who constituted the fighting wing of the party or those who would have nothing to do with a policy of dear bread and who represented from 60 to 70 per cent of the Unionist electorate. Now that he had become leader of the party, Bonar Law found himself obliged to be as cautious and hesitating on this point as Balfour had been and therefore equally incapable of arousing the enthusiasm of the masses. When he launched the programme of tariff reform a great statesman had attached a heavy weight to the neck of his party which it must bear for many a long day.

Hampered though they were by their official programme the Unionist party, despite their double defeat at the polls in 1910 and the apathy the electorate had displayed while the House of Lords was battling for its rights, were not without grounds for hope. The Irish Nationalists, arbiters of Parliament, would demand from the Cabinet their payment for two years' faithful support, the grant of Home Rule. It would therefore not be long before the Irish question would involve the Government in difficulties far more serious than those in which the question of tariff reform had placed the Opposition. Moreover, the subservience of the Labour party to the Liberals was arousing a lively discontent among the working class, which was openly displayed at the end of the year in their denunciations of the machinery set up by the Insurance Bill. The Unionist agents were preparing to turn this discontent to their advantage. And there was another question which ever since 1906 the Unionists had exploited against the Liberals, still suspect of an attachment, unwarranted by the situation, to the traditions of Gladstonian pacifism—the German peril.

The tension between England and Germany had never been greater than at the opening of the year in which Lloyd George carried his great Budget. A semblance of calm had followed until in the summer of 1911 a serious diplomatic incident to which the name of Agadir has remained attached displayed the two countries on the brink of war. We must therefore turn from our study of English domestic politics, to the history of her foreign policy during these three years, so disturbed in both spheres. More than once we shall meet on our way the two great demagogues, the two leaders of the populace, Churchill and Lloyd George. In 1908 and 1909 both had been champions of peace at any price, though continuing nevertheless to make the inevitable concessions to the military party. In 1911 both went over to the war party, Churchill permanently, Lloyd George on a particular occasion, though his temporary change of front was equally significant. It was Lloyd George whom we shall see at the moment of crisis amazing England and Europe by employing in public against Germany the language of the most bellicose patriotism. This redoubtable figure was the hero of the hour. Thrusting his rivals into the background, he held the stage of his time and country.